Doing Business with Pascal

Doing Business with Pascal

Richard Hergert
Douglas Hergert

Berkeley • Paris • Düsseldorf

Cover Design by Michel Jouin
Layout and illustration by Gaynelle B. Grover
Technical illustrations by Margaret Cusick and Sharon Leong

This book describes UCSD Pascal™, which is distributed and licensed for distribution by SofTech Microsystems, Inc., 9494 Black Mountain Road, San Diego, California 92126.

Library of Congress Card Number: 82-62361
ISBN 0-89588-091-1
Printed in the United States of America
10 9 8 7 6 5 4 3 2 1

To Marv and Elaine

Table of Contents

Part III 175

Producing Management Reports: Business Applications in Pascal

Acknowledgments

First, thanks go to our editor, James Compton, who made many contributions to the style, content, and organization of this book. In addition, we would like to thank the following Sybex production staff members for their fine work: Elaine Foster and Donna Scanlon, word processing; Valerie Brewster and Mati Sikk, typesetting; Hilda van Genderen, Cheryl Wilcox, Michael Howard, and Tim Hulihan, proofreading; Gaynelle Grover and Ingrid Owen, art work and design; Sharon Leong and Margaret Cusick, paste-up; and Bret Rohmer, production manager. Finally, thanks go to Dr. Rudolph Langer for his encouragement and support in this project.

Introduction

Doing Business with Pascal is a discussion of two related subjects—the design of a business system to be implemented on microcomputers, and the development and writing of business application programs in Pascal—and the relationship between them. First, important concepts and criteria involved in systems design are outlined; next, UCSD Pascal extensions to the language are used to create a body of routines for common business tasks; finally, these routines are used in a series of application programs to create management reports.

This book will be of interest to three general classes of readers: owners and managers of small or medium-sized businesses, experienced Pascal programmers, and students of either or both subjects. The small-business manager who is about to choose a microcomputer-based system will find the first part the most helpful, and the programmer will be most interested in the second and third. Students (and indeed all readers), however, will probably derive the greatest benefit from reading the entire book as a model for the design, development, and implementation of a system of business software written in UCSD Pascal.

The book is divided into three parts:

Part I, *Building Business Systems: an Introduction,* presents the basic concepts behind the design of business systems, and the criteria used in their evaluation. The major elements of a system are outlined, and their relationships to each other are explained. Managers wil learn what information they must provide to system designers to get the best results, and application programmers will see how their work fits into the system as a whole.

Part II, *Programming for Business Systems: UCSD Pascal and its Extensions,* discusses three features of UCSD Pascal—the precompilable "unit," the long-integer data type, and random-access files—and their importance in business programming. Units are developed for some essential business programming tasks: input/output of dollar-and-cent amounts, calculation of check digits (to ensure the accurate entry of identification numbers), and scalar date conversion (to determine the number of days between two dates). Procedures are developed for sorting and searching methods, and a file-management program is presented. Complete listings of all program modules are provided, and, where necessary, discussed in line-by-line detail.

Part III, *Producing Management Reports: Business Applications in Pascal,* presents a series of interactive application programs that use techniques and program modules from Part II to implement elements of the business system described in Part I. In each chapter, an introductory section explains the application in the context of the system as a whole, then a "sample run" of the program (consisting of the input/output dialogue and the report produced by the program) is presented and discussed, and finally the program itself is listed and explained. These programs work; they were used to generate the sample runs, and many of them can be used by themselves as independent management tools for decision-making.

While the programs are written in UCSD Pascal, so as to take advantage of the extensions mentioned earlier, equivalents to those features are also provided by other commercially available versions of the Pascal compiler. The *Appendix* presents a comparative table of these extensions.

Doing Business with Pascal has several major themes, which are presented both explicitly, through precept, and implicity, through practice. First among these is the idea that a clear understanding of a system's output requirements must precede its design. A related theme is management's need for data to be selected, summarized and abstracted so as to highlight any exceptions to the ordinary course of business. Computers are capable of producing much more information than any individual can digest, so careful planning and selection are essential. The application programs in Part III produce management-oriented exception reports that, unlike the standard accounting reports widely available from commercial software packages, are more commonly produced by minicomputer and mainframe systems.

Another major theme is the value of modular programming and design. Once compiled into program modules (in this case, UCSD Pascal units), routines for tasks that must be performed repeatedly are available wherever they are needed in the system. The revision process is streamlined, because the programmer's efforts can be directed to one "target module," and the rest of the system will be changed accordingly.

We believe that this book is unique in its dual focus on system design and application programming. Design concepts from larger systems are applied, for perhaps the first time, to the design of microcomputer-based systems for the smaller business. The book is suggestive rather than exhaustive. Issues are raised here that you may want to pursue further in the literature. The collection of programs included is extensive, but by no means complete. In short, while *Doing Business with Pascal* does not provide you with a fully integrated business system (which would be beyond the scope of this or any other book), it does provide you with a model of such a system, and lays the groundwork for its development.

EDITOR'S NOTE

A number of typographical conventions have been used throughout this book to distinguish important textual elements. First, the names of all Pascal programs, procedures, functions, etc., are capitalized wherever they appear. Second, lines of program code and output incorporated into the running text are set in Triumvirate type; the running text itself is set in Baskerville. In dialogues between program and user, the user's input appears in **boldface.**

Complete program listings and sample runs (those labeled "figures") are not typeset, but photographed directly from either the authors' tested, executable source code, or the output actually produced by that code. (Lines of dashes have been inserted to separate "screens" in the sample runs.) Program errors that might have been introduced in the typesetting process have thus been avoided.

Part I

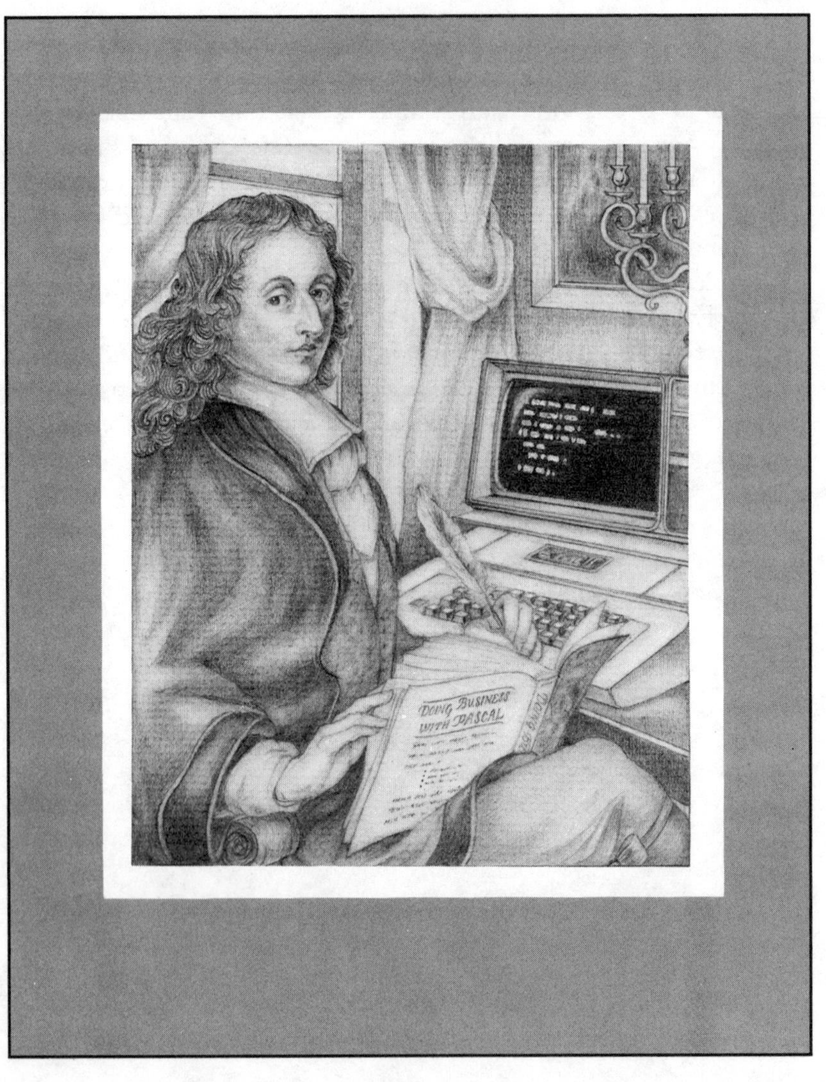

Building Business Systems: An Introduction

Part I of this book comprises two chapters, which together describe how a computerized business system is designed: what the elements of such a system are, what functions they are required to perform, and how they are related to each other to form a system. This section presents design concepts that are important to the business manager and the application programmer alike. It explains what functions of a business can most effectively be computerized, and what kinds of information the management of a business must provide to the system analyst or designer to get the results desired. A major theme of this section is that a detailed specification of a system's requirements must precede its design.

The application chapters in Part III implement elements of the system described in Part I.

Chapter 1

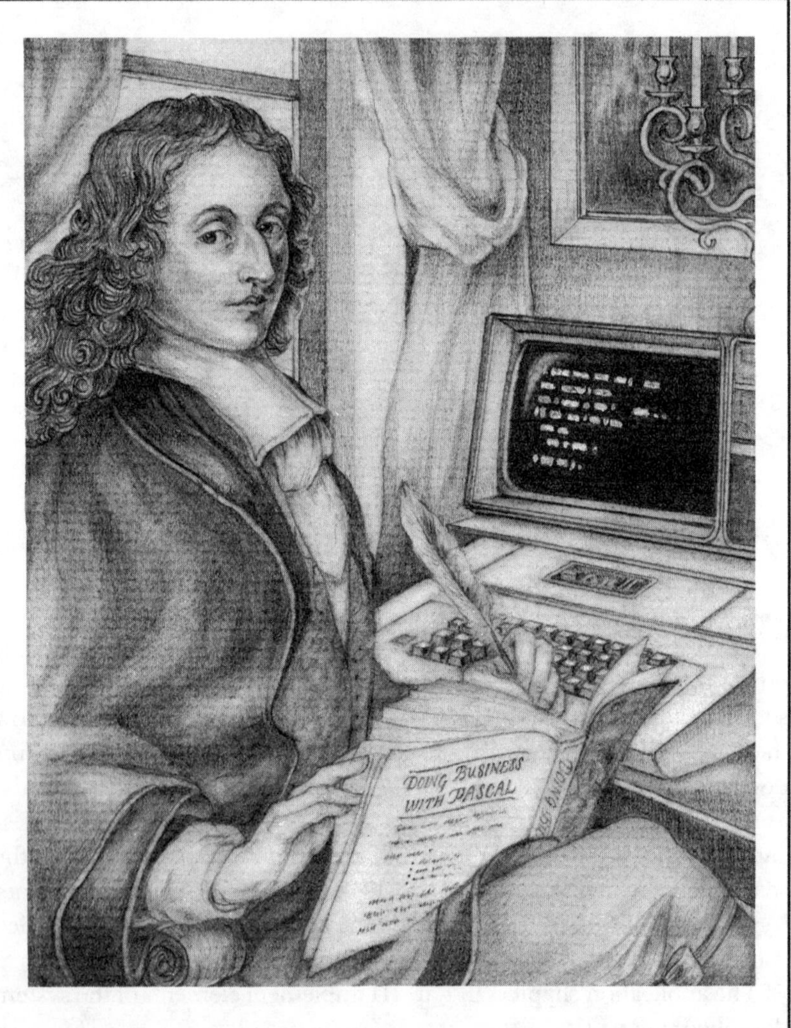

System Design Concepts

INTRODUCTION

This chapter will introduce some important concepts in the design and management of computer systems. We cannot exhaust the subject of "systems" and "systems design" in these few pages. However, the remainder of this book assumes at least a basic knowledge of how and why systems are put together the way they are. Let us map out the road ahead of us. We will begin by defining "system" and some related terms. These definitions will not be exhaustive; but they are important as a basis for understanding the material to come. Next, with both diagrams and text, we will plot out what it means to "think system;" that is, we will describe the design and workings of processes within a system. Third, we will show how these general concepts are applied to the design and management of business computer applications. Finally, we will present a diagram of the business system described in this book, paying particular attention to the relationships between the parts of the system. This last diagram links together the applications. The descriptions that accompany the chapters in Part III, on business applications, each show the relationships of the application to the system as a whole.

DEFINITIONS AND BASIC CONCEPTS

Already we have used some terms that carry special meaning in this book. Let us begin, then, with a few essential definitions.

A *system,* at its most basic level, is an arrangement. The arrangement may or may not be particularly orderly (many business systems fail because of lack of order). The arrangement may not be particularly logical, although systems without logical design are also prone to failure. But since human beings tend to attempt to apply order and logic to what they do, the term "system" usually implies a *good* arrangement. When we *systematize* lists of related data, or when we create system where before there was no organization, we attempt to make an orderly and logical arrangement of things. Systems, however, are orderly and logical because they were planned that way, not because by nature a system contains some magical quality that makes it ordered and logical.

A system has *parts.* If we are developing a system of philosophy or a system within a particular science, those parts might be related ideas or thoughts. In business systems, we are attempting to *do* things (as opposed to thinking about things), so for business systems, the parts are actually processes, interrelated and linked by design and common goal. A *process,* then, is the first level or subdivision of a system.

Like systems, processes are not *inherently* orderly and logical; they must be designed that way. Nor is there anything that demands that a process be mysterious to the uninitiated. A process itself can be broken into components. In business systems for computers these components are programs, subroutines and algorithms. A group of algorithms (in a specific computer code or language) form a subroutine; a group of subroutines together become a program; a group of programs are linked together to form a process; a number of processes together make up a system.

Systems analysis is the task of breaking up the parts of a system into processes, programs, subroutines, and algorithms. It is analysis in the sense that it seeks to describe in detail the workings of the system and its component parts. But systems analysis also goes beyond the simple description of a system and attempts to evaluate the usefulness (or *utility*) of its component parts. If we were to design a completely new computer system for business tasks, the purpose of the analysis would be to study the details of the current business system (be it manual or computerized), and to recommend whatever changes are necessary to meet the goals of the people using the system. If we were already using a computer system, the systems analyst would be required to keep the description of the system up-to-date, to document "bugs" or errors in the system, and to make recommendations for future additions to the computer system. The analyst might even recommend that the system be scrapped as no longer useful to the organization.

User-friendliness is often a goal of systems design. Simply put, a user-friendly system is one that a nontechnical person can use with ease and confidence. It is a system that, on the one hand, makes sense to the user, and, on the other hand, reveals only enough information to be useful and to solve those elementary problems most likely to be encountered. Later we will discuss some of the techniques commonly used to make a computer system user-friendly. User-friendliness has taken on a whole new meaning with the advent of microprocessor-based computers cheap enough to be installed in the home and the small business environment. Software houses are realizing that their products are used by individuals with varying degrees of computer sophistication, from the data entry clerk who needs specific prompts during data entry, to the company manager who guides the system's business goals, to the computer consultant who makes the system answer the company's needs. User-friendliness can often be the deciding factor in the success or failure of systems design, particularly for business software.

The components of a computer system are generally referred to as either *hardware* or *software*. The mechanical and electronic devices that together make a working computer are the hardware. They will normally include a central processing unit (CPU), input-output (I/O) devices such as a cathode-ray tube (CRT), and a keyboard. Data storage is provided by magnetic tape or disks of various types and sizes. A computer and its peripheral devices are linked together to form a computer *configuration*.

All of the hardware in the world will do nothing by itself or of its own accord. It requires instructions, called "software." Software is the body of programs written to make the specific configuration of hardware perform a specific task. Software is usually divided into two types: operating systems software and applications software. Overall systems design must take into account both types of software. Operating systems software is usually sold along with the computer, as part of the initial equipment configuration. Systems software makes it possible to enter data from the keyboard, to see data on the screen, to write data out to the disk and read it back again. Systems software ties together the configuration of the hardware and controls it. Systems software translates English-like program information into signals that the computer's CPU can understand and perform.

HOW TO THINK "SYSTEM"

Earlier we said that a system can be broken into its component parts: processes, programs, subroutines and algorithms. These parts or components represent what might be called the *micro* level of system design. On a *macro* level, a system would be described somewhat differently. And it is to this macro-level description that we now turn. Keep in mind that we are still talking about systems, but looking at the bigger picture.

Figure 1.1 is the basic diagram of any system. It takes an input, does something with that input, and creates an output. An input can take the form of numbers, characters, signs, input from a keyboard, or of signals from some device like a thermostat or circuit. In business systems, it is often raw data from accounting transactions, from time cards, or from the inventory stock room. A process is a task or routine performed on that data. The process may add or subtract sets of numbers, or it may watch for changes in the length or strength of a signal. The output is

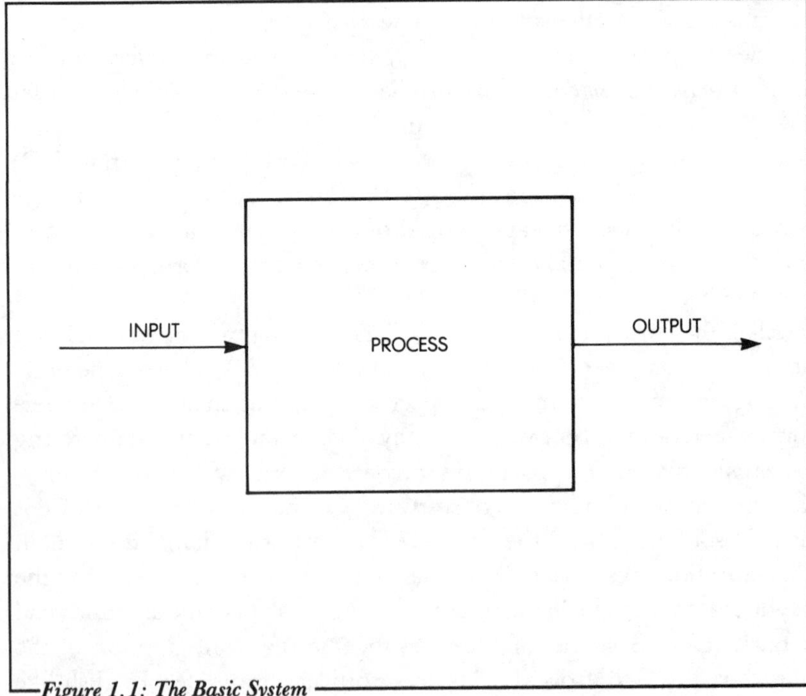

Figure 1.1: The Basic System

the information produced by the process. It is the result of the addition or subtraction, or the signal that sets off a fire alarm.

The process box of the system is often the most confusing to the user. Often the user makes a great effort to ensure that the input is as accurate as possible, only to find the output full of errors, the cause of which is a mystery to the user. The mysterious nature of the process sometimes leads us to call the computer a "black box." Input goes in and output comes out, but how and why is unknown. One of the goals of this book is to make the process easier to understand.

Figure 1.1 is not a complete representation of a system. Figure 1.2 adds three items. Note that for a system to be complete, it must have a *feedback loop*. This is the way that the process monitors the quality of the information that it is producing as output. Certain checks, which are

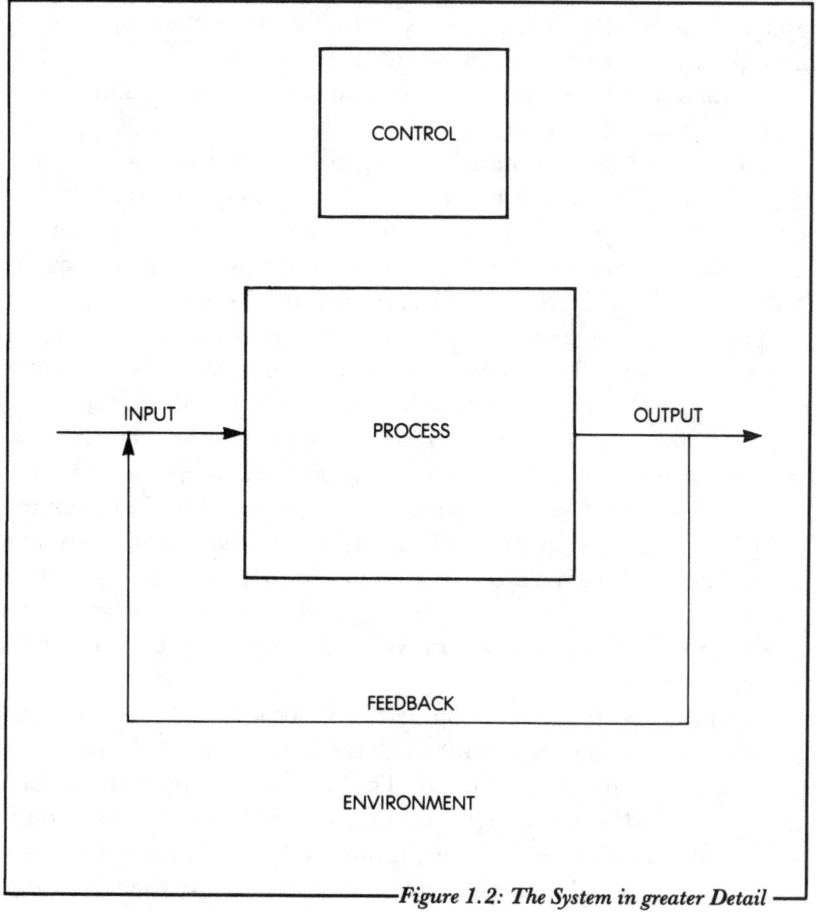

Figure 1.2: The System in greater Detail

designed to ensure the integrity of the output information, are built into the process itself. In addition, the system must have a *control mechanism.* This is often external to the computer itself, and takes the form of operations manuals, policy information, error recovery procedures and the like.

Finally, the entire system has what is called an *environment.* This environment at one level is the computer equipment itself, the components of the hardware. At another level, the environment is the interrelationship or integration of the various processes that make up the system. Information about the environment includes data about the sharing of information between the various processes in the system and about the way in which that information is stored and accessed so that it can be shared.

This basic diagram of the entire system at its "macro" level can also be applied to each component of the system. A process has input and output and performs a task requiring feedback and control within a specifically defined environment. A program and a subroutine and even an algorithm will be the same. Common to each are input, process, and output; feedback and control; and environment.

A few more words are necessary to explain what we mean by "process." Earlier we said that the process is often thought of as the "black box" of the system (just as the computer itself, especially the central processing unit and its related components, is often thought of as the "black box" of the hardware). The process simply does something. But the process can do many different kinds of things. For instance, the process may do fairly detailed error checking of an operator's data entry input. It may check to see that dates are entered correctly, or that numbers are within a legal range. The process may perform advanced mathematical calculations for financial planning or modeling, or for scientific applications. It may also monitor something external to the computer, like the changes in temperature of a room or the variances off course of a jet or rocket. There is almost no limit to what a process can do. What limits the functioning of a process is the specific hardware on which the process must run and the way in which that hardware communicates with the world.

System designers and programmers can choose to make the processes in their systems as complicated or as simple as they want. Some processes are in fact extremely complicated. The process may proceed through many paths and branches so that the total range of possibilities and decisions that the process controls is in the hundreds or thousands. The obvious weakness of this type of design is that a minor change to one section of the process may affect the entire process and even destroy the operations of the system. Often documentation describing exactly what the process does is weak; often the person who designed and wrote the system has been assigned other tasks or is no longer working on the system. So the task of modifying the process is assigned to someone who has limited documentation and who did not originally design and write the system. There is little chance of proceeding without problems.

On the other hand, the processes of a system can each be designed to perform a limited number of simple tasks that may be used in more than one area of the entire system. The key to this type of systems design is a process design that is general enough to be used in several specific routines. For instance, the routine controlling the input of dollar-and-cent values would be written only once, so that any time a program reads such values, the same routine can be used. This requires that the routine be general enough to fit different input situations. In the short run, this kind of planning takes more time, but the value of routines that can be used throughout the entire system soon becomes evident.

These routines with multiple uses in a system are often called *modules*. A module can be designed to perform only one simple task. For instance, on a microcomputer system with a CRT, one useful module might simply clear the screen and position the cursor at the top left corner of the screen. Any time the programmer wants to clear the screen, he simply uses this module and the task is done. Another, more complex, module might perform a "check-digit" calculation on numbers during data entry. An employee number, an invoice number, a vendor number, or a general ledger number might each have appended to it an additional digit that can be used to check the accuracy of the original input. The specific routine or module used to calculate this number need only be written once, and then used by the programmer each time it is needed.

The size and number of modules is related to the complexity of the system and the limitations of hardware. A very complex system may have many hundreds of modules and may link those modules into general types so that similar kinds of tasks are done within the same module. For instance, several kinds of mathematical functions could be put together into one module, and the programmer could use one or more of those functions when the module is used in the program. The routines required to produce reports, with headings, page totals, and summary totals at the end of the report, could all be part of one module. Error checking and error resolution processes could be put into one module and used by the entire system.

A fairly limited hardware configuration might require that modules be very small. In order for a module to run it must be loaded into main memory and then executed. A computer configuration with limited memory will therefore require small modules, loaded one at a time and then abandoned to make room for the next section of program.

Systems planning with modules, sometimes called modular programming, has many advantages. A small module is easier to understand than an entire system or program. A small module might be used many times in the entire system, and would therefore only need to be written once. In a large or complex system, a modular approach to systems planning allows the assignment of tasks to many people, with one person or group charged with ensuring that each module meets the system's overall specifications and that the system is put together into an integrated whole. The process of systems design is more manageable using the modular design.

There are some disadvantages, however. While the process of designing and writing the system is easier and more controllable, the actual execution of the programs on the computer may be somewhat slower. One of the slowest operations that a computer performs (comparatively speaking) is the accessing of information from a storage device. A module, when not in use, would be stored on disk. It would have to be read and loaded into the main memory before it could be run. This slows down the system's operations. In addition, while the process of designing and writing the system in modules is faster, that process requires very strong controls. If a module is to be used in several programs it must be general enough to be used in each of these programs. So a fairly detailed explanation of what the "using" program is going to do must be provided before the "used" module can be produced. The check-digit module mentioned earlier is an example. The maximum size of the number on which the check digit can be calculated must be large enough to allow the routine to be used for any number in the entire system. The worst thing that can happen is to discover that the module was written for a smaller number than required for general ledger account or asset numbers. Rewriting the check-digit module may in fact change its use substantially enough so that it no longer functions properly in the rest of the system.

SOME FEATURES OF THINKING SYSTEM

So far we have discussed some terms commonly used in systems analysis and we have also looked at a pair of diagrams that describe the use of systems. In addition, we have spent some time discussing the design and writing of processes, and suggested that a modular approach to systems design makes the whole process easier and less prone to serious difficulties. Now we need to go somewhat further and discuss the process of doing systems analysis. By extension, this section of the chapter is also an introduction to the task of constructing and writing systems.

Where does the job of systems analysis begin? Refer again to Figure 1.2, our diagram of the system. Note again that a system has input, a process, output, feedback and control, each operating within a defined environment. Where among these features do we begin? *In fact, the whole task of systems design and that of systems analysis begins with a detailed analysis of the required output.* The type of input and even the process itself is secondary to the determination of what the outcome of the process is to be like. What are the reports that the system is to produce? What is the form and content of these reports? Who is to use these reports? What responsibilities and functions will the report address? How is the person going to use the report?

It may seem strange, after all that we have said about the systems diagram and about the careful design of processes into modules, that our starting point is really the output of the system. But the importance of starting from output cannot be overemphasized. It is the design of the output that determines the specific processes that must be run. It is the design and use of reports that gives the system its value. A computer installation can have the fastest-running processes, but if those processes do not produce useful reports and make management analysis easier, the installation does not justify its costs.

The design of a business system is not limited to the standard accounting reports. Business systems often stop at the production of payroll checks, accounts payable checks, a balance sheet, a statement of profit and loss, and a detailed listing of assets or current accounts receivable. While these reports are standard for the operations of most businesses, they do not address some of the management considerations that can—and should—be designed into the system. The system should produce information on the relative productivity of units within a company, be they manufacturing units or sales units. The system should produce information on the maintenance costs for equipment. The system should produce information on vendor quality, like the size of discounts, and the number of back orders and partial orders. The system should produce information on bad debts, summarized by product line, by sales representative, and by geographic area, as well as by age and size of account.

It is this kind of information that allows the manager to control the operations of the company.

After careful consideration has been given to the requirements for the output of the system, the designer next concentrates on the input. What kinds of input are required? What is the form of that input? How will input information be collected? How difficult is the information collection process? Will that difficulty affect the smooth operations of the system? How accurate will that information be?

Many kinds of input are possible. Input could be entered by a manager sitting at the computer, feeding in information that he alone knows, or making requests for processing. Input could be entered from forms completed throughout the business organization and collected for central entry into the computer system. Input could take the form of files of information on disk, files that were produced by other processes or other modules. Input could be entered from files of old or backup information.

The kind of input dictates the amount of error checking that must be done on the data before the process uses that information. *It is important that errors be detected as soon as possible in the input cycle and corrected in a timely and orderly manner.* Data entry operations of payroll time card information, for instance, will typically use several error checking routines. These routines will check for valid dates, for valid time entries, and for the quantity of work hours outside of normal limits. Data entry operations for general ledger transactions will usually check for balanced entries to ensure the integrity of the balance sheet and trial balance. Data entry operations in accounts payable check processing will usually check for valid purchase order numbers and vendor numbers (with a check-digit mechanism). In addition, the total dollar amounts of checks written will be checked against some manually calculated total.

When information is input from a disk file, different errors must be checked for. *Again, the best approach is to do the error checking as early in the process as possible.* This would assume, for instance, that the process that wrote the disk file has in fact already checked for the accuracy of data. All dates would already have been reviewed for acceptable format; numbers would already have been reviewed for check-digit if that was appropriate. The actual reading of data from the disk would then primarily check for errors in the integrity of data and for read/write errors. Normally, these data integrity checks are performed by systems software rather than applications software, but if input accuracy is critical, an application program might also do some data integrity checks.

The next system functions that need design attention are environment and control. Environment, as mentioned earlier, has to do with the specific hardware configuration on which the system will be operating. A new system might need to be run on existing hardware, and so conform to the limitations of that hardware. Size is only one consideration. The types of file structures, the kinds of computer languages supported, and the limitations of those languages are also important considerations of environment. If hardware purchasing is part of the systems design and development process, consideration must be given to the vendors that might provide hardware, and to the costs involved. It should be apparent that only with the careful consideration of the desired output that we discussed earlier can we make an intelligent decision about the kind of hardware that the system would need. The same thing might be said about the input into the system.

Much has been written about the selection of equipment for computer operations. We cannot do more here than mention some important points. The best in hardware is worth nothing without the software to produce the results. Also worth noting is that generally hardware development is many years ahead of software design. This is particularly true with microprocessor-based computers. Pick a hardware vendor for whom software development and support is strong. Do not choose equipment for which there is little in the way of software or software development tools.

Also, stay in the mainstream of computer vendors. The microcomputer industry is a very dynamic one, with vendors appearing and disappearing almost daily. You will need technical support for your computer system, but you will be hard-pressed to find it if the company you purchased the system from is out of business. Do not hesitate to check the financial stability of the company that you choose to use for your computer vendor. The young, hungry entrepreneur may offer a low price on computer equipment, but may not be in business six months later, when something has gone wrong or you need help with your system.

Control elements are also considered before the process is fully designed and probably before much programming code is even written. Determine the kinds of documentation needed, and the error recovery procedures that may be accomplished by users, or by systems designers and programmers. Also determine the kinds of access that might be needed for each type of application, and the security restrictions on that access. Computer misuse and abuse, and fraudulent use of computer functions are facts of life in our society. You will need to determine which employees can rightfully access various applications and what degree of password protection should be designed into the system.

Only with all of these other systems elements considered are we ready to give our attention to the design of the process itself. In any kind of problem-solving, the accurate statement of the problem will make the solution much easier. In systems design, the precision with which the output, input, environment, and control functions are defined will affect the manner in which the process itself is written and designed. Complete definition of these functions will also make the design of the process much easier.

The document that spells out the output, the input, the environment and the control functions is called the system specifications document, or simply the *system specs*. The process section of the systems specs will describe in detail the kinds of functions that the process must complete. If the columns of a report are to be added, then the process description must say so. The exact details of how time cards are calculated, and how taxes and other deductions are processed must be given. In addition, the process specifications must give information on any crucial timing considerations: are there calculations or input which must be completed before the new process can begin?

One important thing to remember when completing the system specifications document is that the computer programmer who does the work may not know very much about the business functions that the system is to assist. While this is a mixed blessing, it is probably preferable that the programmer not second-guess all decisions outlined in the systems specs and pass judgment on the quality of those decisions. If the system specs for the inventory system require that inventory costing be on either FIFO, LIFO or weighted average, the programmer should not be given the opportunity to provide another method of his own choosing or to eliminate any of the prescribed methods. The responsibility for accurate systems-design specification belongs to the user and the systems analyst; the programmer's job is to translate those specifications into computer programs in a language that the hardware will support.

BUSINESS SYSTEMS ORGANIZATION ISSUES

Nearly everything we have said so far relates in a general way to the manner in which all computer systems are designed. All systems have input, a process, and output. All systems have an environment, control functions, and feedback. All systems are composed of the kinds of parts we talked about earlier—the processes, the programs, the subroutines and the algorithms that together form the computer system. The most complicated space vehicle control systems and the computerized video games at your local game center have systems design concepts in common.

Business systems are designed to perform business functions, and to assist the owner or manager in the process of running that business. Most often, business computer systems are organized around the accounting functions of the business rather than around its operations functions. Results of operations are communicated to the business computer system, and the system produces the management reports necessary to assure the stability of the business. The collection and communication of operations results is generally done manually, although some fairly sophisticated computer systems provide for automatic communication of production, payroll, inventory and other types of information into the business system. The small business will generally not require that kind of system sophistication.

Figure 1.3 shows a system organization chart. The specific applications sections in Part III of this book address themselves to one or more of the items on this chart. Here we wish to discuss the ways in which the various applications together form a system.

The rectangular boxes on the chart are subsystems within the business system itself. Each subsystem is made up of several applications, indicated as ovals on the chart. A light line links each application to the subsystem. A heavy line links each subsystem together. Each of the subsystems feeds information to appropriate other subsystems and especially to the general ledger subsystem. Each subsystem requires its own input and produces its own output. Part of that output is the communication of data to other subsystems. This communication of data is usually called the "system interface." Thus, the payroll system may be said to be interfaced to the general ledger system for accounting purposes. The materials management subsystem may be said to be interfaced to the accounts receivable subsystem for the proper debiting of accounts receivable accounts as finished products are shipped.

The general ledger subsystem typically requires interface with each of the other subsystems, for it is the general ledger subsystem that maintains the chart of accounts, and produces the balance sheet, the statement of profit and loss (income and expense) and the statement of sources and applications of funds. Items from payroll, materials management, accounts payable, accounts receivable and capital assets subsystems must be communicated to the general ledger chart of accounts.

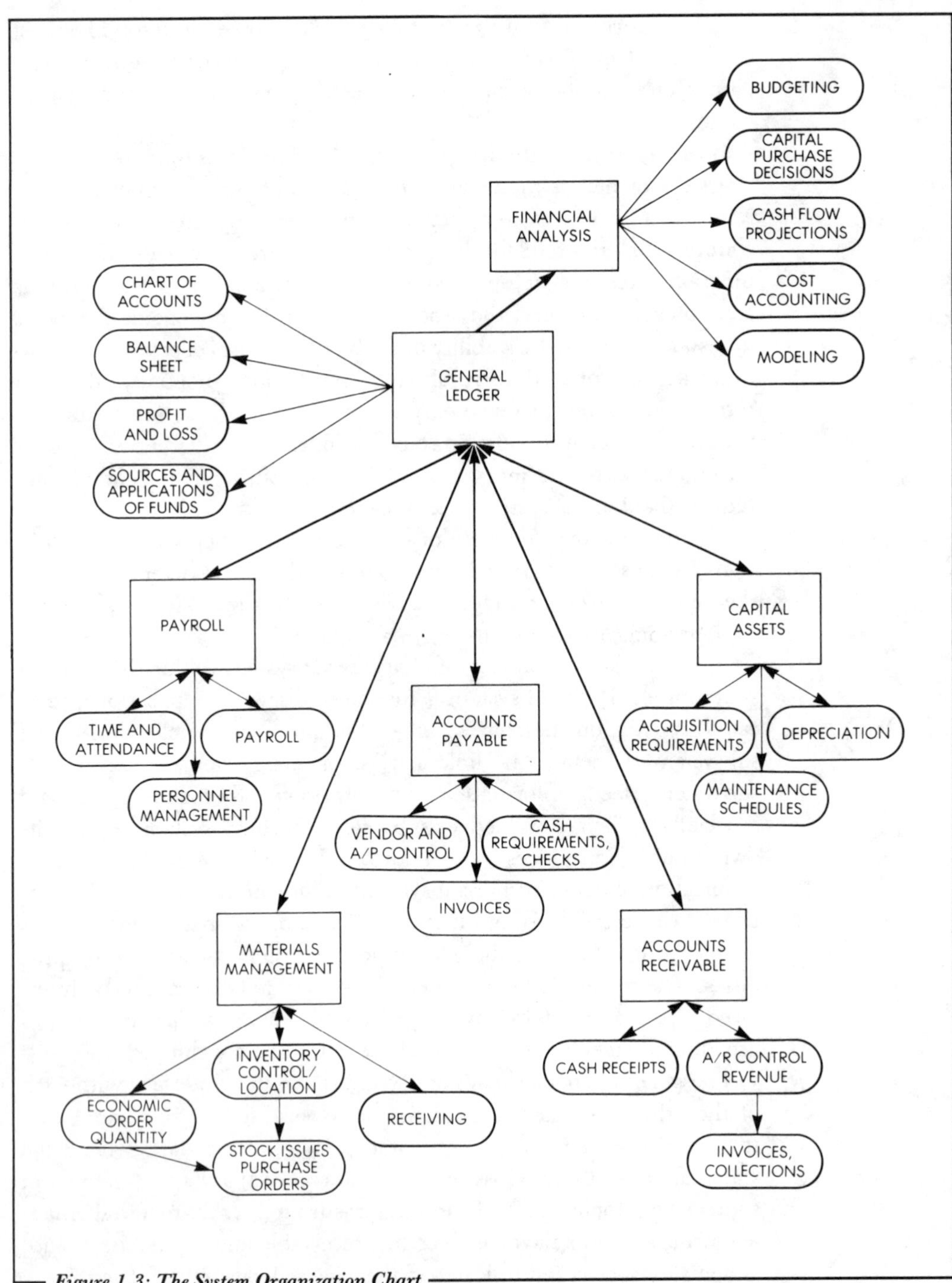

Figure 1.3: The System Organization Chart

Each of the subsystems (other than general ledger) also performs functions of its own. The payroll subsystem will perform the collection of data from the time cards, called the "time and attendance" application. The payroll subsystem will then use that data and produce the weekly or biweekly payroll checks for employees in the "payroll" application. Then, on a monthly schedule, personnel management reports are produced through the "personnel management" application. Note that these applications must be linked or interfaced to each other. The time and attendance application must provide information to the payroll application, which in turn must provide information to the personnel management application.

For now, we are simply calling this communication of data an "interface." In Chapter 2, we will describe in detail how an interface works, and the possibilities in interface design. But it should be clear from what we have said so far that some kind of communication is necessary.

The materials management subsystem maintains information on the company's inventory and shipping and receiving operations. The inventory control application provides information on the location and quantity of all inventory items, both raw materials and finished products. In addition, it provides the mechanism for the inventory costing—information that must be passed to the general ledger for balance sheet accounting. The receiving and stock issues applications must communicate not only with the inventory control applications, but also with the general ledger for appropriate entries; it must also communicate with accounts payable and accounts receivable subroutines. The economic order quantity application performs calculations telling the best time to order stock items. Note again that each of these applications must, through the materials management subsystem, communicate with the general ledger system.

The accounts payable subsystem controls all accounts payable functions. The vendor and A/P control application maintains the list of vendors and the amounts outstanding for each of those vendors. It also keeps information on the way in which discounts are taken and the frequency of back orders or missing orders for a particular vendor. The invoices application provides the mechanism for entering invoices into the accounts payable subsystem, and for checking those invoices against purchase orders and receipts. Note that here the communication is between the accounts payable subsystem and the materials management subsystem. The cash requirements and checks application forecasts the need for cash allocation to the payables accounts and also produces checks for the vendors. It provides the information necessary to relieve the accounts payable account on the general ledger, and also provides information for the source and use of funds application of the general ledger subsystem.

The accounts receivable subsystem maintains information on all accounts outstanding for the business. The A/R control and revenue application maintains information on the relative productivity of members of the sales force, and the sales volume of items of the product line. It also maintains information on the aging of the accounts receivable and, therefore, information on the valuation of accounts receivable and the determination of bad debt. The cash receipts application maintains the control of operations related to cash for the business. Cash from sources other than operations is also controlled here, but posting of that cash does not relate to the accounts receivable files. The invoices and collections application produces bills or invoices to the debtors, and also provides the mechanism that enables the collection department to do its work. Note that there is communication between each of these applications and also between the accounts receivable subsystem and the general ledger.

The capital assets subsystem provides the information necessary for the control of the capital assets of the company. Not only is there a complete listing of all the capital assets in the subsystem, but there are specific applications that perform related functions. The acquisitions and retirement application allows for additions and changes to the capital asset file. Classification of assets into major categories is also necessary. You must be able to distinguish between buildings, major movables, and vehicles, to name a few. In addition, you must be able to determine the location of any asset, and its acquisition date. The depreciation application provides information on the costing of the use of the capital asset over time. Several depreciation methods must be provided for. The maintenance schedules application provides both accounting information on the costs of maintenance and maintenance contracts, and operations information on the scheduling of equipment down-time, for preventive maintenance. Historical information on the reliability of a particular piece of equipment is also maintained.

The general ledger subsystem is the center or hub of the business system. All information from the other subsystems is communicated to and summarized by the general ledger system. In addition, the general ledger subsystem produces the reports necessary for management and external reporting. The chart of accounts application provides the mechanism for adding accounts to the general ledger system, and also for making manual journal entries into the system and making any corrections to the automatic entries from other subsystems. The balance sheet application produces the balance sheet and also maintains comparative data for the previous month's and the previous year's entries. The profit and loss application produces the statement of profit and loss for the business, and maintains comparative data from previous months and years. Together with the balance sheet application it provides information for the sources and applications of funds application.

The financial analysis subsystem receives its information from the general ledger subsystem. The subsystem's applications produce specialized management information and management accounting reports. The budgeting application allows for input of budget information and the comparison of that budget data to actual operations. The capital purchasing application provides information necessary to make the lease/buy decision on capital expenditures, and so uses information from the general ledger subsystem. The cash flow projections application monitors the use of cash for a particular period and projects use of cash in conjunction with budgeted changes in business activities. The cost accounting application allows for the costing of project-oriented productions and for the allocation of overhead expenses to revenue producing areas. The modeling application should provide the ability to determine possible effects of different economic conditions and internal environments on the running of the business.

SUMMARY

The business systems organization we have described is large in its scale and scope. Not every small business will need or want to have all of the capabilities which such a system would provide. Not all small businesses could afford all of these capabilities. But this system organization, as complex as it is, can be implemented in a microcomputer environment. From the discussion of the virtues of modular system designing, we learned that very large programs can be broken up into small bits and pieces and run efficiently with comparatively little computer power.

Chapter 2

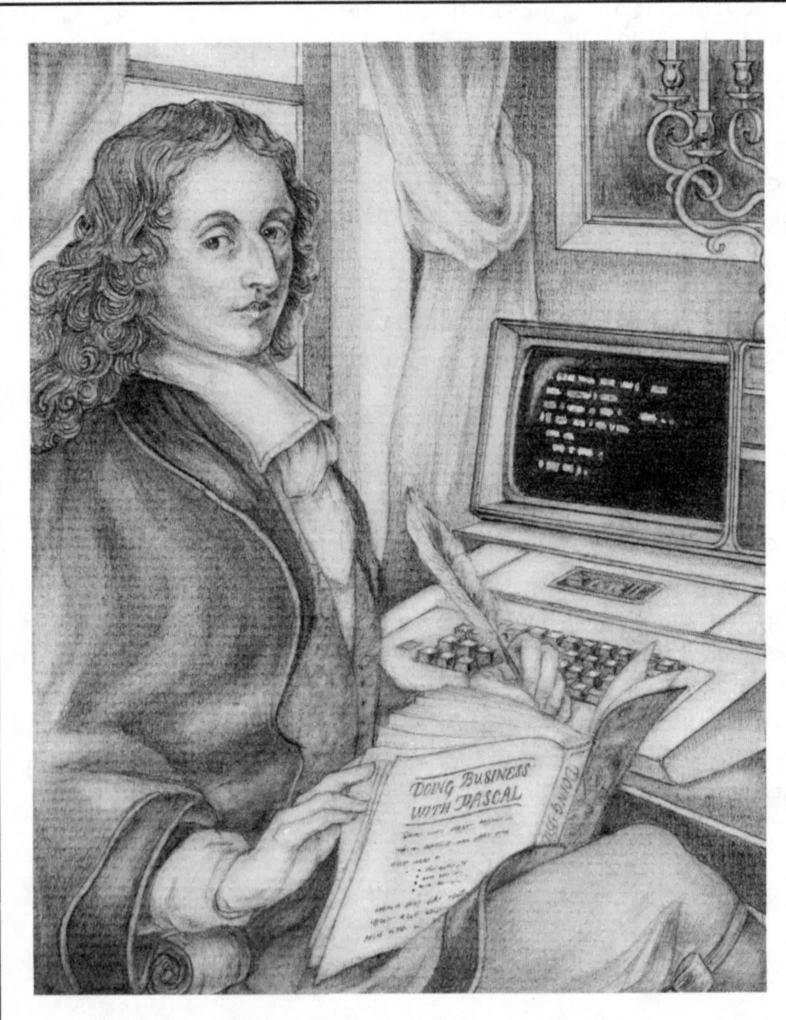

Handling Information within the Business System

INTRODUCTION

In Chapter 1 we discussed some of the basic concepts involved in systems and their design. Of particular importance was the emphasis on the beginning point for all systems design projects: first and foremost the systems analyst must concentrate on the desired output. Our whole discussion of the individual applications in Chapter 1 could have focused solely on reports; in fact, several of the applications chapters in Part III of this book describe ways in which reports are produced. The reports presented in Part III are not necessarily those most commonly included in financial applications. Instead, they are reports oriented toward managers and decision makers in the small business. This is not to say that the standard kinds of operating functions are not also important in a business system, but simply that those kinds of reports are commonly available in microcomputer applications packages. The kinds of management reports included in Part III, however, are most often the products of much larger systems based on minicomputers or even mainframes.

In Chapter 1 we also indicated that the various sections of the business system must communicate with each other. The terms most often used to describe this communication are "interface," "integration," "communications links," and so on. In this chapter we will study the various means of communication between modules and subsystem applications. Specifically, we will deal with the kinds of files commonly found within a business system. Part II of this book includes information on file handling in Pascal. In this chapter we discuss files in more general terms, and give broad guidelines for the control of data destined to be used by application programs.

WHY FILES ARE NECESSARY

We can easily write business application programs that simply accept data from the keyboard, process that data, and then display specific results. In fact, many applications, some of them business-oriented, do just that. Such applications work well when there is no need for permanent storage of results, no need to keep track of other uses of the application, and no need for the current run of the program to know anything about any other programs or applications. Most game applications, for example, are written with little intent or need to maintain information about who ran the game before or what the results were. A computer program that simulates a four-function calculator would not usually maintain results of previous calculations. A program to calculate federal income tax deductions could even be written to do no more than accept input from the keyboard (gross salary, number of dependents claimed, and so on), calculate the tax, and display it on the screen. The operator would then have to transfer that data to a worksheet for later use.

The obvious limitation to, and therefore disadvantage of, this kind of systems design is that human intervention in the process is required at all times. Not only does this requirement open the door to significant errors (suppose the operator transposes a number while writing the tax deduction onto the worksheet), it also keeps the program itself running inefficiently and slowly. Run-time speed will be limited by the speed of the human operator. Speed may not be critical if no one else is using or waiting to use the computer, or if the computer is dedicated to a single task. But in the real world of business applications, that will seldom be the case.

What is needed, then, is an ability to store data in some form for use by applications and subsystems, and also an ability to pass data from one application to another. The length of time the data is stored depends on need, as do the method and place of storage. In general, data must be stored only long enough to be useful and not so long as to get in the way. The specific kinds of files that we will discuss in the remainder of this chapter are typically found in business applications. The exact names may vary from package to package or from one computer installation to another, but the concepts cross over those boundaries.

The System Profile

In any computerized business system, certain specific information about the company and its way of doing business is necessary: the name and address of the company (perhaps in different forms for different purposes), methods of accounting for inventory costing, length of pay periods, specific bank account numbers for business operations, etc. Information like this seldom changes in the normal course of business operations, but the ability to change the data must nevertheless be provided.

That kind of information can be "hard-coded" into each of the applications programs within the system. The programmer can write an application to produce purchase orders, and include in the programming code the name of the company, the address of the company, the address of the receiving department, and so on, so that the company manager would not have to worry that day-to-day users of the system remember that company information is correct. The problem comes when a major change occurs: the company moves, or the receiving department is relocated. The programmer then has to return to the installation and revise the computer code to reflect the new information. The programs must then be recompiled to run properly.

Another disadvantage of including such business profile information in the body of program code is that the same piece of information might well be used in several applications. A business name and address will be common to many programs. A tax identification number might be used in several applications. If this information is hard-coded, the data has to be repeated in each program. Worse, if a change occurs, the programmer has to remember every single location in which that data is used, to ensure that the operations will be completely up-to-date.

The problems created by the hard-coding method can be avoided by writing and maintaining a file of information that can be used by any application or subsystem that needs it. This type of file is called a *system profile.* Chapter 10 provides an example of how a system profile might be created in Pascal. Here, it is important only to note the design considerations behind the use of such a file. If changes must be made to the basic information about the company, those changes are simply made in the profile. One change to one address field will change that address everywhere it appears in the entire system. One change to any profile field will in fact change the entire system's use of that information.

Critical here is the need to document the way in which any item of profile data is used. Before making changes to the profile, the user needs to know the complete effect of that change on the entire system. If another application is written that makes use of profile data, the programmer needs to coordinate that application with the profile data. Possible changes in profile data must be allowed for in the new application.

Profile data must be carefully designed. The primary reason for having a profile at all is to simplify changes in the management or status of the company; however, an important secondary purpose of the profile is to avoid duplication of data. The system may require several addresses; however, it would probably not need a different address for every application. The name of the company may need to be formatted in several ways (on one line, or two, or abbreviated), but probably not in a different way for each subsystem or each application.

A good business system must also be flexible enough to run for more than one company. Business entrepreneurs often own or manage more than one business entity. It is inefficient to have to buy a new computer system for each one of those business enterprises. Nor is it particularly efficient to have to edit the computer source code and recompile the programs for each business. This flexibility will have the effect of making the system less expensive, since the total research and development costs can be spread out over several installations. In addition, such a system typically receives more thorough testing and is thus more reliable.

The System Master Files

Slightly more dynamic than system profile information, which changes seldom in the life of the system, is *master file information,* which can change on a weekly or monthly basis, but probably not much more frequently. So master files are still relatively stable. Unlike system profiles, master files are usually application-dependent. By this we mean that a master file would contain data that is used primarily by one application or one subsystem. A second application may also need that data, and may in fact have access to it, but typically only one application will have modification and control privileges for a given master file, and one application will have primary use of that master file information.

All of the subsystems shown in the system organization chart of Figure 1.3 would thus have their own master files. We will not discuss all of these files in detail, but it is important to look at a few examples to see some of the ways in which master files are organized in business systems, so that the concept of master file handling is clear. The careful and considered design of system master files is absolutely critical to systems design.

The Payroll Subsystem Master Files

Necessary to the operation of a payroll subsystem is the existence of a file of employee master information. This file must have all the required information about each employee—name and address, social security number, rate of pay, and information about tax status, automatic bank deposits, voluntary deductions, and the like. All of this information needs to be accessed when the payroll system is actually operating. There must be mechanisms for modifying the data in that file, with appropriate edit criteria clearly applied.

In fact, modification capability must be part of the design for each master file. Earlier we indicated that checking for accuracy should be done as early as possible in the data-gathering process; further use of that data assumes that the edit process has already been completed and that the data meets system requirements. It follows, then, that the logical time to check the accuracy of the master file information is when data is input into that file. There are several levels of data editing. First, it is important to ensure that the data entered is of the correct data type. Nonnumeric characters cannot be allowed to creep into numeric fields. Second, it is important that fields not be left blank when some value other than spaces is required. Third, values must be checked against predefined legal *ranges.* For instance, dates in the format of month-day-year have legal ranges. A day of the month greater than 31 must be rejected.

Other, more application-specific, edits can also be performed. The first two levels of edit checking are common to the input of nearly all data, while the last level mentioned can be general (as with dates) or very application-specific. Intelligent system design will provide subroutine-type programs for the first two levels of error checking, allowing for greater specificity in the third.

While a given programming language requires specific coding conventions to define files (Pascal has required conventions, as do COBOL, BASIC, FORTRAN, and others), it is usually handy to indicate the structure of the data file in some common format, which is then translated into the specific language requirements. Note that all of this discussion pertains to fixed-length records, without space compression. Large business applications on minicomputers or mainframes will frequently use space compression techniques and dynamic record layouts to manage disk space utilization. Microprocessor applications, especially those written in Pascal, will not generally use these kinds of techniques, so record layout definition is important. The record layout for an employee master file might include information as indicated in Figure 2.1.

The translation of this information into the specific language code (like Pascal) will be different from the format described by the record layout.

However, it is often useful to have a clear picture of the record layout. This layout can be helpful to both the programmer and the person who needs to read and understand file information. The term *offset* is used in Figure 2.1 instead of *length,* although the two are interchangeable. In addition, note that the record layout actually starts with record position zero.

Other information might need to be included in the payroll master file. Some design concepts are illustrated, however, even in this brief example. Note that employee deductions are identified by number and by dollar amount. Typically, the specific deduction description would reside on the system profile, along with information on the frequency, the type, and the priority of the deduction, and so on. This makes it unnecessary to repeat detailed information of this type on each of the employee master file records. The profile is a sort of look-up table for the exact information about the deduction and the way in which the deduction is to be handled.

The employee name is divided into last name, first name, and middle initial. Another name format may also appear as a separate field of the payroll master file: the name as it is to appear on payroll checks (usually first name, middle initial, last name). This duplication of names may

Field Name	Start Point	Offset	Data type
Employee Last Name	0	25	String
Employee First Name	25	15	String
Employee Middle Init	40	1	String
Employee Address	41	40	String
Employee ID#	81	5	Integer
Number of Dependents	86	3	Integer
Hourly Pay	89	5	Real
1st Deduction ID#	94	2	Integer
1st Deduction Amt	96	5	Real
2nd Deduction ID#	101	2	Integer
2nd Deduction Amt	103	5	Real
Married/single/H.H.	108	1	Integer

Figure 2.1: Payroll Master File

in fact be more efficient than developing a specific routine within the program to reformat names. A shorter version of the name (last name, first and middle initial) might also be required for internal reports. The important point to remember is that the payroll master file needs to include sufficient information on the employees for processing reports, both operational and management.

The one-character fields, such as marital status, can often be presented as integers instead of alphabetic codes. Typically these fields will be used as control points for specific processes. In the payroll application, the marital status would indicate the scope of tax deductions for the particular employee. Fields are indicated as integers because systems usually perform comparison operations on integers more efficiently than they do on alphabetic characters. In addition, the use of integers for one-digit fields allows for branching operations within the programming code. The important point is that the design of the master file needs to consider not only data requirements, but also how the data is to be handled within the program and the subsystem. Significant benefits can be realized if data elements are carefully designed.

The payroll master file information would also be needed for personnel applications, which produce information for external reporting (such as EEOC), for internal management (such as position control reports), and so on. However, the personnel master file would be somewhat larger and have greater detail than is required by the payroll applications. It is not efficient to repeat all of the data of one master file in another file. The concepts of sharing common data and providing "pointers" to other files are both important. For payroll/personnel applications, a logical field to use as a pointer is the employee number. Personnel information needs would be filled by simply constructing another file with additional information, making sure that information access to the payroll master file is assured. The personnel application would have access privileges, but not modification privileges in this case. However, the application *would* have modification privileges to any personnel master file information.

To understand the concept of master files, it is necessary to understand the nature of the files themselves. As we indicated earlier, master files are generally stable. They are more subject to change than the system profile would be, but do not require constant updating. In addition, master files provide a medium for sharing information among applications and subsystems. Several programs might have access or update privileges to a particular master file. Usually the processes that update the master files also produce audit trail reports and files about the activity on those master files. But those kinds of files are extremely dynamic and do not themselves constitute master files.

The Vendor Master File

One additional example of a master file will suffice to show the nature of this type of file. Figure 2.2 lists the information that might be part of an accounts payable vendor master file.

Again, this master file is incomplete, but it does add to our illustration of the general nature of master files. Notice that specific entries are provided for both the vendor name as it might appear on purchase orders, and another name format as it might appear on checks. Since our whole system design started with a careful look at reports and output requirements, we know in advance the kinds of information that will be required as input, in this case input from the master file. This shows once again the importance of starting system design with an analysis of output needs.

The use of the fields called *discount rate* and *discount date* is important. The fields are linked together, and in fact the edit process of master file maintenance would probably look for the relationship. The discount rate field could be blank, if the discount date were also blank, but the discount date should not normally be blank if the discount rate is filled in. The discount date is actually a two-digit field indicating the number of

Field Description	Start Point	Offset	Data Type
Vendor Number	0	6	Integer
Vendor Name	6	24	String
Vendor Address	30	20	String
Vendor City	50	20	String
Vendor State	70	2	String
Vendor Zip Code	72	5	Integer
Vendor Name - Checks	77	30	String
1099 Form	107	1	Integer
Discount Rate	108	2	Integer
Discount Date	110	2	Integer
Month-to-Date Dol.	112	7	Real
Year-to-Date Dol.	119	8	Real

Figure 2.2: Vendor Master File

days from the invoice date when the discount can no longer be taken. One data processing convention is to convert all dates from the normal month-day-year format to a sequential "day number" counted from a specific point in time (in this book, January 1, 1901). These are called "scalar" dates. A procedure for scalar data conversion, DATECONVERT, is discussed in Chapter 3. A routine will be required to compare two scalar dates and thus determine the number of days between two given dates. A discount date would, however, be meaningless if no discount rate were filled in.

Another important design consideration is the capacity for data file *revision.* Suppose that the discount policies of a certain vendor changed over time. Or suppose that a vendor had no activity for several years, and its master file needed to be deleted from the records. While we have not specifically mentioned it before, this kind of change clearly illustrates the need for a program to add, modify and delete the records contained in master files. Modifications can be made in two ways: the program can change only the record that needs modifying, leaving all of the rest of the data in the master file the same; or the program can update all records every time the master file is accessed, giving the user an opportunity to review the entire file. Either method would work; the former is probably more efficient and less prone to error.

The *1099 form* field of the vendor master file has two legal values, one meaning "yes" and the other meaning "no." The field has again been defined as an integer type, since integer types can be more efficiently compared than string types. In this case there are only two valid answers, so if the language supports a Boolean variable type (as does Pascal), then that could be used. Otherwise, a value of one (1) could be used to mean yes and a value of zero (0) could be used to mean no. The input routines need to check for valid entries. If a nonlegal value is entered, a branch routine within the program would give error messages and direct the data entry operator to re-key the value. This is a type of program control operation, in that it diverts the program from the "main line" of the program logic and executes some specific error routines.

Also in the vendor master file is an example of how information history can be kept along with the master file information. The month-to-date and year-to-date dollar fields would be used to store current-period and year-to-date information on the activity of the vendor. Daily or weekly transactions posting invoices to an accounts payable file would also need to update information on activity history files. The master file is an ideal place to keep that history. Other kinds of information may be required, some of it rather extensive. Information on a full twelve months of individual activity for a particular vendor, for a particular employee master file, or for some other sort of record keeping may be needed. Activity history should probably be stored in a separate file, accessed only during the actual updating of that history information. If that is done, another file could be created, with individual records related through the account number, the vendor number, or some other such common identification. This relating of records within several files is similar to the operations for linking the personnel master file with the payroll master file. Separate routines would then access the information in the master file for the production of activity-type reports.

Common to all of the master files suggested so far is some sort of identification number. We used an employee number in the payroll master file, a vendor number in the vendor master file. Identifying each entry on a file by number makes it easier to use the file, and to correctly identify each transaction to the correct master. A check-digit calculation can be used on these numbers to ensure that data is entered accurately. Chapters 3 and 5 discuss the construction and use of a check-digit routine. Our check digit is calculated by a MOD-10 operation; other types of check digits are sometimes used. The check-digit routine is part of a module that can be used throughout the entire system.

TRANSACTION FILES

So far we have discussed both the system profile, which contains more or less permanent general information about the company, and system master files, which contain relatively stable information about specific applications. Now we will look at some extremely dynamic files, called *transaction files*. Transactions are records of financial activity within the business. The computerized business system takes these transactions and uses them in the creation of financial and management reports such as those illustrated in section III of this book. There are several modes of transactions processing that a business system might use.

First, there is batch-mode processing. This kind of processing allows for the terminal operator to enter many records of similar type and function at one time into a file called a batch. Specific application programs take those batch records and process them. Much business data processing is done in the batch mode. Typically, time card information is collected in batches and then processed by a payroll program. Cash receipts posting, accounts payable invoice processing, and other kinds of easily grouped tasks are done in a batch mode. Early data processing was almost completely batch-mode processing. Card punch machine operators produced punched cards grouped together for use by the application program.

However, with the rise in popularity of minicomputers and now microcomputers, much of the focus of processing is on what is called *on-line, real-time* processing. These two terms describe the way the person sitting at the computer terminal interacts with the system. *On-line* typically indicates that the actions of the operator have an effect on transaction and master files. *Real-time* means that this effect is immediate, or at least has no appreciable built-in delay. The computer operator knows immediately if an error has been made, and so can make the correction before the error has a chance to affect other operations. Real-time processing can in fact be a form of batch processing. A system of data entry can be developed that allows the computer operator to enter data in batches and, on a real-time basis, have that data edited and monitored for completeness and accuracy. On-line processing, by comparison, does this edit checking but also performs the tasks on the master files and completes the transactions which are requested by the operator. For example, an on-line editing program for the system profile would change the data on that file as the operator is making requests for those changes, and then would display the new information of the updated fields. An on-line editing program for personnel information in the personnel master file would update the employee information as the operator makes requests for a change in that file, and then would display the information which has been changed. On-line editing also takes place in real time; real-time processing is not necessarily on-line.

Microprocessor applications are usually both on-line and real-time. The hardware will usually perform one significant user-oriented task at a time (operating system tasks, like the control of the keyboard and the CRT screen, are of course performed all of the time), and so there are not multiple users competing for CPU time. In addition, since microcomputers are comparatively cheap compared to minicomputers and mainframes, there may be more than one computer, and thus no need for timesharing. Finally, microprocessor business systems often comprise sets of stand-alone module programs which are run independently of one another, with little need for computer resource allocations between concurrent processes.

This is not to say that there is no place in microcomputer-based systems for batch processing. Payroll time cards, for example, can be most efficiently processed independently of the actual payroll calculations necessary to produce payroll checks. The data entry process for time cards would be extremely slow if at each point of entry the entire routine to perform payroll calculations also had to be run. Better design would dictate that the data entry programming (such as the time and attendance program presented in Chapter 11) perform the normal edit checking, and then produce files for other programs to use in completing the payroll process.

On-line, real-time applications need to produce some sort of audit trail to track completed activities and to aid in rebuilding the files and the system, should hardware or software difficulties arise. Audit trails are transaction files in the broadest sense of the term, but they are often handled somewhat differently than the standard transaction files discussed here. Often they are more like print files, meant to be queued up for printing and then stored for later use by auditors.

Transaction files, then, are produced by a particular process for use by that process again, or for use by other processes. Their use is one of the most common ways that subsystems communicate with one another in a business system environment. A payroll application would produce a transaction file, which would be used by the general ledger file to post entries to cash, to accrued liabilities-payroll, and to expense accounts. An inventory application would produce a transaction file to verify that invoiced inventory items were actually received at the loading dock; this file would be used by the accounts payable application. Any application might produce management or statistical information to be used by other subsystems and other applications in the processing of management reports.

Once the particular process that uses a transaction file has completed its tasks, the transaction file may be deleted, or perhaps printed for an audit trail, or it may be saved for further use by some other subsystem application. That application may change some of the data in the transaction file for some future use. It is not necessary to keep several generations of transaction files on disk if in fact only certain data is still being used.

Transaction files are the means of passing large bodies of information from one program to another, from one subsystem to another. They form the key communication and interface link between applications. One application that produces data for a subsequent application must, of course, produce the data in a format that the next application can use conveniently. Intelligent systems design will ensure that the respective files can be accessed and read by whatever applications need them.

In addition, reusable subroutines will be used as much as possible to produce transaction files. This practice not only saves the time that would be required to write new code, it is also a more efficient use of the hardware and systems resources.

Finally, the routines that produce the transaction files must make sure that transaction data is as free from input and production error as possible. Thorough editing and checking of data must be performed, so that the application that uses the transaction files can rely on the data. Always check for data errors as early as possible in any process.

AUDIT TRAIL FILES AND PRINT FILES

We have already briefly touched on the concept of audit trails for checking transactions. Audit trails must give enough detail on the manner in which final results are produced so that internal and external auditors can be assured of system reliability. External auditors or accountants should be involved in the selection or development of a business system. They must be satisfied that the system will not only produce consistent information about the business enterprise, but also that sufficient proof is available of accurate financial reporting. Audit trail reports document the intermediate steps taken to arrive at the final results.

Print file reports are often audit trails, but more frequently are the actual files used to produce the output by the system. They are intermediate files, usually deleted soon after the report itself is printed. Their importance in the system design process is related to the overhead requirements for actually printing reports. A report typically will have the results of many calculations or of accessing information from various files. In addition, the report format will include header information which needs to be repeated at the top and perhaps the bottom of each page. A particular application can do the needed calculations, but it is inefficient for the same application to be driving the printer in the production of the report. Printers are slow devices in the microprocessor environment. No application will run faster than its slowest device. Thus, if an application is dependent on data entry speed, the process time will be limited by that speed. If an application is dependent on printer speed, that process will not be completed any faster than the printer allows. While the total time required to complete the process may not appreciably change, running reports separately from other kinds of functions could provide an opportunity for the operator to carry out other duties, instead of staying at the terminal while all of the processes are being completed.

Often print files include control characters that a specific printer might understand to mean carriage return, top of form, et cetera. A standard routine to print a file could be used for the production of every report. It would then be more efficient to use that routine each time report production is necessary than to write separate code for the actual printing of each report. The printing routine might have several options, relative to width of form, length of page, and other important factors. But the routine need be written only once, and then can be used for nearly any printing job.

It has been stressed that the design of a business system must be based primarily on a clear understanding of output requirements. That is particularly true of reports and print files. Management must decide what information ought to be printed in the first place. Computers in general have the ability to produce pages and pages of reports, very rapidly and rather efficiently. The manager of a small business who is interested in microcomputer technology will thus be faced with the availability of more information than ever before. Thus, the *quality* of information becomes important. The reports that we will illustrate in Part III of this book are all management-oriented, rather than the standard accounting reports. Management reports are most useful if they are *exception* reports, or if they at least show the information in an order or priority that is important to the manager. The detailed reporting of large numbers of transactions is only a detriment to business management. Computers are exceptionally good at producing large amounts of information; only by careful and intelligent systems design (again, starting at the desired results) can the manager avoid an information glut.

FILE INTEGRITY

So far we have discussed the use of a business system profile, the use of master files within a system, and the use of transaction files and audit-trail print files. We have said very little about the maintenance and security of those files in the business system. Files might be lost or damaged in three different circumstances: (1) equipment or software failure; (2) inadvertent operator errors; and (3) willful intent to destroy information. We will discuss each of these in turn.

Equipment or Software Failure

The more we come to depend on computers in our business and even personal lives, the more frequently we will be faced with loss of data and processes because of equipment failure. Much of the equipment that forms a computer system is extremely reliable. Solid-state, integrated circuits are inherently more reliable than mechanical devices, and their use has progressed to the point that much of the computer's circuitry can give many years of service without failure. But some elements of the computer system, particularly the peripherals (the disk drives, the printer, and others), are still mechanical and, therefore, prone to failure. In the event of disk-drive failure, data can be lost permanently. That data may include easily recoverable transaction files, or it may include master file information that is less readily reconstructed. Therefore, there is a need to maintain back-up copies of all system profile information, all master file information, and information on any transaction files that are still needed for future processes. The business system must include utilities for file backup, and for disk copying. The system design might even include some control functions that make backup production a prerequisite to other operations.

Inadvertent File Deletion

The creation of backup files, with copies stored away from the computer operations area, is a positive step toward the recovery from unintentional destruction of files. Maintaining password security of files is a good method of avoiding that problem by ensuring that only the proper people are allowed access to the file information. The system profile application program in Chapter 10 gives an example of password functions for the profile. Other master files may be just as critical to the operations of the system and therefore require password protection. Different levels of password protection can be included, perhaps clearly distinguishing between the ability to access master file information and the ability to change or delete that information.

Password selection is also important, and often given insufficient attention. Very little originality is generally used in the selection of passwords unless the manager of the computer system insists upon it. If you have a list of the names of the spouse, children, near relatives and pets of a computer operator, you can generally discover the password he or she uses in fairly short order. Passwords should also be changed periodically (perhaps every three to six months), and changed immediately if key employees leave the company.

Intentional Sabotage

Keeping back-up copies of files is a good way to protect files from intentional destruction by unhappy or dishonest employees. Password protection will also help. But a clever computer professional can usually find a way around most protective measures used in the small business system environment. Larger systems are using carefully developed methods of protecting data, especially in a multi-user environment. Special codes are used to convert the data, and the codes are modified regularly. But computer crime goes on, in spite of the efforts to prevent it. (The literature on the subject of preventive measures is extensive; some of it is listed in the bibliography.)

Interactive Communications with the Business System

This chapter has dealt with communication among the applications and subsystems of the larger business system. Several file types were discussed, each of which provides methods for passing data between programs.

What we have not yet discussed is interactive communication between the human operator and the business system. Business systems normally require somewhat frequent response from their users. The design of that interactive communication is critical to the usefulness of the computer system. Here, then, are some general principles that will make the system work better.

1. Design menu-driven system modules. A screen full of data, with a question for the operator to answer, can be extremely confusing. A master menu screen like the one shown in Figure 2.3 is much clearer. It is easier to select an option from such a menu than to remember a particular abbreviation for each subsystem, or even

```
              M A S T E R   M E N U   S C R E E N

      A - SYSTEM PROFILE UPDATE
      B - GENERAL LEDGER SUBSYSTEM
      C - ACCOUNTS PAYABLE SUBSYSTEM
      D - PAYROLL SUBSYSTEM
      E - PERSONNEL SUBSYSTEM
      F - INVENTORY SUBSYSTEM
      G - ACCOUNTS RECEIVABLE SUBSYSTEM
      H - CAPITAL ASSETS SUBSYSTEM
      I - STOP PROCESSING

                ENTER SELECTION (A THRU I) -------
```

Figure 2.3: System Master Menu

a program name preceded by some data processing term like *execute* or *run*. Obviously, some error checking needs to be done to make sure that a valid character is entered. Then the program can branch to a specific routine or another set of screens that allow the user to select other processes within each subroutine.

2. Wherever possible, the number of input operations (such as data entry or menu selection) the user must perform for a particular screen should be limited to one or two. The progression from one screen to the next, through a tree-structure logic, lends itself to making very few decisions on each screen. (Operation of batch-type data entry may require more input items per screen.)

3. For batch-type data, design the screen to conform to the input document, so that the data entry operator can follow the format that he or she is looking at and not have to reformat the information during the input operation. Computers can reformat information more easily than people can.

4. At the conclusion of a data-entry operation, give the operator a summary of what has just been accomplished. Then ask if the data is correct. Make sure the operator has the option to either abort the entire operation and go back to the beginning, or go to a particular user-selected point in the process and start again from there.

5. Provide a "help" function. A "help" file can be established, and accessed like other files in the system. A user who needs clarification of a particular choice should be able to call for help from the system. Individual subsystems could provide specialized help. For example, a "help accounts payable" request might even give a listing of the functions available through the accounts payable subsystem without actually requiring that the subsystem be used.

6. Avoid the use of special characters or control characters to direct the functions of the business system. They are difficult to master and add to the possibility that the systems software will function improperly.

SUMMARY

This chapter, like the last one, has presented information on the basic elements of systems design. Much has been written on each of the subjects touched upon, and the bibliography lists some of the important works on systems design. These chapters are intended to be only a summary of some of the issues and subjects that the company manager needs to know about.

Part II

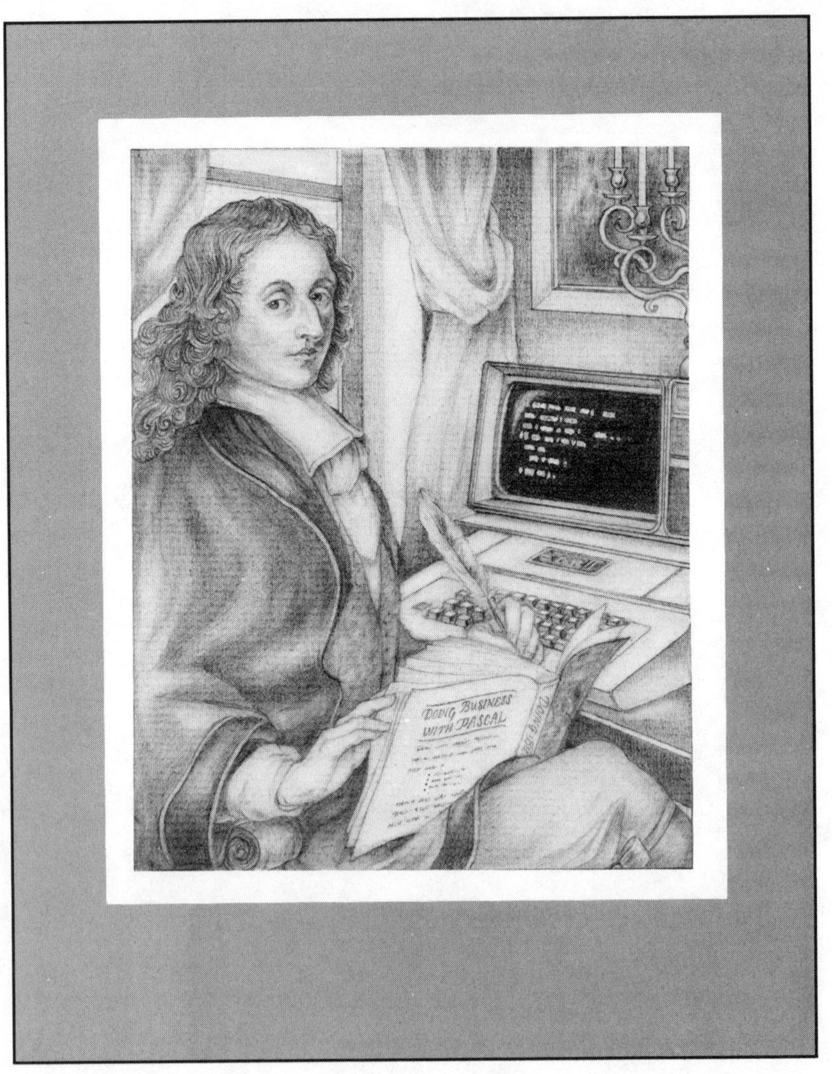

Programming for Business Systems: UCSD Pascal and its Extensions

Now that we have seen how a computerized business system is designed, we are ready to examine some of the issues and techniques involved in building such a system in Pascal. Part II describes and illustrates three important extensions to the Pascal language that are essential to writing business software. These three extensions, as implemented in UCSD Pascal, are:

- the precompilable UNIT module
- the long integer type
- the random access file

Our first concern, then, will be examining the structure and use of units in UCSD Pascal. In Chapters 3 to 6 we will build three units—called MONEYUNIT, CHECKUNIT, and DATEUNIT—to perform certain basic, recurring tasks in business programming. These units include a number of subroutines that deal with the problems of long-integer use. All the subsequent programs in this book will use at least one—and sometimes all three—of the units shown in these chapters.

In Chapters 7, 8, and 9 we will explore the use of random access files in UCSD Pascal. The file update program in Chapter 8 illustrates a technique of indexed file access. (The sorting and searching routines developed in Chapter 7 are tools needed for this indexing process.) Chapter 9 shows how data files provide a means of passing information from one program module to another. The programs in Chapter 9 use the data files—created by the update program in Chapter 8—to write two different reports.

In short, Part II lays the groundwork for business programming in UCSD Pascal. The tools developed in Part II will be used again and again in the application chapters of Part III.

Chapter 3

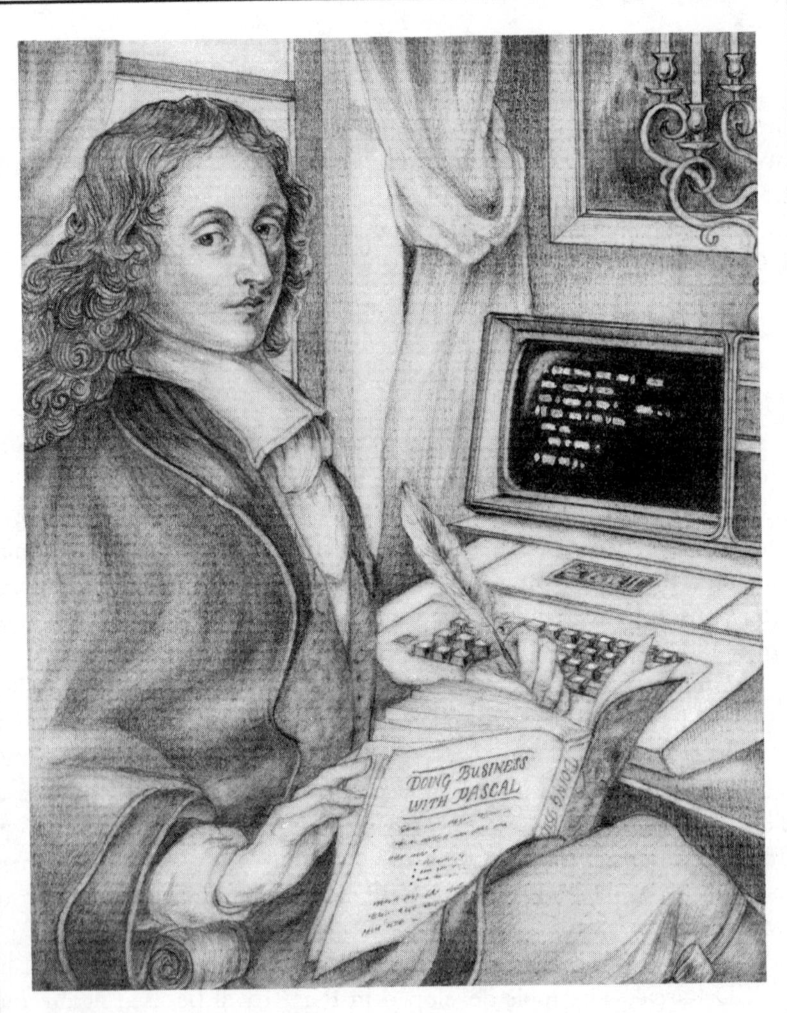

The Unit: Building Subroutine Packages

INTRODUCTION

In this chapter we will introduce a dozen or so important procedures and functions that we will be using throughout this book. These routines are organized into the UCSD Pascal program modules called *units*. The first unit we will look at, MONEYUNIT, provides for input and output of dollar-and-cent values. The next, CHECKUNIT, allows input, output, and verification of identification numbers with check digits. Finally, DATEUNIT includes a scalar date conversion routine that will allow us to calculate the number of days between two dates.

We will examine the use of each of the procedures and functions in these units, and will present three test programs to illustrate how the routines work. In addition, since all three of these units use *long integer* types, we will discuss the reasons for using long integers in financial programs. Finally, we will begin to see why the *precompiled-unit module* is such a convenient way of organizing often used routines in UCSD Pascal programming.

In Chapters 4, 5, and 6, we will examine the inner structure of our three units in turn, and see a complete listing of each. For now, we will simply assume that these units have already been written and that their procedures and functions are available for use in the test programs we will write. Our three goals in this chapter, then, are:

1. to illustrate the importance of units;
2. to discover how and why long integers are used for financial applications; and
3. to begin exploring the use of the procedures and functions of MONEYUNIT, CHECKUNIT, and DATEUNIT.

THE UNIT MODULE

Building a unit is a way of making a group of routines conveniently accessible to any program that needs to use them. The great advantage of a unit is that it can be compiled independently and then used in any program without being recompiled.

A unit has two sections, labeled INTERFACE and IMPLEMENTATION. The INTERFACE section defines all the constants, types, variables, procedures, and functions of the unit that are available to a program that uses the unit. Figure 3.1 shows the INTERFACE section of MONEYUNIT; notice that this particular unit defines one constant, one type, one function, and six procedures. These are referred to as the *public* definitions of the unit. The formal parameter lists and the function type are included here in the INTERFACE section.

The IMPLEMENTATION section of a unit contains the executable code for each of the unit's functions and procedures. In addition, this section may contain other routines that are necessary for implementing

```
(*$S+*)
UNIT MONEYUNIT;

INTERFACE

CONST
  L2 = 15;

TYPE
  LONG2 = INTEGER[L2];

FUNCTION VALUE(CH:CHAR):INTEGER;

PROCEDURE DOLLARFORM(VAL : LONG2;
              VAR    STNUM : STRING);

PROCEDURE INDOLLAR(VAR VAL : LONG2);

PROCEDURE RIGHTFIELD(VAR ST: STRING;
                  FIELDLENGTH: INTEGER);

PROCEDURE FOURCOLUMN(HEAD1, HEAD2,
                     HEAD3, HEAD4 : STRING;
                     FIELD1, FIELD2,
                     FIELD3, FIELD4 : INTEGER);

PROCEDURE LONGMULT(CENTS : LONG2;
                   MULT  : REAL;
               VAR RESULT : LONG2);

PROCEDURE CLEARSCREEN;
```

Figure 3.1: INTERFACE Section of MONEYUNIT

the public routines. The IMPLEMENTATION section, however, is *private*; that is to say, its structure and inner organization are hidden from the user. In this chapter we will only be concerned with the INTERFACE sections of each of our units, because we want to introduce the rationale and *use* of the procedures and functions of these units before we get involved in the details of their implementations. The IMPLEMENTATION section of each unit will be covered in the three chapters that follow.

The USES statement makes a unit available to a program. This statement must be placed just after the program heading, for example:

```
PROGRAM MONEYTEST;
USES MONEYUNIT;
```

With the USES statement, all the procedures of MONEYUNIT become part of program MONEYTEST. However, since MONEYUNIT is already compiled, its procedures do not need to be recompiled for use in MONEYTEST. A program can have only one USES statement, but that statement may include several units, for example:

```
USES MONEYUNIT, CHECKUNIT, DATEUNIT;
```

Depending on the location of the unit code file, we may be required to include a compiler directive before the USES statement:

```
PROGRAM MONEYTEST;
(*$U MONEYUNIT.CODE*)
USES MONEYUNIT;
```

The $U option tells the compiler where to find the unit file. The unit may also have to be explicitly *linked* to the program, using the system's linker utility.

Before we examine the specific routines of our three units, let us briefly discuss an important data structure that appears in all of them—the long integer.

LONG INTEGERS IN FINANCIAL APPLICATIONS

The accuracy of dollar-and-cent values is essential in business applications; for this reason we need a data type capable of representing these values precisely. Integers, while precise, typically have a range of only $2^{15} \pm$ or 32,768. Floating-point numbers (i.e., of type REAL) have a large range, but usually provide only about 6 or 7 digits of precision, which is not accurate enough for large dollar-and-cent values.

Different versions of Pascal offer various kinds of "double precision" types to solve this dilemma. In this book we will use the UCSD *long integer* type. Long integers may be defined with up to 36 digits, and the precision of each digit is guaranteed. We have already seen a long integer definition in the INTERFACE section of unit MONEYUNIT (Figure 3.1). The type LONG2 is a long integer of up to 15 digits:

```
CONST
   L2 = 15;
TYPE
   LONG2 = INTEGER[L2];
```

We will be using variables of type LONG2 to represent monetary values *expressed in cents*. Thus a variable of type LONG2 can represent any amount up to $9,999,999,999,999.99 with perfect accuracy. As we study the procedures of MONEYUNIT, we will discover exactly how these long integer variables can be used. In particular, the implementation of long integers imposes several restrictions that we will have to deal with:

- Only the UCSD Pascal functions TRUNC and STR allow parameters of long integer types. (TRUNC converts a long integer into a regular integer.)
- Functions that return a long integer type are not allowed.
- Long integer types cannot be declared in procedure parameter lists. (Thus, it is necessary to define the type LONG2, which is subsequently used to declare variables in parameter lists.)

All the same, long integers prove to provide a reasonably convenient, and perfectly precise, way of representing dollar-and-cent data.

Now let us begin exploring our three packages—MONEYUNIT, CHECKUNIT, and DATEUNIT.

MONEYUNIT: DOLLAR AND CENT INPUT AND OUTPUT

The routines of MONEYUNIT fall into three functional categories:

1. input (INDOLLAR, VALUE)
2. output (DOLLARFORM, RIGHTFIELD, FOURCOLUMN, CLEARSCREEN)
3. long integer arithmetic (LONGMULT)

We will discuss them in that order.

Procedure INDOLLAR and Function VALUE

A call to procedure INDOLLAR takes the following form:

```
INDOLLAR(LONGVAL)
```

where LONGVAL is defined to be of type LONG2. INDOLLAR performs the following tasks:

1. It reads a dollar-and-cent input value.
2. It determines whether the value is valid.
3. If the value is valid, INDOLLAR converts the value into a long integer representing cents, which is returned in the variable LONGVAL.
4. If the value is not valid, INDOLLAR returns to step 1, above.

INDOLLAR allows a great variety of input formats. The input value may (but is not required to) include leading blanks, a dollar sign, and commas. If the value does not include a decimal point, then it is read as a dollar amount with no cents. If a decimal point is included, then any number of digits may be entered after it; however, the number will be rounded to the nearest cent.

The maximum value INDOLLAR will allow is $999,999,999.99. An attempt to input a larger number will result in the following error messages:

```
*** TOO LONG
*** REDO
?
```

Two bells will also sound. The question mark is the prompt for a new input value. Nonnumeric input (other than the allowable characters '$', '.', and ',') will result in an error message, one bell, and the prompt for a new value.

Function VALUE, which is used by INDOLLAR to convert an input string into a long integer, returns the numeric value of a digit character. We will study the details of VALUE in Chapter 4.

Procedure DOLLARFORM

A call to procedure DOLLARFORM takes two parameters:

```
DOLLARFORM(LONGVAL, ST)
```

where LONGVAL is a long integer of type LONG2, and ST is a string. LONGVAL is assumed to represent cents; DOLLARFORM returns a properly formatted string representing dollars and cents to the variable ST. For example, consider the following sequence:

```
DOLLARFORM(371562115, ST);
WRITELN(ST)
```

The result of these lines would be an output of:

```
$3,715,621.15
```

Procedures RIGHTFIELD, FOURCOLUMN, and CLEARSCREEN

Often in this book we will want to create tables of information, organized in rows and columns. Procedures RIGHTFIELD and FOURCOLUMN are tools that will make this presentation easier to perform in many cases. RIGHTFIELD takes two parameters: a string, ST, and an integer, L:

```
RIGHTFIELD(ST, L);
```

As its name implies, RIGHTFIELD right-justifies the string ST in a field of length L. What actually happens is this: blank characters are inserted to the left of ST until the length of the string reaches L. Note that ST is a VAR parameter, which allows RIGHTFIELD to pass the transformed string back to the calling procedure.

If ST is already more than L characters long at the time of the call to RIGHTFIELD, the "excess" left characters of ST will be chopped off (to give ST a length of L) and the first character of the new ST will be changed to "!" to indicate a loss of characters. For example, the following sequence:

```
ST : = 'TESTING';
RIGHTFIELD(ST,6);
WRITELN(ST)
```

would produce the line:

```
!STING
```

The original string "TESTING," which exceeded the length of L by one character, has apparently lost two: one was dropped, and another was transformed into a flag character.

FOURCOLUMN actually writes a line of output. It takes eight parameters: four strings and four integers (none of them VAR):

```
FOURCOLUMN(ST1,ST2,ST3,ST4,L1,L2,L3,L4)
```

Each string ST will be right-justified in its corresponding field length L.

(RIGHTFIELD is used for this purpose.) In addition, FOURCOLUMN adds one blank character between each field when writing the output line. Thus, the line will be (L1 + 1) + (L2 + 1) + (L3 + 1) + L4 characters long. FOURCOLUMN can actually be used to create tabulations for any number of columns *up to* four. If we want to produce three columns, for example, we simply pass a blank string and a zero length for the fourth column:

```
FOURCOLUMN('ONE','TWO','THREE','',12,12,12,0)
```

Procedure CLEARSCREEN, which takes no parameters, clears the screen of all information, and repositions the cursor at the top-left corner of the screen. (Note: CLEARSCREEN is currently designed for a 25-line screen.)

Procedure LONGMULT

Multiplication of long integers by integers is defined in UCSD Pascal, but multiplication of long integers by real numbers is not. Since we may often need to multiply our long integers (representing cents) by small real numbers (percentages, for example), we need a routine that will perform this operation with acceptable accuracy. Procedure LONGMULT takes three parameters:

```
LONGMULT(LONGVAL, RVAL, RESULT)
```

LONGVAL and RESULT are of type LONG2; RESULT is a VAR parameter. RVAL is the real multiplier. The product of LONGVAL and RVAL is stored in RESULT and returned to the calling procedure. The user must be careful of two restrictions when using this routine: ROUND(RVAL) must not exceed MAXINT, and the product of LONGVAL and RVAL must not overflow LONG2.

A TEST PROGRAM FOR MONEYUNIT

Program MONEYTEST is designed to test all of the routines contained in MONEYUNIT. The program listing is shown in Figure 3.2. The program performs the following tasks:

1. It reads a series of yearly dollar-and-cent input values (INVALUE).
2. It multiplies each value by the corresponding present value factor for that year (LONGMULT).
3. It produces a table of present value factors, the orginal values, and the discounted values (DOLLARFORM and FOURCOLUMN).

```
PROGRAM MONEYTEST;

(*$U MONEYUNIT.CODE*)

USES MONEYUNIT;


  TYPE
    LTABLETYPE = ARRAY[1..30] OF LONG2;
    RTABLETYPE = ARRAY[1..30] OF REAL;

  VAR
    YEARS,
    I         : INTEGER;
    TOTVAL,
    TOTPRES   : LONG2;
    RATE      : REAL;
    VAL,
    PRESVAL   : LTABLETYPE;
    DISCTABLE: RTABLETYPE;
    STVALUE,
    STPRES,
    STDISC,
    STRINDEX,
    ANSWER    : STRING;

PROCEDURE STREAL (VAL : REAL;
              VAR  ST  : STRING);
  VAR
    I : INTEGER;

  BEGIN
    STR(ROUND(VAL * 10000.0), ST);
    IF LENGTH(ST) < 4 THEN
      FOR I := 1 TO (4 - LENGTH(ST)) DO
        INSERT('0', ST, 1);
    INSERT('.',ST,LENGTH(ST)-3)
  END;

PROCEDURE DISCFACS (RATE : REAL;
                    YEARS : INTEGER;
               VAR  DISCOUNT : RTABLETYPE);

  VAR
    INDEX       : INTEGER;
    TEMP        : REAL;

BEGIN
  TEMP := 1.0;
  FOR INDEX := 1 TO YEARS DO
    BEGIN
      TEMP := TEMP * (1.0/(1.0 + RATE/100.0));
      DISCOUNT[INDEX] := TEMP
    END
END;  (* DISCFACS *)
```

Figure 3.2: Listing of Program MONEYTEST

```
BEGIN   (* MAIN PROGRAM *)
  REPEAT
    CLEARSCREEN;
    WRITE   ('HOW MANY YEARS?      ');
    READLN(YEARS);
    WRITE   ('DISCOUNT RATE (%)?  ');
    READLN(RATE);

    (* DISCFACS CALCULATES THE PRESENT
       VALUE FACTORS FOR ALL THE YEARS *)

    DISCFACS(RATE, YEARS, DISCTABLE);

    WRITELN;
    WRITELN('INPUT YEARLY VALUES');
    WRITELN('-------------------');
    WRITELN;

    (* INPUT A VALUE FOR EACH YEAR AND
       MULTIPLY BY APPROPRIATE PRESENT
       VALUE FACTOR *)

    FOR I := 1 TO YEARS DO
      BEGIN
        WRITE('YEAR ',I,'> ');
        INDOLLAR(VAL[I]);
        LONGMULT(VAL[I], DISCTABLE[I], PRESVAL[I])
      END;
    CLEARSCREEN;

    (* PRINT THE TABLE HEADINGS *)

    FOURCOLUMN('YR', 'FACTOR', 'VALUE',
               'PRES VAL', 3, 8, 12, 12);
    FOURCOLUMN('--', '------', '-----',
               '--------', 3, 8, 12, 12);

    TOTVAL := 0;
    TOTPRES := 0;

    (* PRINT EACH LINE OF THE TABLE AND
       ACCUMULATE THE TOTALS *)

    FOR I := 1 TO YEARS DO
      BEGIN
        DOLLARFORM(VAL[I], STVALUE);
        DOLLARFORM(PRESVAL[I], STPRES);
        STR(I,STRINDEX);
        STREAL(DISCTABLE[I],STDISC);
        FOURCOLUMN(STRINDEX, STDISC,
                   STVALUE, STPRES, 3, 8, 12, 12);
        TOTVAL := TOTVAL + VAL[I];
        TOTPRES := TOTPRES + PRESVAL[I]
      END;
```

Figure 3.2: Listing of Program MONEYTEST (cont.)

```
        WRITELN;
        WRITELN;

        (* PRINT THE TOTALS *)

        DOLLARFORM(TOTVAL, STVALUE);
        DOLLARFORM(TOTPRES, STPRES);
        FOURCOLUMN('***', 'TOTALS >', STVALUE, STPRES,
                    3, 8, 12, 12);

        WRITELN;
        WRITE    ('ANOTHER SET OF VALUES? ');
        READLN(ANSWER)
      UNTIL (ANSWER[1] = 'N')

    END.    (* MAIN PROGRAM *)
```

Figure 3.2: Listing of Program MONEYTEST (cont.)

The yearly input values might represent expected future income from an investment; the program calculates the present value of this future income. Let us briefly examine MONEYTEST to see exactly how it uses each of the routines of MONEYUNIT to produce this report. The input values are stored in the array VAL:

```
INDOLLAR(VAL[I]);
```

and are immediately multiplied by the present value factors:

```
LONGMULT(VAL[I], DISCTABLE[I], PRESVAL[I]);
```

The present value factors, stored in the array DISCTABLE, are calculated in procedure DISCFACS. The array PRESVAL, then, contains the discounted values.

DOLLARFORM is used to convert both the original input values and the discounted values into dollar-and-cent strings:

```
DOLLARFORM(VAL[I], STVALUE);
DOLLARFORM(PRESVAL[I], STPRES);
```

MONEYTEST has its own procedure, STREAL, to convert the present value factors (which are of type REAL) into strings:

```
STREAL(DISCTABLE[I], STDISC);
```

FOURCOLUMN is called several times; first to print the table headings:

```
FOURCOLUMN('YR','FACTOR','VALUE','PRESVAL',
                3, 8, 12, 12);
```

then to print each line of the table:

```
FOURCOLUMN(STRINDEX, STDISC, STVALUE, STPRES,
           3, 8, 12, 12);
```

and finally to print the totals:

```
FOURCOLUMN(' * * * ', 'TOTALS > ', STVALUE, STPRES,
           3, 8, 12, 12);
```

These three different uses demonstrate the versatility of FOURCOLUMN. The output from a sample run of this test program is shown in Figure 3.3.

Next we will look at the routines of CHECKUNIT and at a test program for that package.

CHECKUNIT: I.D. NUMBER INPUT AND VERIFICATION

Whenever many long identification numbers must be typed into a computer, the chances are high that typographical errors will be made. One way of reducing these errors is to produce a *check digit* for any given number; if the number is entered incorrectly, then the check digit will probably no longer correspond, and the error will be caught.

```
HOW MANY YEARS?      5
DISCOUNT RATE (%)?   12

INPUT YEARLY VALUES
-------------------

YEAR 1> 225765.34
YEAR 2> 214677.89
YEAR 3>  98754.77
YEAR 4>  50871.88
YEAR 5>  41981.87

 YR    FACTOR          VALUE       PRES VAL
 --    ------          -----       --------
  1     .8929    $225,765.34    $201,585.87
  2     .7972    $214,677.89    $171,141.21
  3     .7118     $98,754.77     $70,293.65
  4     .6355     $50,871.88     $32,329.08
  5     .5674     $41,981.87     $23,820.51


*** TOTALS >     $632,051.75    $499,170.32
```

Figure 3.3: Output from MONEYTEST

The routines in the CHECKUNIT package are designed to perform three basic tasks:

1. accept input of long identification numbers, either with or without check digits;
2. calculate the check digit for any acceptable input number; the calculation is based on a simple algorithm that checks both the value and the position of each digit in the number;
3. verify the correctness of any number that is input *with* a check digit.

The INTERFACE section of CHECKUNIT is shown in Figure 3.4. The unit contains a procedure and two functions, all of which, taken together, perform the input and verification of numbers and check digits. Notice that CHECKUNIT also defines another long integer type—LONG1; long integers of type LONG1 may have up to nine digits.

We will briefly examine calls to these three routines and then run a test program to see how they work.

Procedure INVALUE

INVALUE is the input routine, similar in some ways to INDOLLAR. Unlike INDOLLAR, however, procedure INVALUE takes three parameters:

```
INVALUE(LONGID, L, CH)
```

```
(*$S++)

UNIT CHECKUNIT;

INTERFACE

CONST
  L1 = 9;

TYPE
  LONG1 = INTEGER[L1];

PROCEDURE INVALUE(VAR VAL : LONG1;
                      LWD : INTEGER;
                  VAR  CD : BOOLEAN);

FUNCTION CHECKDIGIT(L: LONG1): INTEGER;

FUNCTION VERIFYCHECK(I : LONG1): BOOLEAN;
```

Figure 3.4: INTERFACE Section of CHECKUNIT

where LONGID is a variable of type LONG1, L is an integer or integer variable, and CH is a Boolean variable. LONGID and CH are VAR parameters.

This input routine is designed to impose a strict format on the numbers it reads. Let us say we are inputting identification numbers that are five digits long plus a check digit—six digits in all. Our call to INVALUE might look like this:

```
INVALUE(LONGID, 6, CH)
```

This call accepts an input value in one of two forms—with or without a check digit. For an input value containing exactly five digits (for example, 12345) the numerical value is assigned to LONGID, and CH becomes false, indicating the absence of a check digit in the input number. An input value *with* a check digit requires a hyphen between the last digit of the identification number and the check digit:

```
12345-5
```

In this case, LONGID receives the six-digit numerical value (hyphen deleted, of course) and CH is switched to true.

Thus, if we wish to make sure the input typist includes a check digit in the input of a five-digit identification number, we might write a sequence of lines as follows:

```
REPEAT
   WRITE('? ');
   INVALUE(LONGID, 6, CH)
UNTIL CH;
```

INVALUE does *not* contain the algorithm that verifies the check digit; that verification is performed by function VERIFYCHECK. INVALUE does, however, contain several input checks:

- the input value must be the correct length; i.e., either (L – 1) digits long or L digits plus a hyphen;
- the hyphen, if it is present, must be in the correct position; i.e., the second-to-last character;
- the input must be numerical, with the exception of the hyphen;
- the first digit of the number may not be zero.

An invalid input will result in an error message and a prompt for another attempt.

Functions CHECKDIGIT and VERIFYCHECK

Both of these functions take a parameter of type LONG1. CHECKDIGIT returns a one-digit integer, the calculated check digit for the long integer that is passed to it. We might use CHECKDIGIT in a WRITELN statement as follows:

```
LONGID := 12345;
WRITELN(LONGID, '-', CHECKDIGIT(LONGID));
```

The output result would be:

```
12345-5
```

We will discuss the details of the check-digit algorithm in Chapter 5. The algorithm is designed to check for two common numerical input errors:

1. typing one incorrect digit;
2. transposing two adjacent digits.

Function VERIFYCHECK assumes that the last digit of the number it receives is in fact the check digit, and that the remaining digits make up the actual identification number. VERIFYCHECK thus returns a value of true or false depending on whether or not the number and the check digit correspond. The following nested REPEAT statements illustrate a method of continuing to display new input prompts until an input six-digit number (five digits, hyphen, and check digit) is both valid and correct:

```
REPEAT
   REPEAT
      WRITE('? ');
      INVALUE(LONGID, 6, CH)
   UNTIL CH
UNTIL VERIFYCHECK(LONGID);
```

A TEST PROGRAM FOR CHECKUNIT

Program CHECKTEST, shown in Figure 3.5, is a very simple programming exercise designed to demonstrate the use of the CHECKUNIT routines. Two FOR loops control the input of numbers. The first loop uses CHECKDIGIT to calculate and display the check digit; the second loop uses VERIFYCHECK to validate the user's input of a number and check digit. Examine the sample run of this program, shown in Figure 3.6, to see the results.

```
PROGRAM CHECKTEST;

(*$U CHECKUNIT.CODE*)

USES CHECKUNIT;

CONST
  BELL = 7;
  LENGTH = 6;

VAR
  NUMBER : LONG1;
  TIMES,
  I      : INTEGER;
  CD,
  DUMMY,
  OK  : BOOLEAN;
  GARBAGE : STRING;

BEGIN (* CHECKTEST *)
  REPEAT
    WRITE('HOW MANY NUMBERS? ');
    GET(INPUT);
    IF INPUT^ IN ['0'..'9'] THEN
      BEGIN
        READLN(TIMES);
        OK := TRUE
      END
    ELSE
      BEGIN
        READLN(GARBAGE);
        OK := FALSE
      END
  UNTIL OK;

  WRITELN;
  WRITELN('INPUT ',TIMES,' NUMBERS, ', LENGTH-1,' DIGITS EACH;');
  WRITELN('THE CHECK DIGIT WILL BE CALCULATED FOR YOU.');
  WRITELN;

  FOR I := 1 TO TIMES DO
    BEGIN
      WRITE('NUMBER? ');
      INVALUE(NUMBER, LENGTH, CD);
      IF NOT CD THEN
        WRITELN('THE FULL NUMBER IS ', NUMBER, '-',CHECKDIGIT(NUMBER))
    END;

  WRITELN;
  WRITELN;
  WRITELN('NOW INPUT ',TIMES, ' NUMBERS OF ',LENGTH-1,' DIGITS');
  WRITELN('PLUS A CHECK DIGIT; THE CHECK WILL BE VERIFIED.');
  WRITELN('YOU MUST USE A HYPHEN TO SEPARATE THE CHECK DIGIT');
  WRITELN('FROM THE REST OF THE NUMBER');
  WRITELN;
```

Figure 3.5: Listing of Program CHECKTEST

```
      FOR I := 1 TO TIMES DO
        BEGIN
          WRITE('NUMBER AND CHECK DIGIT? ');
          INVALUE(NUMBER, LENGTH, CD);
          WHILE NOT CD DO
            BEGIN
              WRITE('*REDO WITH CHECK DIGIT: ');
              INVALUE(NUMBER, LENGTH, CD)
            END;
          IF NOT VERIFYCHECK(NUMBER) THEN
            BEGIN
              WRITE(CHR(BELL));
              WRITELN('*** WRONG CHECK DIGIT');
              WRITELN
            END
        END
    END.       (* CHECKTEST *)
```

Figure 3.5: Listing of Program CHECKTEST (cont.)

```
HOW MANY NUMBERS? 5

INPUT 5 NUMBERS, 5 DIGITS EACH;
THE CHECK DIGIT WILL BE CALCULATED FOR YOU.

NUMBER? 12345
THE FULL NUMBER IS 12345-5
NUMBER? 74139
THE FULL NUMBER IS 74139-8
NUMBER? 88631
THE FULL NUMBER IS 88631-8
NUMBER? 7Y654
*** REDO
? 70654
THE FULL NUMBER IS 70654-0
NUMBER? 21988
THE FULL NUMBER IS 21988-1


NOW INPUT 5 NUMBERS OF 5 DIGITS
PLUS A CHECK DIGIT; THE CHECK WILL BE VERIFIED.
YOU MUST USE A HYPHEN TO SEPARATE THE CHECK DIGIT
FROM THE REST OF THE NUMBER

NUMBER AND CHECK DIGIT? 12345-8
*** WRONG CHECK DIGIT

NUMBER AND CHECK DIGIT? 12345-5
NUMBER AND CHECK DIGIT? 22341-2
NUMBER AND CHECK DIGIT? 11542-7
*** WRONG CHECK DIGIT

NUMBER AND CHECK DIGIT? 11542-8
```

Figure 3.6: Output from Program CHECKTEST

Finally, we should look briefly at a quick and simple method of numerical input validation illustrated by the REPEAT loop at the beginning of CHECKTEST. This method is especially valuable when we are expecting a single-digit numerical input.

Let us say we wish to input a value for TIMES, an INTEGER variable. A simple READLN statement like the following:

```
READLN(TIMES)
```

may be very dangerous. The problem is this: if the user inadvertently types a nonnumeric character in response to this READLN statement, the program may terminate. The simple solution is to GET a one-character record from the implicitly defined file INPUT:

```
GET(INPUT);
```

and then test the value of the INPUT file buffer to make sure the input character is in the appropriate range:

```
IF INPUT   IN ['0'..'9'] THEN
```

If the range is correct, then the input value can safely be assigned to the integer variable TIMES:

```
READLN(TIMES)
```

Otherwise, the value must be read into a string variable (GARBAGE in this case) and another input prompt should be given:

```
READLN(GARBAGE)
```

In Chapters 4, 5, and 6 we will examine more complete and sophisticated methods of numerical input validation; however, we may occasionally make use of this simple method when the need arises.

Now we will look at our last package of routines.

DATEUNIT: DATE INPUT AND OUTPUT, AND SCALAR DATE CONVERSION

The INTERFACE section of DATEUNIT, shown in Figure 3.7, defines two types and three procedures. The first type is yet another long integer, DATELONG, which is required for the scalar date conversion procedure, DATECONVERT. The second type definition, DATEREC, specifies the structure we will use to store dates. DATEREC is a record containing three fields, MONTH, DAY, and YEAR. Notice that all three procedures have parameters of type DATEREC.

There are many ways of approaching the input and output of dates;

the approach illustrated in this package may seem more or less friendly than other approaches. The two essential requirements of a date input/output package are as follows:

1. The user must be given an adequately clear picture of the required date input format.
2. A reasonable amount of checking must be performed on the validity of the date.

We will see how these two requirements are met using our DATEUNIT package.

Procedure INDATE

As we have seen, DATE is a VAR parameter of type DATEREC. A call to procedure INDATE might appear as:

```
INDATE(DATE1)
```

INDATE reads an input string in the following format:

<MM>-<DD>-<YY>

where MM, DD, and YY are integer representations of the month, day, and year, respectively. Notice that the day is written after the month, and the parts of the date are separated by hyphens. An example of correct

```
(*$S+*)
UNIT DATEUNIT;

INTERFACE


TYPE
  DATELONG = INTEGER[5];
  DATEREC = RECORD
            MONTH,
            DAY,
            YEAR   : INTEGER
  END;

PROCEDURE OUTDATE(DATE: DATEREC);

PROCEDURE INDATE (VAR DATE: DATEREC);

PROCEDURE DATECONVERT(DATE:DATEREC;
                VAR SCDATE:DATELONG);
```

Figure 3.7: INTERFACE Section of DATEUNIT

date input for this format is:

```
10-11-83
```

In the case of single-digit months or days, INDATE will accept two forms. Both of the following are correct:

```
01-01-83
```

and

```
1-1-83
```

In addition to the format requirements, INDATE checks the month-day-year values as follows:

1. The month, MM, must be an integer from 1 to 12.
2. The year, YY, must be an integer from 1 to 99.
3. The day, DD, must be an integer from 1 to the maximum number of days in the month represented by MM-YY. For February, INDATE checks to see if YY is a leap year or not.

Thus, this procedure is designed to read and validate any date from January 1, 1901 to December 31, 1999. An illegal date results in an error message and a new date prompt:

```
* * * ILLEGAL DATE
                DATE:
```

Like the other two input routines we have seen, INDATE does not return control to the calling procedure until correct and valid input has been read. The date is stored in the three fields of DATE (i.e., DATE.-MONTH, DATE.DAY, and DATE.YEAR).

Procedure OUTDATE

Given a DATE record, procedure OUTDATE writes the date in the form:

```
MONTH DD, 19YY
```

For example, for the date 10-11-83, OUTDATE writes:

```
OCTOBER 11, 1983
```

In some cases it may be more convenient to output the date in the same format used for input. The following statement can be used in place of OUTDATE, given the record DATE:

```
WRITE(DATE.MONTH,'-',DATE.DAY,'-',DATE.YEAR)
```

Procedure DATECONVERT

We will often need to calculate the number of days between two dates. Procedure DATECONVERT provides a simple method of performing this calculation. A call to this procedure takes the form:

```
DATECONVERT(DATE, SCALAR)
```

where DATE is of type DATEREC and SCALAR, a VAR parameter, is a long integer of type DATELONG. Starting with January 1, 1901 as day one, DATECONVERT counts up the number of days represented by DATE, and assigns that value to SCALAR. For example, April 9, 1982 has a scalar value of 29684, meaning it is the 29,684th day since January 1, 1901.

Why must SCALAR be a long integer? Because December 31, 1999 has a scalar value of 36159, which is outside the range of regular integers. Otherwise, DATECONVERT would be much more convenient to use if it were written as a function:

```
FUNCTION DATECONVERT(DATE: DATEREC): INTEGER;
```

Unfortunately, functions returning long integer types are not permitted.

As we will see in our test program, finding the number of days between two dates, DATE1 and a later DATE2, is a simple task using DATECONVERT. We simply find the difference between the scalar values of the two dates:

```
DATECONVERT(DATE1, SCALAR1);
DATECONVERT(DATE2, SCALAR2);
DIFFERENCE := SCALAR2 - SCALAR1
```

A TEST PROGRAM FOR DATEUNIT

Program DATETEST, shown in Figure 3.8, uses two calls to INDATE for the input of DATE1 and DATE2, a call to DATEDIFF to find the number of days between two dates, and finally two calls to OUTDATE to produce a two-line report for the dates.

Procedure DATEDIFF makes two calls to DATECONVERT and then finds the difference between the two scalar values:

```
IF SCALAR1 > SCALAR2 THEN
   DIFF := SCALAR1 - SCALAR2
ELSE
   DIFF := SCALAR2 - SCALAR1
```

```
PROGRAM DATETEST;

(*$U DATEUNIT.CODE*)

USES DATEUNIT;

VAR
  DATE1,
  DATE2  : DATEREC;
  DIFFERENCE : DATELONG;
  OKANS  : STRING;

PROCEDURE DATEDIFF(D1,D2 : DATEREC;
             VAR  DIFF  : DATELONG);
VAR
  SCALAR1,
  SCALAR2  : DATELONG;

BEGIN
  DATECONVERT(D1,SCALAR1);
  DATECONVERT(D2,SCALAR2);
  IF SCALAR1 > SCALAR2 THEN
    DIFF := SCALAR1 - SCALAR2
  ELSE
    DIFF := SCALAR2 - SCALAR1
END;

BEGIN (* MAIN PROGRAM *)
  REPEAT
    WRITELN;WRITELN;WRITELN;
    WRITELN('INPUT TWO DATES ');
    WRITELN('=============== ');
    WRITELN;
    WRITELN('(<MM>-<DD>-<YY>)');
    WRITELN;
    WRITE('DATE #1: ');
    INDATE(DATE1);
    WRITE('DATE #2: ');
    INDATE(DATE2);
    WRITELN;

    DATEDIFF(DATE1,DATE2,DIFFERENCE);

    WRITELN('THERE ARE ', DIFFERENCE,
            ' DAYS BETWEEN ');
    OUTDATE(DATE1);
    WRITE(' AND ');
    OUTDATE(DATE2);
    WRITELN;WRITELN;
    WRITE('ANOTHER? <Y> OR <N> ');
    READLN(OKANS)
  UNTIL ((OKANS <> 'Y') AND (OKANS <> 'YES'))
END.  (* DATETEST *)
```

Figure 3.8: Listing of Program DATETEST

If these scalar values were not long integers, we could simply have written:

```
DIFF := ABS(SCALAR1 - SCALAR2)
```

However, the predefined Pascal function ABS does not allow long-integer parameters.

Some sample output from DATETEST is shown in Figure 3.9.

```
INPUT TWO DATES
===============

(<MM>-<DD>-<YY>)

DATE #1: 2-27-51
DATE #2: 4-10-82

THERE ARE 11365 DAYS BETWEEN
FEBRUARY 27, 1951 AND APRIL 10, 1982

ANOTHER? <Y> OR <N> Y

----------------------------------------------

INPUT TWO DATES
===============

(<MM>-<DD>-<YY>)

DATE #1: 2-29-81
   *** ILLEGAL DATE
             DATE:     2-28-81
DATE #2: 1-5-83

THERE ARE 676 DAYS BETWEEN
FEBRUARY 28, 1981 AND JANUARY 5, 1983

ANOTHER? <Y> OR <N> N
```

Figure 3.9: Output from Program DATETEST

SUMMARY

In this chapter we have begun to experiment with two of the extensions offered by UCSD Pascal—the *unit* and the *long integer*. These two extensions are clearly essential for building business software. So far we have only seen the INTERFACE sections of our three units, MONEYUNIT, CHECKUNIT, and DATEUNIT. The table shown in Figure 3.10 summarizes the use of the routines provided by these units. In the next three chapters we will look closely at the IMPLEMENTATION sections of the units, to discover exactly how these routines are written.

I. Input Routines

Procedure INDOLLAR

```
VAR LONGVAL : LONG2
```

Dollar-and-cent input; converts input to cents and returns input in LONGVAL.

Procedure INVALUE

```
VAR LONGID : LONG1
          L : INTEGER
VAR      CH : BOOLEAN
```

I.D. number input of length L or (L – 1); Boolean CH indicates whether or not check digit is included in input; returns input in LONGID.

Procedure INDATE

```
VAR DATE : DATEREC
```

Date input;<MM> – <DD> – <YY> returns date in the fields DATE.MONTH, DATE.DAY, and DATE.YEAR.

II. Output Routines

Procedure DOLLARFORM

```
    LONGVAL : LONG2
VAR      ST : STRING
```

Converts LONGVAL cents to dollar-and-cent string (with '$', '.', and ','); returns string in ST.

Procedure RIGHTFIELD

```
VAR      ST : STRING
          L : INTEGER
```

Right-justifies ST in a field of length L.

Procedure FOURCOLUMN

```
ST1, ST2, ST3, ST4 : STRING
L1,  L2,  L3,  L4  : INTEGER
```

Writes one line of output; right-justifies each string in its corresponding field length.

Figure 3.10: Summary of Unit Packages

Procedure FOURCOLUMN

```
ST1, ST2, ST3, ST4 : STRING
L1,  L2,  L3,  L4  : INTEGER
```

Writes one line of output; right-justifies each string in its corresponding field length.

Procedure CLEARSCREEN

Clears screen; positions cursor at upper-left corner.

Procedure OUTDATE

```
DATE : DATEREC
```

Writes date in ' MONTH DD, 19YY' format.

III. Arithmetic Routines

Procedure LONGMULT

```
    LONGVAL : LONG2
       RVAL : REAL
 VAR RESULT : LONG2
```

Returns product of LONGVAL and RVAL in RESULT. Note: ROUND(RVAL) must be smaller than MAXINT.

Function CHECKDIGIT

```
LONGID : LONG1
```

Returns check digit of LONGID.

Function VERIFYCHECK

```
LONGID : LONG1
```

Returns true if last digit of LONGID is correct check digit.

Procedure DATECONVERT

```
       DATE : DATEREC
VAR SCALAR: DATELONG
```

Returns scalar value of DATE in DATELONG. (Value based on 1/1/01 as starting point.)

Figure 3.10: Summary of Unit Packages (cont.)

Chapter 4

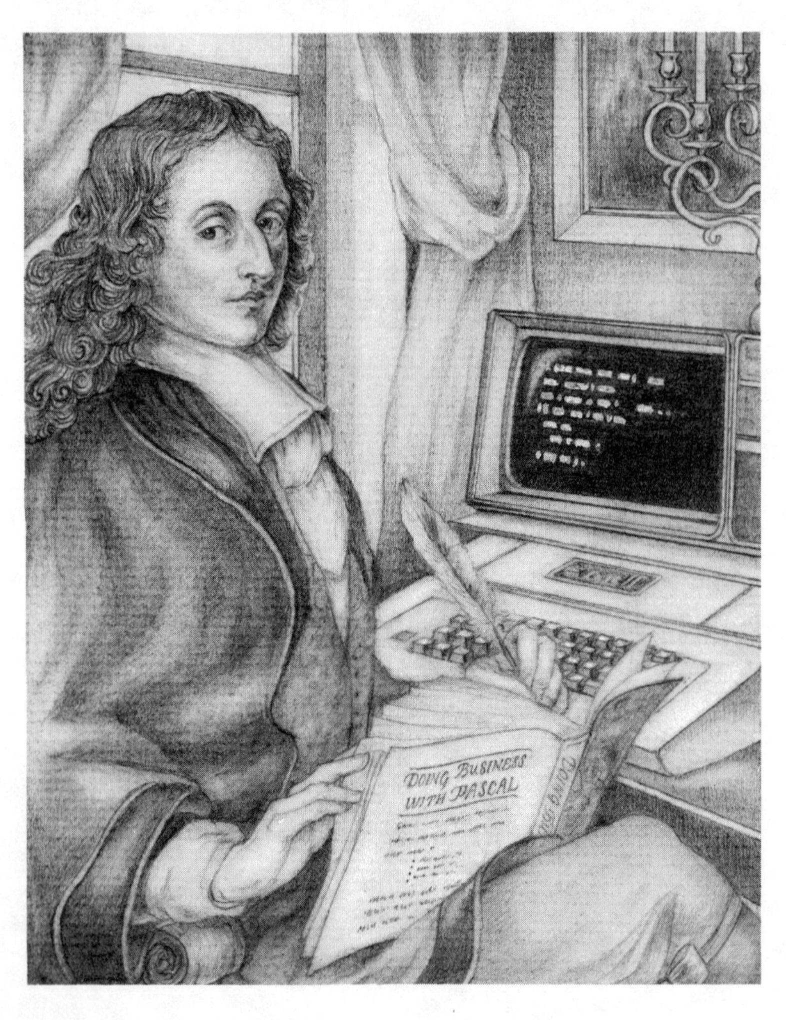

The Implementation of MONEYUNIT

INTRODUCTION

The complete listing for MONEYUNIT is shown in Figure 4.1. Before we begin studying the details of the routines it contains, we should mention three general points of information about units.

First, some early versions of the UCSD Pascal compiler require that the *swapping mode* be activated for unit compilation:

```
(*$S+*)
```

This directive saves memory space during compilation, by "swapping" two parts of the compiler itself in and out of the same active memory space. (It also slows down the compilation process considerably.) In the latest versions of the compiler, swapping is performed automatically whenever necessary, and the $S+ directive can thus be omitted.

Second, notice that the formal parameter lists and function types of public routines are *not* repeated in the IMPLEMENTATION section of the unit. Any private routines would, of course, have to be completely defined within the IMPLEMENTATION section. (All of the routines in MONEYUNIT are public.)

Finally, the IMPLEMENTATION section is completed with a "main program" section. This section provides a place for any initialization tasks that might be necessary at run time. None of the units we will be examining make use of this main program section; however, it must be present all the same:

```
BEGIN
END.
```

```
(*$S+*)
UNIT MONEYUNIT;

INTERFACE

CONST
  L2 = 15;

TYPE
  LONG2 = INTEGER[L2];

FUNCTION VALUE(CH:CHAR):INTEGER;


PROCEDURE DOLLARFORM(VAL : LONG2;
            VAR    STNUM : STRING);

PROCEDURE INDOLLAR(VAR VAL : LONG2);

PROCEDURE RIGHTFIELD(VAR ST: STRING;
                  FIELDLENGTH: INTEGER);

PROCEDURE FOURCOLUMN(HEAD1, HEAD2,
                     HEAD3, HEAD4 : STRING;
                     FIELD1, FIELD2,
                     FIELD3, FIELD4 : INTEGER);

PROCEDURE LONGMULT(CENTS : LONG2;
                   MULT  : REAL;
             VAR RESULT  : LONG2);

PROCEDURE CLEARSCREEN;


IMPLEMENTATION

FUNCTION VALUE;
  BEGIN
    VALUE := ORD(CH) - ORD('0');
  END;

PROCEDURE DOLLARFORM;
  VAR
    L,
    N      : INTEGER;

BEGIN
  STR(VAL,STNUM);
  N := 4;
  L := LENGTH(STNUM);
  IF L < 2 THEN
    INSERT('0',STNUM,1);
  WHILE (L > 5) DO
    BEGIN
      INSERT(',', STNUM, LENGTH(STNUM) - N);
      N := N + 4;
      L := L - 3
    END;
```

Figure 4.1: Complete Listing of MONEYUNIT

```
    INSERT('.', STNUM, LENGTH(STNUM) - 1);
    INSERT('$', STNUM, 1)
  END; (* DOLLARFORM *)

  PROCEDURE INDOLLAR;

  CONST
    BLANK = ' ';
    POINT = '.';
    COMMA = ',';
    DSIGN = '$';
    MAXLENGTH = 11;
    BELL = 7;

  VAR
    TEMP   : LONG2;
    ST     : STRING;
    GOOD,
    MOREBLANKS   : BOOLEAN;
    I,
    COUNT,
    DECIMALPOS,
    PLACES   : INTEGER;

  BEGIN
    REPEAT
      TEMP := 0;
      MOREBLANKS := TRUE;
      GOOD := TRUE;

      READLN(ST);

      (* REMOVE LEADING BLANKS *)

      WHILE GOOD AND MOREBLANKS DO
        IF LENGTH(ST) <> 0 THEN
          IF ST[1] = BLANK THEN
            DELETE(ST,1,1)
          ELSE
            MOREBLANKS := FALSE
        ELSE
          GOOD := FALSE;

      (* REMOVE DOLLAR SIGN AND COMMAS *)

      IF GOOD THEN
        BEGIN
          IF ST[1] = DSIGN THEN
            DELETE(ST,1,1);

          WHILE POS(COMMA,ST) <> 0 DO
            DELETE(ST,POS(COMMA,ST),1);

          (* RECORD POSITION OF DECIMAL PLACE
             AND MAKE APPROPRIATE ADJUSTMENTS *)

          DECIMALPOS := POS(POINT,ST);
          IF DECIMALPOS = 0 THEN
```

Figure 4.1: Complete Listing of MONEYUNIT (cont.)

```
          BEGIN
            PLACES := 0;
            COUNT := LENGTH(ST)
          END
        ELSE
          BEGIN
            PLACES := LENGTH(ST) - DECIMALPOS;
            IF PLACES > 3 THEN
              BEGIN
                DELETE(ST,DECIMALPOS+4,LENGTH(ST)-(DECIMALPOS+3));
                PLACES := 3
              END;
            DELETE(ST,DECIMALPOS,1);
            COUNT := LENGTH(ST)
          END;

        (* ERROR MESSAGE IF NUMBER IS TOO LONG *)

        IF (COUNT > MAXLENGTH + PLACES - 2) THEN
          BEGIN
            WRITE(CHR(BELL));
            WRITELN('*** TOO LONG;');
            GOOD := FALSE
          END
   END;

    (* CHECK FOR NUMERIC INPUT *)

    I := 1;
    WHILE (GOOD AND (I <= COUNT)) DO
      IF ST[I] IN ['0'..'9'] THEN
        BEGIN
          TEMP := TEMP * 10 + VALUE(ST[I]);
          I := I + 1
        END
      ELSE
        GOOD := FALSE;

    IF GOOD THEN
      CASE PLACES OF
        0 : TEMP := TEMP * 100;
        1 : TEMP := TEMP * 10;
        2 : ;
        3 : TEMP := (TEMP + 5) DIV 10
      END
    ELSE
      BEGIN
        WRITE(CHR(BELL));
        WRITELN('*** REDO');
        WRITE  ('? ')
      END

  UNTIL GOOD;

  VAL := TEMP

END;    (* INDOLLAR *)
```

Figure 4.1: Complete Listing of MONEYUNIT (cont.)

```
PROCEDURE RIGHTFIELD;

VAR
  L,
  I  : INTEGER;

BEGIN
  L := LENGTH(ST);
  IF ((L > 0) AND (FIELDLENGTH > 0)) THEN
    BEGIN
      IF (L < FIELDLENGTH) THEN
        FOR I := 1 TO (FIELDLENGTH - L) DO
          INSERT(' ', ST, 1);

      IF (L > FIELDLENGTH) THEN
        BEGIN
          DELETE(ST,1, L - FIELDLENGTH);
          ST[1] := '!'
        END
    END
END; (* RIGHTFIELD *)

PROCEDURE FOURCOLUMN;

CONST
  BLANK = ' ';

BEGIN
  RIGHTFIELD(HEAD1,FIELD1);
  RIGHTFIELD(HEAD2,FIELD2);
  RIGHTFIELD(HEAD3,FIELD3);
  RIGHTFIELD(HEAD4,FIELD4);

  WRITELN(HEAD1,BLANK,HEAD2,BLANK,
          HEAD3,BLANK,HEAD4)

END;  (* FOURCOLUMN *)

PROCEDURE LONGMULT;

CONST
  MAX = 1000;

VAR
  HOLD: LONG2;
  NEWMULT : INTEGER;

BEGIN (* LONGMULT *)
  HOLD := 1;
  WHILE (ROUND(MULT) <= MAX) DO
    BEGIN
      MULT := MULT * 10.0;
      HOLD := HOLD * 10
    END;
  NEWMULT := ROUND(MULT);
  CENTS := CENTS * NEWMULT;
  RESULT := (CENTS + (HOLD DIV 2)) DIV HOLD
END;  (* LONGMULT *)
```

Figure 4.1: Complete Listing of MONEYUNIT (cont.)

```
PROCEDURE CLEARSCREEN;
CONST
  SCREENLENGTH = 25;
VAR
  INDEX : INTEGER;

BEGIN
  FOR INDEX := 1 TO SCREENLENGTH DO
    WRITELN;
  GOTOXY(0,0)
END;

BEGIN

END.
```

Figure 4.1: Complete Listing of MONEYUNIT (cont.)

THE PREDEFINED UCSD PASCAL ROUTINES

The routines of MONEYUNIT make heavy use of six UCSD Pascal string-handling functions and procedures—DELETE, INSERT, LENGTH, ORD, POS, and STR. The following paragraphs provide a quick review of the use of these *predefined* routines. Note that other versions of Pascal include similar string-handling packages.

The DELETE procedure takes three parameters:

```
DELETE(ST, I, L)
```

ST, a VAR parameter, is a string variable; I and L are integer expressions. A total of L characters are deleted from ST, starting from position I.

The INSERT procedure also requires three parameters: two strings and an integer:

```
INSERT(ST1, ST2, I)
```

Only the string variable ST2 is a VAR parameter. The string ST1 is inserted into ST2 starting at position I.

Function LENGTH takes one parameter, a string, and returns an integer representing the number of characters in the string:

```
LENGTH(ST)
```

The ORD function, when used with a parameter of type CHAR, returns the ordinal value of the character. For UCSD Pascal, which uses the ASCII character set, this value will be an integer from 0 to 255.

Function POS takes two string parameters, and returns an integer representing the first occurrence of the first string in the second:

```
POS(ST1, ST2)
```

Significantly, if ST1 is not in ST2, POS returns a zero.

Finally, procedure STR is used to convert an integer to a string:

```
STR(I, ST)
```

ST is a VAR parameter; it is assigned the string equivalent of I. We have already seen that STR takes both regular integers and long integers.

Just as in Chapter 3, we will look at the MONEYUNIT routines in the following order:

1. input routines
2. output routines
3. arithmetic routines.

It may occasionally be useful to refer back to Chapter 3 to review the output from the test programs.

Procedures INDOLLAR and VALUE

Procedure INDOLLAR reads a dollar-and-cent input value as a string, ST:

```
READLN(ST)
```

The procedure removes blanks, commas, dollar sign, and decimal point from ST, and then puts ST through a number of tests to see if it is a valid input. If it is, then its numerical value is calculated and assigned to the long integer TEMP. If ST is invalid, INDOLLAR loops back to start the process over again. Throughout the procedure, the value of the Boolean variable GOOD indicates whether or not the current input has passed all the tests.

First, leading blanks are removed from ST via a WHILE loop. Looping continues until the input has proven to be NOT GOOD or until there are no more leading blanks:

```
WHILE GOOD AND MOREBLANKS DO
```

The WHILE loop consists of two nested IF-THEN-ELSE statements. Remember that each ELSE is paired with the nearest available IF above it. The inner IF deletes the blanks:

```
IF ST[1] = BLANK THEN
   DELETE(ST, 1, 1)
ELSE
   MOREBLANKS := FALSE
```

(The character BLANK, along with POINT, COMMA, and DSIGN, is defined in the CONST section of INDOLLAR.) The outer IF makes sure the length of ST is not zero:

```
IF LENGTH(ST) <> 0 THEN
   ...
ELSE
   GOOD := FALSE;
```

This is an important test. If the user inadvertently typed a simple RETURN in response to the READLN statement—or several blanks and a RETURN—then the length of ST would be zero, once any leading blanks were deleted. In this case, trying to access the first character of ST in the statement:

```
IF ST[1] = BLANK THEN ...
```

would be meaningless and would result in the termination of the program.

The next block of code deletes the dollar sign, commas and decimal point. Notice the use of the POS function to determine first whether or not there are commas in ST, and then the position of those commas for the DELETE procedure:

```
WHILE POS(COMMA, ST) <> 0 DO
   DELETE(ST, POS(COMMA, ST), 1);
```

This WHILE statement continues looping until all the commas are deleted.

Before the decimal point can be deleted, the procedure must record the number of characters after the decimal point. This information is recorded in the variable PLACES. If there is no decimal point, PLACES is set to zero. Otherwise, its value is calculated as the difference between the length of ST and the position of the decimal point in ST:

```
PLACES := LENGTH(ST) - DECIMALPOS;
```

Any decimal places beyond three are considered irrelevant and are deleted:

```
IF PLACES > 3 THEN
   BEGIN
      DELETE(ST,DECIMALPOS + 4,LENGTH(ST) - (DECIMALPOS + 3));
   PLACES := 3
END;
```

PLACES will be used later to convert TEMP to a value representing cents. The next block of code, however, determines whether the final relevant length of ST (assigned to the variable COUNT) is within the length that INDOLLAR allows:

```
IF (COUNT > MAXLENGTH + PLACES - 2) THEN ...
```

(MAXLENGTH is defined in the CONST section. The expression PLACES – 2 is an adjustment based on the upcoming conversion into cents.) If ST is too long, then an error message is printed, the bell is sounded, and GOOD is set to false.

Ringing the bell is programmed by writing the ASCII bell character (BELL = 7 in the CONST section):

```
WRITE(CHR(BELL));
```

Since an input typist may not be looking at the screen while typing in a series of numbers, the bell is an effective way of announcing an input error.

Next the string ST is converted into the long integer TEMP. To be valid, each character of ST must represent a numerical digit:

```
IF ST[I] IN ['0'..'9'] THEN ...
```

If an invalid character is found, then GOOD is set to false. Valid characters are converted to integers (by the function VALUE) and added on to TEMP:

```
TEMP := TEMP * 10 + VALUE(ST[I])
```

Notice that the multiplication by 10 shifts the digits of TEMP to the left.

Function VALUE contains a single statement. The ASCII value of the zero character is subtracted from the ASCII value of the numerical character to determine an integer value from 0 to 9:

```
VALUE := ORD(CH) - ORD('0')
```

In the last block of INDOLLAR, the value of TEMP is converted into cents. A CASE statement is used with PLACES as the case selector. Notice that if PLACES equals 2, TEMP is already in cents, and no action need be taken:

```
2 : ;
```

For three places, TEMP must be rounded up or down to two places:

```
3 : TEMP := (TEMP + 5) DIV 10
```

It is important to recall that no input string has been allowed that would convert into more than eleven digits. Also, note that MAXLENGTH is smaller than L2, the maximum length of LONG2.

If all the characters are valid, then TEMP is finally assigned to VAL. Otherwise, an error message is printed and the user is prompted to try again. An input string that is too long produces two bells; any other input error produces one bell.

We have studied INDOLLAR in careful detail. The input routines of CHECKUNIT (Chapter 5), and DATEUNIT (Chapter 6) have much in common with INDOLLAR, so we will be able to cover them with less effort.

Procedures DOLLARFORM, RIGHTFIELD, FOURCOLUMN, and CLEARSCREEN

These four output procedures are generally much simpler than INDOLLAR.

Procedure DOLLARFORM uses STR to convert the long integer VAL into a string:

```
STR(VAL, STNUM);
```

Once the string conversion has been accomplished, DOLLARFORM simply inserts the appropriate characters in their correct places to make the string look like dollars and cents. The only complexity is posed by the commas, which must be inserted in every fourth position going left from the still nonexistent decimal point. This somewhat intimidating task is performed by a WHILE loop; the best way to see how this loop operates is to choose an arbitrary long integer and walk it through this conversion with pencil and paper. After the commas are in place, two more calls to the INSERT procedure are used to put in the dollar sign and decimal point.

The exceptional case of VAL <10 (that is, LENGTH(VAL) = 1) is also allowed for by insertion of a second zero character into the string:

```
IF L<2 THEN
   INSERT('0', STNUM, 1);
```

For example, for VAL = 0, the final value of STNUM would be:

```
$.00
```

Procedure RIGHTFIELD takes no action at all if the string passed to it has a zero length or if the field length passed to it equals zero:

```
IF ((L > 0) AND (FIELDLENGTH > 0)) THEN ...
```

As we will see, this feature is what allows procedure FOURCOLUMN to produce any number of columns *up to* four.

Given a string that is not null and a nonzero field length, RIGHTFIELD performs one of two blocks of code. If the length of the string is less than the field length, then a FOR loop is used to insert blank characters to the left of the string until its length equals the field length:

```
FOR I := 1 TO (FIELDLENGTH - L) DO
  INSERT(' ', ST, 1);
```

On the other hand, if the string is too long for the field, then the extra characters are deleted from the left, and the first character is changed to '!':

```
DELETE(ST, 1, L - FIELDLENGTH);
ST[1] := '!'
```

Notice that if L = FIELDLENGTH, no action is taken.

Procedure FOURCOLUMN consists simply of four calls to RIGHTFIELD and a WRITELN statement. Each string is fitted to its field, and then one line of output is written.

Procedure CLEARSCREEN is equally simple, but requires the UCSD predefined procedure GOTOXY. A FOR loop clears the screen by calling WRITELN 25 times. GOTOXY repositions the cursor.

Procedure LONGMULT

This procedure must be used somewhat cautiously. As long as it is used for its stated purpose—to multiply long integers by small positive real numbers—it is both useful and accurate. However, the real multiplier, MULT, must meet the following condition:

```
ROUND(MULT) <= MAXINT
```

The value of MAXINT is 32767 in UCSD Pascal.

The method of LONGMULT is to shift the most significant digits of MULT to the left by repeated multiplications by 10, then to convert MULT to an integer by rounding. The rounded value of MULT is assigned to the integer variable NEWMULT, and then multiplied by the long integer CENTS:

```
NEWMULT := ROUND(MULT);
CENTS := CENTS * NEWMULT;
```

The result is then rounded and shifted right to adjust for the previous shift left of MULT:

```
RESULT := (CENTS + (HOLD DIV 2)) DIV HOLD
```

The expression CENTS + (HOLD DIV 2) adds 5 to the leftmost digit that will be eliminated by the shift right. This assures that RESULT will be rounded properly. The value of the variable HOLD (of type LONG2) is a power of 10 representing the extent of the shift.

SUMMARY

Ensuring reliability and user-friendliness in input and output functions proves to be a rather complicated programming task. We will see variations on our I/O routines in the two chapters that follow.

Chapter 5

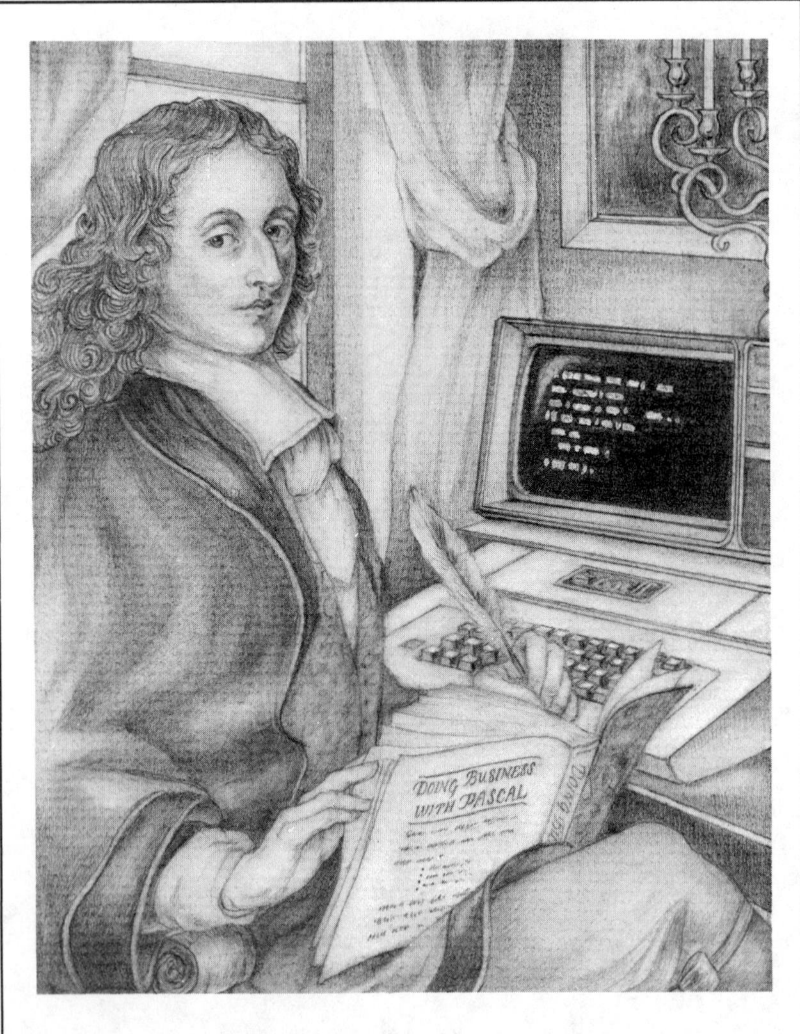

The Implementation of CHECKUNIT

INTRODUCTION

We saw in Chapter 3 that the main tasks performed by the CHECK-UNIT package are the following:

1. to read a long integer I.D. number, with or without a check digit;
2. to produce the check digit for a number that does not have one;
3. to verify the check digit of a number that does have one.

The complete unit is shown in Figure 5.1. Once again, the longest procedure is the input routine, INVALUE.

INVALUE

Recall that INVALUE has three parameters, one of which, LWD ("length with digit") is an integer value passed to INVALUE from the calling procedure. By passing a value to the parameter LWD, the calling procedure tells INVALUE the length of the integer to be read. INVALUE *returns* two values: a long integer, VAL, and a Boolean value, CD. The long integer will have a length of either LWD (in which case CD is true) or LWD − 1 (in which case CD is false).

```
(*$S+*)

UNIT CHECKUNIT;

INTERFACE

CONST
  L1 = 9;

TYPE
  LONG1 = INTEGER[L1];

PROCEDURE INVALUE(VAR VAL : LONG1;
                      LWD : INTEGER;
                  VAR  CD : BOOLEAN);

FUNCTION CHECKDIGIT(L: LONG1): INTEGER;

FUNCTION VERIFYCHECK(I : LONG1): BOOLEAN;

IMPLEMENTATION

FUNCTION VALUE(CH: CHAR):INTEGER;

BEGIN
  VALUE := ORD(CH) - ORD('0')
END;

PROCEDURE INVALUE;

CONST
  BLANK = ' ';
  HYPHEN = '-';

VAR
  TEMP : LONG1;
  ST   : STRING;
  MOREBLANKS,
  GOOD : BOOLEAN;
  COUNT,
  HYPHENPOS,
  INDEX : INTEGER;


BEGIN
  REPEAT
    TEMP := 0;
    READLN(ST);
    MOREBLANKS := TRUE;
    GOOD := TRUE;

    (* CHECK FOR LEADING BLANKS *)

    WHILE GOOD AND MOREBLANKS DO
      IF LENGTH(ST) <> 0 THEN
        IF ST[1] = BLANK THEN
          DELETE(ST,1,1)
```

Figure 5.1: Complete Listing of CHECKUNIT

```
        ELSE
          MOREBLANKS := FALSE
      ELSE
        GOOD := FALSE;

    (* CHECK FOR PRESENCE AND POSITION
       OF HYPHEN *)

    IF GOOD THEN
      BEGIN
        HYPHENPOS := POS(HYPHEN,ST);
        IF HYPHENPOS = 0 THEN
          BEGIN
            COUNT := LENGTH(ST);
            GOOD := (COUNT = LWD - 1);
            CD := FALSE
          END
        ELSE
          BEGIN
            DELETE(ST,HYPHENPOS,1);
            COUNT := LENGTH(ST);
            GOOD := (COUNT = LWD) AND (HYPHENPOS = LWD);
            CD := TRUE
          END;

        (* MAKE SURE FIRST DIGIT IS NONZERO *)

        IF GOOD THEN
          GOOD := ST[1] <> '0'
      END;

      (* CHECK FOR NUMERIC INPUT *)

      INDEX := 1;
      WHILE (GOOD AND (INDEX <= COUNT)) DO
        IF ST[INDEX] IN ['0'..'9'] THEN
          BEGIN
            TEMP := TEMP * 10 +
                    VALUE(ST[INDEX]);
            INDEX := INDEX + 1
          END
        ELSE
          GOOD := FALSE;

    IF NOT GOOD THEN
      BEGIN
        WRITELN('*** REDO');
        WRITE  ('? ')
      END
  UNTIL GOOD;
  VAL := TEMP;

  END;  (* INVALUE *)


  FUNCTION CHECKDIGIT ;
```

Figure 5.1: Complete Listing of CHECKUNIT (cont.)

```
VAR
  N,
  I,
  ALT1,
  ALT2,
  HOLD,
  CARRY,
  TOTAL,
  CHDIG,
  LASTDIGIT : INTEGER;
  S : STRING;


BEGIN  (* CHECKDIGIT *)
  STR(L,S);
  N := LENGTH(S);
  I := N;
  ALT1 := 0;
  ALT2 := 0;
  (*
   * STARTING FROM THE LAST DIGIT,
   * MULTIPLY ALTERNATE DIGITS BY 2;
   * CARRY AS IN REGULAR MULTIPLICATION.
   * STORE THE SUM IN ALT1 *)
   *)
  WHILE (I >= 1) DO
    BEGIN
      HOLD := VALUE(S[I]) * 2;
      IF HOLD < 10 THEN
        CARRY := 0
      ELSE
        BEGIN
          HOLD := HOLD - 10;
          CARRY := 1
        END;
      ALT1 := ALT1 + HOLD + CARRY;
      I := I - 2
    END;
 (*
  * IF THE NUMBER CONTAINS AN ODD NUMBER OF DIGITS
  * AND INCLUDED A CARRY, THEN WE SHOULD HAVE
  * ADDED 10, NOT 1.
  *)

  IF (2 * (N DIV 2) <> N) AND (CARRY = 1) THEN
    ALT1 := ALT1 + 9;

  (* NOW ADD THE REMAINING DIGITS *)

  I := N - 1;
  WHILE (I >= 1) DO
    BEGIN
      ALT2 := ALT2 + VALUE(S[I]);
      I := I - 2
    END;
  TOTAL := ALT1 + ALT2;
```

Figure 5.1: Complete Listing of CHECKUNIT (cont.)

```
    LASTDIGIT := TOTAL MOD 10;
    CHDIG := 10 - LASTDIGIT;
    IF (CHDIG = 10) THEN CHDIG := 0;
    CHECKDIGIT := CHDIG
  END; (* CHECKDIGIT *)

  FUNCTION VERIFYCHECK;

    FUNCTION LONGMODINT(L:LONG1; I: INTEGER) : INTEGER;

    BEGIN
      LONGMODINT := TRUNC(L- ((L DIV I) * I))
    END;

  BEGIN
    IF (CHECKDIGIT(I DIV 10) = LONGMODINT(I,10)) THEN
      VERIFYCHECK := TRUE
    ELSE
      VERIFYCHECK := FALSE
  END; (* VERIFYCHECK *)

  BEGIN

  END.
```

Figure 5.1: Complete Listing of CHECKUNIT (cont.)

There are several similarities between INVALUE and INDOLLAR. The input is read as a string, ST; the Boolean variable GOOD indicates the validity of the current input; the first block of code removes any leading blanks from the string; and, in the end, a valid input is converted into a long integer, TEMP, via an algorithm that shifts the current digits left and adds on the value of the new digit:

```
TEMP := TEMP * 10 + VALUE(ST[INDEX])
```

(Notice that function VALUE is included in CHECKUNIT as a private routine.)

What is unique about INVALUE is the way it tests and makes allowances for the presence or absence of the check digit. We will concentrate on the code that performs this task, located approximately in the center of the procedure.

The presence of a hyphen in the input string is the only valid indicator of a check digit. The string constant HYPHEN is defined in the CONST section:

```
HYPHEN := '-';
```

The UCSD POS function is used to find out if the hyphen is there or not:

```
HYPHENPOS := POS(HYPHEN, ST);
```

Recall that POS returns a zero if the first string is not found in the second. Thus, if HYPHENPOS equals zero, INVALUE assumes that the input string, ST, represents an I.D. number without a check digit. The length of the string is assigned to COUNT:

```
COUNT := LENGTH(ST);
```

GOOD remains true in this case only if COUNT is one less than LWD:

```
GOOD := (COUNT = LWD - 1);
```

and finally, CD, the check-digit indicator, is set to false:

```
CD := FALSE
```

If, on the other hand, HYPHENPOS is not zero, then the hyphen is deleted from the string:

```
DELETE(ST, HYPHENPOS, 1);
```

The new length of ST is assigned to COUNT:

```
COUNT := LENGTH(ST);
```

Now the value of COUNT should be the full length represented by LWD; furthermore, the hyphen, before it was deleted, should have been in the second-to-last position of ST. (The check digit would have been in position LWD + 1.) The value of GOOD, then, depends upon these two conditions:

```
GOOD := (COUNT = LWD) AND (HYPHENPOS = LWD);
```

Finally, CD is set to true:

```
CD := TRUE
```

One last test must be performed before ST is converted into an integer. The procedure requires that the first digit of the number not be a zero:

```
IF GOOD THEN
   GOOD := ST[1] <> '0'
```

Like INDOLLAR, this procedure continues looping until a valid number is read; an error message is written for any invalid input.

CHECKDIGIT

Many different algorithms have been developed to produce check digits. They all have the same rationale—to catch errors in the input of large numbers where accuracy is essential.

The algorithm used in function CHECKDIGIT is a simple one, involving a few steps of basic arithmetic. As we go through the steps, we will calculate the check digit for the number 52743 as an example of how the algorithm works. Remember that the digits are numbered from right to left, as "least significant" to "most significant":

position	5	4	3	2	1
digit	*5*	*2*	*7*	*4*	*3*

1. Starting with the first digit on the right, multiply alternate digits by 2. If the product is greater than or equal to 10 for any given digit except the last, then carry as in regular multiplication. Find the sum of the products and the carries:

digit				*product*	*carry*
3	*	2	=	6	0
7	*	2	=	4	1
5	*	2	=	10	(no carry for last digit)
	sum		=	20	+ 1 = *21*

2. Find the sum of the remaining digits (i.e., alternate digits starting from the second digit on the right):

   sum = 4 + 2 = *6*

3. Add the sums from steps 1 and 2, and subtract the total from the next higher multiple of 10. The result is the check digit (if the sums from steps 1 and 2 add up to a multiple of 10, then the check digit is 0):

   21 + 6 = 27
   30 − 27 = *3*

   Number with check digit = *52743-3*

Function CHECKDIGIT receives the I.D. number as a long integer, L. The first line of the routine converts L to a string:

```
STR(L,S);
```

ALT1 and ALT2, which correspond to the sums in steps 1 and 2, are initialized to zero. The first WHILE loop of the function begins with the rightmost digit and multiplies alternate digits by 2. A call to function VALUE returns the value of each digit:

```
HOLD := VALUE(S[I]) * 2;
```

If the product (HOLD) is less than 10, there is no carry:

```
IF HOLD<10 THEN
   CARRY := 0
```

Otherwise, HOLD becomes the less significant digit, and CARRY is set to 1:

```
ELSE
   BEGIN
      HOLD := HOLD - 10;
      CARRY := 1
   END;
```

All the products and carries are summed up in ALT1:

```
ALT1 := ALT1 + HOLD + CARRY;
```

After this WHILE loop has completed its calculations, the value of CARRY is checked to find out if the last multiplication produced a carry. If it did, and if the I.D. number contains an odd number of digits, we must add 9 to return from the effect of the carry:

```
IF (2 * (N DIV 2) <> N) AND (CARRY = 1) THEN
   ALT1 := ALT1 + 9;
```

The second WHILE loop simply sums up the values of the remaining digits:

```
ALT2 := ALT2 + VALUE(S[I]);
```

After the two sums are added together, a MOD-10 operation isolates the last digit of the result:

```
TOTAL := ALT1 + ALT2;
LASTDIGIT := TOTAL MOD 10;
```

Finally, the last digit is subtracted from 10 to give the check digit. However, if the last digit of the total was a zero, then the check digit will also be zero:

```
CHDIG := 10 - LASTDIGIT;
IF (CHDIG = 10) THEN
   CHDIG := 0;
```

Function CHECKDIGIT returns the value of the check digit:

```
CHECKDIGIT := CHDIG
```

VERIFYCHECK

VERIFYCHECK is a short, elegant function that returns a Boolean value indicating whether or not the number it receives is valid. It assumes that the last digit of the long integer I is the check digit. The method of VERIFYCHECK is to cut off the last digit of I, and send the remaining digits to CHECKDIGIT. If I is a valid number, then the digit returned from CHECKDIGIT will be the same as the last digit of I.

The problem is to isolate the last digit from the rest of I. This problem is solved with the DIV and MOD operations. I DIV 10 shifts all the digits to the right and eliminates the check digit. I MOD 10 produces the check digit. Since the MOD operation is not defined for long integers, we must write our own function LONGMODINT:

```
LONGMODINT := TRUNC(L - ((L DIV I) * I))
```

(The TRUNC function converts a long integer to a regular integer. The long integer argument of TRUNC must, of course, be within the legal range of regular integers.)

With these two methods of isolating first the number from the check digit, and then the check digit from the number, we can write our VERIFYCHECK function in a single statement:

```
IF (CHECKDIGIT(I DIV 10) = LONGMODINT(I,10)) THEN
   VERIFYCHECK := TRUE
ELSE
   VERIFYCHECK := FALSE
```

This statement gives us a glimpse of the real elegance of Pascal as a programming language; that is, the compactness, the brevity with which it can sum up complex operations in a single statement.

SUMMARY

We have seen some interesting programming techniques in CHECKUNIT, particularly in the routines that deal with the check digit itself. We can use this package whenever we need to input long integers that do not represent dollars and cents.

Chapter 6

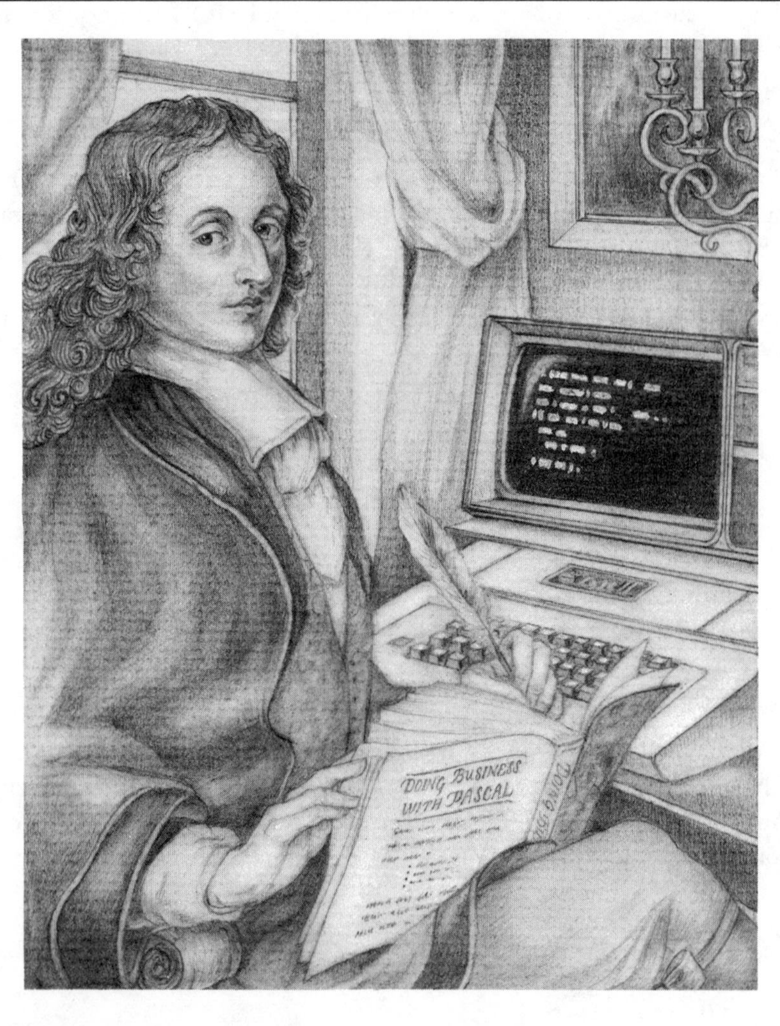

The Implementation of DATEUNIT

INTRODUCTION

The DATEUNIT package provides for the input, validation, and output of dates. Variables of type DATEREC are used to store the dates:

```
DATEREC = RECORD
          MONTH,
          DAY,
          YEAR : INTEGER
END;
```

An additional routine in DATEUNIT, procedure DATECONVERT, performs scalar date conversion. Both INDATE and DATECONVERT make use of function DAYSINMONTH, which is a private routine in DATEUNIT. DAYSINMONTH, as its name implies, determines the number of days in any specified month of any year. Figure 6.1 shows a complete listing of DATEUNIT.

```
(*$S+*)
UNIT DATEUNIT;

INTERFACE


TYPE
  DATELONG = INTEGER[5];
  DATEREC = RECORD
              MONTH,
              DAY,
              YEAR   : INTEGER
  END;

PROCEDURE OUTDATE(DATE: DATEREC);

PROCEDURE INDATE (VAR DATE: DATEREC);

PROCEDURE DATECONVERT(DATE:DATEREC;
                    VAR SCDATE:DATELONG);


IMPLEMENTATION


PROCEDURE OUTDATE;
  VAR
    MOSTRING,
    CENTURY : STRING;

PROCEDURE CHOOSEMONTH(M: INTEGER;
                    VAR NAME: STRING);
  VAR
    TEMP : STRING;

BEGIN
  CASE M OF
    1 : TEMP := 'JANUARY';
    2 : TEMP := 'FEBRUARY';
    3 : TEMP := 'MARCH';
    4 : TEMP := 'APRIL';
    5 : TEMP := 'MAY';
    6 : TEMP := 'JUNE';
    7 : TEMP := 'JULY';
    8 : TEMP := 'AUGUST';
    9 : TEMP := 'SEPTEMBER';
    10: TEMP := 'OCTOBER';
    11: TEMP := 'NOVEMBER';
    12: TEMP := 'DECEMBER'
  END;
  NAME := TEMP
END;


BEGIN (* OUTDATE *)
  WITH DATE DO
```

Figure 6.1: Complete Listing of DATEUNIT

```
    BEGIN
      CHOOSEMONTH(MONTH, MOSTRING);
      IF YEAR >= 10 THEN
        CENTURY := ', 19'
      ELSE
        CENTURY := ', 190';
      WRITE(MOSTRING,' ', DAY, CENTURY, YEAR)
    END
END;

FUNCTION DAYSINMONTH(MO,YR:INTEGER): INTEGER;
  BEGIN
    CASE MO OF
      1,3,5,7,8,10,12 : DAYSINMONTH := 31;
             4,6,9,11 : DAYSINMONTH := 30;
                    2 : IF (YR MOD 4 = 0) THEN
                          DAYSINMONTH := 29
                        ELSE
                          DAYSINMONTH := 28
    END (* CASE *)
  END; (* DAYSINMONTH *)


PROCEDURE INDATE;
  CONST
    SEPARATOR = '-';
  VAR
    OK: BOOLEAN;
    L,
    FIELD,
    PLACE,
    TEMPNUM    : INTEGER;
    TEMPSTRING : STRING;

  FUNCTION GOODDIGIT(L, PLACE:INTEGER): BOOLEAN;
    BEGIN
      IF PLACE <= L THEN
        GOODDIGIT := TEMPSTRING[PLACE] IN ['0'..'9']
      ELSE
        GOODDIGIT := FALSE
    END;

  FUNCTION VALUE(CH: CHAR):INTEGER;
    BEGIN
      VALUE := ORD(CH) - ORD('0')
    END;


BEGIN
  OK := TRUE;
  REPEAT
    READLN(TEMPSTRING);
    L := LENGTH(TEMPSTRING);
    OK := (L <= 8) AND (L >= 6);
    FIELD := 1;
    PLACE := 1;
    WHILE (OK AND (FIELD <= 3)) DO
```

Figure 6.1: Complete Listing of DATEUNIT (cont.)

```
        BEGIN
          TEMPNUM := 0;
          WHILE GOODDIGIT(L, PLACE) DO
            BEGIN
              TEMPNUM := TEMPNUM * 10 + VALUE(TEMPSTRING[PLACE]);
              PLACE := PLACE + 1
            END;
          IF PLACE <= L THEN
            OK := OK AND (TEMPSTRING[PLACE] = SEPARATOR);


          IF OK THEN
            CASE FIELD OF
              1 : IF ((TEMPNUM <= 12) AND
                      (TEMPNUM >= 1)) THEN
                        DATE.MONTH := TEMPNUM
                  ELSE
                        OK := FALSE;

              2 : DATE.DAY := TEMPNUM; (* TEST VALIDITY LATER *)

              3 : IF ((TEMPNUM <= 99) AND
                      (TEMPNUM >= 1)) THEN
                        DATE.YEAR := TEMPNUM
                  ELSE
                        OK := FALSE
            END; (* CASE *)
          PLACE := PLACE + 1;
          FIELD := FIELD + 1
        END; (* WHILE *)

        IF OK THEN
          WITH DATE DO
            OK := DAY <= DAYSINMONTH(MONTH,YEAR);

        IF (NOT OK) THEN
          BEGIN
            WRITELN('   *** ILLEGAL DATE');
            WRITE('                DATE:     ')
          END
    UNTIL OK;
  END; (* INDATE *)


  PROCEDURE DATECONVERT;

  VAR
    TEMP         : DATELONG;
    I            : INTEGER;

  BEGIN
    TEMP := 0;
    WITH DATE DO
    BEGIN
      FOR I := 1 TO YEAR - 1 DO
        IF ((I MOD 4) = 0) THEN
          TEMP := TEMP + 366
```

Figure 6.1: Complete Listing of DATEUNIT (cont.)

```
        ELSE
          TEMP := TEMP + 365;

      FOR I := 1 TO MONTH - 1 DO
        TEMP := TEMP + DAYSINMONTH(I,YEAR);
      TEMP := TEMP + DAY;
      SCDATE := TEMP
    END
  END;  (* DATECONVERT *)


  BEGIN

  END.
```

Figure 6.1: Complete Listing of DATEUNIT (cont.)

INDATE

We noted in Chapter 3 that INDATE imposes a rather strict input format on the user. We might well have chosen to allow any combination of other formats; for example:

APR-14-82

14-APR-82

4/14/82

or even:

APRIL 14, 1982

Certainly we could write a routine to read any one of these date formats, though some of them might be more difficult than others. Writing an input procedure that would allow all of them would be a formidable task, indeed, but also possible. For our purposes we have chosen to allow only two different formats:

4-14-82

or

04-14-82

We will see that even this slight variety in acceptable input adds complexity to our procedure. Our choice represents a compromise between user-friendliness (which would allow input in as many forms as are likely to be used) and the desire to avoid unnecessary complexity in programming.

Like the other input routines we have seen, INDATE is made up of one long REPEAT statement that stops looping only when a valid input has been read; the Boolean variable OK indicates whether or not the input has passed all the validation tests:

```
REPEAT
  ...
UNTIL OK
```

At the beginning of the loop, the input is read into the variable TEMPSTRING. The length of TEMPSTRING, which is assigned to L, must be within the correct number of characters:

```
OK := (L <= 8) AND (L >= 6);
```

The date is validated and converted within two nested WHILE loops. The outer loop isolates each field of the date (i.e., month, day, year); the inner loop uses the local functions GOODDIGIT and VALUE to validate each character of a given field and to convert the field into an integer. Once that conversion is complete, a CASE statement checks the range of each field and makes assignments to the record DATE. The month must be between 1 and 12:

```
CASE FIELD OF
   1 : IF ((TEMPNUM <= 12) AND
          (TEMPNUM >= 1) THEN
             DATE.MONTH := TEMPNUM
```

and the year between 1 and 99:

```
   3 : IF ((TEMPNUM <= 99) AND
          (TEMPNUM >= 1) THEN
             DATE.YEAR := TEMPNUM
```

Range checking for the day, however, depends upon the month and the year, and must therefore be postponed until both of those values are assigned. A call to function DAYSINMONTH determines the appropriate range for the day.

DAYSINMONTH is not a local function in INDATE, because procedure DATECONVERT also uses it. DAYSINMONTH is, however, a private routine in DATEUNIT, so it is defined completely in the IMPLEMENTATION section, and not mentioned in the INTERFACE section. The function has two parameters, MO and YR, both integers; it consists of a single CASE statement. The CASE selector is MO, the month:

```
CASE MO OF
```

These months have 31 days:

```
1,3,5,7,8,10,12 : DAYSINMONTH := 31;
```

and these have 30:

```
4,6,9,11: DAYSINMONTH := 30;
```

Assigning the length of February, the second month, is more complicated. In leap years (when YR MOD 4 = 0) it has 29 days; in other years, 28:

```
2 : IF (YR MOD 4 = 0) THEN
      DAYSINMONTH := 29
    ELSE
      DAYSINMONTH := 28
```

Given a month and a year, then, DAYSINMONTH returns the maximum value of DAY. Notice how the WITH statement in procedure INDATE adds economy to the call to DAYSINMONTH:

```
WITH DATE DO
   OK := DAY = DAYSINMONTH(MONTH,YEAR);
```

Without such a WITH statement, it would be necessary to repeat the record name in each field.

The last block of code in INDATE provides an error message if OK has been switched to FALSE at any point in the procedure. If OK is still TRUE, then a valid date has already been assigned to the record variable DATE, and the task of INDATE is complete.

OUTDATE

Procedure OUTDATE simply writes the date it receives in the form:

```
APRIL 14, 1982
```

Its local procedure CHOOSEMONTH receives the month number and returns the month name in MOSTRING. The string CENTURY is designed to allow for the fact that the integer YEAR may be either one digit or two:

```
IF YEAR >= 10 THEN
   CENTURY := ', 19'
ELSE
   CENTURY := ', 190';
```

Given the month and century strings, and the DAY and YEAR fields of DATE, a WRITE statement outputs the date:

```
WRITE(MOSTRING, ' ', DAY, CENTURY, YEAR)
```

DATECONVERT

Procedure DATECONVERT adds up the number of days up to and including the date passed to it, starting from January 1, 1901. It accumulates this sum in the long integer variable TEMP, initialized to zero. First it adds the years up to the year preceding DATE.YEAR; 366 days for leap years, 365 for others:

```
FOR I := 1 TO YEAR - 1 DO
  IF (I MOD 4 = 0) THEN
    TEMP := TEMP + 366
  ELSE
    TEMP := TEMP + 365
```

Then it adds the months up to the month previous to DATE.MONTH. A call to DAYSINMONTH returns the appropriate number of days to add to TEMP:

```
FOR I := 1 TO MONTH - 1 DO
  TEMP := TEMP + DAYSINMONTH(I,YEAR);
```

Finally, it adds on the days:

```
TEMP := TEMP + DAY;
```

January 1, 1901 is an arbitrary starting point for the scalar date conversion. If there were a reason to do so, we could easily rewrite the routine to go further back in time. Remember, though, that the whole DATEUNIT package as it currently stands assumes that all dates are within the twentieth century. Leap year calculation, in particular, would be more difficult if it had to account for 1900, which meets our MOD 4 = 0 criterion, but is not a leap year in the Gregorian calendar.

SUMMARY

Although a great number of date input functions are possible, we have chosen to keep our INDATE routine simple. In addition to this strictly-formatted input routine, the DATEUNIT package allows us to find the number of days between any two dates in the twentieth century, via the scalar date procedure.

With DATEUNIT we have completed our description of our three unit packages. In Chapter 8 we will be examining a program that uses all three of these units—a file update program. Before moving on to that, however, we will develop two more subroutines that are necessary for file management—a sort routine and a search routine.

Chapter 7

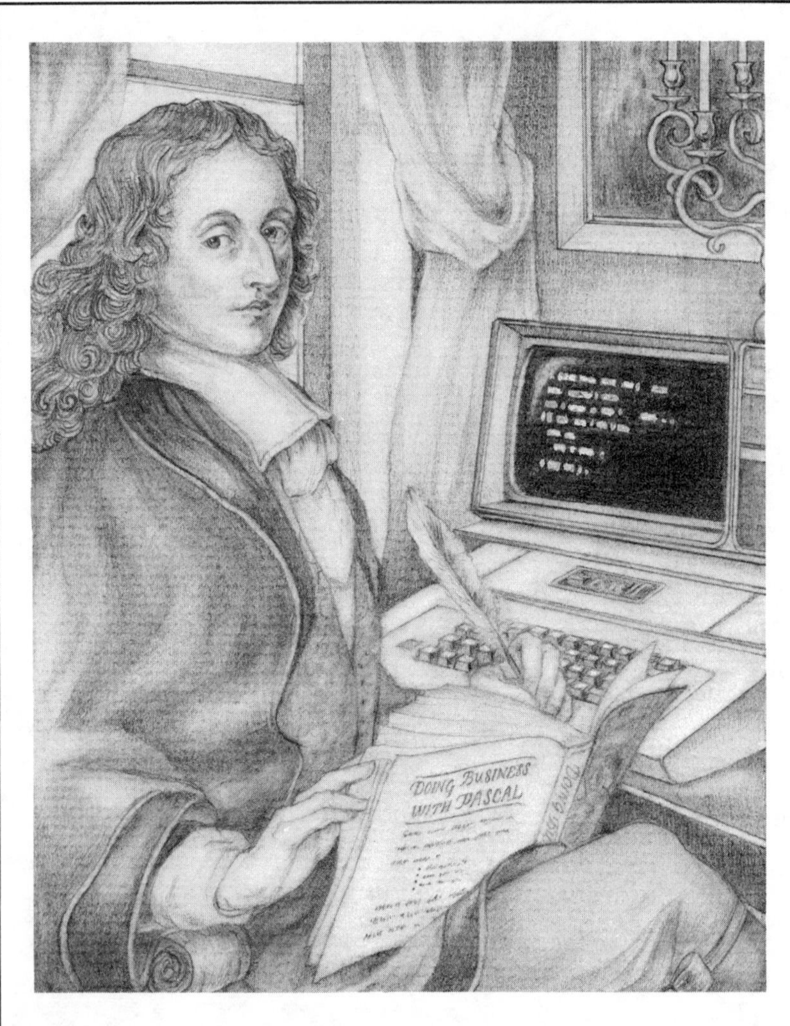

Sorting and Searching

INTRODUCTION

For our file update program, we will be developing an index into a file of records; this index will have to be *sorted*—i.e., arranged in ascending order—at regular intervals. In addition, we will often want to search for a given number in the sorted index. The more efficiently we can perform these two operations—sorting and searching—the more convenient the program will be for the user.

In this chapter, then, we will develop and discuss the two routines that will perform these functions. Since both routines will require a small amount of revision and tailoring to be incorporated into the file update program (or any other program, for that matter), we will not create a unit for them. Instead, we will put them into an *include* file. Unlike the unit module, a UCSD Pascal include file may not be independently compiled; the text of an include file is placed into the main program at compile time. The $I compiler directive is used to tell the compiler where to find an include file. In our example, the file SEARCHSORT.TEXT will be included into program SEARCHTEST as follows:

```
(*$I SEARCHSORT.TEXT*)
```

For purposes of this illustration, we will design both of the procedures in this file to work on an array of strings, defined in program SEARCHTEST as follows:

```
CONST
   N = 100;
TYPE
   ARY = ARRAY[0..N] OF STRING;
VAR
   LIST: ARY;
```

In the file update program, however, we will be sorting and searching numbers, not strings.

SORTING

The bubble sort and the diminishing-increment sort are among the most frequently used sorting algorithms. Both of them operate by comparing and exchanging elements of an array until the array is sorted. When any two elements are found to be out of order, they take each other's places in the array. We will perform this exchange in a procedure named SWAP, which exchanges elements P and Q:

```
HOLD := P;
P := Q;
Q := HOLD;
```

Note that a third variable, HOLD, is required for the exchange. The incorrect sequence:

```
P := Q;
Q := P;
```

would result in both P and Q taking the original value of Q.

The bubble sort (so named because "lighter" elements are said to "float" to the top of the list) is extremely simple to code, but is generally less efficient than other sorting algorithms. In the bubble sort, each element of the array is compared sequentially with every element after it. This comparison is performed in a pair of nested FOR loops. If A is the array to be sorted and N is the number of elements in A, the bubble sort would appear as:

```
FOR I := 1 TO N - 1 DO
   FOR J := I + 1 TO N DO
      IF A[I] > A[J] THEN
         SWAP(A[I], A[J]);
```

For each incrementation of the outer loop, the array is correctly sorted down to element I. By the time I reaches N − 1, the value of J will have reached N, and the list is completely sorted.

In the file update program, we will be sorting lists of 100 elements or fewer. For this purpose the bubble sort might be about as efficient as the diminishing-increment sort. However, for other needs, when the list to be sorted gets longer, the bubble sort is too slow. The problem is that any given value can end up moving up and down the list many times before finding its correct place. In one experimental run, sorting a randomly ordered list of 100 elements, we found that the bubble sort called procedure SWAP over 3,700 times. The best version of the diminishing increment sort, on the other hand, required about 350 calls to SWAP to sort the list.

The diminishing-increment sort (also called the Shell sort, after Donald L. Shell, who first proposed it) is a bit more complicated. Instead of the bulldozer approach of plowing straight through the list element by element, the Shell sort starts by comparing elements that are far away from each other. In each pass through the list, it decreases the distance (or "increment") between the elements it compares. By the time the increment is 1, (i.e., neighboring elements are compared) the list is already nearly sorted.

The trick of using the Shell sort is choosing the best set of decreasing increments to use on the list. Exploring this problem formally turns out to require some rather advanced mathematics. Shell originally suggested using increments based directly on the length, N, of the list. In this approach, the first increment is N, then N/2, N/4, N/8, N/16, and so on until the increment decreases to 1. (The last increment must always be 1.)

We will use what appears experimentally to be a slightly more efficient approach (measuring efficiency in terms of the number of calls to SWAP required for the sort). Our jumps (or increments) will be based on powers of 2. First, we will find the first power of 2 that is greater than *N*, that is:

$$2^k > N$$

This power of 2 will be determined in the short function FIRSTJUMP:

```
TEMP := 1;
WHILE TEMP <= LENGTH DO
   TEMP := TEMP * 2;
```

Actually, FIRSTJUMP is misnamed; 2^k will not be the first jump. The first increment will be $(2^k - 1)/2$. Likewise, each succeeding jump will be calculated from the same formula:

```
JUMP := (JUMP - 1) DIV 2;
```

Let us assume our list has 100 elements. The first power of 2 greater than 100 is 128 (or 2^7). Thus, in this case, the first jump will be (128 − 1) DIV 2, or 63. The entire list of diminishing increments for a list of 100 elements is 63, 31, 15, 7, 3, and 1.

As we have said, this set of increments turns out to be rather efficient to use in the Shell sort. (However, it is still interesting to experiment with other sets.) The listing of our version of the Shell sort is shown in Figure 7.1. The sort is performed in three loops. The inner FOR loop actually makes the comparisons and calls SWAP if necessary. The middle REPEAT loop continues making comparisons with a given increment until all possible exchanges for that increment have been made. The outer WHILE loop controls the increments, and provides a smaller increment for each succeeding "pass" through the list.

Obviously, the number of calls to SWAP is not the only factor that determines the efficiency of the sort; other factors are the number of loops through the list for each increment, and the number of increments. We have designed our sort procedure to document the sort as it proceeds, by displaying certain messages. Each new increment appears on the screen as it is calculated, allowing us to judge approximately how long each pass takes. At the end of the sort, the number of calls to SWAP is also displayed. We will, of course, delete those lines from the procedure when we put it into our file-update program. But for now it will be interesting to see exactly what is happening in the sorting process.

```
PROCEDURE SHELLSORT(VAR A: ARY;
                        N: INTEGER);

VAR
  DONE : BOOLEAN;
  JUMP,
  I,
  J,
  SWNO : INTEGER;

FUNCTION FIRSTJUMP(LENGTH: INTEGER): INTEGER;
VAR
  TEMP : INTEGER;

BEGIN
  TEMP := 1;
  WHILE TEMP <= LENGTH DO
    TEMP := TEMP * 2;
  FIRSTJUMP := TEMP
END;  (* FIRSTJUMP *)

PROCEDURE SWAP (VAR P, Q : STRING);
  VAR
    HOLD : STRING;
  BEGIN
    HOLD := P;
    P := Q;
    Q := HOLD
  END; (* SWAP *)
```

Figure 7.1: Listing of Procedure ***SHELLSORT***

```
BEGIN (* SHELLSORT *)
  SWNO := 0;
  JUMP := FIRSTJUMP(N);
  WRITELN('SORTING ==>');
  WRITE('JUMPS: ');
  WHILE JUMP > 1 DO
  BEGIN
    JUMP := (JUMP - 1) DIV 2;
    WRITE(JUMP, ' ');
      REPEAT
        DONE := TRUE;
          FOR J := 1 TO N - JUMP DO
            BEGIN
              I:= J + JUMP;
              IF A[J] > A[I] THEN
                BEGIN
                  SWNO := SWNO + 1;
                  SWAP(A[J],A[I]);
                  DONE := FALSE
                END (* IF *)
            END (* FOR *)
      UNTIL DONE
  END (* WHILE *);
  WRITELN;
  WRITELN(SWNO,' SWAPS WERE NEEDED.')
END (* SHELLSORT *);
```

Figure 7.1: Listing of Procedure SHELLSORT (cont.)

SEARCHING

Once a list is sorted, we can use a very fast searching algorithm, called the *binary search*, to find any element in the list. The binary search is very simple and elegant. Let us say we have a list of 100 names, and we wish to find the place of a given name that we know is somewhere in the list. (Remember, the names are now in alphabetical order.) We first look at the name in the center of the list—number 50—and compare it with the name we are searching for. From this comparison we will be able to tell whether our name will appear in the first or the last half of the list, so we look next at the name in the center of the appropriate half of the list (either name 25 or 75). We continue cutting parts of the list in half like this until we have found our name.

We can calculate the average number of comparisons that will have to be made to find an element in a list of a given length. For a list of 100 elements, the average is about 6 comparisons. This means that any element can be found very quickly.

The listing of our binary search procedure appears in Figure 7.2. The procedure has five parameters, two of them VAR parameters. VAL is the string we will be searching for in the list. LIST is the array of strings itself, and LENGTH is the number of elements in LIST. The VAR parameter KEY returns the index (i.e., the position) of VAL in LIST, and FOUND is a Boolean value that indicates whether or not VAL was found at all.

Three variables are used to divide up the array. LOWER is the index of the "smallest" (or highest in the alphabet) element in the list, and UPPER is the index of the "largest" (or lowest in the alphabet) element in the list. CENTER is calculated as the index of the element halfway between LOWER and UPPER:

```
CENTER := (LOWER + UPPER) DIV 2;
```

If the CENTER element turns out to be the string we are looking for,

```
PROCEDURE BSEARCH (VAL    : STRING;
                   LENGTH: INTEGER;
                   LIST   : ARY;
               VAR KEY    : INTEGER;
               VAR FOUND  : BOOLEAN);
VAR
  LOWER,
  UPPER,
  CENTER : INTEGER;


BEGIN
  LOWER := 1;
  UPPER := LENGTH;
  FOUND := FALSE;
  WRITE('SEARCHING');

  WHILE (UPPER >= LOWER) AND (NOT FOUND) DO
    BEGIN
      WRITE('.');
      CENTER := (LOWER + UPPER) DIV 2;
      IF VAL = LIST[CENTER] THEN
        BEGIN
          FOUND := TRUE;
          KEY := CENTER
        END
      ELSE
        IF VAL > LIST[CENTER] THEN
          LOWER := CENTER + 1
        ELSE
          UPPER := CENTER - 1
    END (* WHILE *);
    WRITELN
 END (* BSEARCH *);
```

Figure 7.2: Listing of Procedure BSEARCH

the KEY is set to CENTER and FOUND becomes true:

```
IF VAL = LIST[CENTER] THEN
   BEGIN
      FOUND : = TRUE;
      KEY : = CENTER
END
```

Otherwise, if VAL is located lower down in the list than CENTER, then the value of LOWER is dropped down to the element after CENTER:

```
ELSE
   IF VAL >LIST[CENTER] THEN
      LOWER : = CENTER + 1
```

If VAL is higher in the list than CENTER, then UPPER is raised to the element before CENTER:

```
ELSE
   UPPER : = CENTER - 1
```

The WHILE loop that controls this activity ends only when VAL has been found, or when LOWER becomes greater than UPPER, indicating that VAL is not in the list:

```
WHILE (UPPER > = LOWER) AND (NOT FOUND) DO
```

In the course of the search, the procedure writes a message on the screen that shows how many comparisons have been made. The message:

```
SEARCHING.....
```

indicates that the search has gone through five comparisons.

A TEST PROGRAM FOR THE SEARCHING AND SORTING ROUTINES

Program SEARCHTEST, shown in Figure 7.3, is very straightforward. It allows the user to specify how long the list will be, and then prompts for the input of the list. A call to procedure SHELLSORT sorts the list, and then the small procedure PRINTLIST displays the sorted list.

Then the user is given a chance to search for any number of names in the list. Procedure INSEARCH prompts for the name to be searched for, calls BSEARCH to find the name, and writes a message that either gives the location of the name or explains that the name is not in the list.

```
PROGRAM SEARCHTEST;
CONST
  N = 100;
TYPE
  ARY = ARRAY[0..N] OF STRING;
VAR
  I,
  NUM : INTEGER;
  LIST : ARY;
  ANSWER : STRING;

(*$I SEARCHSORT.TEXT*)

PROCEDURE CLEARSCREEN;
CONST
  SCREENLENGTH = 25;
VAR
  INDEX : INTEGER;

BEGIN
  FOR INDEX := 1 TO SCREENLENGTH DO
    WRITELN;
  GOTOXY(0,0)
END;

PROCEDURE PRINTLIST;

VAR
  I : INTEGER;

BEGIN
  WRITELN;
  FOR I := 1 TO NUM DO
    WRITELN(I, ') ', LIST[I]);
  WRITELN
END;

PROCEDURE INSEARCH(J:INTEGER);
VAR
  NAME : STRING;
  KEY  : INTEGER;
  FOUND : BOOLEAN;

BEGIN
  WRITELN;
  WRITELN('SEARCH WHAT NAME? ');
  READLN(NAME);
  BSEARCH(NAME, J, LIST, KEY, FOUND);
  IF FOUND THEN
    BEGIN
      WRITELN(NAME, ' IS NAME #', KEY);
      WRITELN
    END
  ELSE
    BEGIN
      WRITELN(NAME, ' IS NOT IN THE LIST');
      WRITELN
    END
END;
```

Figure 7.3: Listing of SEARCHTEST

```
BEGIN
  WRITE('HOW MANY NAMES? ');
  READLN(NUM);
  WRITELN;
  WRITELN('INPUT ', NUM, ' NAMES');

  FOR I := 1 TO NUM DO
    BEGIN
      WRITE(I,') ');
      READLN(LIST[I])
    END;
  CLEARSCREEN;

  SHELLSORT(LIST,NUM);
  WRITELN;
  WRITE('PRESS <RETURN> WHEN READY.');
  READLN(ANSWER);
  WRITELN('SORTED LIST');
  WRITELN('===========');
  WRITELN;
  PRINTLIST;

  WRITE('TYPE <RETURN> TO CONTINUE');
  READLN(ANSWER);
  CLEARSCREEN;

  REPEAT
    INSEARCH(NUM);
    WRITE('ANOTHER SEARCH? ');
    READLN(ANSWER);
    CLEARSCREEN
  UNTIL ANSWER = 'N';
END.  (* SEARCHTEST *)
```

Figure 7.3: Listing of SEARCHTEST (cont.)

Notice that the value of the Boolean variable FOUND, returned from BSEARCH, is used to determine which message to write:

```
IF FOUND THEN
  BEGIN
    WRITELN(NAME, ' IS NAME #', KEY);
    WRITELN
  END
ELSE
  BEGIN
    WRITELN(NAME, ' IS NOT IN THE LIST');
    WRITELN
  END
```

A run of the program for a list of 100 names appears in Figure 7.4. Note in particular the messages supplied by the sort and search routines.

```
HOW MANY NAMES? 100

INPUT 100 NAMES
1) PREVOST
2) ROSTAND
3) CASANOVA
4) ANDERSON
5) ZOLA
6) TYNAN
7) WALDMAN
8) IRVING
9) CAEN
10) LAUTREAMONT
11) TZARA
12) DURAS
13) SWINBURNE
14) BLOCH
15) STEFFENS
16) WORDSWORTH
17) FOURIER
18) LEDUC
19) BARNES
20) RABELAIS
21) BAUDELAIRE
22) LENIN
23) GIBRAN
24) JOZSEF
25) SMART
26) LUKACS
27) BECKETT
28) WELTY
29) TOYNBEE
30) WEBSTER
31) MAYAKOVSKY
32) JAMES
33) FRANCE
34) SYNGE
35) AMIS
36) CAVAFY
37) DINESEN
38) WILDER
39) GRAUBERRY
40) HALEY
41) BACCHELLI
42) CROSBY
43) STOKER
44) ABELARD
45) BRONTE
46) FIELDING
47) STAEL
48) ROLVAAG
49) SHAKESPEARE
50) NABOKOV
51) DONLEAVY
52) TROLLOPE
53) WARREN
54) MARE
55) DEFOE
56) WITTGENSTEIN
57) LOOS
58) ALEIXANDRE
59) JONG
60) GIBBON
61) WOLLSTONECRAFT
62) FITTS
63) NEWTON
64) HEARST
65) MCKUEN
66) TOKLAS
67) RANSOM
68) DANTE
69) ADDISON
70) HELLER
71) SOUTHERN
72) NOVALIS
73) BENN
74) MACHIAVELLI
75) MANN
76) KIERKEGAARD
77) MARX
78) ROETHKE
79) FREUD
80) TAGORE
81) JARRELL
82) BROWNING
83) MACLEISH
84) WILSON
85) GARY
86) SNYDER
87) PYNCHON
88) BARRIE
89) GASSET
90) BERRIGAN
91) BERLIN
92) LEAR
93) ROSSETTI
94) VOZNESENSKY
95) HEINE
96) DAUDET
97) MAURIER
98) KOSTELANETZ
99) BOSWELL
100) JOHNSON

SORTING ==>
JUMPS: 63 31 15 7 3 1
```

Figure 7.4: Sample Run of SEARCHTEST

```
377 SWAPS WERE NEEDED.

PRESS <RETURN> WHEN READY.

------------------------------

SORTED LIST
===========


1) ABELARD
2) ADDISON
3) ALEIXANDRE
4) AMIS
5) ANDERSON
6) BACCHELLI
7) BARNES
8) BARRIE
9) BAUDELAIRE
10) BECKETT
11) BENN
12) BERLIN
13) BERRIGAN
14) BLOCH
15) BOSWELL
16) BRONTE
17) BROWNING
18) CAEN
19) CASANOVA
20) CAVAFY
21) CROSBY
22) DANTE
23) DAUDET
24) DEFOE
25) DINESEN
26) DONLEAVY
27) DURAS
28) FIELDING
29) FITTS
30) FOURIER
31) FRANCE
32) FREUD
33) GARY
34) GASSET
35) GIBBON
36) GIBRAN
37) GRAUBERRY
38) HALEY
39) HEARST
40) HEINE
41) HELLER
42) IRVING
43) JAMES
44) JARRELL
45) JOHNSON
46) JONG
47) JOZSEF
48) KIERKEGAARD
49) KOSTELANETZ
50) LAUTREAMONT
51) LEAR
52) LEDUC
53) LENIN
54) LOOS
55) LUKACS
56) MACHIAVELLI
57) MACLEISH
58) MANN
59) MARE
60) MARX
61) MAURIER
62) MAYAKOVSKY
63) MCKUEN
64) NABOKOV
65) NEWTON
66) NOVALIS
67) PREVOST
68) PYNCHON
69) RABELAIS
70) RANSOM
71) ROETHKE
72) ROLVAAG
73) ROSSETTI
74) ROSTAND
75) SHAKESPEARE
76) SMART
77) SNYDER
78) SOUTHERN
79) STAEL
80) STEFFENS
81) STOKER
82) SWINBURNE
83) SYNGE
84) TAGORE
85) TOKLAS
86) TOYNBEE
87) TROLLOPE
88) TYNAN
89) TZARA
90) VOZNESENSKY
91) WALDMAN
92) WARREN
93) WEBSTER
94) WELTY
95) WILDER
96) WILSON
97) WITTGENSTEIN
98) WOLLSTONECRAFT
99) WORDSWORTH
100) ZOLA
```

Figure 7.4: Sample Run of SEARCHTEST (cont.)

```
TYPE <RETURN> TO CONTINUE
------------------------------

SEARCH WHAT NAME?
TOKLAS
SEARCHING.......
TOKLAS IS NAME #85

ANOTHER SEARCH? Y


------------------------------


SEARCH WHAT NAME?
MACHIAVELLI
SEARCHING....
MACHIAVELLI IS NAME #56

ANOTHER SEARCH? Y


------------------------------


SEARCH WHAT NAME?
DICKENS
SEARCHING.......
DICKENS IS NOT IN THE LIST

ANOTHER SEARCH? Y

------------------------------


SEARCH WHAT NAME?
ZOLA
SEARCHING.......
ZOLA IS NAME #100

ANOTHER SEARCH? N
```

Figure 7.4: Sample Run of SEARCHTEST (cont.)

SUMMARY

Sorting and searching, two of the classic problems of computer programming, provide us with some interesting exercises in Pascal. We will see both of these routines again in Chapter 8 in the file update program.

Chapter 8

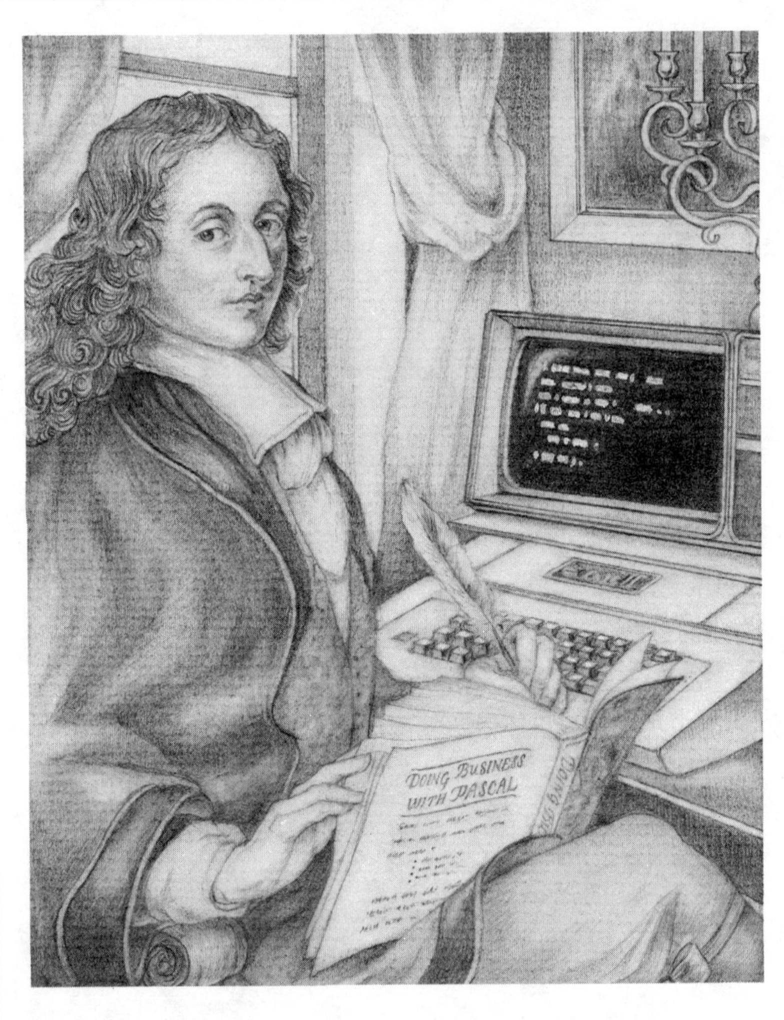

Data File Management

INTRODUCTION

We have concentrated so far in Part II on two Pascal extensions that are essential to business applications—a double-precision numeric data type (represented by the *long integer* in UCSD Pascal), and a separately compiled program module (the *unit* in UCSD Pascal). In this chapter we will discuss a third important extension—*random access files*. Standard Pascal, as defined by Jensen and Wirth, provides only *sequential files*. The records of a sequential file are accessed one by one, from the beginning of the file to the end. The records of a random access file, on the other hand, may be read or written in any order. In addition, random access files in UCSD Pascal may be opened for both input and output operations simultaneously. As we will see in this chapter, the random access feature is essential for files that require frequent updating.

We will be examining a file management program called UPDATE. This is the longest and most complete program in this book. In its present form, UPDATE is designed specifically to maintain a file of fixed assets. Each record of the file will contain four fields: the identification number, the name, the acquisition date, and the initial cost of an asset. (To input and output the data for these fields, we will use the I/O procedures and functions of the three units we developed in Chapters 3 through 6.)

UPDATE also creates an index for the asset file, and stores this index in a separate file of its own. Since the asset records might be stored in a random order, the index provides a means of locating any record in the asset file. The sort and search programs from Chapter 7 are used (in revised forms) to manage the index. The use of an index to locate records in a random access file is sometimes called an *indexed sequential access method* (or ISAM). We will see that the present version of UPDATE implements only an abbreviated form of ISAM; however, we will outline the details of an expanded ISAM that could be created for the UPDATE program.

Let us begin, then, by examining some interactive dialogue from the UPDATE program.

CREATING AND UPDATING FILES

UPDATE has two modes of operation, a creation mode and an update mode. The user chooses the mode at the beginning of the program run by typing a C or a U:

```
ASSET FILE MANAGEMENT PROGRAM
=================================
C(REATE OR U(PDATE?
```

The program pauses to give the user a chance to put the correct data disk into the second disk drive (note that the present version of UPDATE assumes that two drives are available):

```
PUT DISK IN DRIVE B:
PRESS <RETURN> WHEN READY.
```

The two files created (or updated) by this program are called ASSETS and INDEX in the disk directory. It is the user's responsibility to make sure that both files are available on the disk before running the program in the update mode. Thus, in this mode, the additional reminder:

```
(MUST CONTAIN FILES 'ASSETS' AND 'INDEX')
```

appears on the screen. In the creation mode, any previous versions of ASSETS and INDEX will be destroyed. The program will terminate with an I/O error message if both files are not available for the update mode. We will discuss alternative, and perhaps friendlier, approaches to opening the UPDATE program when we look at its initialization procedures.

Figure 8.1 shows a sample run of the program in the creation mode. (Note that each block of this output represents a screenful of information.) The creation mode only allows the user to *add* records to the new file; thus there are only two different screen formats in this mode—the input and the echo.

The input screen simply prompts the user to type in the data for the four fields of the record. The I.D. number comes first. If the user types a

```
ASSET FILE MANAGEMENT PROGRAM
===== ==== ========== =======

C(REATE OR U(PDATE? C

PUT DISK IN DRIVE B:

PRESS <RETURN> WHEN READY.

CREATING INDEX FILE...
OPENING ASSET FILE...

--------------------------------------------------

I.D. NUMBER:     82510
I.D. NUMBER WITH CHECK DIGIT: 82510-0
NAME OF ASSET:              TRUCK#1
DATE OF ACQUISITION:        1-5-67
ORIGINAL COST OF ASSET: 12650

--------------------------------------------------
ID#:     825100

1) NAME:    TRUCK#1
2) DATE:    JANUARY 5, 1967
3) COST:    $12,650.00


OK TO SAVE? Y
SORTING INDEX

SAVING RECORD...
ADD ANOTHER? Y

--------------------------------------------------

I.D. NUMBER:     61123
I.D. NUMBER WITH CHECK DIGIT: 61123-7
NAME OF ASSET:              COPIER
DATE OF ACQUISITION:        8-20-69
ORIGINAL COST OF ASSET: 19845

--------------------------------------------------
ID#:     611237

1) NAME:    COPIER
2) DATE:    AUGUST 20, 1969
3) COST:    $19,845.00


OK TO SAVE? Y
SORTING INDEX.

SAVING RECORD...
ADD ANOTHER? Y

--------------------------------------------------
```

Figure 8.1: Output in Creation Mode

```
I.D. NUMBER:     75619
I.D. NUMBER WITH CHECK DIGIT: 75619-8
NAME OF ASSET:              MACHINE#1
DATE OF ACQUISITION:        5-4-72
ORIGINAL COST OF ASSET: 25980

----------------------------------------------------

ID#:     756198

1) NAME:    MACHINE#1
2) DATE:    MAY 4, 1972
3) COST:    $25,980.00


OK TO SAVE? Y
SORTING INDEX.

SAVING RECORD...
ADD ANOTHER? Y

____________________________________________________

I.D. NUMBER:     32115
I.D. NUMBER WITH CHECK DIGIT: 32115-8
NAME OF ASSET:              COMPUTER
DATE OF ACQUISITION:        9520
   *** ILLEGAL DATE
                   DATE:    6-8-79
ORIGINAL COST OF ASSET: 9520

----------------------------------------------------

ID#:     321158

1) NAME:    COMPUTER
2) DATE:    JUNE 8, 1979
3) COST:    $9,520.00


OK TO SAVE? Y
SORTING INDEX.

SAVING RECORD...
ADD ANOTHER? Y


----------------------------------------------------

I.D. NUMBER:     19786
I.D. NUMBER WITH CHECK DIGIT: 19786-3
NAME OF ASSET:              MACHINE#2
DATE OF ACQUISITION:        2-3-73
ORIGINAL COST OF ASSET: 5780

----------------------------------------------------
```

Figure 8.1: Output in Creation Mode (cont.)

```
ID#:     197863

1) NAME:   MACHINE#2
2) DATE:   FEBRUARY 3, 1973
3) COST:   $5,780.00

OK TO SAVE? Y
SORTING INDEX..

SAVING RECORD...
ADD ANOTHER? Y
-------------------------------------------------------

I.D. NUMBER:     45521
I.D. NUMBER WITH CHECK DIGIT: 45521-2
NAME OF ASSET:              BUILDING#1
DATE OF ACQUISITION:        5-10-75
ORIGINAL COST OF ASSET: 115,650

-------------------------------------------------------

ID#:     455212

1) NAME:   BUILDING#1
2) DATE:   MAY 10, 1975
3) COST:   $115,650.00

OK TO SAVE? Y
SORTING INDEX..

SAVING RECORD...
ADD ANOTHER? Y
-------------------------------------------------------

I.D. NUMBER:     61152
I.D. NUMBER WITH CHECK DIGIT: 61152-6
NAME OF ASSET:              CAMERA
DATE OF ACQUISITION:        2-10-80_
    *** ILLEGAL DATE
                  DATE:     2-10-80
ORIGINAL COST OF ASSET: 2890

-------------------------------------------------------
ID#:     611526

1) NAME:   CAMERA
2) DATE:   FEBRUARY 10, 1980
3) COST:   $2,890.00

OK TO SAVE? Y
SORTING INDEX..

SAVING RECORD...
ADD ANOTHER? Y

-------------------------------------------------------
```

Figure 8.1: Output in Creation Mode (cont.)

```
I.D. NUMBER:     23611
I.D. NUMBER WITH CHECK DIGIT: 23611-7
NAME OF ASSET:              BUILDING#2
DATE OF ACQUISITION:        87500
   *** ILLEGAL DATE
                 DATE:      3-25-75
ORIGINAL COST OF ASSET: 87500

---------------------------------------------------

ID#:     236117

1) NAME:   BUILDING#2
2) DATE:   MARCH 25, 1975
3) COST:   $87,500.00


OK TO SAVE? Y
SORTING INDEX..

SAVING RECORD...
ADD ANOTHER? Y

---------------------------------------------------

I.D. NUMBER:     23611
I.D. NUMBER WITH CHECK DIGIT: 23611-7
THIS I.D. NUMBER IS ALREADY IN THE FILE.

I.D. NUMBER:     52665
I.D. NUMBER WITH CHECK DIGIT: 52665-8
NAME OF ASSET:              TRUCK#2
DATE OF ACQUISITION:        4-4-78
ORIGINAL COST OF ASSET: 15450

---------------------------------------------------

ID#:     526658

1) NAME:   TRUCK#2
2) DATE:   APRIL 4, 1978
3) COST:   $15,450.00
OK TO SAVE? Y
SORTING INDEX...

SAVING RECORD...
ADD ANOTHER? Y

---------------------------------------------------

I.D. NUMBER:     99113
I.D. NUMBER WITH CHECK DIGIT: 99113-4
NAME OF ASSET:              MACHINE#3
DATE OF ACQUISITION:        10-25-81
ORIGINAL COST OF ASSET: 63980

---------------------------------------------------
```

Figure 8.1: Output in Creation Mode (cont.)

```
ID#:      991134

1) NAME:     MACHINE#3
2) DATE:     OCTOBER 25, 1981
3) COST:     $63,980.00


OK TO SAVE? Y
SORTING INDEX...

SAVING RECORD...
ADD ANOTHER? N
```

Figure 8.1: Output in Creation Mode (cont.)

five-digit number without the check digit, then the program supplies the complete number:

I.D. NUMBER: **61123**

I.D. NUMBER WITH CHECK DIGIT: 61123-7

At this point the user should make note of the check digit; it *will* be required for some options of the update mode.

After the input of the I.D. number, the program searches the index to make sure it is a new number. If it is not, then an error message appears along with a prompt for a new number:

THIS I.D. NUMBER IS ALREADY IN THE FILE.

I.D. NUMBER:

The program then reads the other three fields—the name, acquisition date, and cost of the asset. The name may be up to ten characters long. Input validation is performed on all the data (using the input procedures from our units); in the case of an input error, the user is prompted to try again. (Note that the sample run contains several such errors.)

When all four fields have been read, the screen is cleared, and an *echo* of the input appears. Notice that the output formats for the date and the cost are more elaborate than the input formats; this formatting is also done by the units introduced in Chapter 3. The intention is to draw attention to these fields and to simplify verification. After the echo, a question appears on the screen:

OK TO SAVE?

At this point the user may save the record as it stands by typing a Y. If, on the other hand, an examination of the echo reveals an error in one or more of the fields, the user types an N to abandon the record. Depending, then, on the answer to this question, the program either saves the record and sorts the index again:

```
SORTING INDEX...
SAVING RECORD...
```

or throws the record out:

```
ABANDONING RECORD
```

After each save, the index must be re-sorted so that the program can check for duplicate I.D. numbers during the input process. We will discuss this point further when we examine the program itself.

Finally, the question:

```
ADD ANOTHER?
```

appears. At this point, the user may either continue to input new records, or end the run of the program.

Once the asset and index files have been created (by running UPDATE in the creation mode), subsequent runs of the program should be in the update mode. This mode offers a recurring menu of five options, all of which are illustrated in the sample run of Figure 8.2. The user may examine, revise, add, or remove a record, or terminate the program. The correct response to the menu is thus an integer from 1 to 5:

```
OPTIONS:
-------

1) EXAMINE A RECORD
2) REVISE A RECORD
3) ADD A RECORD
4) REMOVE A RECORD
5) QUIT
                              ?
```

We will look briefly at how each of these options works.

The *examine* option begins with a prompt for the I.D. number of the desired record. The user is not required to input the check digit in order to examine a record; it will be supplied if it is not included:

```
EXAMINE A RECORD
================

I.D. NUMBER: 23611
I.D. NUMBER WITH CHECK DIGIT: 23611-7
```

```
ASSET FILE MANAGEMENT PROGRAM
===== ==== ========== =======

C(REATE OR U(PDATE? U

PUT DISK IN DRIVE B:
(MUST CONTAIN FILES 'ASSETS' AND 'INDEX')

PRESS <RETURN> WHEN READY.

OPENING ASSET FILE...
--------------------------------------------------
OPTIONS:
--------
1) EXAMINE A RECORD
2) REVISE A RECORD
3) ADD A RECORD
4) REMOVE A RECORD
5) QUIT
                          ? 1
--------------------------------------------------
EXAMINE A RECORD
======= = ======

I.D. NUMBER:    23611
I.D. NUMBER WITH CHECK DIGIT: 23611-7

--------------------------------------------------
ID#:    236117

1) NAME:   BUILDING#2
2) DATE:   MARCH 25, 1975
3) COST:   $87,500.00


PRESS <RETURN> TO CONTINUE.

--------------------------------------------------
OPTIONS:
--------
1) EXAMINE A RECORD
2) REVISE A RECORD
3) ADD A RECORD
4) REMOVE A RECORD
5) QUIT
                          ? 2

--------------------------------------------------
REVISE A RECORD
====== = ======

I.D. NUMBER:    61152
  *** CHECK DIGIT REQUIRED.
I.D. NUMBER:    61152-6

--------------------------------------------------
```

Figure 8.2: Output in Update Mode

```
ID#:     611526

1) NAME:    CAMERA
2) DATE:    FEBRUARY 10, 1980
3) COST:    $2,890.00

PRESS <RETURN> TO CONTINUE.

REVISE WHICH ITEM?
1, 2, 3, OR Q(UIT ==> 1

NAME:    PHOTOEQUIP
REVISE WHICH ITEM?
1, 2, 3, OR Q(UIT ==> 3

COST:    6750
REVISE WHICH ITEM?
1, 2, 3, OR Q(UIT ==> Q
---------------------------------------------------
ID#:     611526

1) NAME:    PHOTOEQUIP
2) DATE:    FEBRUARY 10, 1980
3) COST:    $6,750.00

OK TO SAVE NEW RECORD? Y

PRESS <RETURN> TO CONTINUE.
---------------------------------------------------
OPTIONS:
--------
1) EXAMINE A RECORD
2) REVISE A RECORD
3) ADD A RECORD
4) REMOVE A RECORD
5) QUIT
                             ? 1
---------------------------------------------------
EXAMINE A RECORD
======= = ======

I.D. NUMBER:    61152-6
---------------------------------------------------
ID#:     611526
1) NAME:    PHOTOEQUIP
2) DATE:    FEBRUARY 10, 1980
3) COST:    $6,750.00

PRESS <RETURN> TO CONTINUE.
---------------------------------------------------
```

Figure 8.2: Output in Update Mode (cont.)

```
OPTIONS:
--------
1) EXAMINE A RECORD
2) REVISE A RECORD
3) ADD A RECORD
4) REMOVE A RECORD
5) QUIT
                          ? 4

---------------------------------------------------

REMOVE A RECORD
====== = ======

I.D. NUMBER:    75619-8

---------------------------------------------------

ID#:     756198

1) NAME:    MACHINE#1
2) DATE:    MAY 4, 1972
3) COST:    $25,980.00

PRESS <RETURN> TO CONTINUE.
REMOVE THIS RECORD? Y
REMOVING RECORD
SORTING INDEX...

PRESS <RETURN> TO CONTINUE.

---------------------------------------------------

OPTIONS:
--------
1) EXAMINE A RECORD
2) REVISE A RECORD
3) ADD A RECORD
4) REMOVE A RECORD
5) QUIT
                          ? 3

---------------------------------------------------

ADD A RECORD
=== = ======

I.D. NUMBER:    63125
I.D. NUMBER WITH CHECK DIGIT: 63125-0


NAME OF ASSET:            NEW-MACH
DATE OF ACQUISITION:      1-1-82
ORIGINAL COST OF ASSET:   52840

---------------------------------------------------
```

Figure 8.2: Output in Update Mode (cont.)

```
ID#:     631250

1) NAME:    NEW-MACH
2) DATE:    JANUARY 1, 1982
3) COST:    $52,840.00

OK TO SAVE? Y
SORTING INDEX...

SAVING RECORD...

----------------------------------------------------
OPTIONS:
--------
1) EXAMINE A RECORD
2) REVISE A RECORD
3) ADD A RECORD
4) REMOVE A RECORD
5) QUIT
                              ? 5
```

Figure 8.2: Output in Update Mode (cont.)

After this short dialogue, the screen clears, and an echo of the record appears in the format we have already seen. In the event that the user types an I.D. number that is not yet in the file, the program displays the following message and prompt:

* * * NOT FOUND IN FILE

PRESS <RETURN> TO CONTINUE.

The *revise* option allows the user to change any field of a record except the I.D. number. To identify a record for revision, the user must type the complete I.D. number (including the check digit):

REVISE A RECORD

====== = =======

I.D. NUMBER: **61152**

* * * CHECK DIGIT REQUIRED.

I.D. NUMBER: **61152-6**

Following this input, the corresponding record appears on the screen:

I.D.#: **611526**

1) NAME: CAMERA

2) DATE: FEBRUARY 10, 1980

3) COST: $2,890.00

The user then identifies the item for revision by typing a '1', '2', or '3':

REVISE WHICH ITEM?

1, 2, 3, OR Q(UIT = => **1**

and a prompt appears for the new value of the field:

NAME:

Typing a 'Q' in response to the *revise* menu results in termination of the revision dialogue and an echo of the new version of the record. Then a question is displayed:

OK TO SAVE NEW RECORD?

Thus, the user may either save the revised version or keep the old version. If the revision is saved, the old version is lost, of course.

The *add* option produces the sequence we have already seen in the creation mode: an input screen and an echo screen. The user is not required to input a check digit.

The *remove* option, like the *revise* option, does require a check digit for identification of the target record. The rationale for this is clear: any time an existing record might be changed or deleted, the check digit is required as added insurance that the correct record will be found. The *remove* option echoes the record and asks:

REMOVE THIS RECORD?

to give the user a chance to change his mind. An answer of 'Y' removes the record; an 'N' keeps the record in place.

Since this program enables users to make major changes in information about the company, access to the program should be controlled by means of a password, or even a series of passwords for different levels of access. The current version of this program does not include a password access system; however, Chapter 10, "The System Profile," provides a model for password use that could be applied to this program also.

In the remaining sections of this chapter we will discuss the structure and implementation of this program. Look through the sample runs carefully before reading on; it is important to understand what the program does and how it operates before studying the details of the code itself.

UCSD FILE HANDLING PROCEDURES

First, let us review briefly four of the basic UCSD Pascal file-handling procedures: REWRITE, RESET, GET, and PUT. They differ from their standard Pascal equivalents in several important details.

The REWRITE procedure, which opens a new file, and the RESET procedure, which opens an already existing file, can take two parameters in UCSD Pascal: a file variable and a string. These parameters enable us to associate a program file variable with a file name on a disk directory. For example, in UPDATE, the two file variables ASSETFILE and INDEXFILE are first opened (in the creation mode) by REWRITE as follows:

```
REWRITE(ASSETFILE, '#5:ASSETS');
REWRITE(INDEXFILE, '#5:INDEX');
```

These statements open the files on volume #5, the second disk drive. In the update mode, which assumes that both files already exist, the RESET procedure is used to open the files:

```
RESET(ASSETFILE, '#5:ASSETS');
RESET(INDEXFILE, '#5:INDEX');
```

The RESET procedure performs a GET on the first record in the file. That is, the record at position zero is transferred to the file buffer, and then the pointer is moved forward by one position.

UCSD Pascal files allow both input and output operations after a REWRITE or RESET. The GET procedure transfers a record from the file to the file buffer, and the PUT procedure transfers the contents of the buffer to the file. In both cases, the file pointer is moved forward *after* the transfer (unlike standard Pascal). This design feature ensures proper coordination between GET, PUT, and SEEK. We will review the SEEK procedure in the following section.

AN INDEX INTO THE FILE

We have already referred several times to the index created by the update program. In this section we will outline one approach to indexed sequential access methods.

The purpose of the index is to provide the simplest means possible of locating any record in the main asset file. To do so, the index must keep track of the *position* of each record in the file. These positions are represented by sequential nonnegative integers starting from 0.

Given the position, POSN, of a record in ASSETFILE, we can access that record using the SEEK and GET procedures:

```
SEEK(ASSETFILE,POSN);
GET(ASSETFILE);
ASSET := ASSETFILE^;
```

Briefly, this sequence of instructions operates as follows: SEEK moves the file pointer to position POSN; GET transfers the record at POSN to the buffer variable ASSETFILE^ (and then advances the pointer); and the third statement assigns the value of the buffer to the record variable ASSET. Clearly, the SEEK procedure is essential for random access file processing in UCSD Pascal; but in order to use SEEK we need to keep an efficient list of the position of each record in the file.

The data structure we use for this index in program UPDATE is an array of records. The records in this array contain two fields, POSN and NUM:

```
ISAMREC = RECORD
   POSN : INTEGER;
   NUM : LONG1
END;
```

The field NUM holds the I.D. number of an asset. (Recall that type LONG1 is defined globally in CHECKUNIT.) POSN holds the integer value that represents the position of that asset record in ASSETFILE. The index data type, ISAMARY, is defined as follows:

```
ISAMARY = ARRAY[0..N] OF ISAMREC;
```

With N set at 100 (in the CONST section of the program), this array can keep track of the locations of 100 different records in the asset file. We will use the zeroth element of this array to store information about the length of the file and the number of "empty" positions in the file.

At the beginning of the update program, we must initialize the index to a completely empty state. The variable INDEX (of type ISAMARY) represents the index. The fields of the zeroth element of the array are set to zero:

```
INDEX[0].POSN := 0; (* NUMBER OF RECORDS *)
INDEX[0].NUM := 0; (* NUMBER OF EMPTY POSITIONS *)
```

For reasons we will discuss shortly, it will be convenient to assign special "flag" variables to the rest of the index. The POSN fields are thus assigned the value 999 and the NUM fields the value 999999:

```
FOR I := 1 TO N DO
  BEGIN
    INDEX[I].POSN := 999;
    INDEX[I].NUM := 999999;
END;
```

(Note that 999999 is *not* a legal asset I.D. number; the check digit for 99999 would be 6. Thus, there is no danger of confusing the "flag" with an actual I.D. number.)

As we add asset records to the asset file, we will store their I.D. numbers and positions in the index. Each time we add or remove an index entry, we will have to re-sort the index, in ascending order, using the I.D. numbers (INDEX[I].NUM) as the key. Furthermore, each time we wish to access a record in the asset file we will first have to search for its I.D. number in the index, and then refer to its position (stored in the index) in order to SEEK the record in the asset file. We will use the sorting and searching routines we developed in Chapter 7 to perform these tasks. The revised versions of these routines appear in Figures 8.3 and 8.4. The algorithms of these two routines remain essentially unchanged; only the data types are new. We will incorporate both of these procedures into our program via an include file statement:

```
(*$I SRCHSRT.TEXT*)
```

```
PROCEDURE SHELLSORT(VAR A: ISAMARY;
                        N: INTEGER);

VAR
  DONE : BOOLEAN;
  JUMP,
  I,
  J    : INTEGER;

FUNCTION FIRSTJUMP(LENGTH: INTEGER): INTEGER;
VAR
  TEMP : INTEGER;

BEGIN
  TEMP := 1;
  WHILE TEMP <= LENGTH DO
    TEMP := TEMP * 2;
  FIRSTJUMP := TEMP
END;  (* FIRSTJUMP *)


PROCEDURE SWAP (VAR P, Q : ISAMREC);
  VAR
    HOLD : ISAMREC;
  BEGIN
    HOLD := P;
    P := Q;
    Q := HOLD
  END; (* SWAP *)
```

Figure 8.3: Procedure SHELLSORT for Use in Program UPDATE

```
BEGIN (* SHELLSORT *)
  JUMP := FIRSTJUMP(N);
  WRITE('SORTING INDEX');
  WHILE JUMP > 1 DO
  BEGIN
    JUMP := (JUMP - 1) DIV 2;
    WRITE('.');
      REPEAT
        DONE := TRUE;
          FOR J := 1 TO N - JUMP DO
            BEGIN
              I:= J + JUMP;
              IF A[J].NUM > A[I].NUM THEN
                BEGIN
                  SWAP(A[J],A[I]);
                  DONE := FALSE
                END (* IF *)
            END (* FOR *)
      UNTIL DONE
  END (* WHILE *);
  WRITELN;
END (* SHELLSORT *);
```

Figure 8.3: Procedure SHELLSORT for Use in Program UPDATE (cont.)

```
PROCEDURE BSEARCH (VAL    : LONG1;
                   LENGTH: INTEGER;
                   LIST   : ISAMARY;
               VAR POSN   : INTEGER;
               VAR FOUND  : BOOLEAN);
VAR
  LOWER,
  UPPER : INTEGER;
  (* CENTER IS GLOBAL *)

BEGIN
  LOWER := 1;
  UPPER := LENGTH;
  FOUND := FALSE;

  WHILE (UPPER >= LOWER) AND (NOT FOUND) DO
    BEGIN
      CENTER := (LOWER + UPPER) DIV 2;
      IF VAL = LIST[CENTER].NUM THEN
        BEGIN
          FOUND := TRUE;
          POSN := LIST[CENTER].POSN
        END
      ELSE
        IF VAL > LIST[CENTER].NUM THEN
          LOWER := CENTER + 1
        ELSE
          UPPER := CENTER - 1
    END (* WHILE *);
END (* BSEARCH *);
```

Figure 8.4: Procedure BSEARCH for Use in Program UPDATE

This means that both procedures must be available on disk under the file name SRCHSRT.TEXT. They will be inserted into the program at compile time.

Each time we make a change in the main asset file, then, we must also update the index. Two different update procedures are actually necessary—one for *adding* an asset record, and another for *removing* a record. We will discuss the record-removal procedure first, since it reorganizes the index in a way that is essential to the record-addition procedure.

When we remove a record from the asset file, we would like to keep track of the position it occupied so that we can reuse that "empty" position later on for new records. This information is stored in the index rather than in the asset file itself. Here is the sequence of steps for updating the index after removal of a record from the asset file:

1. Search for the target I.D. number in the index.
2. Set the NUM field of this element to 999999; do not change the POSN field.
3. Re-sort the index; the index entry of the record that has been removed will sink to the bottom of the index (for example, if there are 10 records in the file, then the removed record will be found in the 11th element in the index array).
4. Decrement INDEX[0].POSN, the number of records in the file.
5. Increment INDEX[0].NUM, the number of empty positions in the asset file.

If we search the index for the I.D. number of the removed asset now, we will not find it, since its number has been changed to 999999 and sorted out of the range of index references. It is important to understand that this record is no longer available to the program, even if we do nothing to remove it from the actual asset file. If the index reference to an asset record has been removed, it is as though the asset record itself had been removed. Our only way of finding asset records in the UPDATE program is via the index.

However, one piece of information about the removed asset record remains in the index. Notice that when we set the NUM field to 999999, we left the POSN field alone. Thus, we still know the location of the record that was removed. This is an important point for the second index updating procedure, which we will use when we *add* records to the file.

The steps of this second update algorithm are as follows:

1. Examine INDEX[0].NUM to see if there are any empty positions in the asset file (if INDEX[0].NUM equals 0 then there are no empties).
2. If empty positions exist, then look at the first 999999 NUM entry in the index; the POSN field associated with this entry will contain the position of a previously removed asset record. We will PUT the new asset record (which is currently being added to the file) into this vacated position in the asset file, and store the asset's I.D. number (along with its position, POSN) in the index. We must also decrement INDEX[0].NUM, the number of empty positions.
3. If there are no empty positions, then we simply create a new position at the end of the asset file, PUT the new record in this position, and store its I.D. number and position in the index.
4. Increment INDEX[0].POSN, the number of records in the file.
5. Sort the index.

(We will review these steps from a slightly different perspective when we look at the actual code that implements them.)

In short, the index is a tool we use for processing a random-access file. The information contained in the index serves two important functions: It allows us to find the position of any record in the file, no matter what order the records are in; and it encourages optimal use of file storage space by keeping track of vacated record positions that can be reused for new records.

In the context of our file management system, the asset file is almost useless without its index. We must therefore store the index permanently in an external file of its own. We have already mentioned that the name of this file on the disk directory is INDEX. The file variable in the program is defined as follows:

```
INDEXFILE : FILE OF ISAMARY;
```

In the current version of the update program, we store our index in the zeroth position of this file. As it is written, this index is limited to files of no more than 100 records. For longer files, we would have to devise a more sophisticated indexing system, one that would comprise several *pages* of index. In the following section we will outline the design of a multi-page index.

Expanding the Index

The idea of a multi-page index is simple, but its actual implementation can be complicated. Let us say we wish to expand our indexing system to allow up to 1000 asset records in the file. To do so, we can initialize ten index arrays, or *pages*, each capable of referencing 100 asset records. But then we need some way of determining which page of the index will contain the reference to a given asset. Thus, we must set up a page index that will tell us which page of the index to access to search for the asset number we are looking for. This page index is sometimes called the *coarse* index (as opposed to the *fine* index, which references the asset files indexed on a given page). The page index would have ten elements—one for each page. It would contain the location of each page in the index file, and the highest I.D. number referenced by each page. Thus, to find an asset file, we would first refer to the page index to find the correct page. Then we would GET this page and search for the asset record reference just as we did with the simpler one-page index.

Updating this multi-page index would require careful planning, in order to minimize the need to shift index references from one page to another as some pages become filled to capacity.

Our approach to this updating procedure might depend on the range of the I.D. numbers that we will be indexing. If we expect our thousand I.D. numbers to be evenly distributed over a range (say 10000-9 to 99999-6), we might simply divide this range into ten equal subranges and assign the limits of each page when we initialize the index. Then we must hope that no one page fills up much faster than another. Unfortunately, we are not likely to have such a simple arrangement of records, so we must devise some system of shifting data from one page of the index to another.

A different approach would be to maintain approximately the same number of references in each page of the index during the process of building the file. We would start by putting the first fifty references in the first page of the index. At the time the fifty-first record is stored in the file, we would divide the index references in half and put the upper half in a newly-created second page of the index. When both of these pages contained fifty references, we would create a third page and transfer the top third of the references to it. In this approach, all ten pages would be initialized by the time the first 500 records had been stored.

For the purposes of this chapter, we have avoided these complications by limiting our index to a single page of references. This will allow us to concentrate on other aspects of the file management program. However, to create a realistic program we would have to add a multi-page storage capacity to our index.

In the next section we will begin looking at our program. A brief look at the main program section will show us the overall structure; then we will proceed step by step through each routine of the program.

THE MAIN PROGRAM AND A STRUCTURE CHART

The main program section appears in Figure 8.5; the accompanying structure chart, in Figure 8.6, illustrates the structural division of the program into two modes. The main program begins by displaying the title and prompting for the input of the mode indicator, C or U. Notice how a REPEAT loop is used to validate this single-character input:

```
REPEAT
  WRITE('C(REATE OR U(PDATE? ');
  READLN(MODE)
UNTIL (MODE IN ['C','U']);
```

The prompt is displayed repeatedly until MODE is in the set ['C','U']—that is, until the user types a C or a U at the keyboard.

```
BEGIN (* MAIN PROGRAM *)
  CLEARSCREEN;
  WRITELN('ASSET FILE MANAGEMENT PROGRAM');
  WRITELN('===== ==== ========== =======');
  WRITELN;
  REPEAT
    WRITE('C(REATE OR U(PDATE? ');
    READLN(MODE)
  UNTIL (MODE IN ['C','U']);
  IF (MODE = 'C') THEN
    BEGIN
      INIT1;
      REPEAT
        CLEARSCREEN;
        ADD;
        WRITE('ADD ANOTHER? ');
        READLN(OKANS)
      UNTIL (OKANS = 'N')
    END
  ELSE
    BEGIN
      INIT2;
      REPEAT
        CLEARSCREEN;
        MENU(FINISHED)
      UNTIL FINISHED
    END;
    CLOSE(ASSETFILE,LOCK)
END. (* MAIN PROGRAM *)
```

Figure 8.5: Main Program Section of UPDATE

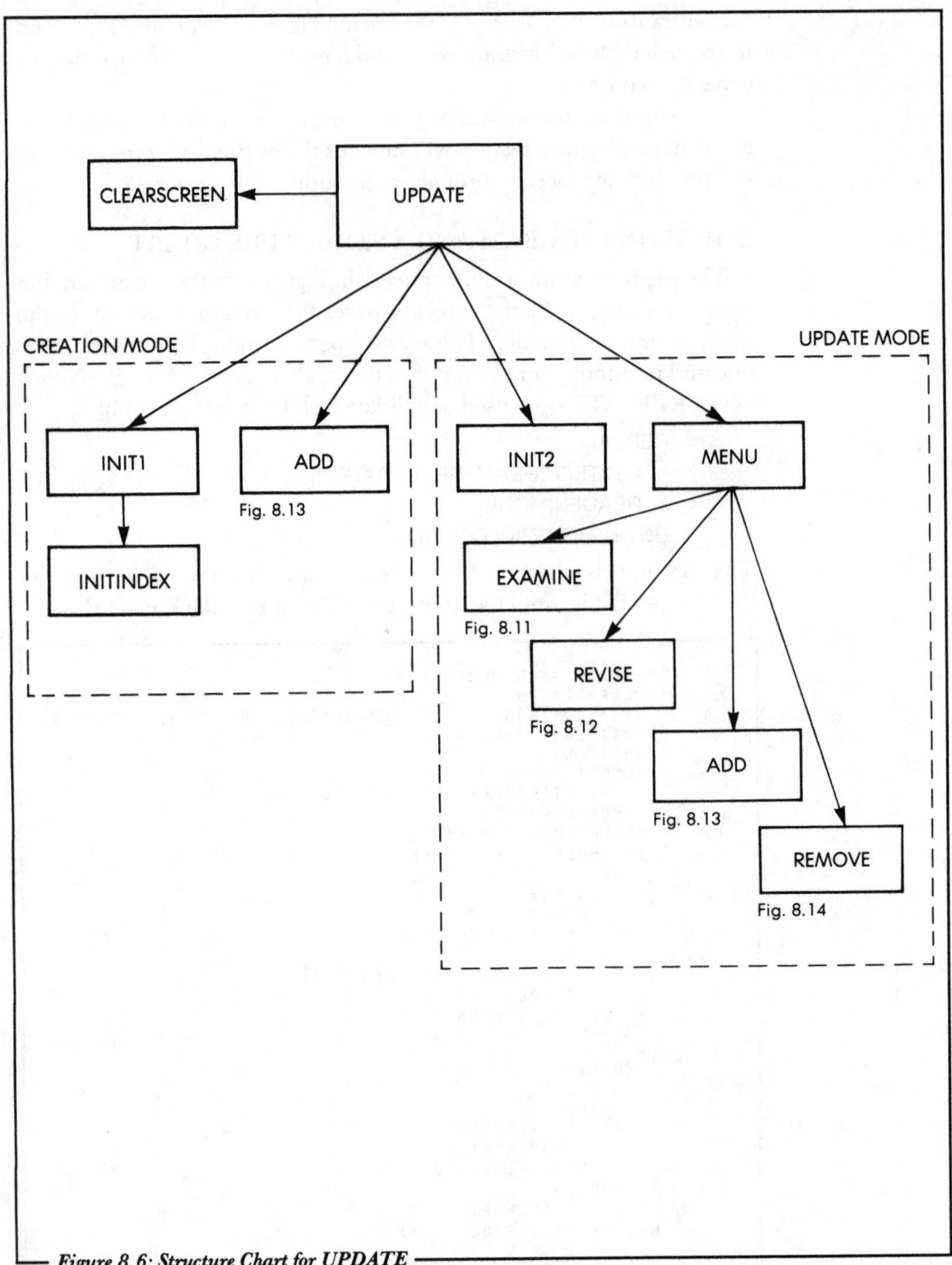

Figure 8.6: Structure Chart for UPDATE

An IF/THEN/ELSE statement controls the rest of the action of the program. For the creation mode (IF (MODE = 'C')), procedure INIT1 is called to open the files, and procedure ADD is called repeatedly until the user indicates that input is complete. Otherwise, for the update mode, INIT2 opens the asset file, and procedure MENU is called repeatedly until it returns a value of true to the Boolean variable FINISHED.

We will see the initialization procedures INIT1 and INIT2 in the next section of this chapter. Procedure MENU is shown in Figure 8.7. The

```
PROCEDURE MENU(VAR FINISHED : BOOLEAN);
  VAR
    OPTION : CHAR;
    FOUND  : BOOLEAN;

BEGIN
  FINISHED := FALSE;
  WRITELN('OPTIONS:');
  WRITELN('--------');
  WRITELN('1) EXAMINE A RECORD');
  WRITELN('2) REVISE A RECORD');
  WRITELN('3) ADD A RECORD');
  WRITELN('4) REMOVE A RECORD');
  WRITELN('5) QUIT');
  REPEAT
    WRITE('                          ? ');
    READLN(OPTION)
  UNTIL (OPTION IN ['1'..'5']);

  CASE OPTION OF

    '1':BEGIN
          CLEARSCREEN;
          WRITELN('EXAMINE A RECORD');
          WRITELN('======= = ======');
          WRITELN;
          EXAMINE(FOUND,FALSE)
        END;

    '2':BEGIN
          CLEARSCREEN;
          WRITELN('REVISE A RECORD');
          WRITELN('====== = ======');
          WRITELN;
          REVISE
        END;

    '3':BEGIN
          CLEARSCREEN;
          WRITELN('ADD A RECORD');
          WRITELN('=== = ======');
          WRITELN;
          ADD
        END;
```

Figure 8.7: Procedure MENU

```
            '4':BEGIN
                   CLEARSCREEN;
                   WRITELN('REMOVE A RECORD');
                   WRITELN('====== = ======');
                   WRITELN;
                   REMOVE
                 END;

            '5':FINISHED := TRUE

        END (* CASE *)
    END;   (* MENU *)
```

Figure 8.7: Procedure MENU (cont.)

first part of this procedure simply displays the menu and reads the user's input for the option choice. Once again, a REPEAT loop verifies this input; OPTION must be a character from '1' to '5'. The second part of procedure MENU is a CASE statement that uses OPTION as the case selector, and calls one of four procedures: EXAMINE, REVISE, ADD, or REMOVE. The Pascal CASE statement is a simple and clear way of organizing such multi-path choices. Some programmers prefer to avoid the CASE statement, because it produces uncertain results if the value of the case selector falls outside of the range expressed by the case labels. (In UCSD Pascal, the CASE statement performs no action at all if the value of the selector does not match one of the labels.) In MENU, however, we have used a REPEAT statement to insure that OPTION will always be a valid selector.

Notice that the fifth case label is the one that ends the program:

```
'5' : FINISHED : = TRUE
```

When MENU returns a true to the main program in the variable FINISHED, the REPEAT loop that calls MENU is terminated. The last statement of the main program, which is executed for both modes, closes the asset file:

```
CLOSE(ASSETFILE,LOCK)
```

We will see in the next section how the files are opened and initialized by procedures INIT1 and INIT2.

THE FILE INITIALIZATION PROCEDURES

Procedure INIT1 is shown in Figure 8.8. Since this procedure is called in the creation mode, before either of the files exists, it uses the REWRITE procedure to open the files. The local procedure INITINDEX initializes the index in the way we have already described. Notice that this procedure stores the initialized index with a PUT statement and then actually closes INDEXFILE. We will find throughout this program that INDEXFILE is always defined locally in the procedures that reference the index. (ASSETFILE, on the other hand, is defined globally.) Only five routines in the whole program actually need to refer to the index. One reason for isolating the index locally in a small number of routines is to make it easier to expand the indexing system for use with an asset file larger than 100 records. Another reason is to economize on run-time memory space.

INIT2, shown in Figure 8.9, simply opens the already-created asset file with the RESET procedure. (INIT2 has no reason to open the index file.) We have already mentioned that the program will terminate with an I/O error message if both files are not on line for the update mode. One possible way to prevent this in UCSD Pascal is to suppress I/O error

```
PROCEDURE INIT1;

  PROCEDURE INITINDEX;
    VAR
      I : INTEGER;
      INDEX : ISAMARY;
      INDEXFILE : FILE OF ISAMARY;

    BEGIN
      FOR I := 1 TO N DO
        BEGIN
          INDEX[I].POSN := 999;
          INDEX[I].NUM := 999999
        END;
      INDEX[0].POSN := 0; (* NUMBER OF RECORDS *)
      INDEX[0].NUM := 0; (* NUMBER OF EMPTY RECORDS *)
      REWRITE(INDEXFILE,'#5:INDEX');
      INDEXFILE^ := INDEX;
      PUT(INDEXFILE);
      CLOSE(INDEXFILE,LOCK);
    END;

BEGIN
  WRITELN;
  WRITELN('PUT DISK IN DRIVE B:');
  WRITELN;
  WRITE('PRESS <RETURN> WHEN READY.');
  READLN(OKANS);
  WRITELN;
  WRITELN('CREATING INDEX FILE...');
  INITINDEX;
  WRITELN('OPENING ASSET FILE...');
  REWRITE(ASSETFILE,'#5:ASSETS')
END; (* INIT1 *)
```

Figure 8.8: Procedure INIT1

checking with the $I – compiler option:

```
(*$I-*)
```

When this option is used, we can check the built-in function IORESULT after any input or output operation. IORESULT returns an integer value from 0 to 15. The value 0 indicates that the I/O operation was performed without error. The other values indicate various I/O errors. The error we are looking for, that the requested file is not on line, is indicated by the value 10. Knowing this, we might consider revising INIT2 to avoid termination of the program in the event that the user puts the wrong disk into the drive. The following is a simple example of the use of IORESULT:

```
(*$I-*)
REPEAT
   WRITELN('PUT DISK IN DRIVE B.');
   WRITE('PRESS <RETURN> WHEN READY.');
   READLN(OKANS);
   RESET(ASSETFILE, '#5:ASSETS');
   IOMESSAGE := IORESULT;
   IF (IOMESSAGE = 10) THEN
      WRITELN('FILE ''ASSETS'' NOT FOUND.')
   ELSE
      IF (IOMESSAGE = 0) THEN
         WRITELN('''ASSETS'' OPEN.')
      ELSE
         WRITELN('I/0 ERROR; TRY AGAIN.')
UNTIL (IOMESSAGE = 0);
(*$I+*)
```

```
PROCEDURE INIT2;

BEGIN
  WRITELN;
  WRITELN('PUT DISK IN DRIVE B:');
  WRITELN('(MUST CONTAIN FILES ''ASSETS'' AND ''INDEX'')');
  WRITELN;
  WRITE('PRESS <RETURN> WHEN READY.');
  READLN(OKANS);
  WRITELN;
  WRITELN('OPENING ASSET FILE...');
  RESET(ASSETFILE,'#5:ASSETS')
END; (* INIT2 *)
```

Figure 8.9: Procedure INIT2

Notice that the error-checking code is reactivated after the REPEAT loop.

We have now studied the main program, the menu procedure, and the file initialization procedures. We are finally ready to look at the implementation of the four options—*examine*, *revise*, *add*, and *remove*.

The entire listing of program UPDATE is shown in Figure 8.10.

```
(*$S++)

PROGRAM UPDATE;

USES
              (*$U MONEYUNIT.CODE*)
MONEYUNIT,
              (*$U CHECKUNIT.CODE*)
CHECKUNIT,
              (*$U DATEUNIT.CODE*)
DATEUNIT;


CONST
  S1 = 10;
  N  = 100;
  L = 6;

TYPE
  AREC = RECORD
    NAME : STRING[S1];
    NUMBER : LONG1;
    DATE : DATEREC;
    COST : LONG2
  END;

  ISAMREC = RECORD
    POSN : INTEGER;
    NUM : LONG1
  END;

  ISAMARY = ARRAY[0..N] OF ISAMREC;

VAR
  ASSET : AREC;
  ASSETFILE : FILE OF AREC;
  OKANS    : STRING;
  ANSWER,
  MODE     : CHAR;
  POINTER,
  CENTER : INTEGER;
  FINISHED : BOOLEAN;

PROCEDURE INIT1;

  PROCEDURE INITINDEX;
    VAR
      I : INTEGER;
```

Figure 8.10: Program UPDATE

```
        INDEX : ISAMARY;
        INDEXFILE : FILE OF ISAMARY;

      BEGIN
        FOR I := 1 TO N DO
          BEGIN
            INDEX[I].POSN := 999;
            INDEX[I].NUM := 999999
          END;
        INDEX[0].POSN := 0; (* NUMBER OF RECORDS *)
        INDEX[0].NUM := 0; (* NUMBER OF EMPTY RECORDS *)
        REWRITE(INDEXFILE,'#5:INDEX');
        INDEXFILE^ := INDEX;
        PUT(INDEXFILE);
        CLOSE(INDEXFILE,LOCK);
      END;

  BEGIN
    WRITELN;
    WRITELN('PUT DISK IN DRIVE B:');
    WRITELN;
    WRITE('PRESS <RETURN> WHEN READY.');
    READLN(OKANS);
    WRITELN;
    WRITELN('CREATING INDEX FILE...');
    INITINDEX;
    WRITELN('OPENING ASSET FILE...');
    REWRITE(ASSETFILE,'#5:ASSETS')
  END; (* INIT1 *)


  PROCEDURE INIT2;

  BEGIN
    WRITELN;
    WRITELN('PUT DISK IN DRIVE B:');
    WRITELN('(MUST CONTAIN FILES ''ASSETS'' AND ''INDEX'')');
    WRITELN;
    WRITE('PRESS <RETURN> WHEN READY.');
    READLN(OKANS);
    WRITELN;
    WRITELN('OPENING ASSET FILE...');
    RESET(ASSETFILE,'#5:ASSETS')
  END; (* INIT2 *)

  (*$I SRCHSRT.TEXT*)


  PROCEDURE ECHORECORD;
    VAR
      DOLLCENT  : STRING;

  BEGIN
    CLEARSCREEN;
    WRITELN('ID#:     ', ASSET.NUMBER);
    WRITELN;
    WRITELN('1) NAME:    ', ASSET.NAME);
```

Figure 8.10: Program UPDATE (cont.)

```
    WRITE('2) DATE:     ');
    OUTDATE(ASSET.DATE);
    WRITELN;
    DOLLARFORM(ASSET.COST, DOLLCENT);
    WRITELN('3) COST:     ', DOLLCENT);
    WRITELN;
  END;


  PROCEDURE INIDNO(REQUIRED: BOOLEAN;
               VAR NUM     : LONG1);
    VAR
      CHECK,
      OK     : BOOLEAN;
      ST     : STRING;
      CHDIG  : INTEGER;

  BEGIN
    IF REQUIRED THEN
      REPEAT
        WRITE('I.D. NUMBER:     ');
        INVALUE(NUM,L,CHECK);
        IF NOT CHECK THEN
          WRITELN('   *** CHECK DIGIT REQUIRED.')
        ELSE (* IF INPUT INCLUDED CHECK DIGIT *)
          IF (NOT (VERIFYCHECK(NUM))) THEN
            BEGIN
              WRITELN('   *** CHECK DIGIT DOES NOT MATCH.');
              OK := FALSE
            END
          ELSE (* IF CHECK DIGIT MATCHES *)
            OK := TRUE
      UNTIL OK
    ELSE  (* IF CHECK DIGIT IS NOT REQUIRED *)
      REPEAT
        WRITE('I.D. NUMBER:     ');
        INVALUE(NUM,L,CHECK);
        IF CHECK (* DIGIT WAS INPUT ANYWAY *) THEN
          IF (NOT (VERIFYCHECK(NUM))) THEN
            BEGIN
              WRITELN('   *** CHECK DIGIT DOES NOT MATCH.');
              OK := FALSE
            END
          ELSE (* IF CHECK DIGIT MATCHES *)
            OK := TRUE
        ELSE (* IF CHECK DIGIT WAS NOT INCLUDED IN INPUT *)
          BEGIN
            CHDIG := CHECKDIGIT(NUM);
            WRITE('I.D. NUMBER WITH CHECK DIGIT: ');
            WRITELN(NUM,'-',CHDIG);
            NUM := NUM * 10 + CHDIG;
            OK := TRUE
          END
      UNTIL OK
  END; (* INIDNO *)
```

Figure 8.10: Program UPDATE (cont.)

```
PROCEDURE EXAMINE(VAR FOUND : BOOLEAN;
                      CDREQ : BOOLEAN);
  VAR
    ID : LONG1;
    INDEX : ISAMARY;
    INDEXFILE : FILE OF ISAMARY;

BEGIN

  (*
   * CDREQ INDICATES WHETHER OR NOT
   * THE USER IS REQUIRED TO INPUT
   * THE CHECK DIGIT ALONG WITH THE
   * I.D. NUMBER.
   *)

  INIDNO(CDREQ,ID);
  RESET(INDEXFILE,'#5:INDEX');
  INDEX := INDEXFILE^;
  CLOSE(INDEXFILE,LOCK);
  BSEARCH(ID, INDEX[0].POSN, INDEX, POINTER, FOUND);
  IF FOUND THEN
    BEGIN
      SEEK(ASSETFILE, POINTER);
      GET(ASSETFILE);
      ASSET := ASSETFILE^;
      ECHORECORD
    END
  ELSE
    WRITELN('*** NOT FOUND IN FILE');

  WRITELN;
  WRITE('PRESS <RETURN> TO CONTINUE.');
  READLN(OKANS)
END; (* EXAMINE *)


PROCEDURE REVISE;
  VAR
    FOUND : BOOLEAN;
    TEMPNAME : STRING;

BEGIN
  EXAMINE(FOUND,TRUE); (* CHECK DIGIT REQUIRED *)
  IF FOUND THEN
    BEGIN
      WRITELN;
      REPEAT
        REPEAT
          WRITELN('REVISE WHICH ITEM?');
          WRITE('1, 2, 3, OR Q(UIT ==> ');
          READLN(ANSWER)
        UNTIL (ANSWER IN ['1'..'3','Q']);
        WRITELN;
        CASE ANSWER OF
```

Figure 8.10: Program UPDATE (cont.)

```
            '1' : BEGIN
                    REPEAT
                      WRITE('NAME:   ');
                      READLN(TEMPNAME)
                    UNTIL (LENGTH(TEMPNAME) <= S1);
                    ASSET.NAME := TEMPNAME
                  END;
            '2' : BEGIN
                    WRITE('DATE:    ');
                    INDATE(ASSET.DATE)
                  END;
            '3' : BEGIN
                    WRITE('COST:    ');
                    INDOLLAR(ASSET.COST)
                  END;
            'Q' :;
          END (* CASE *)
        UNTIL (ANSWER = 'Q');

        ECHORECORD;
        WRITELN;
        WRITE('OK TO SAVE NEW RECORD? ');
        READLN(OKANS);
        IF ((OKANS = 'Y') OR (OKANS = 'YES')) THEN
          BEGIN
            SEEK(ASSETFILE, POINTER);
            ASSETFILE^ := ASSET;
            PUT(ASSETFILE)
          END
        ELSE
          BEGIN
            WRITELN;
            WRITELN('KEEPING OLD RECORD')
          END;
        WRITELN;
        WRITE('PRESS <RETURN> TO CONTINUE. ');
        READLN(OKANS);
      END
END; (* REVISE *)


PROCEDURE INRECORD(VAR NEW : BOOLEAN);
  VAR
    TEMPSTRING : STRING;

  FUNCTION USED: BOOLEAN;
    VAR
      DUMMY : INTEGER;
      FOUND : BOOLEAN;
      INDEX : ISAMARY;
      INDEXFILE : FILE OF ISAMARY;

    BEGIN
      RESET(INDEXFILE,'#5:INDEX');
      INDEX := INDEXFILE^;
```

Figure 8.10: Program UPDATE (cont.)

```
        CLOSE(INDEXFILE,LOCK);
        BSEARCH(ASSET.NUMBER,INDEX[0].POSN,INDEX,DUMMY,FOUND);
        USED := FOUND
      END;

  BEGIN
    INIDNO(FALSE,ASSET.NUMBER); (* CHECK DIGIT NOT REQUIRED *)

    IF NOT USED THEN
      BEGIN
        REPEAT
          WRITE('NAME OF ASSET:            ');
          READLN(TEMPSTRING)
        UNTIL (LENGTH(TEMPSTRING) <= S1);
        ASSET.NAME := TEMPSTRING;
        WRITE('DATE OF ACQUISITION:     ');
        INDATE(ASSET.DATE);
        WRITE('ORIGINAL COST OF ASSET: ');
        INDOLLAR(ASSET.COST);
        NEW := TRUE
      END
    ELSE
      BEGIN
        WRITELN('THIS I.D. NUMBER IS ALREADY IN THE FILE.');
        WRITELN;
        NEW := FALSE
      END
  END; (* INRECORD *)


  PROCEDURE SAVERECORD;
    VAR
      INDXFULL : BOOLEAN;

    PROCEDURE UPDATEINDEX(VAR FULL: BOOLEAN);
      VAR
        POSITION,
        NEWPOS    : INTEGER;
        EMPTIES   : LONG1;
        INDEX     : ISAMARY;
        INDEXFILE : FILE OF ISAMARY;
        (* MODE IS GLOBAL *)

       (*
        * SETPOINTER IS USED TO
        * REPOSITION THE ASSETFILE POINTER,
        * BUT ONLY IN THE UPDATE MODE.
        *)

    PROCEDURE SETPOINTER;
    BEGIN
      IF INDEX[0].POSN > 0 THEN
        BEGIN
          SEEK(ASSETFILE,INDEX[0].POSN-1);
          GET(ASSETFILE)
        END
    END;
```

Figure 8.10: Program UPDATE (cont.)

```
  BEGIN
    RESET(INDEXFILE,'#5:INDEX');
    INDEX := INDEXFILE^;
    POSITION := INDEX[0].POSN;
    EMPTIES := INDEX[0].NUM;
    NEWPOS := POSITION + 1;

    IF (NEWPOS > N) AND (EMPTIES = 0) THEN
       (* THE INDEX IS FULL *)
      BEGIN
        FULL := TRUE;
        CLOSE(INDEXFILE,LOCK);
        WRITELN('INDEX IS FULL')
      END
    ELSE
      BEGIN
        FULL := FALSE;
        IF EMPTIES = 0 THEN
          (* NO EMPTY POSITIONS IN THE ASSETFILE *)
          BEGIN
            INDEX[NEWPOS].POSN := POSITION;
            IF MODE = 'U' THEN
              SETPOINTER
          END
        ELSE (* THERE ARE EMPTY POSITIONS IN ASSETFILE *)
          BEGIN
            (*
             * POSITION THE ASSETFILE POINTER
             * AT THE MOST RECENTLY VACATED
             * EMPTY POSITION.
             *)
            SEEK(ASSETFILE,INDEX[NEWPOS].POSN);
            INDEX[0].NUM := EMPTIES - 1
          END;
        INDEX[NEWPOS].NUM := ASSET.NUMBER;
        INDEX[0].POSN := NEWPOS;
        SHELLSORT(INDEX,INDEX[0].POSN);
        SEEK(INDEXFILE,0);
        INDEXFILE^ := INDEX;
        PUT(INDEXFILE);
        CLOSE(INDEXFILE,LOCK)
      END
  END; (* UPDATEINDEX *)

BEGIN
  UPDATEINDEX(INDXFULL);
  IF NOT INDXFULL THEN
    BEGIN
      WRITELN;
      WRITELN('SAVING RECORD...');
      ASSETFILE^ := ASSET;
      PUT(ASSETFILE)
    END
END; (* SAVERECORD *)

PROCEDURE ADD;
  VAR
    OKREC : BOOLEAN;
```

Figure 8.10: Program UPDATE (cont.)

```
BEGIN
  REPEAT
    INRECORD(OKREC)
  UNTIL OKREC;
  ECHORECORD;
  WRITELN;
  WRITE('OK TO SAVE? ');
  READLN(OKANS);
  IF ((OKANS = 'Y') OR (OKANS = 'YES')) THEN
    SAVERECORD
  ELSE
    BEGIN
      WRITELN;
      WRITELN('ABANDONING RECORD')
    END
END; (* ADD *)


PROCEDURE REMOVE;
  VAR
    FOUND : BOOLEAN;
    INDEX : ISAMARY;
    INDEXFILE : FILE OF ISAMARY;
     (* CENTER IS GLOBAL *)


  BEGIN
    EXAMINE(FOUND,TRUE); (* CHECK DIGIT REQUIRED *)
    IF FOUND THEN
      BEGIN
        WRITE('REMOVE THIS RECORD? ');
        READLN(OKANS);
        IF ((OKANS = 'Y') OR (OKANS = 'YES')) THEN
          BEGIN
            WRITELN('REMOVING RECORD');
            RESET(INDEXFILE,'#5:INDEX');
            INDEX := INDEXFILE^;

             (* THE VALUE OF CENTER COMES FROM BSEARCH *)
            INDEX[CENTER].NUM := 999999;
            SHELLSORT(INDEX,INDEX[0].POSN);
            INDEX[0].POSN := INDEX[0].POSN - 1; (* DECRMNT # OF RECORDS *)
            INDEX[0].NUM := INDEX[0].NUM + 1; (* INCRMNT # OF EMPTIES *)

            (*
             * THE NUMBER OF THE ASSET
             * IS SET TO ZERO IN THE
             * ASSET FILE. THIS WILL SERVE
             * AS A FLAG FOR PROGRAM REPORT1.
             *)

            SEEK(INDEXFILE,0);
            INDEXFILE^ := INDEX;
            PUT(INDEXFILE);
            CLOSE(INDEXFILE,LOCK);
```

Figure 8.10: Program UPDATE (cont.)

```
            SEEK(ASSETFILE,POINTER);
            GET(ASSETFILE);
            ASSET := ASSETFILE^;
            ASSET.NUMBER := 0;
            SEEK(ASSETFILE,POINTER);
            ASSETFILE^ := ASSET;
            PUT(ASSETFILE)
          END
        ELSE
          WRITELN('LEAVING RECORD IN FILE.');
        WRITELN;
        WRITE('PRESS <RETURN> TO CONTINUE.');
        READLN(OKANS)
      END
END;  (* REMOVE *)



PROCEDURE MENU(VAR FINISHED : BOOLEAN);
  VAR
    OPTION : CHAR;
    FOUND  : BOOLEAN;


BEGIN
  FINISHED := FALSE;
  WRITELN('OPTIONS:');
  WRITELN('--------');
  WRITELN('1) EXAMINE A RECORD');
  WRITELN('2) REVISE A RECORD');
  WRITELN('3) ADD A RECORD');
  WRITELN('4) REMOVE A RECORD');
  WRITELN('5) QUIT');
  REPEAT
    WRITE('                              ? ');
    READLN(OPTION)
  UNTIL (OPTION IN ['1'..'5']);

  CASE OPTION OF

    '1':BEGIN
          CLEARSCREEN;
          WRITELN('EXAMINE A RECORD');
          WRITELN('======= = ======');
          WRITELN;
          EXAMINE(FOUND,FALSE)
        END;

    '2':BEGIN
          CLEARSCREEN;
          WRITELN('REVISE A RECORD');
          WRITELN('====== = ======');
          WRITELN;
          REVISE
        END;
```

Figure 8.10: Program UPDATE (cont.)

```
        '3':BEGIN
              CLEARSCREEN;
              WRITELN('ADD A RECORD');
              WRITELN('=== = ======');
              WRITELN;
              ADD
            END;

        '4':BEGIN
              CLEARSCREEN;
              WRITELN('REMOVE A RECORD');
              WRITELN('====== = ======');
              WRITELN;
              REMOVE
            END;

        '5':FINISHED := TRUE

      END (* CASE *)
  END;  (* MENU *)



  BEGIN (* MAIN PROGRAM *)
    CLEARSCREEN;
    WRITELN('ASSET FILE MANAGEMENT PROGRAM');
    WRITELN('===== ==== ========== =======');
    WRITELN;
    REPEAT
      WRITE('C(REATE OR U(PDATE? ');
      READLN(MODE)
    UNTIL (MODE IN ['C','U']);
    IF (MODE = 'C') THEN
      BEGIN
        INIT1;
        REPEAT
          CLEARSCREEN;
          ADD;
          WRITE('ADD ANOTHER? ');
          READLN(OKANS)
        UNTIL (OKANS = 'N')
      END
    ELSE
      BEGIN
        INIT2;
        REPEAT
          CLEARSCREEN;
          MENU(FINISHED)
        UNTIL FINISHED
      END;
      CLOSE(ASSETFILE,LOCK)
  END. (* MAIN PROGRAM *)
```

Figure 8.10: Program UPDATE (cont.)

Notice that the swapping compiler option is activated:

```
(*$S+*)
```

Also note that all three of our units are included in the USES statement. The type definition of the asset record uses three data types that are defined globally in the units—LONG1, DATEREC, and LONG2:

```
TYPE
  AREC = RECORD
    NAME : STRING[S1]
    NUMBER : LONG1;
    DATE : DATEREC;
    COST : LONG2
  END;
    ...
VAR
  ASSET : AREC;
  ASSETFILE : FILE OF AREC;
```

We will present a separate structure chart for each of the four menu options of our program; the main structure chart for program UPDATE (Figure 8.6) refers forward to the figures containing the subsidiary structure charts. These five charts together describe the entire program. Let us begin, then, with the *examine* option. The structure chart for the *examine* options appears in Figure 8.11.

Examining a Record

Briefly, procedure EXAMINE calls three procedures: INIDNO to read the number of the asset record that the user wishes to look at; then BSEARCH to find the reference to that number in the index; and finally ECHORECORD to display the record on the screen. EXAMINE itself is actually called from three different places in the update program. Procedure MENU calls it to implement the *examine* option:

```
EXAMINE(FOUND, FALSE);
```

Procedures REVISE and REMOVE call it to read the I.D. number, find the record, and display the echo:

```
EXAMINE(FOUND, TRUE);
```

The first of the two Boolean arguments is a VAR parameter; it returns a value of true to the calling procedure if EXAMINE actually finds the record the user wants. The second parameter is a Boolean value the calling procedure passes to EXAMINE. It indicates whether or not EXAMINE should require the user to input a check digit with the I.D. number. The *examine* option itself does not require the check digit, but both procedures REVISE and REMOVE do require it. Procedure EXAMINE receives this Boolean value in the variable CDREQ ("check digit required") and in turn passes it on to procedure INIDNO:

```
INIDNO(CDREQ, I.D.);
```

INIDNO calls the three routines of CHECKUNIT—INVALUE, VERIFYCHECK, and CHECKDIGIT—to read and verify the input of an I.D. number. Recall that INVALUE takes three parameters:

```
INVALUE(NUM, L, CHECK);
```

NUM, a VAR parameter, returns the value of the I.D. number. L is the

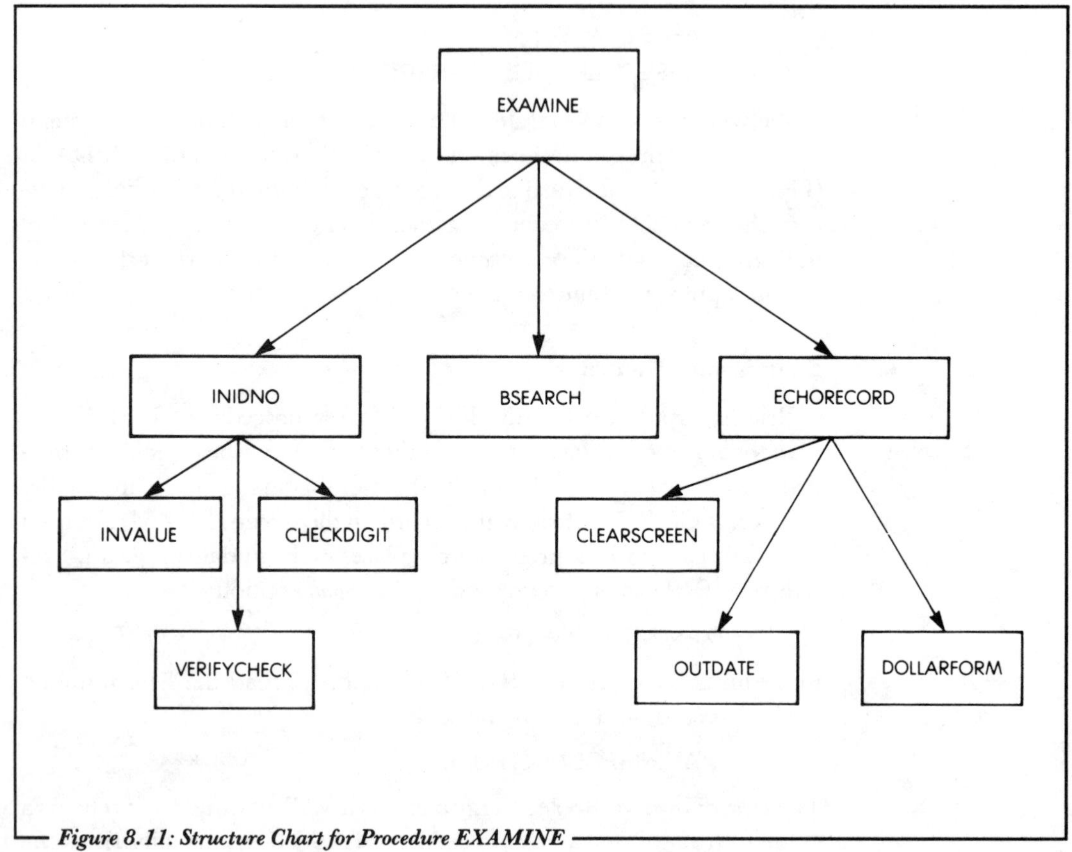

Figure 8.11: Structure Chart for Procedure EXAMINE

desired length of the number, including the check digit. CHECK, also a VAR parameter, is a Boolean value that indicates whether or not a check digit was included in the input.

The logic of INIDNO may seem a little complicated at first glance, since the procedure contains several levels of nested IF statements. We might write a pseudocode description of the procedure as follows:

```
IF a check digit is required THEN
  REPEAT
    calls to INVALUE
  UNTIL a complete I.D. number with a
      valid check digit is returned

    ELSE if a check digit is not required, then
      REPEAT
        calls to INVALUE;
        IF a check digit is included in the input THEN
          make sure it is valid and correct
        ELSE if no check digit is included in the input
          THEN
        calculate the check digit and
        display it on the screen
      UNTIL a complete and valid I.D. number is available
```

Procedure EXAMINE receives the complete identification number in the variable ID. The next step is to open the index file, access the index array, and call procedure BSEARCH to look in the index for the I.D. number:

```
BSEARCH(ID, INDEX[0].POSN, INDEX, POINTER, FOUND);
```

Let us review the parameters of BSEARCH. The first, ID, is the number we are searching for. The second represents the number of elements we must search through. Recall that the length of the index is always stored in INDEX[0].POSN. The third parameter is the array itself, in this case INDEX. The fourth and fifth parameters are of type VAR: POINTER in this case returns the POSN field of the index record, and FOUND is a Boolean value that tells whether or not ID was found in the index. Thus, if FOUND is true, then POINTER contains the position of the desired record in the asset file. (Look back at Figure 8.4 for a review of procedure BSEARCH.)

Depending on the value of FOUND, then, EXAMINE either GETs

the record from the asset file and displays it, or prints a message indicating that the file was not found:

```
IF FOUND THEN
   BEGIN
      SEEK(ASSETFILE, POINTER);
      GET(ASSETFILE);
      ASSET := ASSETFILE   ;
      ECHORECORD
   END
ELSE
   WRITELN(' * * * NOT FOUND IN FILE');
```

ASSET is a global variable, so procedure ECHORECORD requires no parameters. ECHORECORD simply clears the screen and writes each of the fields of ASSET. It calls OUTDATE (from DATEUNIT) to convert the date to the desired output format:

```
WRITE('2) DATE:  ');
OUTDATE(ASSET.DATE);
WRITELN;
```

and DOLLARFORM (from MONEYUNIT) to produce the expected dollar-and-cent output format for the cost:

```
DOLLARFORM(ASSET.COST, DOLLCENT);
WRITELN('3) COST:  ', DOLLCENT);
```

Finally, procedure EXAMINE allows the user to take as much time as necessary looking at the record:

```
WRITE ('PRESS <RETURN > TO CONTINUE.');
READLN(OKANS)
```

Revising a Record

Figure 8.12 shows the structure chart for procedure REVISE. The first line of REVISE is a call to EXAMINE. If EXAMINE returns a false to FOUND, indicating that the input I.D. number was not found in the file, REVISE performs no further action. (EXAMINE displays an error message and allows the user to try again.)

If FOUND is true, REVISE can make changes in the global value of ASSET. A pair of nested REPEAT loops and a CASE statement control the revision dialogue. The inner REPEAT loop presents the revision menu and reads the user's menu choice:

```
REPEAT
   WRITELN('REVISE WHICH ITEM? ');
   WRITE('1, 2, 3, OR Q(UIT = => ');
   READLN(ANSWER)
UNTIL (ANSWER IN ['1'..'3','Q']);
```

Just as in procedure MENU, we use the set operator IN to verify the menu choice. The input must be a character from '1' to '3' or a 'Q'. Once a valid choice has been made, ANSWER becomes the selector in a CASE statement.

An answer of '1' results in revision of the NAME field:

```
'1' : BEGIN
     REPEAT
        WRITE('NAME: ');
        READLN(TEMPNAME)
     UNTIL (LENGTH(TEMPNAME) <= S1);
     ASSET.NAME := TEMPNAME
     END;
```

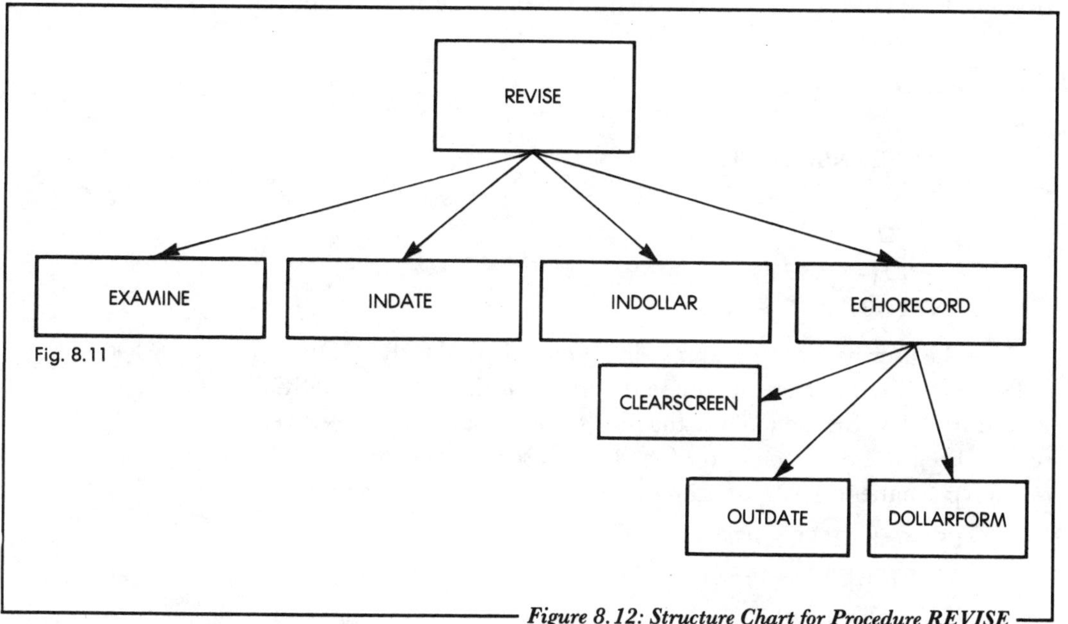

Figure 8.12: Structure Chart for Procedure REVISE

Since the string ASSET.NAME is limited to ten characters, we do not simply write:

```
READLN(ASSET.NAME)
```

Instead, we read the name into a temporary string variable, and make sure the length of the string is within the correct range before we assign it to ASSET.NAME.

A '2' revises the DATE field, using procedure INDATE to read the input:

```
'2' : BEGIN
       WRITE('DATE: ');
       INDATE(ASSET.DATE)
      END;
```

A '3' revises the COST field; procedure INDOLLAR reads the input:

```
'3' : BEGIN
       WRITE('COST: ');
       INDOLLAR(ASSET.COST)
      END;
```

A value of 'Q' ends the revision input dialogue. However, since the outer REPEAT loop is designed to continue reading revisions until ANSWER equals 'Q', the CASE statement itself performs no action for a 'Q':

```
REPEAT
   . . .
   CASE ANSWER OF
      . . .
      'Q' : ;
   END (* CASE *)
UNTIL (ANSWER = 'Q');
```

Once the user has completed revising a record, ECHORECORD is called to display the current (revised) version of that record, ASSET. Procedure REVISE then allows the user to either save the revised version or keep the old version on file. If the user chooses to make the revision permanent, REVISE stores the current ASSET in the asset file:

```
SEEK(ASSETFILE,POINTER);
ASSETFILE^ := ASSET;
PUT(ASSETFILE)
```

Otherwise, REVISE simply displays a message, and makes no change in the file:

```
WRITELN('KEEPING OLD RECORD')
```

Adding a Record

The *add* and *remove* options are more complicated than the others, because both the asset file and the index must be updated. The structure chart for procedure ADD appears in Figure 8.13. ADD itself is short and simple. It calls INRECORD repeatedly until a complete, new record has been read into ASSET. Then it calls ECHORECORD to display the new record, and finally SAVERECORD to update the two files. (It also gives the user a chance to abandon the new record after the echo.)

Procedure INRECORD is also fairly simple. It begins with a call to INIDNO. Notice that the check digit is not required in the input:

```
INIDNO(FALSE, ASSET.NUMBER);
```

INRECORD then calls its own local function USED to see if the I.D. number returned by INIDNO is already part of the file. USED simply opens the index file, and calls procedure BSEARCH to find out if ASSET.NUMBER is already in the index. USED then returns the Boolean value of FOUND from BSEARCH: if false, INRECORD can continue the input dialogue; if true, an error message is displayed:

```
IF NOT USED THEN
   input the rest of the record
ELSE
   print an error message—this I.D. number already exists in the file
```

Procedure SAVERECORD has a local procedure, UPDATEINDEX, which performs the somewhat complicated task of recording the new record information in the index. UPDATEINDEX also sends SAVERECORD a message (via the Boolean variable INDXFULL) when the index is filled to capacity. As long as that point has not been reached, SAVERECORD stores the new record in the asset file:

```
UPDATEINDEX(INDXFULL);
IF NOT INDXFULL THEN
   save the new record in the asset file
```

Otherwise, an error message is displayed.

Procedure UPDATEINDEX actually performs several different tasks. In the update mode, it repositions the asset file pointer so that

SAVERECORD will PUT the new record in the appropriate place in ASSETFILE. This action depends on whether any empty positions have been created by removal of previous records. Thus, UPDATEINDEX

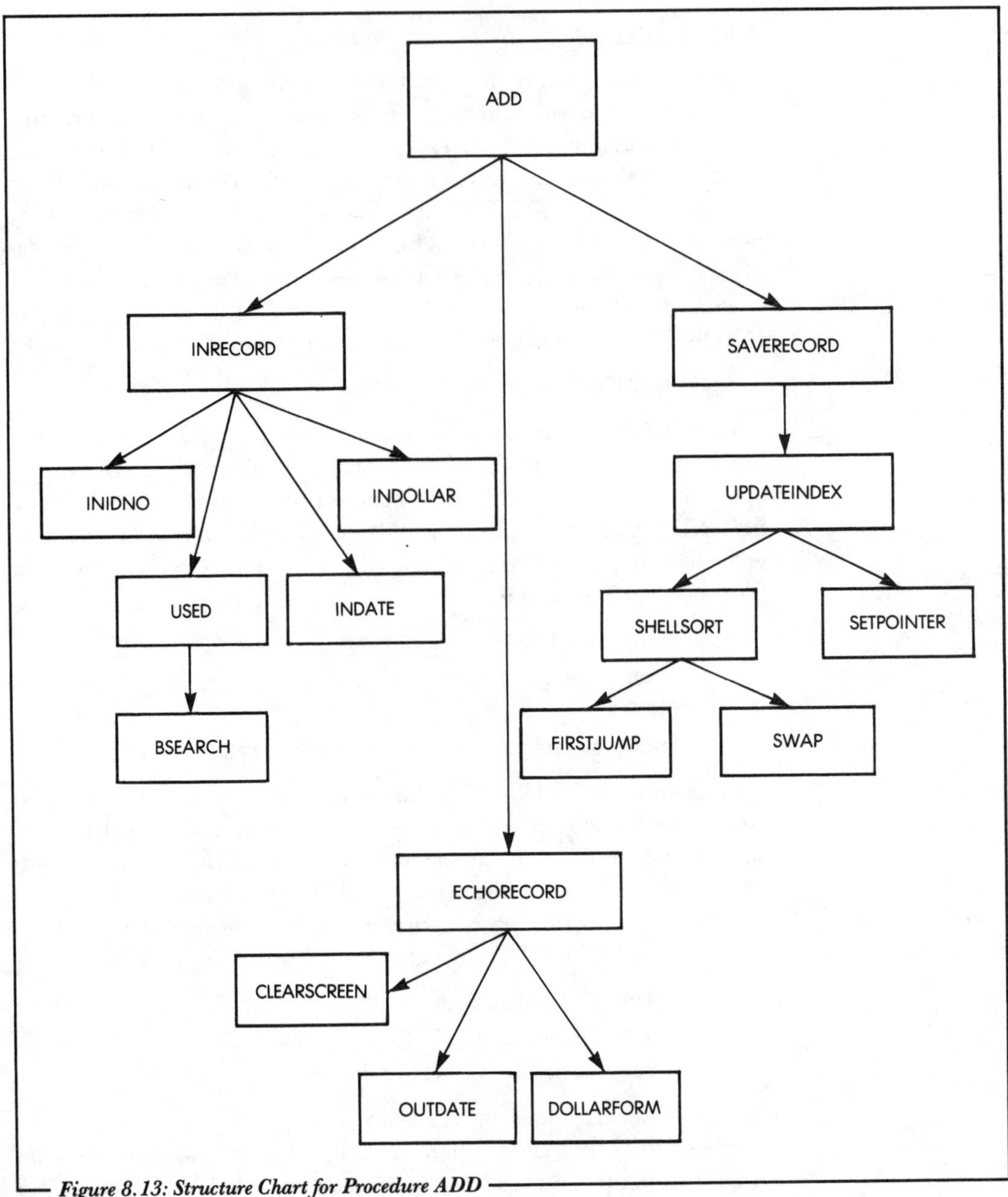

Figure 8.13: Structure Chart for Procedure ADD

must be flexible enough to deal with several different situations. It uses three variables to keep track of the current status of the file: POSITION is the number of records in the file; EMPTIES is the number of empty record positions in the file, waiting to be filled with new records; and NEWPOS is the number of records there will be in the file when the new record is added:

```
POSITION := INDEX[0].POSN;
EMPTIES := INDEX[0].NUM;
NEWPOS := POSITION + 1;
```

UPDATEINDEX first determines if there is any room in the index:

```
IF (NEWPOS > N) AND (EMPTIES = 0) THEN
```

If the index is full, procedure UPDATEINDEX closes the index and writes an error message. Otherwise, it checks next to see if there are any empty record positions in the asset file. If there are none, POSITION represents the number of the next new position in the asset file. (Remember that a file begins at position 0; thus, the nth record is stored in position $n - 1$.)

If ADD is being used in the update mode, there is a further detail to attend to at this point. Any of the other options (*examine*, *revise*, *remove*) may have moved the asset file pointer away from the end of the file. If we are to store the new record at the end of the file, then we must position the pointer properly. This is the job of the small procedure SETPOINTER:

```
IF MODE = 'U' THEN
  SETPOINTER
```

SETPOINTER simply SEEKs the last record in the file and then performs a GET to move the file pointer forward one more position:

```
SEEK(ASSETFILE, INDEX[0].POSN - 1);
GET(ASSETFILE)
```

Finally, if there *are* some empty positions to be filled in the asset file, UPDATEINDEX moves the file pointer to the most recently vacated of those positions:

```
SEEK(ASSETFILE, INDEX[NEWPOS].POSN);
```

and decrements the number of empty positions:

```
INDEX[0].NUM := EMPTIES - 1
```

After all of these different situations have been tested and accounted for, then the new asset number is stored in the index, the number of records is incremented, and the index is sorted:

```
INDEX[NEWPOS].NUM := ASSET.NUMBER;
INDEX[0].POSN := NEWPOS;
SHELLSORT(INDEX, INDEX[0].POSN);
```

Removing a Record

The structure chart for procedure REMOVE is shown in Figure 8.14. REMOVE calls EXAMINE to find and display the target record. If the record is found, and if the user still wants to delete it (recall that the program asks the user to verify the choice), the I.D. number of the record is changed to 999999 in the index, and the index is sorted:

```
INDEX[CENTER].NUM := 999999;
SHELLSORT(INDEX, INDEX[0].POSN);
```

CENTER is a global variable representing the most recently accessed element of the index array; its value is determined in BSEARCH. Next, the number of records is decremented, the number of empties is incremented, and the new index is saved in the index file.

For the purpose of this program, no further action need be taken by procedure REMOVE. When the asset number is removed from the

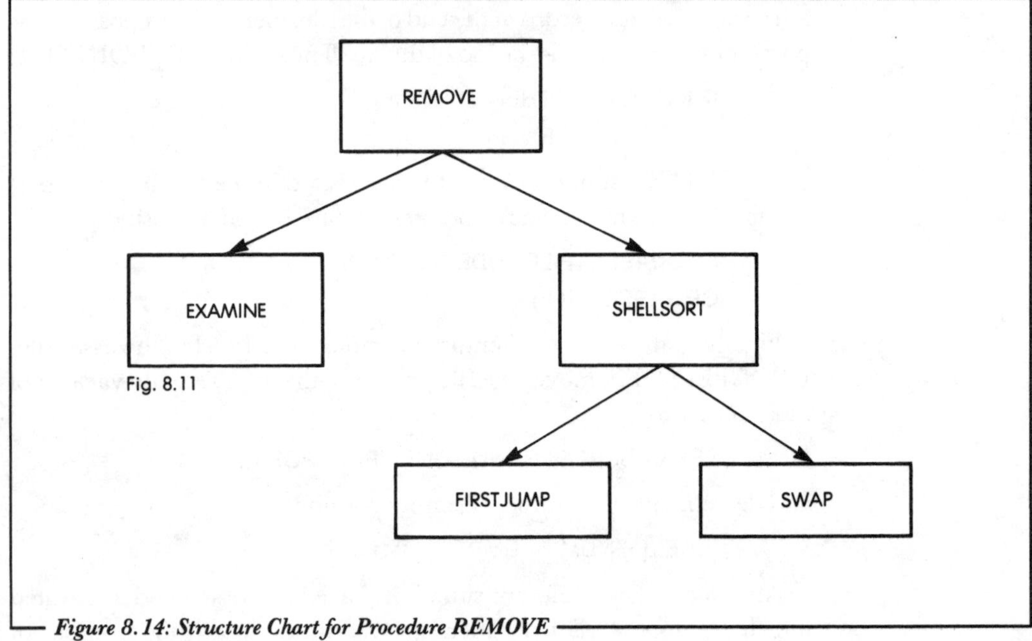

Figure 8.14: Structure Chart for Procedure REMOVE

index, the record is as good as gone. However, we will soon be looking at another program that will produce a report from the asset file. This program will not refer to the index at all, and so will need some way of finding out if a given record in the asset file has actually been deleted. For this reason, REMOVE actually goes into the asset file, sets the removed asset number to zero, and re-saves the record:

```
SEEK(ASSETFILE,POINTER);
GET(ASSETFILE);
ASSET : = ASSETFILE^;
ASSET.NUMBER : = 0;
SEEK(ASSETFILE, POINTER);
ASSETFILE^ : = ASSET;
PUT(ASSETFILE)
```

This zero will serve as a flag to the report-producing program.

SUMMARY

We have taken a detailed look at a file management program in this chapter. The main features of the program are:

- It has two modes of operation: creation and update.
- The update mode offers four options: *examine*, *revise*, *add*, and *remove*.
- The program creates an index in order to find records in the main file; the binary search and Shell sort procedures are used to maintain this index.
- To assure user-friendliness, the program uses the procedures of MONEYUNIT, CHECKUNIT, and DATEUNIT for input and output.

The main limitation of this program is that its index restricts it to small files. We have discussed ways of expanding the indexing system to a multi-page arrangement, but they would add considerable complexity to the program.

In Chapter 9 we will examine two programs that generate reports from the asset file. We will use these reports to verify the algorithms of the update program.

Chapter 9

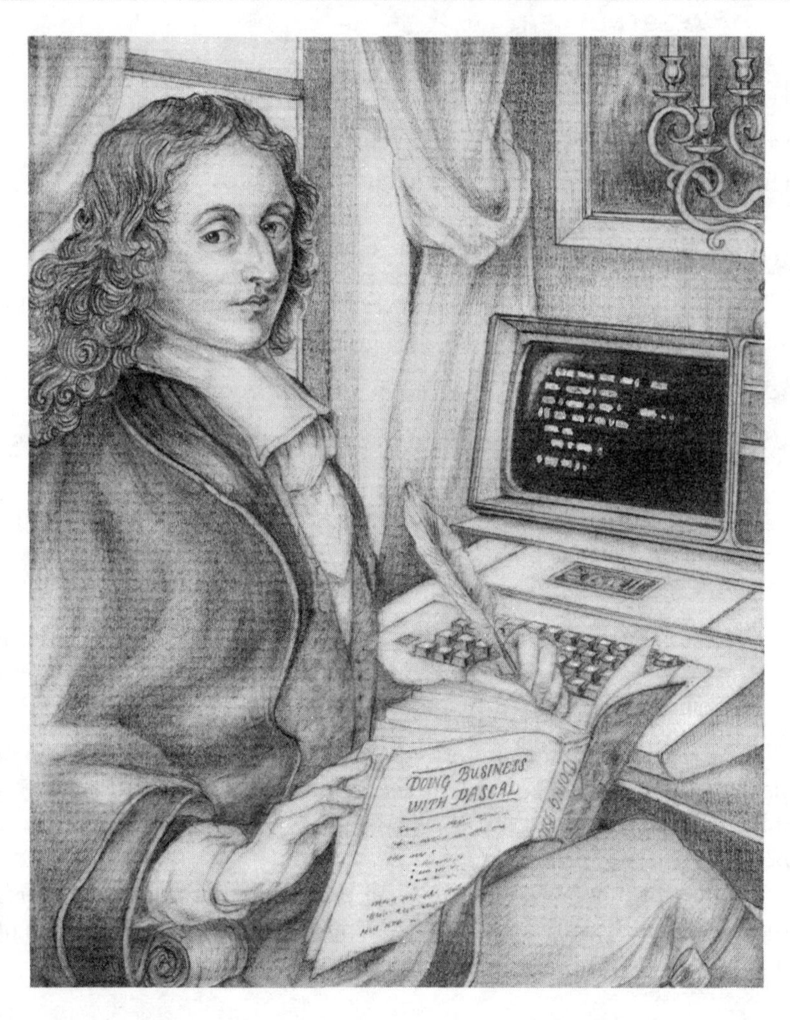

Producing Reports From a Data File

INTRODUCTION

The two programs presented in this chapter, REPORT1 and REPORT2, both create tables from data stored in an asset file. REPORT1 simply reads the records in the file sequentially and presents them in an unsorted order. REPORT2 uses the index to present the records sorted in the ascending order of their I.D. numbers.

We will test these two programs using the asset file created in Chapter 8. Refer back to Figures 8.1 and 8.2 to review the two runs of the program that created the file. Here is a summary of the sequence they produced:

1. The first run of the program was in the creation mode (Figure 8.1). Ten records were placed in the file.
2. The second run, in the update mode (Figure 8.2), made three changes in the file: one record was revised (I.D. #611526), one record was removed (I.D. #756198), and one record was added to the file (I.D. #631250). The record that was removed was originally the third record placed in the file.

Some of the details of this update history will show up in the output from REPORT1.

THE FIRST REPORT—SEQUENTIAL ACCESS

Both programs REPORT1 and REPORT2 produce tables, with one line for each record of the file. The line contains the name, the I.D. number, the cost, and the age (in years) of the asset. In order to calculate the age, the programs begin by prompting the user to input the current date.

A sample run of REPORT1 is shown in Figure 9.1. The order in which the records are actually stored in the asset file is the order in which this program presents them. We can see the three changes that were made in the file during the second run of the update program. The name and cost of record #611526 have been revised. Record #756198 ("MACHINE#1") has been deleted. In its place—that is, in the *third* position of the asset file—we find the record #631250 ("NEW-MACH"), the record that was added *last* to the file. Our update program is working just as we expected it to: vacant positions in the asset file are used up by new additions, and the length of the file is increased only when there are no empty positions left to fill.

The complete listing of program REPORT1 appears in Figure 9.2. The program uses several routines (and data structures) from our units—including INDATE, DATECONVERT, CLEARSCREEN, FOURCOLUMN, and DOLLARFORM. We can follow the action of the program by reading through the main program section. After a prompt for the date is written, procedure INDATE reads the date, and procedure DATECONVERT calculates the scalar date equivalent, storing it

```
TODAY'S DATE: 5-2-82

NAME          NUMBER          COST       YEARS
====          ======          ====       =====

TRUCK#1       825100    $12,650.00         15
COPIER        611237    $19,845.00         12
NEW-MACH      631250    $52,840.00          0
COMPUTER      321158     $9,520.00          2
MACHINE#2     197863     $5,780.00          9
BUILDING#1    455212   $115,650.00          6
PHOTOEQUIP    611526     $6,750.00          2
BUILDING#2    236117    $87,500.00          7
TRUCK#2       526658    $15,450.00          4
MACHINE#3     991134    $63,980.00          0

PRESS <RETURN> TO CLOSE FILE
```

Figure 9.1: Output from Program REPORT1

```
(*$S+*)
PROGRAM REPORT1;

USES
                (*$U MONEYUNIT.CODE*)
MONEYUNIT,
                (*$U CHECKUNIT.CODE*)
CHECKUNIT,
                (*$U DATEUNIT.CODE*)
DATEUNIT;

CONST
  S1 = 10;
  L  = 6;

TYPE
  AREC = RECORD
    NAME : STRING[S1];
    NUMBER : LONG1;
    DATE : DATEREC;
    COST : LONG2
  END;

VAR
  ASSET : AREC;
  ASSETFILE : FILE OF AREC;
  TODAY : DATEREC;
  SCTODAY : DATELONG;
  OKANS : STRING;


PROCEDURE OUTLINE;
  VAR
    SCDATE : DATELONG;
    AGE,
    STCOST,
    STNUM  : STRING;
    I,
    L,
    AGEDIF      : INTEGER;

  PROCEDURE SPACE;
    BEGIN
      WRITE(' ')
    END;

BEGIN
  WRITE(ASSET.NAME);
  L := LENGTH(ASSET.NAME);
  FOR I := 1 TO (11 - L) DO
    SPACE;
  DATECONVERT(ASSET.DATE,SCDATE);
  AGEDIF := TRUNC((SCTODAY - SCDATE) DIV 365);
  STR(AGEDIF,AGE);
  STR(ASSET.NUMBER,STNUM);
  DOLLARFORM(ASSET.COST,STCOST);
  FOURCOLUMN(STNUM,STCOST,AGE,'',6,14,6,0);
END;
```

Figure 9.2: Listing of Program REPORT1

```
PROCEDURE HEADING;
  BEGIN
    WRITELN;
    WRITE('NAME          ');
    FOURCOLUMN('NUMBER','COST     ','YEARS','',6,14,6,0);
    WRITE('====          ');
    FOURCOLUMN('======','====     ','=====','',6,14,6,0);
    WRITELN
  END;  (* HEADING *)

BEGIN (* MAIN PROGRAM *)
  CLEARSCREEN;
  WRITELN;
  WRITE('TODAY''S DATE: ');
  INDATE(TODAY);
  DATECONVERT(TODAY,SCTODAY);
  CLEARSCREEN;
  WRITELN;
  RESET(ASSETFILE,'#5:ASSETS');

  HEADING;

  WHILE (NOT (EOF(ASSETFILE))) DO
    BEGIN
      ASSET := ASSETFILE^;
      IF ASSET.NUMBER <> 0 THEN
        OUTLINE;
      GET(ASSETFILE)
    END; (* WHILE *)

  WRITELN;
  WRITE('PRESS <RETURN> TO CLOSE FILE ');
  READLN(OKANS);
  CLOSE(ASSETFILE,LOCK)
END.  (* MAIN PROGRAM *)
```

*Figure 9.2: Listing of Program **REPORT1** (cont.)*

in SCDATE:

```
WRITE('TODAY''S DATE: ');
INDATE(TODAY);
DATECONVERT(TODAY,SCDATE);
```

Notice that TODAY is of type DATEREC and SCTODAY is of type DATELONG.

Next, the main program opens the asset file (with a RESET statement) and calls procedure HEADING to produce the table heading. The records of the asset file are read and displayed one by one within a WHILE loop that uses the UCSD Pascal EOF function to test for the end of the file:

```
WHILE (NOT (EOF(ASSETFILE))) DO
```

In UCSD Pascal, the EOF function returns a true when the file pointer points to a position *beyond* the last record, and a GET is performed on the empty record position. For this reason, the GET appears as the last statement of the WHILE loop:

```
WHILE (NOT (EOF(ASSETFILE))) DO
  BEGIN
    ASSET := ASSETFILE ^;
    IF ASSET.NUMBER <> 0 THEN
      OUTLINE;
    GET(ASSETFILE)
  END;
```

The GET that accesses the last record of the file transfers the record to the buffer and moves the pointer forward to the position beyond the last record, but does not yet set EOF to true. The *next* iteration of the WHILE loop prints that last record; EOF finally returns a true when GET is performed on a position that does not contain a record.

Procedure OUTLINE, which writes one line of output for each record, is called unless the asset number is zero. That is why we took the trouble, in program UPDATE, to go into the asset file and set the NUMBER field to zero when we were removing a record. If it were not for this feature, REPORT1 would have to access the index to find out which records of the asset file were still valid and which had been removed.

Procedure OUTLINE calculates the age of the asset, converts all the numeric data to strings, and calls FOURCOLUMN to write the line of output. Actually, FOURCOLUMN is only used to produce three of the columns of information. The first column, the name of the asset, is left-justified; the other columns are right-justified. After writing the name, we must space forward to the beginning of the next column. The number of spaces depends on the length of the name:

```
WRITE(ASSET.NAME);
L := LENGTH(ASSET.NAME);
FOR I := 1 TO (11 - L) DO
  SPACE;
```

Then FOURCOLUMN writes the rest of the line; notice that the last string parameter of the call to FOURCOLUMN is null, and that the last integer parameter is zero:

```
FOURCOLUMN(STNUM, STCOST, AGE, '', 6, 14, 6, 0)
```

To calculate the age of the asset, OUTLINE calls DATECONVERT to find SCDATE, the scalar value of the acquisition date. This value is subtracted from SCTODAY, the scalar value of the current date, and then DIV 365 produces the number of whole years. In UCSD Pascal, the DIV operation is defined for long integers, and the quotient of a long-integer DIV operation is itself a long integer. The built-in function TRUNC may therefore be used to convert this long integer to a regular integer:

```
AGEDIF := TRUNC((SCTODAY - SCDATE) DIV 365);
```

The second report program, REPORT2, is very similar to REPORT1; it performs essentially the same functions. The difference is that REPORT2 uses the file index to access the asset records, and thus to produce a sorted list.

THE SECOND REPORT—DIRECT ACCESS

The output from REPORT2 is shown in Figure 9.3, and the listing of the program is shown in Figure 9.4. The new procedure in REPORT2 is GETINDEX, which opens the index file and makes it available to the program. Since INDEX[0].POSN contains the number of records in the file, the main program can use a FOR loop rather than a WHILE loop to read and display the records:

```
FOR I := 1 TO INDEX[0].POSN DO
```

This loop simply goes down the index, from beginning to end, SEEKs

```
TODAY'S DATE: 5-2-82


NAME          NUMBER           COST       YEARS
====          ======           ====       =====

MACHINE#2     197863        $5,780.00         9
BUILDING#2    236117       $87,500.00         7
COMPUTER      321158        $9,520.00         2
BUILDING#1    455212      $115,650.00         6
TRUCK#2       526658       $15,450.00         4
COPIER        611237       $19,845.00        12
PHOTOEQUIP    611526        $6,750.00         2
NEW-MACH      631250       $52,840.00         0
TRUCK#1       825100       $12,650.00        15
MACHINE#3     991134       $63,980.00         0

PRESS <RETURN> TO CLOSE FILE
```

Figure 9.3: Output from Program REPORT2

each record in turn, and calls OUTLINE to produce the display:

```
SEEK(ASSETFILE, INDEX[I].POSN);
GET(ASSETFILE);
ASSET : = ASSETFILE ^;
OUTLINE
```

Since the index is sorted, the records are ordered by asset number in this report.

```
(*$S+*)
PROGRAM REPORT2;

USES
                (*$U MONEYUNIT.CODE*)
MONEYUNIT,
                (*$U CHECKUNIT.CODE*)
CHECKUNIT,
                (*$U DATEUNIT.CODE*)
DATEUNIT;

CONST
  S1 = 10;
  L  = 6;
  N  = 100;

TYPE
  AREC = RECORD
    NAME : STRING[S1];
    NUMBER : LONG1;
    DATE : DATEREC;
    COST : LONG2
  END;

  ISAMREC = RECORD
    POS : INTEGER;
    NUM : LONG1
  END;

  ISAMARY = ARRAY[0..N] OF ISAMREC;

VAR
  ASSET : AREC;
  ASSETFILE : FILE OF AREC;
  TODAY : DATEREC;
  SCTODAY : DATELONG;
  OKANS : STRING;
  INDEX : ISAMARY;
  I     : INTEGER;



PROCEDURE GETINDEX;
  VAR
    INDEXFILE : FILE OF ISAMARY;
```

Figure 9.4: Listing of Program REPORT2

```
BEGIN
  RESET(INDEXFILE,'#5:INDEX');
  INDEX := INDEXFILE^;
  CLOSE(INDEXFILE,LOCK);
END;  (* GETINDEX *)

PROCEDURE OUTLINE;
  VAR
    SCDATE : DATELONG;
    AGE,
    STCOST,
    STNUM  : STRING;
    I,
    L,
    AGEDIF      : INTEGER;

  PROCEDURE SPACE;
    BEGIN
      WRITE(' ')
    END;

BEGIN
  WRITE(ASSET.NAME);
  L := LENGTH(ASSET.NAME);
  FOR I := 1 TO (10 - L + 1) DO
    SPACE;
  DATECONVERT(ASSET.DATE,SCDATE);
  AGEDIF := TRUNC((SCTODAY - SCDATE) DIV 365);
  STR(AGEDIF,AGE);
  STR(ASSET.NUMBER,STNUM);
  DOLLARFORM(ASSET.COST,STCOST);
  FOURCOLUMN(STNUM,STCOST,AGE,'',6,14,6,0);
END;



PROCEDURE HEADING;
  BEGIN
    WRITELN;
    WRITE('NAME        ');
    FOURCOLUMN('NUMBER','COST  ','YEARS','',6,14,6,0);
    WRITE('====        ');
    FOURCOLUMN('======','====  ','=====','',6,14,6,0);
    WRITELN
  END;  (* HEADING *)


BEGIN (* MAIN PROGRAM *)
  CLEARSCREEN;
  WRITELN;
  WRITE('TODAY''S DATE: ');
  INDATE(TODAY);
  DATECONVERT(TODAY,SCTODAY);
  CLEARSCREEN;
  WRITELN;
```

Figure 9.4: Listing of Program REPORT2 (cont.)

```
    GETINDEX;

    RESET(ASSETFILE,'#5:ASSETS');
    HEADING;

    FOR I := 1 TO INDEX[0].POS DO
      BEGIN
        SEEK(ASSETFILE,INDEX[I].POS);
        GET(ASSETFILE);
        ASSET := ASSETFILE^;
        OUTLINE
      END;

    WRITELN;
    WRITE('PRESS <RETURN> TO CLOSE FILE ');
    READLN(OKANS);
    CLOSE(ASSETFILE,LOCK)
  END.  (* MAIN PROGRAM *)
```

Figure 9.4: Listing of Program REPORT2 (cont.)

SUMMARY

Once a data file is created, we may want to produce any number of different reports from it. The design of both the data file and its index should be planned in advance with the goal of making report writing as convenient as possible.

Part III

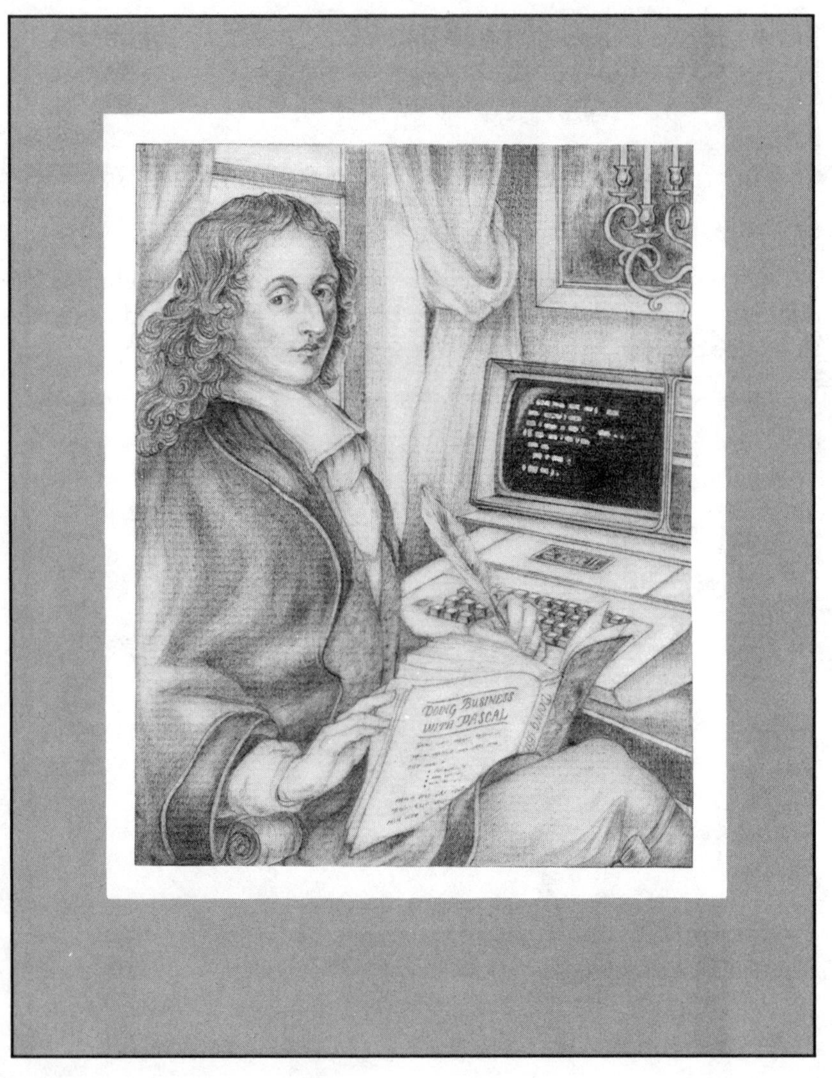

Producing Management Reports: Business Applications in Pascal

Part III presents a series of eleven application programs, each one illustrating one of the modules of the business system described in Part I of this book. These programs are all interactive; that is, they all create input dialogues and read their required data from the keyboard. In this sense, they differ from the system modules described in Chapters 1 and 2, which would read and create a system of data files that would, in turn, form the backbone of a working business system.

These programs illustrate a number of the business algorithms essential to a business system. Most of these programs organize, calculate, and present data, creating management-oriented reports that focus on efficient decision-making. Many of these programs will be useful as stand-alone tools for business management.

Each chapter in Part III is divided into three sections:

— *The Application* describes the program in the context of the business system. The files and the modules that the program would use and interact with in a working system are outlined and discussed.

— *The Sample Run* presents some actual dialogue and output from the program, and suggests uses—and often modifications—possible for this module.

— *The Program* gives a complete listing of the program, and describes its essential algorithms in line-by-line detail. Important elements of UCSD Pascal are described and explained as they occur in the programs.

Chapter 10

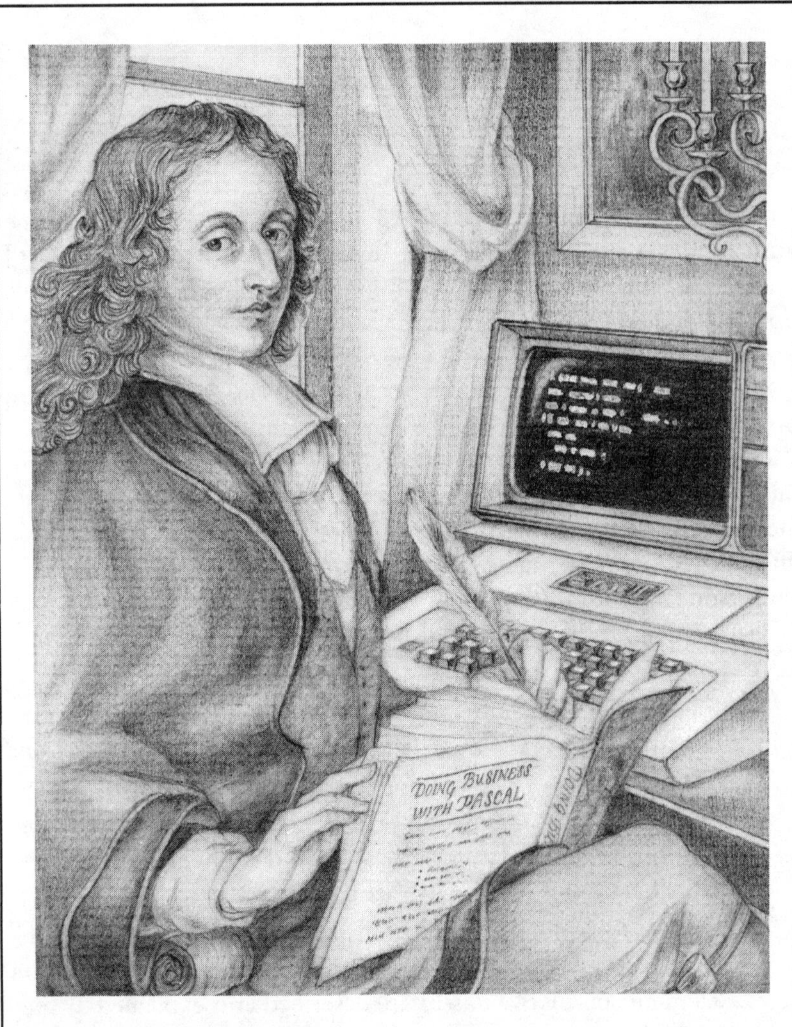

The System Profile

THE APPLICATION

We discussed the function of the system profile and some of the criteria for its design in Chapter 2. It is designed to provide information of a fairly static and constant nature to the entire system as needed. The specific items included in this system profile program are presented for the purpose of illustration only. In a real business system, the list would be much longer. Any item that is common to two or more business programming applications should be placed in the profile.

Several elements of good system design are evident in this application program. First is the need for security within the system. The password function implemented within this program might well be used elsewhere, perhaps in some of the applications within the payroll subsystem. The ability to change a password might itself require another password. System security is usually critical if more than one person has access to the computer.

Second, the screen configuration illustrates some of the output design considerations mentioned in Chapter 2. The system user is given relatively few decisions to make on each screen, and those decisions are indicated by as few characters as possible. The report produced by the profile translates all of the selections into intelligible text, rather than merely repeating the option codes from the menu. This allows the user to double-check the accuracy of the input information.

Not included in the example, but of some importance in a complete business system, is the need for an audit trail of all on-line changes to the profile. This might be accomplished by storing one or two previous versions of the profile on disk and making them accessible to viewing (but not to further changing). Within that previous version might be kept the date of the next profile revision, and the name of the individual who actually made the changes. Audit trail information might also be provided through a specific report that would be generated each time changes are made to the system profile. The report could give before-and-after information on the specific fields that were changed, along with the date and the name of the individual who made the changes.

The system profile is the key to the design and development of the business system. The ability to revise general business information at a single place in the profile—and to be assured that the change will be made throughout the system—is essential. The alternative—having to change the information everywhere it occurs—would not be acceptable.

THE SAMPLE RUN

The system profile maintained by this program includes a sampling of the kinds of general business information that would typically be stored in a profile. All of this information must be accessible to individuals who need to see or change it. In addition, parts of the profile can be designed to supply information or option choices to other modules of the system.

This profile contains fourteen items of company information, divided into three categories:

1. general (name, address, telephone number, founding date)
2. payroll/employee information (number of hours per pay period; overtime calculation method; number of employees; maximum payroll check amount; employee evaluation scheduling information)
3. accounting/reporting option (reporting periods for accounts receivable; inventory costing method; date of oldest fixed asset acquisition).

In addition, the profile stores the password and the date of the last profile revision. Two sample runs of the system profile program are presented; the first is shown in Figure 10.1.

For security reasons, the user must enter the password correctly in order to access or revise profile information. As we see in the first sample run, the program begins by prompting the user to input two pieces of information: the current date, and then the password. The password does not appear on the screen as the user types it in; instead, a string of asterisks appears, one asterisk for each character of the password:

```
===>********
```

```
SYSTEM PROFILE UPDATE PROGRAM
====== ======= ====== =======

TODAY'S DATE? 6-10-82

PLEASE TYPE PASSWORD TO ACCESS PROFILE.

   ===> ********

*** WELCOME TO THE SYSTEM PROFILE ***

----------------------------------------------------

CURRENT STATUS OF SYSTEM PROFILE
------- ------ -- ------ -------

 ==> LAST PROFILE REVISION ON MAY 10, 1982

COMPANY NAME:
-------------
JONES, INC.

STREET ADDRESS:
---------------
15 MAPLE DRIVE

CITY, STATE, ZIP:
-----------------
SMALLTOWN, CA 99912

TELEPHONE #:
------------
(321) 987-6543

FOUNDING DATE:
--------------
MARCH 5, 1977

TYPE <RETURN> TO CONTINUE.
----------------------------------------------------

HOURS PER PAY PERIOD:
---------------------
80 HOURS

OVERTIME CALCULATION METHOD:
----------------------------
BY PAY PERIOD

NUMBER OF EMPLOYEES:
--------------------
48 EMPLOYEES

NET PAY FLAG AMOUNT:
--------------------
FLAG PAYROLL GREATER THAN $3,500.00
```

Figure 10.1: First Sample Run of System Profile Program

```
EMPLOYEE EVALUATION DATES:
--------------------------
FIRST QUARTER, THEN ANNUALLY


TYPE <RETURN> TO CONTINUE.

----------------------------------------------------

ACCOUNT AGING REPORTING PERIODS:
--------------------------------
PERIOD 1: 30 DAYS
PERIOD 2: 30 DAYS
PERIOD 3: 30 DAYS

INVENTORY COSTING METHOD:
-------------------------
FIFO

DEPRECIATION METHOD:
--------------------
FIXED PERCENTAGE ON DECLINING BASE

OLDEST ACQUISITION DATE:
------------------------
MAY 5, 1977


TYPE <RETURN> TO CONTINUE.

----------------------------------------------------


REVISE ANY ITEM? Y

1) COMPANY NAME
2) STREET ADDRESS
3) CITY, STATE, ZIP
4) TELEPHONE #
5) FOUNDING DATE
6) HOURS PER PAY PERIOD
7) OVERTIME CALCULATION METHOD
8) NUMBER OF EMPLOYEES
9) NET PAY FLAG AMOUNT
10) EMPLOYEE EVALUATION DATES
11) ACCOUNT AGING REPORTING PERIODS
12) INVENTORY COSTING METHOD
13) DEPRECIATION METHOD
14) OLDEST ACQUISITION DATE

15) NO MORE REVISIONS

    REVISE WHICH ITEM? 2


STREET ADDRESS? 236 PINE STREET

----------------------------------------------------
```

Figure 10.1: First Sample Run of System Profile Program (cont.)

```
1) COMPANY NAME
2) STREET ADDRESS
3) CITY, STATE, ZIP
4) TELEPHONE #
5) FOUNDING DATE
6) HOURS PER PAY PERIOD
7) OVERTIME CALCULATION METHOD
8) NUMBER OF EMPLOYEES
9) NET PAY FLAG AMOUNT
10) EMPLOYEE EVALUATION DATES
11) ACCOUNT AGING REPORTING PERIODS
12) INVENTORY COSTING METHOD
13) DEPRECIATION METHOD
14) OLDEST ACQUISITION DATE

15) NO MORE REVISIONS

    REVISE WHICH ITEM? 8


HOW MANY EMPLOYEES? 57

----------------------------------------------------


1) COMPANY NAME
2) STREET ADDRESS
3) CITY, STATE, ZIP
4) TELEPHONE #
5) FOUNDING DATE
6) HOURS PER PAY PERIOD
7) OVERTIME CALCULATION METHOD
8) NUMBER OF EMPLOYEES
9) NET PAY FLAG AMOUNT
10) EMPLOYEE EVALUATION DATES
11) ACCOUNT AGING REPORTING PERIODS
12) INVENTORY COSTING METHOD
13) DEPRECIATION METHOD
14) OLDEST ACQUISITION DATE

15) NO MORE REVISIONS

    REVISE WHICH ITEM? 13


FIXED ASSET DEPRECIATION METHOD:
1) STRAIGHT-LINE
2) SUM-OF-THE-YEARS'-DIGITS
3) DOUBLE-DECLINING-BALANCE
4) FIXED PERCENTAGE ON A DECLINING BASE

          ? 3

----------------------------------------------------
```

Figure 10.1: First Sample Run of System Profile Program (cont.)

```
1) COMPANY NAME
2) STREET ADDRESS
3) CITY, STATE, ZIP
4) TELEPHONE #
5) FOUNDING DATE
6) HOURS PER PAY PERIOD
7) OVERTIME CALCULATION METHOD
8) NUMBER OF EMPLOYEES
9) NET PAY FLAG AMOUNT
10) EMPLOYEE EVALUATION DATES
11) ACCOUNT AGING REPORTING PERIODS
12) INVENTORY COSTING METHOD
13) DEPRECIATION METHOD
14) OLDEST ACQUISITION DATE

15) NO MORE REVISIONS

    REVISE WHICH ITEM? 15

----------------------------------------------------

CHANGE PASSWORD? Y

PLEASE TYPE NEW PASSWORD THREE TIMES:

1> ********
2> ********
3> ********


SAVE REVISIONS? Y
```

Figure 10.1: First Sample Run of System Profile Program (cont.)

The user has three tries at typing in the correct password. A welcome message appears if the password is correct:

* * * WELCOME TO THE SYSTEM PROFILE * * *

If the password is still incorrect after three attempts, however, the program execution ends without giving access to the profile:

```
===>********
===>********
===>********
```

* * * WRONG PASSWORD! ACCESS NOT GRANTED * * *

A correct password is followed by a display of the current status of the system profile. The program supplies a screenful of information at a time and allows the user to examine each screen for as long as necessary. In the case of items that represent options, the option is described in words;

for example:

```
DEPRECIATION METHOD:
--------------
FIXED PERCENTAGE ON DECLINING BASE
```

In the file itself this option is simply recorded as an integer.

Following the initial display of the profile, a revision dialogue begins. Note that in the current version of this program, any individual who knows the one password can both access and revise the profile. For some companies, it might be preferable to have two or three passwords, representing different levels of access or authority to revise. For example, one password might be required to access the profile, another to make changes in the profile, and a third to change the passwords themselves. As we will see, the password algorithms are carefully isolated into routines of their own in this program, so these design revisions would be relatively easy to make.

If the user answers with a 'Y' to the question:

```
REVISE ANY ITEM?
```

then a menu of the revisable items appears on the screen. To select an item for revision, the user types its number, from 1 to 14. The fifteenth line of the revision menu supplies a way of ending the revision dialogue:

```
15) NO MORE REVISIONS
```

Some of the revisions simply involve typing in a new piece of information about the company; for example, a change in the number of employees:

```
REVISE WHICH ITEM? 8

HOW MANY EMPLOYEES? 57
```

Others involve indicating a new menu option for an accounting method:

```
REVISE WHICH ITEM? 13

FIXED ASSET DEPRECIATION METHOD:
1) STRAIGHT-LINE
2) SUM-OF-THE-YEARS'-DIGITS
3) DOUBLE-DECLINING-BALANCE
4) FIXED-PERCENTAGE-ON-A-DECLINING BASE
        ? 3
```

The user may revise any number of items; typing '15' ends the revision dialogue.

Next, the user is allowed to change the password:

CHANGE PASSWORD?

Since it would not be desirable for the new password to appear on the screen (or, more to the point, on paper, if a hard copy of the program dialogue is being produced), some method of verifying the new password is necessary. The method chosen here is to request the user to enter the new password three times:

PLEASE TYPE NEW PASSWORD THREE TIMES:

1 >********

2 >********

3 >********

The program checks the three entries to make sure they are all the same. If they are, then the new password is recorded. If not, then an error message appears, and the user must type the password three more times:

THESE THREE WORDS DID NOT MATCH.
PLEASE TRY AGAIN.

Finally, the program asks for confirmation before saving any revision on disk:

SAVE REVISIONS?

This gives the user a chance to abandon the entire revision dialogue if anything has gone wrong.

The second sample run, shown in Figure 10.2, shows how the profile was revised by the dialogue of the first run. The new password was needed to access the profile for the second run.

When we examine the listing itself, we will see that the program actually runs in two different modes, like the data file management program of Chapter 8. The profile update program can be used to *create* a profile if one does not yet exist. When the program is run, it begins by checking to see if the profile is on line or not. If the profile is not available, then the following message appears on the screen:

NO PROFILE ON LINE.
DO YOU WISH TO INITIALIZE PROFILE?

After an affirmative answer, the program conducts an input dialogue for the complete profile, including the password. Following the input, the new profile information is echoed, and the user has the option of saving it on file or not.

This creation mode is incorporated into the program to illustrate how the profile would be initialized. However, in the interests of security, it might be wiser to separate the profile creation program routines into a program module of their own.

```
SYSTEM PROFILE UPDATE PROGRAM
====== ======= ====== =======

TODAY'S DATE? 6-12-82

PLEASE TYPE PASSWORD TO ACCESS PROFILE.

   ===> ********

*** WELCOME TO THE SYSTEM PROFILE ***

--------------------------------------------------

CURRENT STATUS OF SYSTEM PROFILE
------- ------ -- ------ -------

 ==> LAST PROFILE REVISION ON JUNE 10, 1982

COMPANY NAME:
-------------
JONES, INC.

STREET ADDRESS:
---------------
236 PINE STREET

CITY, STATE, ZIP:
-----------------
SMALLTOWN, CA 99912

TELEPHONE #:
------------
(321) 987-6543

FOUNDING DATE:
--------------
MARCH 5, 1977

TYPE <RETURN> TO CONTINUE.
--------------------------------------------------
```

Figure 10.2: Second Sample Run of System Profile Program

```
HOURS PER PAY PERIOD:
---------------------
80 HOURS

OVERTIME CALCULATION METHOD:
----------------------------
BY PAY PERIOD

NUMBER OF EMPLOYEES:
--------------------
57 EMPLOYEES

NET PAY FLAG AMOUNT:
--------------------
FLAG PAYROLL GREATER THAN $3,500.00

EMPLOYEE EVALUATION DATES:
--------------------------
FIRST QUARTER, THEN ANNUALLY


TYPE <RETURN> TO CONTINUE.
------------------------------------------------------


ACCOUNT AGING REPORTING PERIODS:
--------------------------------
PERIOD 1: 30 DAYS
PERIOD 2: 30 DAYS
PERIOD 3: 30 DAYS

INVENTORY COSTING METHOD:
-------------------------
FIFO

DEPRECIATION METHOD:
--------------------
DOUBLE DECLINING BALANCE

OLDEST ACQUISITION DATE:
------------------------
MAY 5, 1977


TYPE <RETURN> TO CONTINUE.
------------------------------------------------------



REVISE ANY ITEM? N



CHANGE PASSWORD? N
```

Figure 10.2: Second Sample Run of System Profile Program (cont.)

THE PROGRAM

A structure chart for program SYSPROFILE appears in Figure 10.3. The listing of the program is shown in Figure 10.4. The routines of this program fall loosely into three functional categories—the password routines, the creation-mode routines, and the revision-mode routines; however, several of the routines serve more than one function. The profile record type, PROFREC, contains thirteen fields of various types, designed to hold all the profile items. (Note that this number is not the same as NUMFIELDS. Four menu items have been combined into one field; and the date and password are included in the record.) PROFILE is the record variable, and FPROF is the file variable:

```
VAR
   PROFILE : PROFREC;
   FPROF   : FILE OF PROFREC;
```

The program is relatively long, but we can look to the main program section for a summary of the action:

```
IF NOPROFILE THEN
   NEWPROFILE
ELSE
   IF OKPW THEN
      ACCESSPROFILE
```

Function NOPROFILE searches for the profile on disk, and returns a true value if the profile is *not* on line. In this case, the profile-creation routine NEWPROFILE is called. If the profile *is* found, function OKPW prompts the user to input the password. Function NOPROFILE thus determines which mode—creation or revision—the program will run in. OKPW returns a true value only if the user enters the correct password, and then the access and revision routine, ACCESSFILE, is called. If the user does not know the password, OKPW returns a value of false, and execution of the program ends without giving access to the profile.

At the beginning of NOPROFILE, I/O checking is switched off, and an attempt is made to open the profile with a RESET statement:

```
(*$I- *)
RESET(FPROF,'#5:PROFILE');
```

IORESULT indicates the result of the RESET statement. A zero means

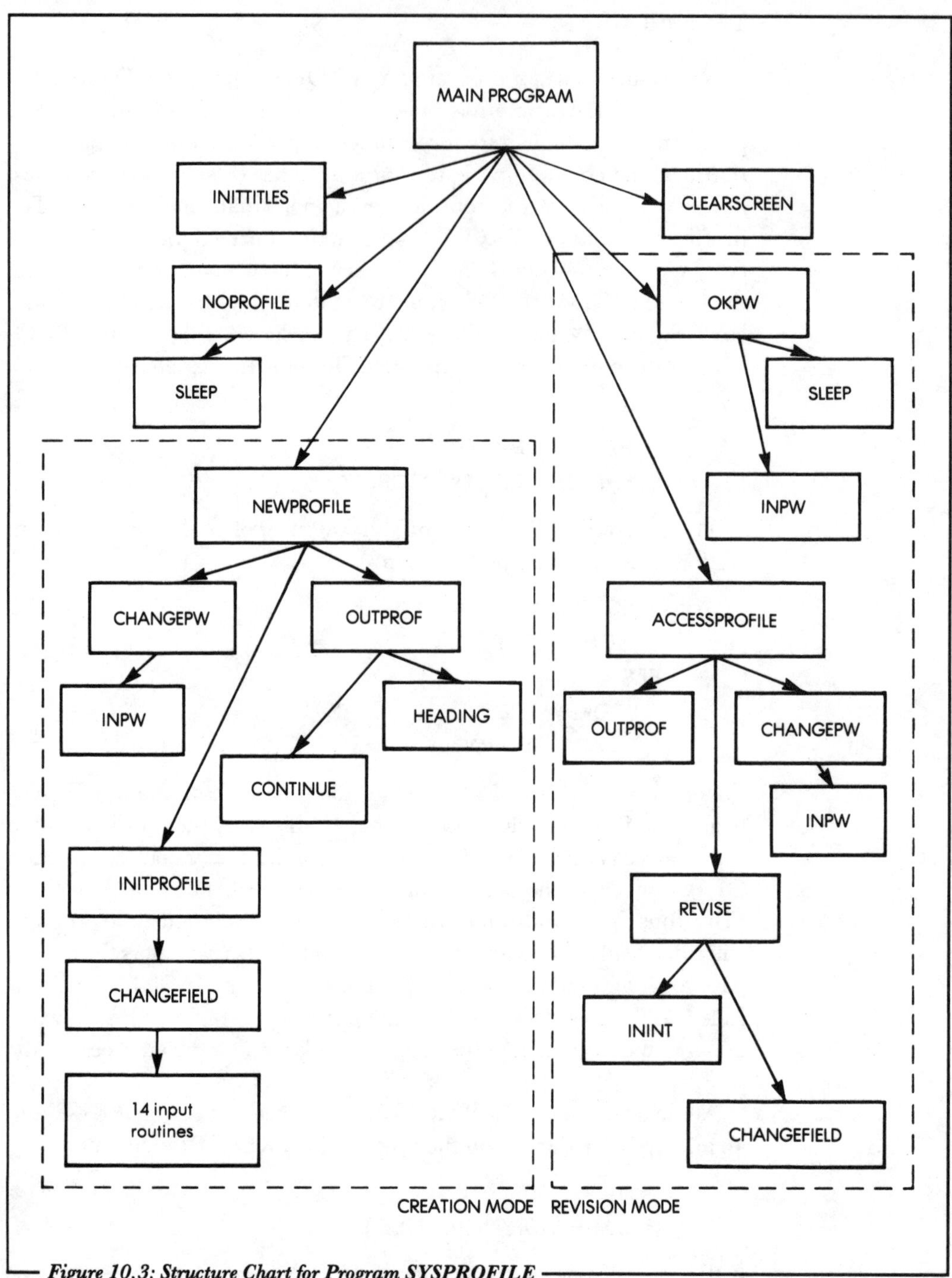

Figure 10.3: Structure Chart for Program SYSPROFILE

the file was found and opened; the next step is to GET the record and assign it to PROFILE:

```
IF IORESULT = 0 THEN
  BEGIN
    NOPROFILE := FALSE;
    GET(FPROF);
    PROFILE := FPROF^
  END
```

An IORESULT value of 10 means that the file was not found on the disk:

```
ELSE
  IF IORESULT = 10 THEN
    NOPROFILE := TRUE
```

Any other IORESULT value indicates some other I/O error. The program is simply terminated with an EXIT statement in this case:

```
ELSE
  BEGIN
    ...
    EXIT(PROGRAM)
  END
```

Notice that I/O checking is switched back on again at the end of function NOPROFILE:

```
(*$I+*)
```

The three password routines in this program are INPW, OKPW, and CHANGEPW. The input routine, INPW, uses the UCSD Pascal predefined file type KEYBOARD to read the characters of the password without echoing them on the screen:

```
READ(KEYBOARD,PW[I]);
```

Function OKPW calls INPW to read the user's input, and assigns a Boolean value to GOOD, which indicates whether or not the user's password corresponds to the correct profile password:

```
INPW(USERPW);
GOOD := USERPW = PROFILE.PASSWORD;
```

Procedure CHANGEPW records three different entries for a new password:

```
FOR I := 1 TO 3 DO
   BEGIN
      WRITE(I,'>');
      INPW(NEWPW[I])
   END;
```

All three entries must be the same before the password change can be recorded:

```
IF (NEWPW[1] = NEWPW[2]) AND (NEWPW[1] = NEWPW[3])
   THEN
   ...
```

Procedure NEWPROFILE is the driver routine for the creation mode. It calls CHANGEPW to initialize the password and then INITPROFILE to read all the items of the profile. Procedure INITPROFILE consists of a single FOR loop that makes NUMFIELDS (a constant with the value of 14, the number of profile items) calls to CHANGEFIELD:

```
FOR I := 1 TO NUMFIELDS DO
   BEGIN
      CHANGEFIELD(I);
      ...
   END
```

Procedure CHANGEFIELD, then, is the actual input routine for the items of the profile. It consists of 14 small specialized input routines, one for each item. It determines which of these routines to call via a CASE statement; the case selector, FIELD, is the parameter value that CHANGEFIELD receives from the procedure that calls it:

```
CASE FIELD OF
...
```

CHANGEFIELD is thus designed to be used conveniently in either the creation mode or the revision mode. Procedure REVISE presents the menu of revisable profile items, and reads the user's menu choice into WHICH. This integer variable then becomes the parameter of a call to CHANGEFIELD:

```
CHANGEFIELD(WHICH);
```

The main driver routine for the revision/access mode is ACCESS-

PROFILE. It begins with a call to OUTPROF, which displays the current status of the entire profile. Then REVISE is called until the user ends the revision dialogue:

```
REPEAT
   REVISE(FINISHED)
UNTIL FINISHED;
```

CHANGEPW is called if the user wants to change the password. Finally, ACCESSPROFILE saves the new version of the profile on disk:

```
SEEK(FPROF,0);
FPROF ^ := PROFILE;
PUT(FPROF)
```

```
(*$S++*)
PROGRAM SYSPROFILE;

USES
            (*$U MONEYUNIT.CODE*)
MONEYUNIT,
            (*$U DATEUNIT.CODE*)
DATEUNIT;

CONST
  NUMFIELDS = 14;


TYPE
  PROFREC = RECORD
    LASTCHANGE : DATEREC;    (* DATE OF LAST PROFILE REVISION *)
    PASSWORD   : STRING;
    NADDTEL    :  ARRAY[1..4] OF STRING; (* NAME,ADDRESS,TELE *)
    FOUNDED    : DATEREC;    (* FOUNDING DATE OF COMPANY *)

    (* PAYROLL INFORMATION *)

    PERIODHRS  : INTEGER;    (* HOURS PER PAY PERIOD *)
    OVRTIMEOPT : '1'..'3';   (* OVERTIME CALCULATION OPTION *)
    NUMEMPS    : INTEGER;    (* NUMBER OF EMPLOYEES *)
    NETPAYFLAG : LONG2;      (* MAXIMUM PAY CHECK AMOUNT *)
    EMPEVALOPT : '1'..'3';   (* EMPLOYEE EVALUATION SCHEDULING *)

    (* A/R AGING CATEGORIES *)

    ACCAGE      :  ARRAY[1..3] OF  INTEGER;   (* A/R REPORTING *)

    (* INVENTORY COSTING *)

    INVENT      : '1'..'3';   (* LIFO,FIFO, OR WEIGHTED AVE. *)
```

Figure 10.4: Listing of Program SYSPROFILE

```
      (* FIXED ASSETS *)

      DEPMETHOD  : '1'..'4';   (* DEPRECIATION METHODS *)
      OLDEST     : DATEREC     (* OLDEST FIXED ASSET *)
    END;      (* PROFREC *)


  VAR
    TITLE : ARRAY[1..NUMFIELDS] OF STRING;
    PROFILE : PROFREC;
    FPROF   : FILE OF PROFREC;
    TODAY   : DATEREC;

  PROCEDURE CONTINUE;

  (*
   * STOPS OUTPUT DISPLAY AND WAITS
   * FOR USER RESPONSE.
   *)

  VAR
    CONT : STRING;

  BEGIN
    WRITELN;
    WRITE('TYPE <RETURN> TO CONTINUE.');
    READLN(CONT);
    WRITELN; WRITELN
  END;


  PROCEDURE INITTITLES;

  (*
   * STRINGS USED BOTH FOR THE REVISION
   * MENU AND FOR THE PROFILE OUTPUT
   * DISPLAY.
   *)

  BEGIN
    TITLE[1] := 'COMPANY NAME';
    TITLE[2] := 'STREET ADDRESS';
    TITLE[3] := 'CITY, STATE, ZIP';
    TITLE[4] := 'TELEPHONE #';
    TITLE[5] := 'FOUNDING DATE';
    TITLE[6] := 'HOURS PER PAY PERIOD';
    TITLE[7] := 'OVERTIME CALCULATION METHOD';
    TITLE[8] := 'NUMBER OF EMPLOYEES';
    TITLE[9] := 'NET PAY FLAG AMOUNT';
    TITLE[10] := 'EMPLOYEE EVALUATION DATES';
    TITLE[11] := 'ACCOUNT AGING REPORTING PERIODS';
    TITLE[12] := 'INVENTORY COSTING METHOD';
    TITLE[13] := 'DEPRECIATION METHOD';
    TITLE[14] := 'OLDEST ACQUISITION DATE'
  END;
```

Figure 10.4: Listing of Program SYSPROFILE (cont.)

```
PROCEDURE ININT(VAR VAL : INTEGER);

(*
 * INTEGER INPUT VALIDATION.
 *)

  VAR
    GARBAGE : STRING;

BEGIN
  GET(INPUT);
  IF INPUT^ IN ['0'..'9'] THEN
    READLN(VAL)
  ELSE
    BEGIN
      READLN(GARBAGE);
      WRITELN('*** REDO ');
      WRITE  ('       ? ');
      ININT(VAL)
    END
END;       (* ININT *)



PROCEDURE SLEEP(T : INTEGER);

(*
 * PAUSES A FEW SECONDS (DEPENDING ON VALUE
 * OF PARAMETER T) TO ALLOW USER TO READ A
 * MESSAGE ON THE SCREEN.
 *)

VAR
  I,
  J  : INTEGER;

BEGIN
  T := T * 10;
  FOR I := 1 TO T DO
    FOR J := 1 TO T DO
      BEGIN
      END
END;


PROCEDURE INPW(VAR ST : STRING);

(*
 * PASSWORD INPUT.
 *)

CONST
  MAX = 10;         (* MAXIMUM NUMBER OF LETTERS IN PASSWORD *)
  HIDECHR = '*';    (* CHARACTER THAT APPEARS ON THE SCREEN  *)
  SPACE = 32;       (* ASCII SPACE *)
  RETURN = 13;      (* ASCII CARRIAGE RETURN *)
```

Figure 10.4: Listing of Program SYSPROFILE (cont.)

```
VAR
  I,
  LEN : INTEGER;
  PW : ARRAY[1..MAX] OF CHAR;

BEGIN
  I := 1;
  LEN := MAX;

  WHILE I <= LEN DO
    BEGIN
      READ(KEYBOARD,PW[I]);
      IF (PW[I] IN [CHR(SPACE),CHR(RETURN)]) THEN
        LEN := I - 1
      ELSE
        BEGIN
          WRITE(HIDECHR);
          I := I + 1
        END
    END;

  WRITELN;
  ST := '           ';
  FOR I := 1 TO LEN DO
    ST[I] := PW[I];
  WHILE (POS(' ',ST) <> 0) DO
    DELETE(ST,POS(' ',ST),1)
END;  (* INPW *)

PROCEDURE CHANGEPW(VAR PW : STRING);

(*
 * INPUT DIALOGUE FOR CHANGING THE PASSWORD.
 *)

VAR
  NEWPW : ARRAY[1..3] OF STRING;
  I : INTEGER;
  OKPW : BOOLEAN;

BEGIN

  WRITELN;

  WRITELN('PLEASE TYPE NEW PASSWORD THREE TIMES:');
  WRITELN;
 REPEAT
   FOR I := 1 TO 3 DO
     BEGIN
       WRITE(I,'> ');
       INPW(NEWPW[I])
     END;

   (*
    * MAKE SURE ALL THREE PASSWORD ENTRIES
    * ARE THE SAME.
    *)
```

Figure 10.4: Listing of Program SYSPROFILE (cont.)

```
IF (NEWPW[1] = NEWPW[2]) AND (NEWPW[1] = NEWPW[3]) THEN
  OKPW := TRUE
ELSE
  BEGIN
    OKPW := FALSE;
    WRITELN;
    WRITELN('THESE THREE WORDS DID NOT MATCH.');
    WRITELN('PLEASE TRY AGAIN.');
    WRITELN
  END

UNTIL OKPW;

PW := NEWPW[1]

END;  (* CHANGEPW *)


PROCEDURE CHANGEFIELD(FIELD:INTEGER);

(*
 * REVISION OF PROFILE ITEMS.
 * CONTAINS ONE PROCEDURE FOR EACH ITEM.
 *)

PROCEDURE INNAME;

BEGIN
  WRITE('COMPANY NAME? ');
  READLN(PROFILE.NADDTEL[1])
END;


PROCEDURE INSTADDR;

BEGIN
  WRITE('STREET ADDRESS? ');
  READLN(PROFILE.NADDTEL[2]);
END;


PROCEDURE INCITST;

BEGIN
  WRITE('CITY, STATE <ZIP>? ');
  READLN(PROFILE.NADDTEL[3])
END;



PROCEDURE INTELE;

BEGIN
  WRITE('TELEPHONE NUMBER? ');
  READLN(PROFILE.NADDTEL[4])
END;
```

Figure 10.4: Listing of Program SYSPROFILE (cont.)

```
PROCEDURE INFOUND;

BEGIN
  WRITE('FOUNDING DATE OF COMPANY? ');
  INDATE(PROFILE.FOUNDED)
END;


PROCEDURE INPHRS;

BEGIN
  WRITE('HOW MANY HOURS PER PAY PERIOD? ');
  ININT(PROFILE.PERIODHRS)
END;


PROCEDURE INOVRTM;

  VAR
    OPTION : CHAR;

BEGIN
  WITH PROFILE DO
    BEGIN
      WRITELN('OVERTIME CALCULATION METHOD:');
      WRITELN;
      WRITELN('1) BASED ON 8 HOURS PER DAY.');
      WRITELN('2) BASED ON 40 HOURS PER WEEK.');
      WRITELN('3) BASED ON ',PERIODHRS,' PER PERIOD.');
      WRITELN;
      REPEAT
        WRITE('            ? ');
        READLN(OPTION)
      UNTIL (OPTION IN ['1'..'3']);
      OVRTIMEOPT := OPTION
    END
END;


PROCEDURE INNUMEMPS;

BEGIN
  WRITE('HOW MANY EMPLOYEES? ');
  ININT(PROFILE.NUMEMPS)
END;


PROCEDURE INNETFLAG;

BEGIN
  WRITE('UPPER-LIMIT NET SALARY AMOUNT? ');
  INDOLLAR(PROFILE.NETPAYFLAG)
END;


PROCEDURE INEMPEVAL;
```

Figure 10.4: Listing of Program SYSPROFILE (cont.)

```
  VAR
    OPTION : CHAR;

BEGIN
  WRITELN('EMPLOYEE EVALUATION DATE OPTIONS.');
  WRITELN;
  WRITELN('1) NEW EMPLOYEE EVALUATION AFTER 90 DAYS;');
  WRITELN('   REGULAR EVALUATIONS ANNUALLY.');
  WRITELN('2) REGULAR EVALUATIONS EVERY SIX MONTHS.');
  WRITELN('3) NO REGULAR EVALUATION DATES.');
  WRITELN;
  REPEAT
    WRITE('            ? ');
    READLN(OPTION)
  UNTIL (OPTION IN ['1'..'3']);
  PROFILE.EMPEVALOPT := OPTION
END;



PROCEDURE INACCAGE;

  VAR
    I : INTEGER;

BEGIN
  WRITELN('DAYS PER PERIOD FOR ');
  WRITELN('ACCOUNTS RECEIVABLE AGING REPORT?');
  WRITELN;
  FOR I := 1 TO 3 DO
    BEGIN
      WRITE('PERIOD #',I,'? ');
      ININT(PROFILE.ACCAGE[I])
    END
END;


PROCEDURE ININVCOST;

  VAR
    OPTION : CHAR;

BEGIN
  WRITELN('INVENTORY COSTING METHOD:');
  WRITELN('1) LIFO');
  WRITELN('2) FIFO');
  WRITELN('3) WEIGHTED AVERAGE');
  WRITELN;
  REPEAT
    WRITE('       ? ');
    READLN(OPTION)
  UNTIL (OPTION IN ['1'..'3']);
  PROFILE.INVENT := OPTION
END;


PROCEDURE INDEPMETH;
```

Figure 10.4: Listing of Program SYSPROFILE (cont.)

```
    VAR
      OPTION : CHAR;

  BEGIN
    WRITELN('FIXED ASSET DEPRECIATION METHOD:');
    WRITELN('1) STRAIGHT-LINE');
    WRITELN('2) SUM-OF-THE-YEARS''-DIGITS');
    WRITELN('3) DOUBLE-DECLINING-BALANCE');
    WRITELN('4) FIXED PERCENTAGE ON A DECLINING BASE');
    WRITELN;
    WRITELN;
    REPEAT
      WRITE('            ? ');
      READLN(OPTION)
    UNTIL (OPTION IN ['1'..'4']);
    PROFILE.DEPMETHOD := OPTION
  END;

  PROCEDURE INOLDEST;

  BEGIN
    WRITE('DATE OF OLDEST FIXED ASSET? ');
    INDATE(PROFILE.OLDEST)
  END;

  BEGIN (* CHANGEFIELD *)

    (*
     * CASE STATEMENT ALLOWS CHANGEFIELD TO
     * BE USED BY BOTH PROCEDURES REVISE AND
     * INITPROFILE.
     *)

    CASE FIELD OF
      1: INNAME;
      2: INSTADDR;
      3: INCITST;
      4: INTELE;
      5: INFOUND;
      6: INPHRS;
      7: INOVRTM;
      8: INNUMEMPS;
      9: INNETFLAG;
      10: INEMPEVAL;
      11: INACCAGE;
      12: ININVCOST;
      13: INDEPMETH;
      14: INOLDEST
    END     (* CASE *)
  END;      (* CHANGEFIELD *)


  PROCEDURE OUTPROF;

  (*
   * DISPLAYS THE ENTIRE PROFILE.
   *)
```

Figure 10.4: Listing of Program SYSPROFILE (cont.)

```
VAR
  I, J : INTEGER;
  STFLAG : STRING;

  PROCEDURE HEADING;
    BEGIN
      WRITELN('CURRENT STATUS OF SYSTEM PROFILE');
      WRITELN('------- ------ -- ------ -------');
      WRITELN;
      WRITE  (' ==> LAST PROFILE REVISION ON ');
      OUTDATE(PROFILE.LASTCHANGE);
      WRITELN;
      WRITELN;
    END;


BEGIN
  HEADING;
  FOR I := 1 TO NUMFIELDS DO
    BEGIN
      WRITELN(TITLE[I],':');
      FOR J := 1 TO LENGTH(TITLE[I])+1 DO
        WRITE('-');
      WRITELN;

      WITH PROFILE DO
        CASE I OF
          1,2,3,4 : WRITELN(NADDTEL[I]);
          5       : BEGIN
                      OUTDATE(FOUNDED);
                      WRITELN
                    END;
          6       : WRITELN(PERIODHRS,' HOURS');
          7       : CASE OVRTIMEOPT OF
                      '1':WRITELN('DAILY');
                      '2':WRITELN('WEEKLY');
                      '3':WRITELN('BY PAY PERIOD');
                    END;
          8       : WRITELN(NUMEMPS,' EMPLOYEES');
          9       : BEGIN
                      DOLLARFORM(NETPAYFLAG,STFLAG);
                      WRITELN('FLAG PAYROLL GREATER THAN ',STFLAG);
                    END;
          10      : CASE EMPEVALOPT OF
                      '1':WRITELN('FIRST QUARTER, THEN ANNUALLY');
                      '2':WRITELN('SEMI-ANNUALLY');
                      '3':WRITELN('NO REGULAR EVALUATION DATES')
                    END;
          11      : FOR J := 1 TO 3 DO
                      WRITELN('PERIOD ',J,': ',ACCAGE[J],' DAYS');
          12      : CASE INVENT OF
                      '1' : WRITELN('LIFO');
                      '2' : WRITELN('FIFO');
                      '3' : WRITELN('WEIGHTED AVERAGE')
                    END;
```

Figure 10.4: Listing of Program SYSPROFILE (cont.)

```
            13  : CASE DEPMETHOD OF
                    '1' : WRITELN('STRAIGHT LINE');
                    '2' : WRITELN('SUM OF YEARS'' DIGITS');
                    '3' : WRITELN('DOUBLE DECLINING BALANCE');
                    '4' : WRITELN('FIXED PERCENTAGE ON DECLINING BASE');
                  END;
            14  : BEGIN
                    OUTDATE(OLDEST);
                    WRITELN
                  END
          END; (* CASE *)

      WRITELN;

      (* SCREENFULL AT A TIME *)

      IF (I MOD 5 = 0) THEN
        CONTINUE;

    END   (* FOR I *)

  END;   (* OUTPROF *)



  PROCEDURE REVISE(VAR DONE : BOOLEAN);

  (*
   * CONDUCTS THE REVISION DIALOGUE.
   *)

    VAR
      I,
      WHICH  : INTEGER;

  BEGIN
    DONE := FALSE;

    (* DISPLAY THE MENU *)

    FOR I := 1 TO NUMFIELDS DO
      WRITELN(I, ') ', TITLE[I]);

    WRITELN;

    (* WAY OUT *)

    WRITELN(NUMFIELDS+1,') NO MORE REVISIONS');
    WRITELN;

    REPEAT
      WRITE('    REVISE WHICH ITEM? ');
      ININT(WHICH)
    UNTIL (WHICH >= 1) AND (WHICH <= NUMFIELDS+1);
    IF WHICH <= NUMFIELDS THEN
      BEGIN
        CLEARSCREEN;
```

Figure 10.4: Listing of Program SYSPROFILE (cont.)

```
      (* CHANGEFIELD READS THE ACTUAL REVISION *)

      CHANGEFIELD(WHICH);
      CLEARSCREEN
    END
  ELSE
    DONE := TRUE

END;      (* REVISE *)


PROCEDURE INITPROFILE;

(*
 * CREATES THE PROFILE.
 * CALLED ONLY IF THE PROFILE IS NOT FOUND ON LINE.
 *)

  VAR
    I : INTEGER;

BEGIN
  FOR I := 1 TO NUMFIELDS DO
    BEGIN
      CHANGEFIELD(I);
      WRITELN;
      WRITELN
    END
END;         (* INITPROFILE *)


FUNCTION NOPROFILE : BOOLEAN;

(*
 * LOOKS FOR THE PROFILE ON DISK.
 * IF IT'S THERE, OPENS IT; OTHERWISE
 * RETURNS A TRUE, INDICATING NO PROFILE.
 *)

BEGIN
  (*$I-*)

  RESET(FPROF,'#5:PROFILE');

  IF IORESULT = 0 THEN  (* PROFILE FOUND *)
    BEGIN
      NOPROFILE := FALSE;
      GET(FPROF);
      PROFILE := FPROF^
    END
  ELSE
    IF IORESULT = 10 THEN   (* PROFILE NOT FOUND *)
      NOPROFILE := TRUE
    ELSE     (* SOME OTHER I/O ERROR *)
```

Figure 10.4: Listing of Program SYSPROFILE (cont.)

```
        BEGIN
          WRITELN;
          WRITELN('I/O ERROR.');
          SLEEP(5);
          EXIT(PROGRAM)
        END
  (*$I+*)
END;          (* NOPROFILE *)

PROCEDURE NEWPROFILE;

(*
 * DRIVER ROUTINE FOR CREATION MODE
 *)

  VAR
    ANSWER : CHAR;

BEGIN
  WRITELN('NO PROFILE ON LINE.');
  WRITE('DO YOU WISH TO INITIALIZE PROFILE? ');
  READLN(ANSWER);
  IF ANSWER = 'Y' THEN
    BEGIN
      CLEARSCREEN;
      CHANGEPW(PROFILE.PASSWORD);
      PROFILE.LASTCHANGE := TODAY;
      CLEARSCREEN;
      INITPROFILE;
      CLEARSCREEN;
      OUTPROF;
      WRITELN;
      WRITE('DO YOU WANT TO SAVE THIS VERSION? ');
      READLN(ANSWER);
      IF ANSWER = 'Y' THEN
        BEGIN
          REWRITE(FPROF,'#5:PROFILE');
          FPROF^ := PROFILE;
          PUT(FPROF);
          CLOSE(FPROF,LOCK)
        END
    END
END;        (* NEWPROFILE *)


FUNCTION OKPW : BOOLEAN;

(*
 * PASSWORD VERIFICATION.
 *)

  VAR
    I : INTEGER;
    GOOD : BOOLEAN;
    USERPW : STRING;
```

Figure 10.4: Listing of Program SYSPROFILE (cont.)

```
BEGIN
  WRITELN('PLEASE TYPE PASSWORD TO ACCESS PROFILE.');
  WRITELN;
  I := 1;
  GOOD := FALSE;

  (*
   * ALLOWS THREE TRIES.
   *)

  WHILE (I <= 3) AND NOT GOOD DO
    BEGIN
      WRITE('    ===> ');
      INPW(USERPW);
      GOOD := USERPW = PROFILE.PASSWORD;
      I := I + 1
    END;

  WRITELN; WRITELN;

  IF GOOD THEN
    WRITELN('*** WELCOME TO THE SYSTEM PROFILE ***')
  ELSE
    WRITELN('*** WRONG PASSWORD!  ACCESS NOT GRANTED ***');

  SLEEP(5);

  OKPW := GOOD
END;                    (* OKPW *)


PROCEDURE ACCESSPROFILE;

(*
 * PROFILE ACCESS ROUTINE.
 * CALLED IF THE USER INPUTS THE
 * CORRECT PASSWORD.
 *)

  VAR
    ANS1,
    ANS2,
    ANS3  : CHAR;
    FINISHED : BOOLEAN;


BEGIN
  CLEARSCREEN;
  OUTPROF;    (* DISPLAY THE PROFILE *)
  CONTINUE;
  CLEARSCREEN;
  WRITELN;
  WRITE('REVISE ANY ITEM? ');
  READLN(ANS1);
  WRITELN;
```

Figure 10.4: Listing of Program SYSPROFILE (cont.)

```
      (* PROFILE REVISION *)

      IF ANS1 = 'Y' THEN
        REPEAT
          REVISE(FINISHED)
        UNTIL FINISHED;

      CLEARSCREEN;

      (* PASSWORD REVISION *)

      WRITE('CHANGE PASSWORD? ');
      READLN(ANS2);


      (*
       * SAVE CHANGES OR ABANDON THEM
       * AND KEEP OLD PROFILE.
       *)


      IF ANS2 = 'Y' THEN
        CHANGEPW(PROFILE.PASSWORD);

      CLEARSCREEN;

      IF (ANS1 = 'Y') OR (ANS2 = 'Y') THEN
        BEGIN
          WRITE('SAVE REVISIONS? ');
          READLN(ANS3);
          IF ANS3 = 'Y' THEN
            BEGIN
              PROFILE.LASTCHANGE := TODAY;
              SEEK(FPROF,0);
              FPROF^ := PROFILE;
              PUT(FPROF)
            END
        END;

    CLOSE(FPROF,LOCK)
  END;                    (* ACCESSPROFILE *)



  BEGIN (* MAIN PROGRAM *)

    INITTITLES;
    CLEARSCREEN;
    WRITELN('SYSTEM PROFILE UPDATE PROGRAM');
    WRITELN('====== ======= ====== =======');
    WRITELN;

    WRITE('TODAY''S DATE? ');
    INDATE(TODAY);
    WRITELN; WRITELN;
```

Figure 10.4: Listing of Program SYSPROFILE (cont.)

```
  IF NOPROFILE THEN
    NEWPROFILE
  ELSE
    IF OKPW THEN
      ACCESSPROFILE

END.    (* MAIN PROGRAM *)
```

Figure 10.4: Listing of Program SYSPROFILE (cont.)

Chapter 11

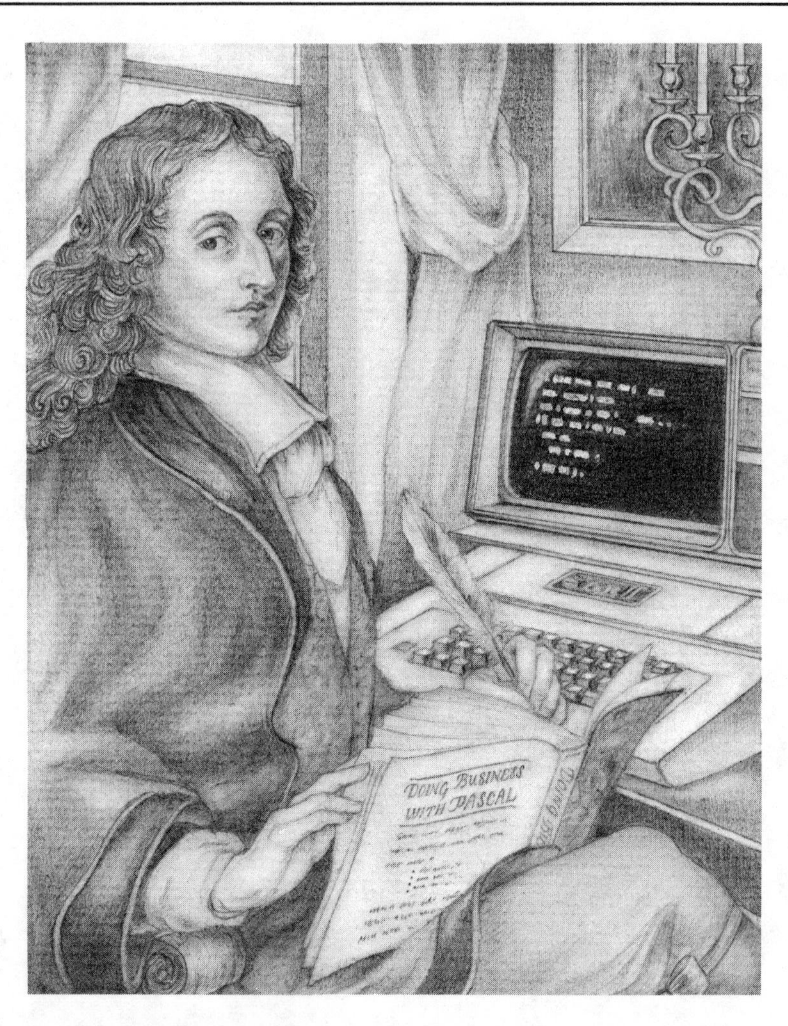

Time and Attendance System

THE APPLICATION

One of the more tedious tasks in any accounting department is calculating time-card information and summarizing that information for payroll input. Typically, the task is done manually. The application program presented in this chapter provides a mechanism for the automatic calculation of pay-period information, which would then be passed to the payroll application to calculate the proper deductions and produce the paychecks. All of the input here is done through carefully designed screens.

In an actual business system, two files would pass information to this application. First, the system profile would provide information on business policy. The number of hours in a standard pay period would be recorded in the system profile. Thus, if a company changed from a weekly pay cycle to a biweekly or even monthly cycle, that information would be changed within the profile and then would automatically update the processing within this program. The system profile could also include information on the method of overtime calculation: Is overtime based on daily hours or period hours? Are sick and holiday pay included in, or excluded from, overtime calculation? How soon after hiring date is the employee eligible for sick and holiday pay?

Second, the employee master file of the payroll application would supply the employee name. All the user of the time and attendance application should need to know is the employee number (including check-digit). When the name of that employee is automatically displayed on the screen, the user can verify that the time card itself has the same name.

The time and attendance application itself would pass its information to the payroll application, through a transaction record for each employee time card.

The assurance of correct time card calculation and correct application of company policy with regard to overtime is important to management. With few changes, the program could actually supply input for specific management reports. Work-hours could be assigned to a particular department or a particular project, and thus be used for input on cost or productivity reports. Overtime information would certainly be summarized for management, by department and perhaps also by project. Use of sick hours and of vacation and holiday hours could be monitored by management and used as supplemental information on productivity. Overall, the design of the time and attendance application as an information-gathering tool is quite important, for it will provide information for the reporting needs of the rest of the system, as well as eliminating the rather mundane task of calculating time card information.

THE SAMPLE RUN

This program presents a series of screens, carefully organized to allow easy input of employee hours during a given pay period. The sample run appears in Figure 11.1. We will look briefly at each screen.

The first screen shows the title of the program and prompts the user for the beginning and ending dates of the pay period. From these two dates, the program calculates the number of days in the period (including both the first and the last day), the day of the week (Monday through Friday) of each date, and the number of regular work hours in the period, based on a 40-hour work week. The second screen echoes all this information in the form of the following message:

```
ENTER EMPLOYEE HOURS FOR
THE 7-DAY PERIOD
BEGINNING MONDAY, MAY 3, 1982
AND ENDING SUNDAY, MAY 9, 1982.
```

and then gives the user the chance to confirm or reject the calculated number of regular hours:

```
TOTAL REGULAR HOURS IN PERIOD = 40.00?
```

In this case, if the number of regular hours is more or less than 40, the user may answer N, and then enter the correct number of hours. This number is important for the calculation of overtime hours.

Once the pay period has been established, the user may begin entering information about individual employees. Consequently, the next screen prompts for the name and identification number of an employee. The I.D. number must be four digits long, including the required check digit. The program verifies the number before continuing. All subsequent screens that involve this employee will now begin with an echo of the employee's number and name:

```
EMPLOYEE #1230
=========>CONRAD, RONALD P.
```

The input dialogue is menu-driven. The user may choose one of four different input categories, or, when the input is complete for a given employee, request a summary report:

```
MENU
====
        R(EGULAR TIME
        V(ACATION TIME
        H(OLIDAY TIME
        S(ICK TIME
        ------ ---
        D(ISPLAY REPORT (INPUT COMPLETE)
```

The menu appears on the screen after each input activity. Any input category on the menu may be chosen more than once, if the user wishes to input a category again for any reason. In that case, the previous input for the category is abandoned in favor of the new input.

In our sample run, the first input category chosen is *regular time*. For this category, the program prompts for two clock-in times and two clock-out times for each day of the pay period. The input might represent, for example, clocking in and out in the morning, breaking for lunch, and then clocking in and out in the evening:

```
MONDAY
-----

IN: 8
OUT: 12

IN: 13
OUT: 17
```

Notice that the program expects the clock times to be on a 24-hour basis. The user may either type a single integer representing the hour (as above), or two integers—in the form <HH> , <MM> —representing hours and minutes:

```
WEDNESDAY
---------

IN: 8,30
OUT: 12,30

IN: 13,30
OUT: 18,15
```

In either case, the program calculates the total number of hours worked, converts the hours and minutes to hours (in decimal fractions of two places) and displays the results for each day:

```
TOTAL TIME FOR WEDNESDAY = 8.75
```

The program can also calculate hours for work days that begin in the evening and end the following morning:

```
MONDAY
------

IN: 21,30
OUT: 1,30

IN: 2,30
OUT: 6,30

TOTAL TIME FOR MONDAY = 8.00
```

The other three input categories—*vacation time*, *holiday time*, and *sick time*—simply read the number of hours to be credited to the specific time category. For example:

```
SICK TIME
---------

HOURS? 12.5
```

Notice that this input, which may include decimal fractions of an hour, is not the same as the hour-and-minute clock-in and clock-out format of the *regular time* category.

When input for a given employee is complete, the user may type a menu choice of D to display the report for the employee. Before the report can be displayed, however, the program requires an additional piece of information affecting overtime calculations. Overtime hours may be computed on a daily basis or on a period basis; the user inputs a D or a P:

OVERTIME HOURS (IF ANY):
BASED ON D(AILY OR P(ERIOD TOTALS?

For daily overtime, the program allocates overtime hours for any day when the employee worked more than 8 hours. For period overtime, the program records overtime hours only if the total number of hours the employee worked during the period exceeds the number of regular working hours for the period.

After the user has indicated the overtime calculation method, the report is displayed. The report includes a line for each time category that applies to the employee, and a total line.

Finally, in order to continue running the program for additional employees, the user types a Y in response to the question:

ANOTHER EMPLOYEE?

```
EMPLOYEE TIME CARD REPORTS
======== ==== ==== =======

BEGINNING DATE OF PAY PERIOD: 5-3-82
=> ENDING DATE OF PAY PERIOD: 5-9-82
-----------------------------------------------


*****************************************

ENTER EMPLOYEE HOURS FOR
THE 7-DAY PERIOD
BEGINNING MONDAY, MAY 3, 1982
AND ENDING SUNDAY, MAY 9, 1982.

*****************************************

TOTAL REGULAR HOURS IN PERIOD =  40.00? Y

PRESS <RETURN> TO CONTINUE.
-----------------------------------------------
```

Figure 11.1: Sample Run of Time and Attendance System Program

```
EMPLOYEE'S NAME: CONRAD, RONALD P.
         I.D. #: 123-0
------------------------------------------------------


******************************************

EMPLOYEE #1230
========> CONRAD, RONALD P.

******************************************


MENU
====

      R(EGULAR TIME
      V(ACATION TIME
      H(OLIDAY TIME
      S(ICK TIME
      --------------
      D(ISPLAY REPORT (INPUT COMPLETE)

******************************************

                     ? R
------------------------------------------------------


******************************************

EMPLOYEE #1230
========> CONRAD, RONALD P.

******************************************


REGULAR TIME
======= ====


MONDAY
------

IN:  8
OUT: 12

IN:  13
OUT: 17


TOTAL TIME FOR MONDAY =  8.00
```

Figure 11.1: Sample Run of Time and Attendance System Program (cont.)

```
TUESDAY
-------

IN:  8
OUT: 12

IN:  13
OUT: 17

TOTAL TIME FOR TUESDAY =  8.00

WEDNESDAY
---------

IN:  8,30
OUT: 12,30

IN:  13,30
OUT: 17,30

TOTAL TIME FOR WEDNESDAY =  8.00

THURSDAY
--------

IN:  8,30
OUT: 12,30

IN:  13,30
OUT: 18,15

TOTAL TIME FOR THURSDAY =  8.75

FRIDAY
------

IN:  8
OUT: 12

IN:  13
OUT: 17

TOTAL TIME FOR FRIDAY =  8.00

SATURDAY
--------

IN:  8,30
OUT: 12

IN:  0
OUT: 0

TOTAL TIME FOR SATURDAY =  3.50
```

Figure 11.1: Sample Run of Time and Attendance System Program (cont.)

```
SUNDAY
------

IN:  0
OUT: 0

IN:  0
OUT: 0

TOTAL TIME FOR SUNDAY =  0.00

****************************************

EMPLOYEE #1230
========> CONRAD, RONALD P.

****************************************

MENU
====

      R(EGULAR TIME
      V(ACATION TIME
      H(OLIDAY TIME
      S(ICK TIME
      --------------
      D(ISPLAY REPORT (INPUT COMPLETE)

****************************************

                     ? D
---------------------------------------------------

****************************************

EMPLOYEE #1230
========> CONRAD, RONALD P.

****************************************

OVERTIME HOURS (IF ANY):
BASED ON D(AILY OR P(ERIOD TOTALS? P
---------------------------------------------------

****************************************

EMPLOYEE #1230
========> CONRAD, RONALD P.

****************************************

REGULAR TIME =    40.00

OVERTIME =       4.25


TOTAL TIME =      44.25
```

Figure 11.1: Sample Run of Time and Attendance System Program (cont.)

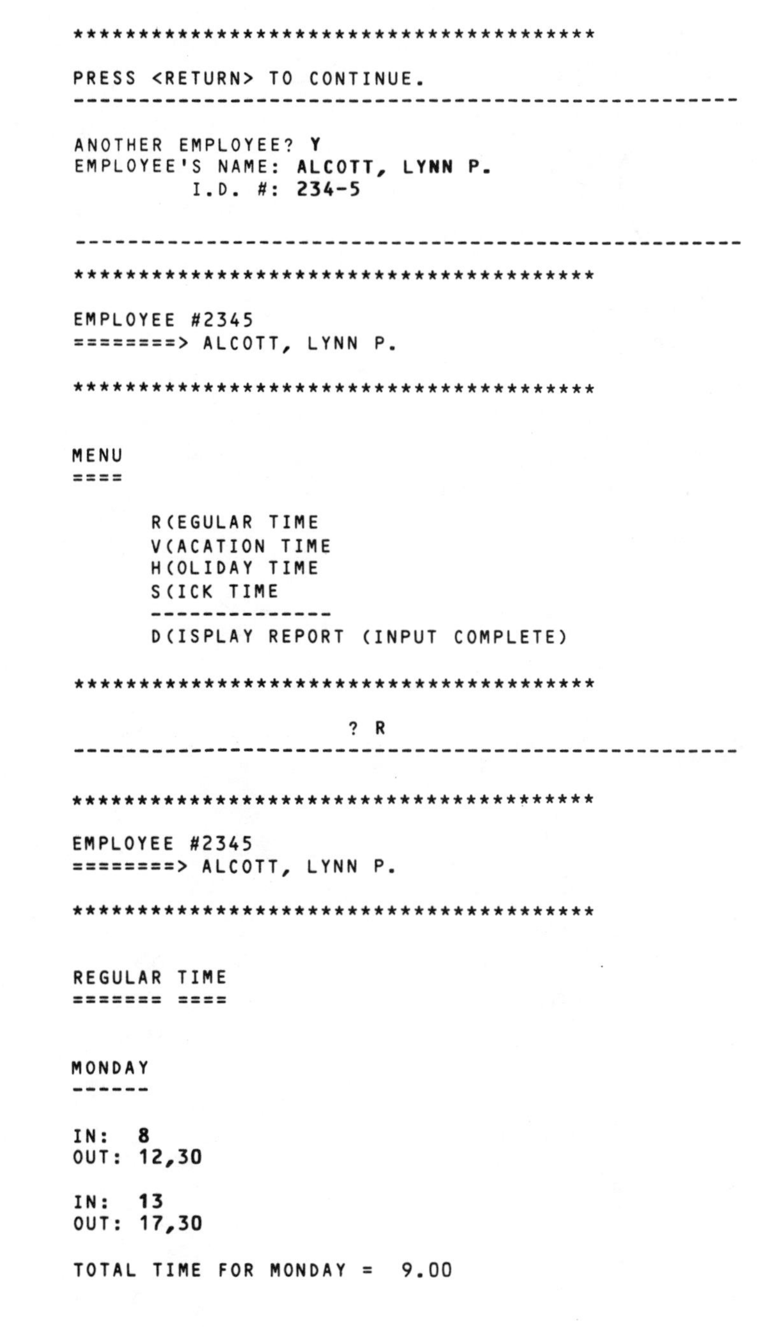

```
****************************************

PRESS <RETURN> TO CONTINUE.
---------------------------------------------------

ANOTHER EMPLOYEE? Y
EMPLOYEE'S NAME: ALCOTT, LYNN P.
         I.D. #: 234-5

---------------------------------------------------
****************************************

EMPLOYEE #2345
========> ALCOTT, LYNN P.

****************************************


MENU
====

      R(EGULAR TIME
      V(ACATION TIME
      H(OLIDAY TIME
      S(ICK TIME
      --------------
      D(ISPLAY REPORT (INPUT COMPLETE)

****************************************

                     ? R
---------------------------------------------------

****************************************

EMPLOYEE #2345
========> ALCOTT, LYNN P.

****************************************


REGULAR TIME
======= ====


MONDAY
------

IN:  8
OUT: 12,30

IN:  13
OUT: 17,30

TOTAL TIME FOR MONDAY =  9.00
```

Figure 11.1: Sample Run of Time and Attendance System Program (cont.)

```
TUESDAY
-------

IN:  0
OUT: 0

IN:  0
OUT: 0

TOTAL TIME FOR TUESDAY =  0.00

WEDNESDAY
---------

IN:  0
OUT: 0

IN:  13
OUT: 17

TOTAL TIME FOR WEDNESDAY =  4.00

THURSDAY
--------

IN:  8
OUT: 12

IN:  13
OUT: 17

TOTAL TIME FOR THURSDAY =  8.00

FRIDAY
------

IN:  8,30
OUT: 12,30

IN:  13
OUT: 17

TOTAL TIME FOR FRIDAY =  8.00

SATURDAY
--------

IN:  0
OUT: 0

IN:  0
OUT: 0

TOTAL TIME FOR SATURDAY =  0.00
```

Figure 11.1: Sample Run of Time and Attendance System Program (cont.)

```
SUNDAY
------

IN:  0
OUT: 0

IN:  0
OUT: 0

TOTAL TIME FOR SUNDAY =  0.00



****************************************

EMPLOYEE #2345
========> ALCOTT, LYNN P.

****************************************


MENU
====

      R(EGULAR TIME
      V(ACATION TIME
      H(OLIDAY TIME
      S(ICK TIME
      --------------
      D(ISPLAY REPORT (INPUT COMPLETE)

****************************************

                    ? S
---------------------------------------------------



****************************************

EMPLOYEE #2345
========> ALCOTT, LYNN P.

****************************************


SICK TIME
==== ====

HOURS? 12

SICK TIME =  12.00

PRESS <RETURN> TO CONTINUE.
---------------------------------------------------
```

Figure 11.1: Sample Run of Time and Attendance System Program (cont.)

```
****************************************

EMPLOYEE #2345
========> ALCOTT, LYNN P.

****************************************


MENU
====

      R(EGULAR TIME
      V(ACATION TIME
      H(OLIDAY TIME
      S(ICK TIME
      --------------
      D(ISPLAY REPORT (INPUT COMPLETE)

****************************************

                     ? D
---------------------------------------------------


****************************************

EMPLOYEE #2345
========> ALCOTT, LYNN P.

****************************************

OVERTIME HOURS (IF ANY):
BASED ON D(AILY OR P(ERIOD TOTALS? D
---------------------------------------------------


****************************************

EMPLOYEE #2345
========> ALCOTT, LYNN P.

****************************************

REGULAR TIME =    28.00

SICK TIME =       12.00
OVERTIME =       1.00


TOTAL TIME =      41.00

****************************************

PRESS <RETURN> TO CONTINUE.
---------------------------------------------------
```

Figure 11.1: Sample Run of Time and Attendance System Program (cont.)

THE PROGRAM

Program EMPHOURS consists primarily of specialized input and output routines. (It also uses the I/O routines from our three units; notice that the program begins with a USES statement). The input routines in EMPHOURS are INPERIOD, INEMPLOYEE, INHOURS, and INTIME. We will examine each one briefly.

Procedure INPERIOD is responsible for the first two screens of the program run—that is, the input of the period's beginning and ending dates, and the message displayed on the second screen. INPERIOD uses all three of the routines from DATEUNIT: INDATE for the date input, DATECONVERT to calculate the scalar date equivalents, and OUTDATE to display the dates in word format.

Perhaps the most interesting algorithm of procedure INPERIOD is the one that finds the day of the week of each date. This algorithm requires function LONGMODINT and the array DAYSTRING, both defined earlier in the program. Function LONGMODINT is modeled on a function of the same name that is used privately in the IMPLEMENTATION section of CHECKUNIT. Both versions of the function perform a MOD operation between a long integer and an integer; however, the two versions work on differently defined long integer types. Here, LONGMODINT receives a long integer of type DATELONG, the scalar date data structure.

The lines that calculate the days of the week for the first day and the last day of the pay period are:

```
FIRSTNUM := LONGMODINT(SCFIRST,7) + 1;
LASTNUM  := LONGMODINT(SCLAST,7) + 1;
```

The values of FIRSTNUM and LASTNUM are then used to access the correct day in the array DAYSTRING. The elements of DAYSTRING are initialized in procedure DAYINIT; DAYSTRING[1] is 'MONDAY'. The algorithm for finding the days is based on the fact that day 1 in the scalar date conversion, January 1, 1901, is a Tuesday. (Review DATEUNIT to confirm that this is true.) If day 1 were any other day of the week, we would have to adjust the order of the elements of DAYSTRING appropriately.

Procedure INEMPLOYEE reads the employee's name, and uses the procedures of CHECKUNIT to read and verify the identification number.

Procedures INHOURS and INTIME read two distinct forms of numerical input: a real number representing hours (INHOURS), and one or two integers representing a clock-in or clock-out time (INTIME). INHOURS employs a simple, quick technique for numerical input validation. It GETs the first character of the input and checks the implicitly defined buffer variable INPUT^ before reading the value into the real variable CATEGORY:

```
GET(INPUT);
IF INPUT^ IN ['0'..'9'] THEN
   READLN(CATEGORY)
```

If the first character is not a valid digit, then the input value is read into the string variable GARBAGE, and a recursive call to INHOURS is executed:

```
ELSE
   BEGIN
      READLN(GARBAGE);
      INHOURS(CATEGORY)
   END
```

This sequence avoids the run-time error that would result from trying to read a string input value into a variable of type REAL. INHOURS is called from procedure MENU for the input of VACATION, HOLIDAY and SICK hours.

Procedure INTIME, which is local to procedure REGTIME, is designed to read hour-and-minute inputs in several different formats. For example, all of the following are acceptable:

```
08
8
8,30
8,30
12,5
12,05
```

INTIME is similar in its logical complexity to INDOLLAR (in MONEYUNIT) and INVALUE (in CHECKUNIT). It begins by reading the input into the string variable TIME, and then performs its conversion in four steps:

1. It removes any spaces from the string TIME.
2. It looks for a comma separating hours from minutes; if there is no comma, it assumes that the value represents whole hours.

3. It converts the characters to the left of the comma to an integer value and assigns that value to the variable HOURS; likewise, the characters to the right of the comma are converted and assigned to MINS.
4. It returns the value expressed in hours—i.e., HOURS + MINS / 60.

Procedure REGTIME, which conducts the input dialogue for regular time, uses INTIME to read the clock-in and clock-out values. We have noted that REGTIME expects input based on a 24-hour clock. The reason for this is the following: if CLOCKOUT is less than CLOCKIN, then REGTIME assumes that the two clock times represent a night-to-morning work shift:

```
IF CLOCKOUT >= CLOCKIN THEN
   TEMPTIME := TEMPTIME +
               (CLOCKOUT - CLOCKIN)
ELSE
   TEMPTIME := TEMPTIME +
               ((24.0 - CLOCKIN) + CLOCKOUT);
```

The output procedures in program EMPHOURS are all quite simple. Procedure LINEOFSTARS prints a line of asterisks across the screen. Procedure CONTINUE provides a means of stopping the program run while the user examines a screenful of information. It displays the message:

```
PRESS <RETURN> TO CONTINUE.
```

and waits for a response from the keyboard. Procedure OUTEMPLOYEE provides a recurring echo of the employee's name and number at the top of each screen.

Finally, procedure REPORT produces the summary of the employee's hours, and displays it on the screen. REPORT has a local procedure, OVERCALC, which computes the overtime hours based on the user's instructions. When the daily regular hours are read in procedure REGTIME, they are stored in the array REGULAR. This leaves OVERCALC the choice of calculating either daily overtime hours or period overtime hours. If REGTIME had simply tallied up a total number of hours for the period, the daily figures would have been lost.

The main program section of EMPHOURS conducts the dialogue via a pair of nested WHILE loops. The inner loop makes repeated calls to MENU for a given employee; the outer loop continues iterating until all the employees have been accounted for. Notice that INITHOURS resets the global hour variables—REGULAR, REG, OVERTIME, VACATION, and SICK—to zero for each new employee. Program EMPHOURS is shown in Figure 11.2

```
(*$S++)
PROGRAM EMPHOURS;

USES
           (*$U MONEYUNIT.CODE*)
MONEYUNIT,
           (*$U CHECKUNIT.CODE*)
CHECKUNIT,
           (*$U DATEUNIT.CODE*)
DATEUNIT;

VAR
  REGULAR : ARRAY[1..31] OF REAL;     (* REGULAR TIME FOR EACH DAY *)
  DAYSTRING : ARRAY[1..7] OF STRING; (* INITIALIZED IN DAYINIT *)
  ANSWER : CHAR;
  FINISHED,
  OK        : BOOLEAN;
  FIRSTDAY,
  LASTDAY   : DATEREC;
  SCFIRST,
  SCLAST    : DATELONG;
  PERIOD,                     (* NUMBER OF DAYS IN PAY PERIOD *)
  FIRSTNUM,                   (* INDEX INTO DAYSTRING FOR FIRST DAY *)
  LASTNUM   : INTEGER;        (* INDEX INTO DAYSTRING FOR LAST DAY *)
  NUM       : LONG1;          (* EMPLOYEE I.D. NUMBER *)
  NAME      : STRING;
  REGTOT,                     (* THE HOUR VARIABLES *)
  REG,
  OVERTIME,
  VACATION,
  HOLIDAY,
  SICK      : REAL;

PROCEDURE LINEOFSTARS;

(*
 * PRINTS A LINE OF ASTERISKS
 * ACROSS THE SCREEN.
 *)

VAR
  I : INTEGER;
BEGIN
  FOR I := 1 TO 40 DO
    WRITE('*');
  WRITELN
END; (* LINEOFSTARS *)
```

Figure 11.2: Listing of Program EMPHOURS

```
FUNCTION LONGMODINT(L: DATELONG;
                    I: INTEGER): INTEGER;

(*
 * LONG INTEGER (OF TYPE DATELONG)
 * MOD INTEGER; USED TO FIND THE
 * DAY OF THE WEEK.
 *)

  BEGIN
    LONGMODINT := TRUNC(L - (L DIV I) * I)
  END;



PROCEDURE CONTINUE;

(*
 * STOPS PROGRAM TO ALLOW USER
 * TO EXAMINE A SCREEN OF INFORMATION.
 *)

VAR
  OKANS : STRING;

BEGIN
  WRITELN;
  WRITE('PRESS <RETURN> TO CONTINUE.');
  READLN(OKANS);
  WRITELN
END;




PROCEDURE DAYINIT;

(*
 * THE ARRAY DAYINIT IS USED IN
 * THE DAY-OF-THE-WEEK ALGORITHM.
 *)

BEGIN
  DAYSTRING[1] := 'MONDAY';
  DAYSTRING[2] := 'TUESDAY';
  DAYSTRING[3] := 'WEDNESDAY';
  DAYSTRING[4] := 'THURSDAY';
  DAYSTRING[5] := 'FRIDAY';
  DAYSTRING[6] := 'SATURDAY';
  DAYSTRING[7] := 'SUNDAY';
END;



PROCEDURE INHOURS (VAR CATEGORY: REAL);
```

Figure 11.2: Listing of Program EMPHOURS (cont.)

```
(*
 * USED FOR INPUT OF VACATION, HOLIDAY,
 * AND SICK TIME.
 *)

VAR
  GARBAGE : STRING;
  OKANS   : CHAR;

BEGIN
  WRITE('HOURS? ');
  GET(INPUT);
  IF INPUT^ IN ['0'..'9'] THEN
     READLN(CATEGORY)
  ELSE
    BEGIN
      READLN(GARBAGE);
      INHOURS(CATEGORY)
    END
END;    (* INHOURS *)

PROCEDURE INPERIOD;
  VAR
    ANS : CHAR;
BEGIN
  REPEAT

(* READ THE PERIOD INFORMATION *)

    OK := TRUE;
    WRITE('BEGINNING DATE OF PAY PERIOD: ');
    INDATE(FIRSTDAY);
    WRITE('=> ENDING DATE OF PAY PERIOD: ');
    INDATE(LASTDAY);
    DATECONVERT(FIRSTDAY,SCFIRST);
    DATECONVERT(LASTDAY,SCLAST);
    PERIOD := TRUNC(SCLAST - SCFIRST + 1);

 (*
  * THE PERIOD MUST NOT BE LONGER THAN 31 DAYS.
  * A SINGLE DAY IS OK.
  *)

    IF (PERIOD < 1) OR (PERIOD > 31) THEN
      BEGIN
        WRITELN;
        WRITELN('*** PLEASE RE-ENTER DATES');
        CONTINUE;
        CLEARSCREEN;
        OK := FALSE
      END
  UNTIL OK;

  CLEARSCREEN;
  LINEOFSTARS;
  WRITELN;
```

Figure 11.2: Listing of Program EMPHOURS (cont.)

```
(*
 * FIND THE DAY OF THE WEEK FOR THE FIRST
 * AND LAST DAY OF THE PERIOD.
 *)


  FIRSTNUM := LONGMODINT(SCFIRST,7) + 1;
  LASTNUM  := LONGMODINT(SCLAST,7) + 1;


(* DISPLAY THE PERIOD INFORMATION *)


  WRITELN('ENTER EMPLOYEE HOURS FOR');
  WRITELN('THE ', PERIOD, '-DAY PERIOD');
  WRITE('BEGINNING ', DAYSTRING[FIRSTNUM], ', ');
  OUTDATE(FIRSTDAY);
  WRITELN;
  WRITE('AND ENDING ', DAYSTRING[LASTNUM], ', ');
  OUTDATE(LASTDAY);
  WRITE('.');
  WRITELN;
  WRITELN;
  LINEOFSTARS;
  WRITELN;


(*
 * FIND THE NUMBER OF REGULAR HOURS IN THE PERIOD,
 * EITHER BY CALCULATION OR BY INPUT.
 *)


  REGTOT := (PERIOD DIV 7) * 40;
  WRITE('TOTAL REGULAR HOURS IN PERIOD = ', REGTOT:2:2, '? ');
  READLN(ANS);
  IF ANS <> 'Y' THEN
    INHOURS(REGTOT);
  CONTINUE;
  CLEARSCREEN
END; (* INPERIOD *)


PROCEDURE INEMPLOYEE;


(*
 * INPUT NAME AND I.D. NUMBER OF EMPLOYEE;
 * USES ROUTINES FROM CHECKUNIT.
 *)
```

Figure 11.2: Listing of Program EMPHOURS (cont.)

```
VAR
  CHECK : BOOLEAN;

BEGIN
  WRITE('EMPLOYEE''S NAME: ');
  READLN(NAME);
  WRITE('          I.D. #: ');
  REPEAT
    INVALUE(NUM, 4, CHECK);
    IF NOT CHECK THEN
      BEGIN
        WRITELN('MUST INCLUDE CHECK DIGIT.');
        WRITE('          I.D. #: ')
      END
    ELSE
      IF NOT (VERIFYCHECK(NUM)) THEN
        BEGIN
          WRITELN('CHECK DIGIT INCORRECT.');
          WRITE('          I.D. #: ');
          CHECK := FALSE
        END
  UNTIL CHECK;
  CLEARSCREEN
END; (* INEMPLOYEE *)



PROCEDURE OUTEMPLOYEE;


(*
 * ECHO THE EMPLOYEE INFORMATION.
 *)



BEGIN
  LINEOFSTARS;
  WRITELN;
  WRITELN('EMPLOYEE #',NUM);
  WRITELN('========> ',NAME);
  WRITELN;
  LINEOFSTARS;
  WRITELN
END;  (* OUTEMPLOYEE *)



PROCEDURE REGTIME;



(*
 * REGTIME CONDUCTS THE INPUT DIALOGUE FOR
 * REGULAR TIME.
 *)
```

Figure 11.2: Listing of Program EMPHOURS (cont.)

```
  VAR
    I,
    J,
    K,
    DAY : INTEGER;
    TEMPTIME,
    CLOCKIN,
    CLOCKOUT : REAL;

PROCEDURE INTIME(VAR REALTIME : REAL);

CONST
  BLANK = ' ';
  COMMA = ',';
  BELL  = 7;

VAR
  HOURS,
  MINS,
  BPOS,
  L,
  CPOS,
  I       : INTEGER;

  TIME    : STRING;
  GOOD    : BOOLEAN;

BEGIN

REPEAT
  HOURS := 0;
  MINS  := 0;

  READLN(TIME);

  (* ELIMINATE ALL BLANKS FROM THE STRING *)

  BPOS := POS(BLANK,TIME);

  WHILE BPOS <> 0 DO
    BEGIN
      DELETE(TIME,BPOS,1);
      BPOS := POS(BLANK,TIME)
    END;

  L := LENGTH(TIME);

  GOOD := (L > 0) AND (L <= 5);

  IF GOOD THEN
    BEGIN
      (* FIND THE COMMA IF THERE IS ONE *)
      CPOS := POS(COMMA,TIME);
      IF CPOS = 0 THEN
        IF L <= 2 THEN
          BEGIN
```

Figure 11.2: Listing of Program EMPHOURS (cont.)

```
            (*
             * IF THERE IS NO COMMA, ASSUME THE
             * INPUT IS AN EVEN HOUR.
             *)
            I := 1;
            WHILE (GOOD AND (I <= L)) DO
              IF TIME[I] IN ['0'..'9'] THEN
                BEGIN
                   HOURS := HOURS * 10 + VALUE(TIME[I]);
                   I := I + 1
                 END
               ELSE
                 GOOD := FALSE
           END
         ELSE
           GOOD := FALSE
       ELSE
         (*
          * IF THERE'S A COMMA IN TIME, DIVIDE THE
          * TIME STRING BETWEEN HOURS AND MINUTES.
          *)
         BEGIN
           I := 1;
           WHILE (GOOD AND (I < CPOS)) DO
             IF TIME[I] IN ['0'..'9'] THEN
               BEGIN
                 HOURS := HOURS * 10 + VALUE(TIME[I]);
                 I := I + 1
               END
             ELSE
               GOOD := FALSE;
           I := CPOS + 1;
           WHILE (GOOD AND (I <= L)) DO
             IF TIME [I] IN ['0'..'9'] THEN
               BEGIN
                 MINS := MINS * 10 + VALUE(TIME[I]);
                 I := I + 1
               END
             ELSE
               GOOD := FALSE;
         END
     END;

     GOOD := GOOD AND (HOURS < 24) AND (MINS < 60);

     (* CONVERT TO THE DECIMAL FORM OF REALTIME *)
     IF GOOD THEN
       BEGIN
         REALTIME := HOURS; (* TYPE CONVERSION *)
         REALTIME := (ROUND((REALTIME + MINS / 60)*100))/100
       END
     ELSE
       BEGIN
         WRITE(CHR(BELL));
         WRITELN('*** REDO');
         WRITE  ('? ')
       END
```

Figure 11.2: Listing of Program EMPHOURS (cont.)

```
    UNTIL GOOD

    END;  (* INTIME *)



    BEGIN (* REGTIME *)
      FOR I := 1 TO PERIOD DO
        BEGIN
          WRITELN;
          (* DISPLAY THE DAY OF THE WEEK *)
          DAY := (FIRSTNUM + I - 2) MOD 7 + 1;
          WRITELN(DAYSTRING[DAY]);
          FOR K := 1 TO LENGTH(DAYSTRING[DAY]) DO
            WRITE('-');
          WRITELN;
          WRITELN;
          TEMPTIME := 0.0;
          (*
           * TWO CLOCK-IN ENTRIES, AND
           * TWO CLOCK-OUT ENTRIES.
           *)
          FOR J := 1 TO 2 DO
            BEGIN
              WRITE('IN:  ');
              INTIME(CLOCKIN);
              WRITE('OUT: ');
              INTIME(CLOCKOUT);
              IF CLOCKOUT >= CLOCKIN THEN   (* DAY SHIFT *)
                TEMPTIME := TEMPTIME +
                            (CLOCKOUT - CLOCKIN)
              ELSE  (* NIGHT SHIFT *)
                TEMPTIME := TEMPTIME +
                            ((24.0 - CLOCKIN) + CLOCKOUT);
              WRITELN
            END;
            (* DISPLAY THE TOTAL HOURS FOR THE DAY *)
            WRITELN('TOTAL TIME FOR ',DAYSTRING[DAY], ' = ', TEMPTIME:2:2);
            WRITELN;
            WRITELN;
            REGULAR[I] := TEMPTIME
          END;

    END;  (* REGTIME *)



    PROCEDURE MENU (VAR DONE : BOOLEAN);


    VAR
      OK : BOOLEAN;
      MENUCHOICE : CHAR;
```

Figure 11.2: Listing of Program EMPHOURS (cont.)

```
BEGIN
  DONE := FALSE;
  OUTEMPLOYEE;
  WRITELN;
  WRITELN('MENU');
  WRITELN('====');
  WRITELN;
  WRITELN('      R(EGULAR TIME');
  WRITELN('      V(ACATION TIME');
  WRITELN('      H(OLIDAY TIME');
  WRITELN('      S(ICK TIME');
  WRITELN('      --------------');
  WRITELN('      D(ISPLAY REPORT (INPUT COMPLETE)');
  WRITELN;
  LINEOFSTARS;
  WRITELN;
  REPEAT
    WRITE('                           ? ');
    READLN(MENUCHOICE);
  UNTIL (MENUCHOICE IN ['R','V','H','S','D']);



  CASE MENUCHOICE OF
    'R' : BEGIN
            CLEARSCREEN;
            OUTEMPLOYEE;
            WRITELN;
            WRITELN('REGULAR TIME');
            WRITELN('======= ====');
            WRITELN;
            REGTIME;
            CLEARSCREEN
          END;



    'V' : BEGIN
            CLEARSCREEN;
            OUTEMPLOYEE;
            WRITELN;
            WRITELN('VACATION TIME');
            WRITELN('======== ====');
            WRITELN;
            INHOURS(VACATION);
            WRITELN;
            WRITELN('VACATION TIME = ', VACATION:2:2);
            CONTINUE;
            CLEARSCREEN
          END;
```

Figure 11.2: Listing of Program EMPHOURS (cont.)

```
     'H' : BEGIN
              CLEARSCREEN;
              OUTEMPLOYEE;
              WRITELN;
              WRITELN('HOLIDAY TIME');
              WRITELN('======= ====');
              WRITELN;
              INHOURS(HOLIDAY);
              WRITELN;
              WRITELN('HOLIDAY TIME = ', HOLIDAY:2:2);
              CONTINUE;
              CLEARSCREEN
           END;



     'S' : BEGIN
              CLEARSCREEN;
              OUTEMPLOYEE;
              WRITELN;
              WRITELN('SICK TIME');
              WRITELN('==== ====');
              WRITELN;
              INHOURS(SICK);
              WRITELN;
              WRITELN('SICK TIME = ', SICK:2:2);
              CONTINUE;
              CLEARSCREEN
           END;

     'D' : BEGIN
              DONE := TRUE;
              CLEARSCREEN
           END;
  END

END;  (* MENU *)



PROCEDURE INITHOURS;
(*
 * INITIALIZES ALL THE HOUR VARIABLES
 * TO ZERO FOR EACH NEW EMPLOYEE.
 *)




VAR
  I : INTEGER;
```

Figure 11.2: Listing of Program EMPHOURS (cont.)

```
BEGIN
  FOR I := 1 TO 31 DO
    REGULAR[I] := 0.0;
  REG := 0;
  OVERTIME := 0;
  VACATION := 0;
  HOLIDAY := 0;
  SICK := 0
END;  (* INITHOURS *)


PROCEDURE REPORT;

PROCEDURE OVERCALC;

  VAR
    OVERANS : CHAR;
    I : INTEGER;
    TOTTIME : REAL;

  BEGIN
    WRITELN('OVERTIME HOURS (IF ANY):');
    REPEAT
      WRITE('BASED ON D(AILY OR P(ERIOD TOTALS? ');
      READLN(OVERANS)
    UNTIL OVERANS IN ['D','P'];

    IF OVERANS = 'D' THEN
      FOR I := 1 TO PERIOD DO
        IF REGULAR[I] > 8.0 THEN
          BEGIN
            REG := REG + 8.0;
            OVERTIME := OVERTIME + (REGULAR[I] - 8)
          END
        ELSE
          REG := REG + REGULAR[I]
    ELSE (* IF OVERANS = 'P' *)
      BEGIN
        FOR I := 1 TO PERIOD DO
          REG := REG + REGULAR[I];
        TOTTIME := REG + VACATION + HOLIDAY + SICK;
        IF TOTTIME > REGTOT THEN
          BEGIN
            OVERTIME := REG - REGTOT;
            REG := REGTOT
          END
      END
  END; (* OVERCALC *)

BEGIN (* REPORT *)
  OUTEMPLOYEE;
  OVERCALC;
  CLEARSCREEN;
```

Figure 11.2: Listing of Program EMPHOURS (cont.)

```
    OUTEMPLOYEE;
    WRITELN('REGULAR TIME =     ', REG:2:2);
    WRITELN;
    IF SICK <> 0.0 THEN
      WRITELN('SICK TIME =        ',SICK:2:2);
    IF HOLIDAY <> 0.0 THEN
      WRITELN('HOLIDAY TIME =     ',HOLIDAY:2:2);
    IF VACATION <> 0.0 THEN
      WRITELN('VACATION TIME =    ',VACATION:2:2);
    IF OVERTIME <> 0.0 THEN
      WRITELN('OVERTIME =         ',OVERTIME:2:2);
    WRITELN;
    WRITELN;
    WRITELN('TOTAL TIME =       ',(REG+SICK+VACATION+HOLIDAY+OVERTIME):2:2);
    WRITELN;
    LINEOFSTARS;

    CONTINUE;
    CLEARSCREEN
  END; (* REPORT *)



  BEGIN (* MAIN PROGRAM *)
    DAYINIT;
    CLEARSCREEN;
    WRITELN;
    WRITELN('EMPLOYEE TIME CARD REPORTS');
    WRITELN('======== ==== ==== =======');
    WRITELN;
    INPERIOD;

    WHILE ANSWER <> 'N' DO
      BEGIN
        INEMPLOYEE;
        INITHOURS;
        FINISHED := FALSE;
        WHILE NOT FINISHED DO
          MENU(FINISHED);
        REPORT;
        WRITE('ANOTHER EMPLOYEE? ');
        READLN(ANSWER);
      END
  END. (* MAIN PROGRAM *)
```

Figure 11.2: Listing of Program EMPHOURS (cont.)

Chapter 12

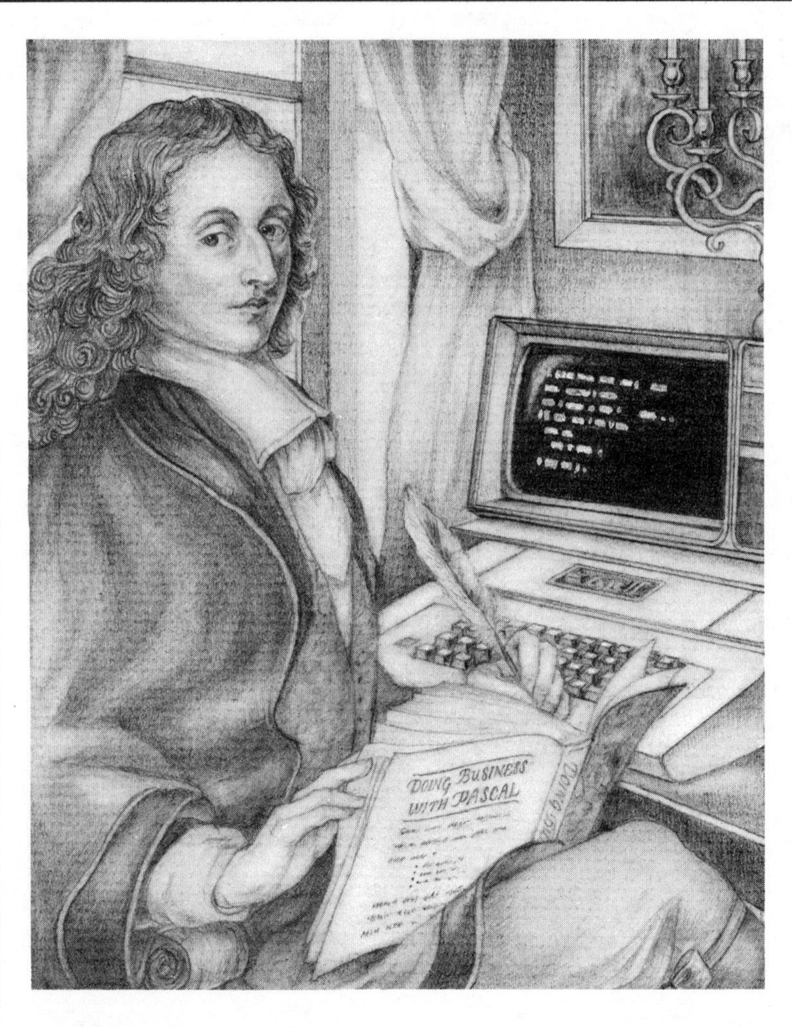

Employee Evaluation Dates

THE APPLICATION

The scheduling of employee evaluations is strictly a personnel department activity, and is therefore often left out of computer-based business systems. But it is a fairly simple application to implement, as the information required for the program itself would be supplied from the payroll programs. In order to illustrate the reporting in a run-time environment, the application given here requires manual input of data; but, as in other applications, the business system would naturally provide most of that input.

Refer again to the system organization chart (Figure 1.3). Included in the personnel master file would be fields for the employee name (actually referenced from the payroll master file, as indicated in Chapter 2), hiring date, and last evaluation date. Included in the system profile would be detailed information on the company's evaluation policies. While we have included the specific policy information in the program in our example, this kind of information would ordinarily be part of the profile itself. At run-time, the application would access the system profile for the specific policy information, and then search through the entire personnel master file to create the report.

Several aspects of this application program illustrate system design criteria discussed in Part I. First, the report can be used as an exception report, in that overdue evaluations are clearly flagged, and appear at the beginning of the report. Thus, it meets one of the prime requirements of management-level reporting, that the manager's attention be directed to exceptions, rather than masses of data. Second, it is a report that might typically be given on demand only. Every month, the personnel department of the company would request the report for the next 30 days of required evaluations.

With a full business system implemented, the only information that would be input by the system user is the request for the report and the range of dates that the report is to cover. The application program itself would then complete the process of gathering information from the various master files. Note that the program would have a read-only access to the files. No changes could be made to any data files from this application.

A full personnel subsystem would include many other applications. For example, reports could be produced containing position control information for use in recruiting and hiring, and summarizing employee turnover rates by job category or by department. The system design provides the required information through the various master files; all that must be constructed is the application program to access the information and write the report.

THE SAMPLE RUN

This program implements a specific policy for employee evaluation dates, which can be summarized as follows:

1. Each employee must be evaluated annually, on or near the anniversary of his or her hiring date. The evaluation may occur as early as 30 days before or as late as 30 days after the anniversary.

2. New employees must also receive a first-quarter evaluation on or near the 90th day of employment.

The program thus produces a schedule of evaluations for a given list of employees. To produce the schedule, the program requires two dates for each employee on the list: the date the employee was hired, and the date of the employee's last evaluation. If these two dates are the same, the program assumes that the employee is new and has not yet received a first-quarter evaluation.

In an actual business application, these dates would be stored in the employee master file, and the program would access this file for the information. For the purposes of illustration, however, the present version of this program simply reads information input from the keyboard for 20 employees, and then produces a schedule based on this input.

The sample run of the program, shown in Figure 12.1, contains two distinct parts. The first part is the input dialogue. The user types in the current date, and then a name and two dates for each of 20 employees. (Notice that several new employees in this list have not been evaluated yet.)

The second part of the sample run is the output produced: the schedule. The program prints a three-line message for each employee, including the date hired, the date of the last evaluation, and a description of the next evaluation:

```
BARNES,E.
------   HIRED JUNE 25, 1980.
      LAST EVALUATION HELD ON JULY 1, 1981.
      2-YEAR EVALUATION DUE IN 4 WEEKS.
```

Overdue evaluations are flagged with an arrow:

```
ADDISON,A.
------   HIRED MAY 1, 1980.
      LAST EVALUATION HELD ON MAY 4, 1981.
      2-YEAR EVALUATION OVERDUE BY 3 WEEKS. <===
```

The program presents these messages in the order of urgency: the overdue evaluations come first; then the evaluations that are only days away; and finally those that are still weeks or months away. (The names were originally entered in alphabetical order.) This list thus provides the manager or personnel officer with a conveniently organized schedule of evaluations for the year ahead.

```
EMPLOYEE EVALUATION SCHEDULING
-------- ---------- ----------

TODAY'S DATE? 5-26-82


EMPLOYEE'S NAME?          ABELARD,J.
DATE HIRED?               3-20-75
LAST EVALUATION DATE
(OR DATE HIRED)?          4-2-82

EMPLOYEE'S NAME?          ADDISON,A.
DATE HIRED?               5-1-80
LAST EVALUATION DATE
(OR DATE HIRED)?          5-4-81

EMPLOYEE'S NAME?          ALEXANDER,H.
DATE HIRED?               3-22-82
LAST EVALUATION DATE
(OR DATE HIRED)?          3-22-82
```

Figure 12.1: Sample Run of Employee Evaluation Program

```
EMPLOYEE'S NAME?           AMIS,S.
DATE HIRED?                2-15-82
LAST EVALUATION DATE
(OR DATE HIRED)?           2-15-82

EMPLOYEE'S NAME?           ANDERSON,K.
DATE HIRED?                5-22-72
LAST EVALUATION DATE
(OR DATE HIRED)?           5-27-81

EMPLOYEE'S NAME?           BACH,D.
DATE HIRED?                1-12-81
LAST EVALUATION DATE
(OR DATE HIRED)?           1-2-82

EMPLOYEE'S NAME?           BARNES,E.
DATE HIRED?                6-25-80
LAST EVALUATION DATE
(OR DATE HIRED)?           7-1-81

EMPLOYEE'S NAME?           BAUDELAIRE,R.
DATE HIRED?                2-27-78
LAST EVALUATION DATE
(OR DATE HIRED)?           3-5-82

EMPLOYEE'S NAME?           BECKETT,D.
DATE HIRED?                5-1-82
LAST EVALUATION DATE
(OR DATE HIRED)?           5-1-82

EMPLOYEE'S NAME?           BENN,S.
DATE HIRED?                9-5-73
LAST EVALUATION DATE
(OR DATE HIRED)?           9-10-81

EMPLOYEE'S NAME?           BERLIN,L.
DATE HIRED?                1-30-79
LAST EVALUATION DATE
(OR DATE HIRED)?           2-10-82

EMPLOYEE'S NAME?           BERRIGAN,B.
DATE HIRED?                5-26-81
LAST EVALUATION DATE
(OR DATE HIRED)?           8-24-81

EMPLOYEE'S NAME?           BLOCH,J.
DATE HIRED?                5-24-82
LAST EVALUATION DATE
(OR DATE HIRED)?           5-24-82

EMPLOYEE'S NAME?           BRONTE,E.
DATE HIRED?                6-15-76
LAST EVALUATION DATE
(OR DATE HIRED)?           6-14-81
```

Figure 12.1: Sample Run of Employee Evaluation Program (cont.)

```
EMPLOYEE'S NAME?         BROWNING,E.
DATE HIRED?              3-2-81
LAST EVALUATION DATE
(OR DATE HIRED)?         3-26-82

EMPLOYEE'S NAME?         CAEN,B.
DATE HIRED?              7-7-80
LAST EVALUATION DATE
(OR DATE HIRED)?         7-15-81

EMPLOYEE'S NAME?         CASANOVA,C.
DATE HIRED?              5-1-80
LAST EVALUATION DATE
(OR DATE HIRED)?         5-5-81

EMPLOYEE'S NAME?         CAVAFY,E.
DATE HIRED?              5-5-81
LAST EVALUATION DATE
(OR DATE HIRED)?         8-7-81

EMPLOYEE'S NAME?         CROSBY,M.
DATE HIRED?              3-8-82
LAST EVALUATION DATE
(OR DATE HIRED)?         5-24-82

EMPLOYEE'S NAME?         DANTE,G.
DATE HIRED?              8-6-71
LAST EVALUATION DATE
(OR DATE HIRED)?         8-15-81

-------------------------------------------


          EVALUATION DATES
          ========== =====



ADDISON,A.
----------     HIRED MAY 1, 1980.
     LAST EVALUATION HELD ON MAY 4, 1981.
     2-YEAR EVALUATION OVERDUE BY 3 WEEKS.  <===


CASANOVA,C.
-----------     HIRED MAY 1, 1980.
     LAST EVALUATION HELD ON MAY 5, 1981.
     2-YEAR EVALUATION OVERDUE BY 3 WEEKS.  <===


CAVAFY,E.
---------     HIRED MAY 5, 1981.
     LAST EVALUATION HELD ON AUGUST 7, 1981.
     1-YEAR EVALUATION OVERDUE BY 3 WEEKS.  <===
```

Figure 12.1: Sample Run of Employee Evaluation Program (cont.)

```
AMIS,S.
-------      HIRED FEBRUARY 15, 1982.
     NEW EMPLOYEE:
     FIRST-QUARTER EVALUATION OVERDUE BY 10 DAYS. <===


ANDERSON,K.
-----------      HIRED MAY 22, 1972.
     LAST EVALUATION HELD ON MAY 27, 1981.
     10-YEAR EVALUATION OVERDUE BY 6 DAYS.  <===


BERRIGAN,B.
-----------      HIRED MAY 26, 1981.
     LAST EVALUATION HELD ON AUGUST 24, 1981.
     1-YEAR EVALUATION OVERDUE BY TODAY.  <===


BRONTE,E.
---------      HIRED JUNE 15, 1976.
     LAST EVALUATION HELD ON JUNE 14, 1981.
     6-YEAR EVALUATION DUE IN 19 DAYS.


ALEXANDER,H.
------------      HIRED MARCH 22, 1982.
     NEW EMPLOYEE:
     FIRST-QUARTER EVALUATION DUE IN 3 WEEKS.


BARNES,E.
---------      HIRED JUNE 25, 1980.
     LAST EVALUATION HELD ON JULY 1, 1981.
     2-YEAR EVALUATION DUE IN 4 WEEKS.


CAEN,B.
-------      HIRED JULY 7, 1980.
     LAST EVALUATION HELD ON JULY 15, 1981.
     2-YEAR EVALUATION DUE IN 6 WEEKS.


BECKETT,D.
----------      HIRED MAY 1, 1982.
     NEW EMPLOYEE:
     FIRST-QUARTER EVALUATION DUE IN 9 WEEKS.


DANTE,G.
--------      HIRED AUGUST 6, 1971.
     LAST EVALUATION HELD ON AUGUST 15, 1981.
     11-YEAR EVALUATION DUE IN 9 WEEKS.


BLOCH,J.
--------      HIRED MAY 24, 1982.
     NEW EMPLOYEE:
     FIRST-QUARTER EVALUATION DUE IN 12 WEEKS.
```

Figure 12.1: Sample Run of Employee Evaluation Program (cont.)

```
BENN,S.
-------      HIRED SEPTEMBER 5, 1973.
     LAST EVALUATION HELD ON SEPTEMBER 10, 1981.
     9-YEAR EVALUATION DUE IN 14 WEEKS.


BACH,D.
-------      HIRED JANUARY 12, 1981.
     LAST EVALUATION HELD ON JANUARY 2, 1982.
     2-YEAR EVALUATION DUE IN 7 MONTHS.


BERLIN,L.
---------      HIRED JANUARY 30, 1979.
     LAST EVALUATION HELD ON FEBRUARY 10, 1982.
     4-YEAR EVALUATION DUE IN 8 MONTHS.


BAUDELAIRE,R.
-------------      HIRED FEBRUARY 27, 1978.
     LAST EVALUATION HELD ON MARCH 5, 1982.
     5-YEAR EVALUATION DUE IN 9 MONTHS.


BROWNING,E.
-----------      HIRED MARCH 2, 1981.
     LAST EVALUATION HELD ON MARCH 26, 1982.
     2-YEAR EVALUATION DUE IN 9 MONTHS.


CROSBY,M.
---------      HIRED MARCH 8, 1982.
     LAST EVALUATION HELD ON MAY 24, 1982.
     1-YEAR EVALUATION DUE IN 9 MONTHS.


ABELARD,J.
----------      HIRED MARCH 20, 1975.
     LAST EVALUATION HELD ON APRIL 2, 1982.
     8-YEAR EVALUATION DUE IN 9 MONTHS.
```

Figure 12.1: Sample Run of Employee Evaluation Program (cont.)

THE PROGRAM

The central data structure of program EMPEVAL (which appears in Figure 12.2) is the employee record:

```
EMPLOYEE = RECORD
   NAME : STRING[15];
   HIRED,
   LASTEVAL : DATEREC;
   EVALDUE : INTEGER
END;
```

The two dates, HIRED and LASTEVAL, are of type DATEREC (defined in DATEUNIT). EVALDUE, calculated by the program, represents the number of days until the next evaluation is due. (We will see that EVALDUE is negative if the evaluation is overdue.) EMPARY is a global array of employee records:

```
TYPE
  ARY = ARRAY[1..NUMEMPLOYEES] OF EMPLOYEE;
  VAR
    EMPARY : ARY;
```

Program EMPEVAL contains three important subroutines: SHELLSORT, INEMP, and OUTEMP. SHELLSORT is a version of the sort routine we developed in Chapter 6. Tailored to the problem at hand, this version uses the field EVALDUE as the key for sorting EMPARY:

```
IF A[J].EVALDUE > A[I].EVALDUE THEN . . .
```

Procedure INEMP reads the input information for each employee record, and then computes a value for the field EVALDUE. Determining this value involves several intermediate calculations. First, both dates are converted to their scalar equivalents:

```
DATECONVERT(HIRED,SCHIRED);
DATECONVERT(LASTEVAL,SCLASTEVAL);
```

Then, three integer values are determined from these two scalar dates (along with SCTODAY, the scalar value of today's date, which was input and converted in the main program section): First, the number of days the employee has been on the job:

```
DAYSONJOB : = TRUNC(SCTODAY - SCHIRED);
```

then the number of days since the employee's last evaluation:

```
EVALGAP : = TRUNC(SCTODAY - SCLASTEVAL);
```

and finally the number of days since the employee's last anniversary:

```
THISYEAR : = DAYSONJOB MOD 365;
```

Given these values, a pair of IF statements determine which of three methods will be used to calculate EVALDUE. If the employee is new (i.e., has never been evaluated), EVALDUE is the number of days to the first-quarter evaluation:

```
IF SCHIRED = SCLASTEVAL THEN
  EVALDUE : = 90 - DAYSONJOB
```

If an "old" employee has recently had an anniversary (within the last 30 days) but has not yet been evaluated, EVALDUE will be a negative number representing the number of days overdue:

```
ELSE
   IF (THISYEAR < = 30) AND
      EVALGAP > THISYEAR + 30) THEN
      EVALDUE : = 0 - THISYEAR
```

Otherwise, EVALDUE is calculated as the number of days to the *next* anniversary:

```
ELSE
   EVALDUE : = 365 - THISYEAR
```

Procedure OUTEMP prints the appropriate message for each employee. Its local procedure PRINTGAP gives it the ability to write the time period in days, weeks, or months, depending on the size of EVALDUE. For a negative EVALDUE, OUTEMP prints an overdue message; otherwise it displays the number of days (or weeks, or months) to the next evaluation.

```
(*$S+*)
PROGRAM EMPEVAL;

USES
            (*$U DATEUNIT.CODE*)
DATEUNIT;


CONST
  NUMEMPLOYEES = 20;

TYPE
  EMPLOYEE = RECORD
    NAME    : STRING[15];
    HIRED,
    LASTEVAL   : DATEREC;
    EVALDUE    : INTEGER
  END;

  ARY = ARRAY[1..NUMEMPLOYEES] OF EMPLOYEE;


VAR
  TODAY : DATEREC;
  SCTODAY : DATELONG;
```

Figure 12.2: Listing of Program EMPEVAL

```
      EMPARY : ARY;

      I   : INTEGER;

    PROCEDURE SHELLSORT(VAR A : ARY;
                            N : INTEGER);

      VAR
        DONE : BOOLEAN;
        JUMP,
        I,
        J     : INTEGER;

      FUNCTION FIRSTJUMP(LENGTH: INTEGER): INTEGER;

        VAR
          TEMP : INTEGER;

        BEGIN
          TEMP := 1;
          WHILE TEMP < LENGTH DO
            TEMP := TEMP * 2;
          FIRSTJUMP := TEMP
        END;    (* FIRSTJUMP *)

      PROCEDURE SWAP (VAR P, Q : EMPLOYEE);

        VAR
          HOLD : EMPLOYEE;

        BEGIN
          HOLD := P;
          P := Q;
          Q := HOLD
        END;

      BEGIN (* SHELLSORT *)
        JUMP := FIRSTJUMP(N);
        WHILE JUMP >= 1 DO
          BEGIN
            JUMP := (JUMP - 1) DIV 2;
            REPEAT
              DONE := TRUE;
              FOR J := 1 TO N - JUMP DO
                BEGIN
                  I := J + JUMP;
                  IF A[J].EVALDUE > A[I].EVALDUE THEN
                    BEGIN
                      SWAP(A[J],A[I]);
                      DONE := FALSE
                    END (* IF *)
                END (* FOR *)
            UNTIL DONE
          END (* WHILE *)
      END; (* SHELLSORT *)
```

Figure 12.2: Listing of Program EMPEVAL (cont.)

```
PROCEDURE INEMP(VAR EMP: EMPLOYEE);

  VAR
    DAYSONJOB,
    THISYEAR,
    EVALGAP     : INTEGER;
    SCHIRED,
    SCLASTEVAL  : DATELONG;

BEGIN
  WITH EMP DO
    BEGIN
      WRITE('EMPLOYEE''S NAME?        ');
      READLN(NAME);
      WRITE('DATE HIRED?              ');
      INDATE(HIRED);
      DATECONVERT(HIRED,SCHIRED);
      DAYSONJOB := TRUNC(SCTODAY - SCHIRED);
      WRITELN('LAST EVALUATION DATE');
      WRITE('(OR DATE HIRED)?         ');
      INDATE(LASTEVAL);
      WRITELN;
      DATECONVERT(LASTEVAL,SCLASTEVAL);
      EVALGAP := TRUNC(SCTODAY - SCLASTEVAL);
      THISYEAR := DAYSONJOB MOD 365;


      (*
       * FIND NUMBER OF DAYS TO
       * NEXT EVALUATION, OR NUMBER
       * OF DAYS OVERDUE.
       *)


      IF SCHIRED = SCLASTEVAL THEN (* A NEW EMPLOYEE *)
        EVALDUE := 90 - DAYSONJOB
      ELSE  (* NOT A NEW EMPLOYEE *)
        IF (THISYEAR <= 30) AND
           (EVALGAP > THISYEAR + 30) THEN  (* EVALUATION OVERDUE *)
          EVALDUE := 0 - THISYEAR
        ELSE  (* FIND DAYS TO NEXT EVALUATION *)
          EVALDUE := 365 - THISYEAR
    END (* WITH *)
END;   (* INEMP *)



PROCEDURE OUTEMP;

  VAR
    SCHIRED : DATELONG;
    DAYSONJOB,
    J          : INTEGER;

  PROCEDURE PRINTGAP (DAYS : INTEGER);
```

Figure 12.2: Listing of Program EMPEVAL (cont.)

```
        BEGIN
          IF DAYS = 0 THEN
            WRITE('TODAY')
          ELSE
            IF DAYS = 1 THEN
              WRITE(DAYS,' DAY')
            ELSE
              IF DAYS < 21 THEN
                WRITE(DAYS,' DAYS')
              ELSE
                IF DAYS < 120 THEN
                  WRITE(DAYS DIV 7,' WEEKS')
                ELSE
                  WRITE(DAYS DIV 30,' MONTHS')
        END;   (* PRINTGAP *)

      BEGIN
        WITH EMPARY[I] DO
          BEGIN
            DATECONVERT(HIRED, SCHIRED);
            DAYSONJOB := TRUNC(SCTODAY - SCHIRED);
            WRITELN;
            WRITELN(NAME);
            FOR J := 1 TO LENGTH(NAME) DO
              WRITE('-');
            WRITE('     HIRED ');
            OUTDATE(HIRED);
            WRITELN('.');
            IF HIRED = LASTEVAL THEN
              BEGIN
                WRITELN('     NEW EMPLOYEE:');
                WRITE  ('     FIRST-QUARTER EVALUATION ');
                IF EVALDUE <= 0 THEN
                  BEGIN
                    WRITE('OVERDUE BY ');
                    PRINTGAP(ABS(EVALDUE));
                    WRITELN('.  <===')
                  END
                ELSE
                  BEGIN
                    WRITE('DUE IN ');
                    PRINTGAP(EVALDUE);
                    WRITELN('.')
                  END
              END
            ELSE
              BEGIN
                WRITE('     LAST EVALUATION HELD ON ');
                OUTDATE(LASTEVAL);
                WRITELN('.');
                IF EVALDUE <= 0 THEN
                  BEGIN
                    WRITE('     ');
                    WRITE(DAYSONJOB DIV 365,'-YEAR EVALUATION OVERDUE BY ');
                    PRINTGAP(ABS(EVALDUE));
                    WRITELN('.  <===')
                  END
```

Figure 12.2: Listing of Program EMPEVAL (cont.)

```
            ELSE
              BEGIN
                WRITE('      ');
                WRITE(DAYSONJOB DIV 365 + 1,'-YEAR EVALUATION DUE IN ');
                PRINTGAP(EVALDUE);
                WRITELN('.')
              END
          END;
        WRITELN
      END  (* WITH *)
END;  (* OUTEMP *)



PROCEDURE CLEARSCREEN;

  CONST
    LENGTH = 24;

  VAR
    I : INTEGER;

BEGIN
  FOR I := 1 TO LENGTH DO
    WRITELN;
  GOTOXY(0,0)
END;            (* CLEARSCREEN *)


BEGIN    (* MAIN PROGRAM *)

  WRITELN('EMPLOYEE EVALUATION SCHEDULING');
  WRITELN('-------- ---------- ----------');
  WRITELN;
  WRITE('TODAY''S DATE? ');
  INDATE(TODAY);
  DATECONVERT(TODAY,SCTODAY);
  WRITELN;
  WRITELN;

  FOR I := 1 TO NUMEMPLOYEES DO
    INEMP(EMPARY[I]);

  SHELLSORT(EMPARY,NUMEMPLOYEES);

  CLEARSCREEN;

  WRITELN;
  WRITELN('          EVALUATION DATES');
  WRITELN('          ========== =====');
  WRITELN;
  WRITELN;

  FOR I := 1 TO NUMEMPLOYEES DO
    OUTEMP

END.     (* MAIN PROGRAM *)
```

Figure 12.2: Listing of Program EMPEVAL (cont.)

Chapter 13

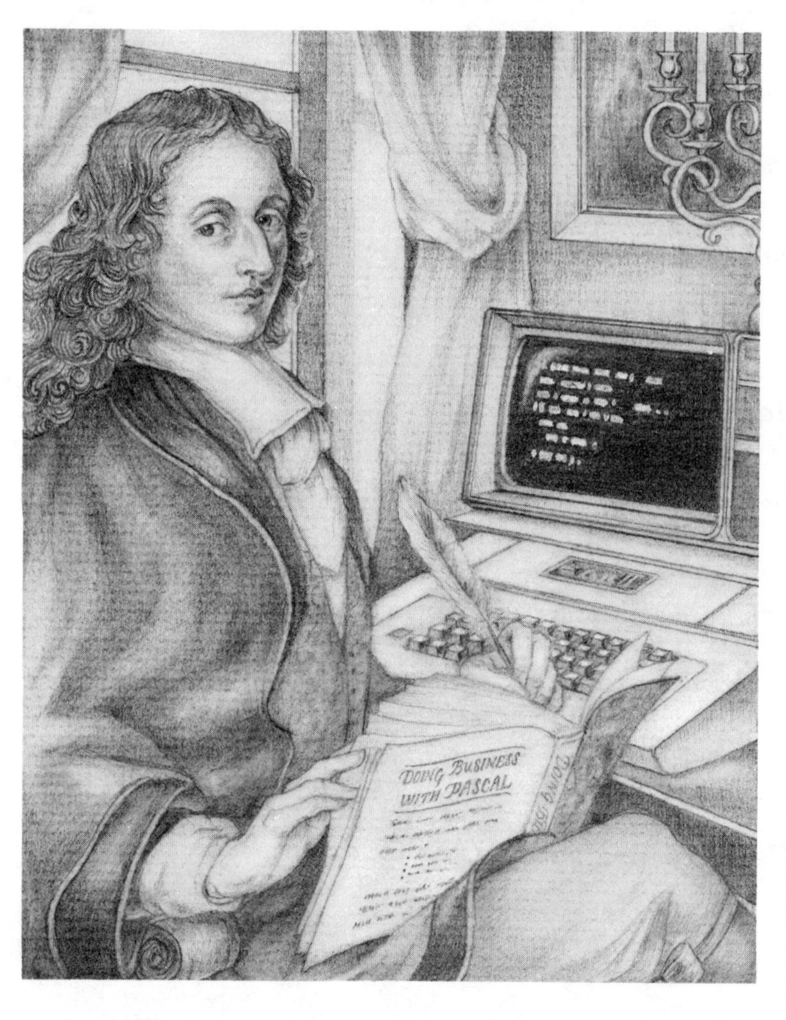

Vendor Performance Analysis

THE APPLICATION

This application provides another example of a management-level report that can be generated from existing data. The materials manager or purchasing agent, when choosing among similar vendors, needs information about the prior performance of those vendors. The program itself allows the manager to focus either on a single vendor, analyzing performances for all products ordered, or on a particular product that is ordered from several vendors, comparing vendor performance for the delivery of the product. The three reporting categories—the days required for delivery of ordered goods, and the two types of discrepancies between purchase order and invoice—have been chosen arbitrarily and could easily be changed or expanded to meet the needs of a particular company's materials management.

The data in this example is input through the keyboard. In a real system, however, the data would come from several sources. The stock issues/purchase order application would keep a record of purchase orders for each vendor for a predetermined period (related directly to the amount of disk space available). The receiving application would keep information on the actual items received, and the date of receipt. This application, vendor performance analysis, would simply combine the six pieces of information required and report them to the materials manager. Note also that the actual name of the vendor would normally be held in the vendor/AP control master file—an application that is part of a different subsystem (the accounts payable subsystem). To make the vendor master file available to the materials management subsystem might require some disk shifting on a small computer system, but such a link is certainly possible to implement. There is often a need for subsystems to communicate. The means of that communication, as stressed in Chapter 2, is the use of files.

Other kinds of reports would also be produced within the materials management subsystem. Chapters 14 and 15 discuss two other management-level reports, on inventory costing and economic order quantity. These reports would supplement the standard accounting office reports within materials management—stock-issues reports, inventory reports, and the like.

Even independently of a complete business system, this application example can be implemented on a small computer so as to provide information for the materials manager. While the input would have to be manual, the report would still be useful.

THE SAMPLE RUN

Given data from purchase order, invoice, and shipment documents, this program evaluates and summarizes vendor performance. The evaluation is expressed in terms of the days required for delivery of ordered goods, and discrepancies in price and number of units delivered between purchase order and invoice. The program can be used either to evaluate the delivery performance of a single vendor, or to compare the performances of several competing vendors for delivery of a given product.

The sample run, shown in Figure 13.1, illustrates the two different uses of the program. The first evaluation is of one vendor, SlowCo, Inc., which filled five orders for a certain product during a period of several months. To evaluate the vendor, we input six pieces of information about each order: the date of the order, the unit price quoted, and the number of units ordered; the date the goods were received, the unit price invoiced, and the number of units received. The program reads this information for all the purchases from a given vendor, and calculates three statistics on the vendor's performance:

1. the average number of days the vendor takes to deliver;
2. the average percent difference between the unit purchase price quoted and the unit price actually invoiced;
3. the average percent difference between the number of units ordered and the number of units delivered.

The program presents this data in a table that appears on the screen after the input dialogue. In the case of SlowCo, we see that the company has taken an average of 26 days to deliver goods, and has shown discrepancies of 2% and 6% in the unit price and quantity delivered, respectively.

The second report in the sample run compares the performance of five vendors that have supplied the same product over a half-year period. We see from the evaluation table that three of the vendors—Parts,Inc., FastCo, and ReliCo—have taken about the same time to deliver. Among these three, ReliCo has the best performance record for filling orders accurately.

```
      VENDOR PERFORMANCE ANALYSIS
      ====== =========== ========


HOW MANY VENDORS? 1


NAME OF VENDOR #1? SLOWCO,INC.
HOW MANY PURCHASES FROM SLOWCO,INC? 5

PURCHASE #1: PURCHASE ORDER

  DATE OF ORDER?        2-1-82
  QUOTED UNIT PRICE?    1.88
  UNITS ORDERED?        200

PURCHASE #1: RECEIPT OF GOODS

  DATE RECEIVED?        3-5-82
  INVOICE UNIT PRICE?   1.95
  UNITS RECEIVED?       175

PURCHASE #2: PURCHASE ORDER

  DATE OF ORDER?        3-8-82
  QUOTED UNIT PRICE?    1.96
  UNITS ORDERED?        500

PURCHASE #2: RECEIPT OF GOODS

  DATE RECEIVED?        4-9-82
  INVOICE UNIT PRICE?   2.03
  UNITS RECEIVED?       450

PURCHASE #3: PURCHASE ORDER

  DATE OF ORDER?        4-13-82
  QUOTED UNIT PRICE?    2.05
  UNITS ORDERED?        400
```

Figure 13.1: Sample Run of Vendor Performance Analysis Program

```
PURCHASE #3: RECEIPT OF GOODS

  DATE RECEIVED?        5-3-82
  INVOICE UNIT PRICE? 2.05
  UNITS RECEIVED?       400

PURCHASE #4: PURCHASE ORDER

  DATE OF ORDER?        5-5-82
  QUOTED UNIT PRICE?  2.06
  UNITS ORDERED?        300

PURCHASE #4: RECEIPT OF GOODS

  DATE RECEIVED?        6-4-82
  INVOICE UNIT PRICE? 2.08
  UNITS RECEIVED?       275

PURCHASE #5: PURCHASE ORDER

  DATE OF ORDER?        6-7-82
  QUOTED UNIT PRICE?  2.08
  UNITS ORDERED?        450

PURCHASE #5: RECEIPT OF GOODS

  DATE RECEIVED?        6-25-82
  INVOICE UNIT PRICE? 2.08
  UNITS RECEIVED?       450

----------------------------------------------
            VENDOR EVALUATIONS
            ====== ===========

             AVERAGE    AVERAGE     AVERAGE
             DAYS TO    % PRICE   % QUANTITY
  VENDOR     DELIVER  DIFFERENCE  DIFFERENCE
---------- ---------- ----------  ----------

SLOWCO,INC     26          2           6


ANOTHER REPORT? Y

----------------------------------------------

HOW MANY VENDORS? 5


NAME OF VENDOR #1? PARTS,INC.
HOW MANY PURCHASES FROM PARTS,INC.? 3

PURCHASE #1: PURCHASE ORDER

  DATE OF ORDER?        1-4-82
  QUOTED UNIT PRICE?  1.25
  UNITS ORDERED?        300
```

Figure 13.1: Sample Run of Vendor Performance Analysis Program (cont.)

```
PURCHASE #1: RECEIPT OF GOODS

  DATE RECEIVED?         1-13-82
  INVOICE UNIT PRICE? 1.25
  UNITS RECEIVED?        300

PURCHASE #2: PURCHASE ORDER

  DATE OF ORDER?         1-29-82
  QUOTED UNIT PRICE?  1.25
  UNITS ORDERED?         500

PURCHASE #2: RECEIPT OF GOODS

  DATE RECEIVED?         2-3-82
  INVOICE UNIT PRICE? 1.27
  UNITS RECEIVED?        480

PURCHASE #3: PURCHASE ORDER

  DATE OF ORDER?         3-29-82
  QUOTED UNIT PRICE?  1.27
  UNITS ORDERED?         500

PURCHASE #3: RECEIPT OF GOODS

  DATE RECEIVED?         4-5-82
  INVOICE UNIT PRICE? 1.27
  UNITS RECEIVED?        495


NAME OF VENDOR #2? FASTCO
HOW MANY PURCHASES FROM FASTCO? 3

PURCHASE #1: PURCHASE ORDER

  DATE OF ORDER?         1-12-82
  QUOTED UNIT PRICE?  1.14
  UNITS ORDERED?         500

PURCHASE #1: RECEIPT OF GOODS

  DATE RECEIVED?         1-28-82
  INVOICE UNIT PRICE? 1.18
  UNITS RECEIVED?        450

PURCHASE #2: PURCHASE ORDER

  DATE OF ORDER?         4-7-82
  QUOTED UNIT PRICE?  1.12
  UNITS ORDERED?         550

PURCHASE #2: RECEIPT OF GOODS

  DATE RECEIVED?         4-12-82
  INVOICE UNIT PRICE? 1.12
  UNITS RECEIVED?        550
```

Figure 13.1: Sample Run of Vendor Performance Analysis Program (cont.)

```
PURCHASE #3: PURCHASE ORDER

  DATE OF ORDER?       4-15-82
  QUOTED UNIT PRICE?  1.20
  UNITS ORDERED?       600

PURCHASE #3: RECEIPT OF GOODS

  DATE RECEIVED?       4-21-82
  INVOICE UNIT PRICE? 1.20
  UNITS RECEIVED?      575


NAME OF VENDOR #3? SLOWCO
HOW MANY PURCHASES FROM SLOWCO? 2

PURCHASE #1: PURCHASE ORDER

  DATE OF ORDER?       2-3-82
  QUOTED UNIT PRICE?  1.22
  UNITS ORDERED?       350

PURCHASE #1: RECEIPT OF GOODS

  DATE RECEIVED?       2-25-82
  INVOICE UNIT PRICE? 1.24
  UNITS RECEIVED?      325

PURCHASE #2: PURCHASE ORDER

  DATE OF ORDER?       2-26-82
  QUOTED UNIT PRICE?  1.25
  UNITS ORDERED?       400

PURCHASE #2: RECEIPT OF GOODS

  DATE RECEIVED?       3-26-82
  INVOICE UNIT PRICE? 1.27
  UNITS RECEIVED?      300


NAME OF VENDOR #4? DISTRICO
HOW MANY PURCHASES FROM DISTRICO? 2

PURCHASE #1: PURCHASE ORDER

  DATE OF ORDER?       4-23-82
  QUOTED UNIT PRICE?  1.10
  UNITS ORDERED?       1000

PURCHASE #1: RECEIPT OF GOODS

  DATE RECEIVED?       5-13-82
  INVOICE UNIT PRICE? 1.10
  UNITS RECEIVED?      900
```

Figure 13.1: Sample Run of Vendor Performance Analysis Program (cont.)

```
PURCHASE #2: PURCHASE ORDER

  DATE OF ORDER?        6-1-82
  QUOTED UNIT PRICE?    1.12
  UNITS ORDERED?        800

PURCHASE #2: RECEIPT OF GOODS

  DATE RECEIVED?        6-25-82
  INVOICE UNIT PRICE?   1.14
  UNITS RECEIVED?       800


NAME OF VENDOR #5? RELICO
HOW MANY PURCHASES FROM RELICO? 2

PURCHASE #1: PURCHASE ORDER

  DATE OF ORDER?        5-17-82
  QUOTED UNIT PRICE?    1.15
  UNITS ORDERED?        400

PURCHASE #1: RECEIPT OF GOODS

  DATE RECEIVED?        5-28-82
  INVOICE UNIT PRICE?   1.15
  UNITS RECEIVED?       400

PURCHASE #2: PURCHASE ORDER

  DATE OF ORDER?        6-28-82
  QUOTED UNIT PRICE?    1.16
  UNITS ORDERED?        550

PURCHASE #2: RECEIPT OF GOODS

  DATE RECEIVED?        7-2-82
  INVOICE UNIT PRICE?   1.16
  UNITS RECEIVED?       550

---------------------------------------------
            VENDOR EVALUATIONS
            ====== ===========

             AVERAGE     AVERAGE     AVERAGE
             DAYS TO     % PRICE   % QUANTITY
  VENDOR     DELIVER   DIFFERENCE  DIFFERENCE
---------- ---------- ---------- ----------

PARTS,INC.       7          1           2
FASTCO           9          1           5
SLOWCO          25          2          16
DISTRICO        22          1           5
RELICO           8          0           0

ANOTHER REPORT? N
```

Figure 13.1: Sample Run of Vendor Performance Analysis Program (cont.)

THE PROGRAM

The listing of program VENDEVAL is shown in Figure 13.2. The central data structure of VENDEVAL is VENDOR, a record that contains four fields:

```
VENDOR = RECORD
   NAME : STRING[10];
   DAYS : INTEGER;
   PRICEDIF,
   QUANTDIF : REAL
END;
```

The fields DAYS, PRICEDIF, and QUANTDIF are designed to store the statistical data calculated on the vendor's performance; they are initialized to zero.

In the current version of the program, up to twenty vendors may be evaluated in any one report. The array VENDARY holds the vendor records:

```
CONST
   MAXVEND = 20;
   ...
VAR
   VENDARY : ARRAY[1..MAXVEND] OF VENDOR;
```

Procedure INVEND does most of the work of this program. It reads the input values, calculates the performance statistics, and stores them in VENDARY. These tasks are organized within a pair of nested loops. The outer loop deals one at a time with each vendor for a given report:

```
FOR I := 1 TO NUMVEND DO
   WITH VENDARY[I] DO
```

and the inner loop covers each of the transactions for a given vendor:

```
FOR J := 1 TO TRANSACTIONS DO
```

The input routines INDATE, INDOLLAR, and ININT are used to read the data. DATECONVERT produces the scalar date values SCORDDATE, for the order date, and SCRECDATE, for the receiving date. From these two values, INVEND computes the delivery time and assigns it to the record field DAYS:

```
DAYS := DAYS + TRUNC(SCRECDATE - SCORDDATE);
```

If there is a discrepancy between the quoted unit purchase price and the price on the invoice document, the percent difference must be calculated. To do so, INVALUE uses two long-integer arithmetic routines, LONGABSDIF and LDIVL. Procedure LONGABSDIF finds the absolute value of the difference between the two long integers, and function LDIVL divides one long integer by another and returns a REAL result:

```
IF QUOTEPRICE <> INVPRICE THEN
  BEGIN
    LONGABSDIF(QUOTEPRICE,INVPRICE,DIF);
    PRICEDIF := PRICEDIF + LDIVL(DIF,QUOTEPRICE)
  END;
```

The same calculation must be performed for the number of units; however, this case is easier because UNITSORD and UNITSREC are simple integers:

```
IF UNITSORD <> UNITSREC THEN
  QUANTDIF := QUANTDIF +
  ABS(UNITSORD - UNITSREC)/UNITSORD;
```

Finally, after all the transactions are recorded, INVEND calculates the three averages:

```
DAYS := ROUND(DAYS/TRANSACTIONS);
PRICEDIF := PRICEDIF / TRANSACTIONS;
QUANTDIF := QUANTDIF / TRANSACTIONS;
```

Procedure OUTVEND produces the evaluation report. It simply prints one line of the table for each record in VENDARY.

```
(*$S+*)

PROGRAM VENDEVAL;

USES
          (*$U MONEYUNIT.CODE*)
MONEYUNIT,
          (*$U DATEUNIT.CODE*)
DATEUNIT;


CONST
  MAXVEND = 20;    (* MAXIMUM NUMBER OF VENDORS *)
```

Figure 13.2: Listing of Program VENDEVAL

```
TYPE
  VENDOR = RECORD
    NAME : STRING[10];
    DAYS : INTEGER;    (* DAYS TAKEN TO DELIVER GOODS *)
    PRICEDIF,
    QUANTDIF : REAL    (* DECIMAL PERCENTAGES *)
  END;

VAR
  VENDARY : ARRAY[1..MAXVEND] OF VENDOR;
  NUMVEND : INTEGER;    (* NUMBER OF VENDORS ON A REPORT *)
  ANS  : STRING;



PROCEDURE INIT;

  (*
   * INITIALIZES THE ARRAY OF VENDORS
   * TO ZERO VALUES.
   *)

  VAR
    I : INTEGER;

BEGIN
  FOR I := 1 TO MAXVEND DO
    WITH VENDARY[I] DO
      BEGIN
        DAYS := 0;
        PRICEDIF := 0.0;
        QUANTDIF := 0.0
      END  (* WITH *)
END; (* INIT *)


PROCEDURE ININT(VAR VAL: INTEGER);

(*
 * INTEGER INPUT ROUTINE.
 *)

  VAR
    GARBAGE : STRING;

  BEGIN
    GET(INPUT);
    IF INPUT^ IN ['0'..'9'] THEN
      READLN(VAL)
    ELSE
      BEGIN
        READLN(GARBAGE);
        WRITELN('*** REDO');
        WRITE('    ? ');
        ININT(VAL)
      END
  END;     (* ININT *)
```

Figure 13.2: Listing of Program VENDEVAL (cont.)

```
PROCEDURE INVEND;

(*
 * CONDUCTS THE INPUT DIALOGUE.
 *)

  VAR
    TRANSACTIONS,
    I, J,
    UNITSORD,
    UNITSREC   : INTEGER;

    ORDDATE,
    RECDATE   : DATEREC;

    SCORDDATE,
    SCRECDATE   : DATELONG;

    DIF,
    QUOTEPRICE,
    INVPRICE    : LONG2;


  PROCEDURE LONGABSDIF(L1,L2: LONG2;
                    VAR  DIF   : LONG2);


   (*
    * FINDS THE ABSOLUTE VALUE
    * OF THE DIFFERENCE BETWEEN
    * TWO LONG INTEGERS.
    *)


  BEGIN
    IF L1 >= L2 THEN
      DIF := L1 - L2
    ELSE
      DIF := L2 - L1
  END;      (* LONGABSDIF *)



  FUNCTION LDIVL(L1,L2 : LONG2): REAL;


  (*
   * DIVIDES L1 BY L2 AND RETURNS A REAL
   * QUOTIENT. ASSUMES L1 < L2.
   *)


   VAR
     HOLD1,
     HOLD2   : LONG2;
     R       : REAL;
```

Figure 13.2: Listing of Program VENDEVAL (cont.)

```
    BEGIN
      HOLD1 := 1;
      WHILE L1 > MAXINT DO
        BEGIN
          L1 := L1 DIV 10;
          HOLD1 := HOLD1 * 10
        END;

      HOLD2 := 1;
      WHILE L2 > MAXINT DO
        BEGIN
          L2 := L2 DIV 10;
          HOLD1 := HOLD1 * 10
        END;

      R := TRUNC(L1)/TRUNC(L2);

      HOLD2 := HOLD2 DIV HOLD1;

      WHILE HOLD2 > 1 DO
        BEGIN
          R := R / 10.0;
          HOLD2 := HOLD2 DIV 10
        END;

      LDIVL := R
    END;   (* LDIVL *)


  BEGIN (* INVEND *)
    FOR I := 1 TO NUMVEND DO
      WITH VENDARY[I] DO
        BEGIN
          WRITE('NAME OF VENDOR #',I,'? ');
          READLN(NAME);
          WRITE('HOW MANY PURCHASES FROM ', NAME, '? ');
          ININT(TRANSACTIONS);
          WRITELN;


          FOR J := 1 TO TRANSACTIONS DO
            BEGIN
              WRITELN('PURCHASE #',J,': PURCHASE ORDER');
              WRITELN;
              WRITE('  DATE OF ORDER?       ');
              INDATE(ORDDATE);
              DATECONVERT(ORDDATE,SCORDDATE);
              WRITE('  QUOTED UNIT PRICE?  ');
              INDOLLAR(QUOTEPRICE);
              WRITE('  UNITS ORDERED?       ');
              ININT(UNITSORD);
              WRITELN;
```

Figure 13.2: Listing of Program VENDEVAL (cont.)

```
                WRITELN('PURCHASE #',J,': RECEIPT OF GOODS');
                WRITELN;
                WRITE('  DATE RECEIVED?        ');
                INDATE(RECDATE);
                DATECONVERT(RECDATE,SCRECDATE);
                WRITE('  INVOICE UNIT PRICE? ');
                INDOLLAR(INVPRICE);
                WRITE('  UNITS RECEIVED?       ');
                ININT(UNITSREC);
                WRITELN;

                (*
                 * ACCUMULATE DELIVERY DAYS.
                 *)

                DAYS := DAYS + TRUNC(SCRECDATE - SCORDDATE);

                (*
                 * FIND ANY PRICE OR QUANTITY DISCREPANCIES (%).
                 *)

                IF QUOTEPRICE <> INVPRICE THEN
                  BEGIN
                    LONGABSDIF(QUOTEPRICE,INVPRICE,DIF);
                    PRICEDIF := PRICEDIF + LDIVL(DIF,QUOTEPRICE)
                  END;

                IF UNITSORD <> UNITSREC THEN
                  QUANTDIF := QUANTDIF +
                              ABS(UNITSORD - UNITSREC)/UNITSORD
            END; (* FOR J *)
            WRITELN;

            (*
             * FIND AVERAGE DAYS, AND
             * AVERAGE PRICE AND QUANTITY DISCREPANCIES (%).
             *)

            DAYS := ROUND(DAYS/TRANSACTIONS);
            PRICEDIF := PRICEDIF / TRANSACTIONS;
            QUANTDIF := QUANTDIF / TRANSACTIONS;
        END  (* WITH *)
    END;  (* INVEND *)


    PROCEDURE OUTVEND;

      (*
       * PRINTS THE EVALUATION TABLE.
       *)
```

Figure 13.2: Listing of Program VENDEVAL (cont.)

```
VAR
  I,
  J  : INTEGER;

PROCEDURE HEADING;

  CONST
    LINE = '----------';

  BEGIN
    WRITELN('VENDOR EVALUATIONS':30);
    WRITELN('====== ===========':30);
    WRITELN;
    FOURCOLUMN(' ','AVERAGE ','AVERAGE ','AVERAGE ',
               10,10,10,10);
    FOURCOLUMN(' ','DAYS TO ','% PRICE ','% QUANTITY',
               10,10,10,10);
    FOURCOLUMN('VENDOR   ','DELIVER ','DIFFERENCE','DIFFERENCE',
               10,10,10,10);
    FOURCOLUMN(LINE,LINE,LINE,LINE,10,10,10,10);
    WRITELN
  END;  (* HEADING *)


BEGIN (* OUTVEND *)
  HEADING;
  FOR I := 1 TO NUMVEND DO
    WITH VENDARY[I] DO
      BEGIN
        WRITE(NAME);
        FOR J := 1 TO (10-LENGTH(NAME)+1) DO
          WRITE(' ');
        WRITELN(DAYS:6, ROUND(PRICEDIF*100.0):10,
                  ROUND(QUANTDIF*100.0):11)
      END
END;  (* OUTVEND *)



BEGIN (* MAIN PROGRAM *)

  CLEARSCREEN;

    WRITELN;
    WRITELN('VENDOR PERFORMANCE ANALYSIS':33);
    WRITELN('====== =========== ========':33);
    WRITELN;

    REPEAT
      INIT;

      REPEAT
        WRITE('HOW MANY VENDORS? ');
        ININT(NUMVEND)
      UNTIL NUMVEND <= MAXVEND;
      WRITELN;
      WRITELN;
```

Figure 13.2: Listing of Program VENDEVAL (cont.)

```
    INVEND;
    CLEARSCREEN;
    OUTVEND;

    WRITELN;
    WRITELN;
    WRITE('ANOTHER REPORT? ');
    READLN(ANS);
    CLEARSCREEN
  UNTIL (ANS = 'N')
END.  (* MAIN PROGRAM *)
```

Figure 13.2: Listing of Program VENDEVAL (cont.)

Chapter 14

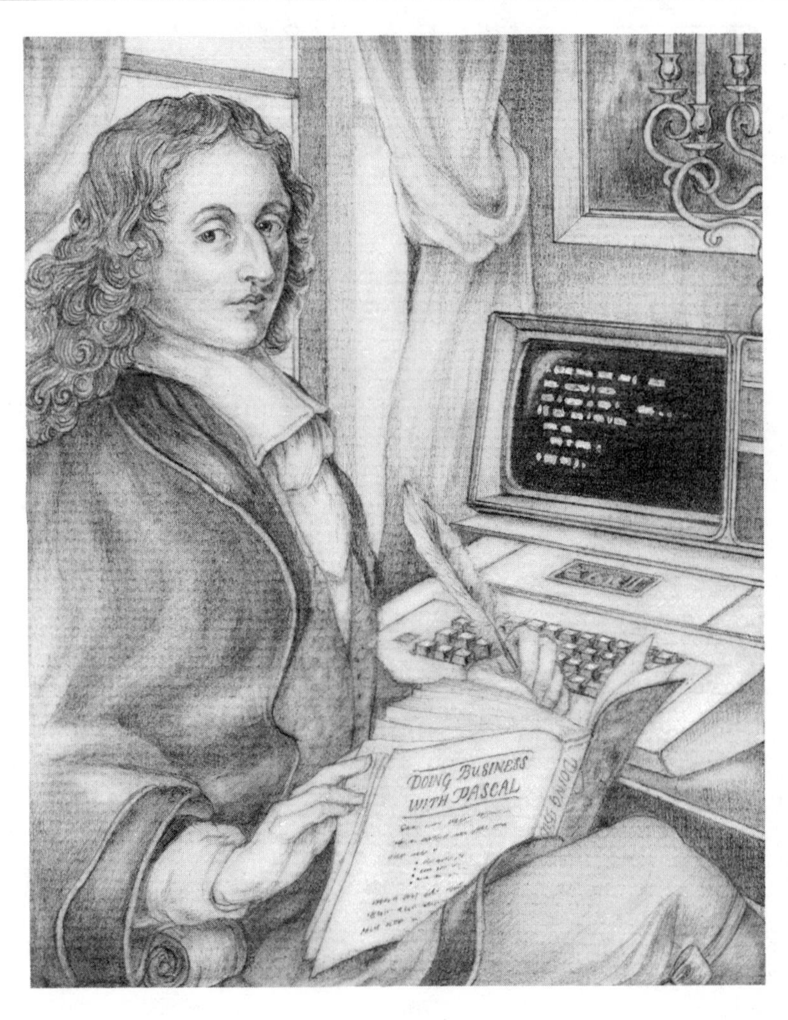

Costing Methods for Units Issued from Inventory

THE APPLICATION

The application program described in this chapter, besides performing the specific tasks needed to cost out stock issues, illustrates how one program might be used for several functions. For example, the program could easily be modified to calculate the value of remaining inventories. A periodic physical inventory would verify the inventory stock items as shown on the inventory master file. Then the same application could automatically calculate the value of the inventory on hand and provide input for adjustments to the numbers on the general ledger.

In its present form, the application also lets the user compare the results of different inventory costing methods. While the information for comparing the inventory value or cost of issues may occasionally be a topic for managerial concern, the costing method is commonly standard for the whole organization. Thus, the specific method used could easily become part of the system profile, which would provide the menu choice for this program.

The inventory master file would normally be the source of much of the information that is input from the keyboard in this program. In an on-line, real-time environment, the application might still require the input of the inventory item number. However, the name of the inventory item (with perhaps its location among several stock rooms), along with the quantity and cost of previous purchases, would come from the inventory master file. That file in turn would be periodically updated by transactions processed through the inventory receiving application. The inventory costing program could also be used for processes requiring only start-up information from the user, and could then give either value or cost information as needed.

The functions performed by this program require combinations of data that might not otherwise be associated together, and thus clearly illustrate the need for communication between the various subsystems through master files and transaction files. The inventory control application would keep records of the history of inventory purchases. The receiving application would provide information about actual shipments, and the accounts payable subsystem's invoices application would pass information on the unit cost for each item. Finally, the stock issues application would pass information to the inventory control application. Without the proper funneling of information, considerable manual input would be required.

Other potentially valuable kinds of management reporting might be produced by the inventory control and stock issues applications. A management report showing the duplication of stock items over several inventory locations could show whether a particular stock location is used more often than another. Similar reporting could show excess inventories or "private" inventories of specific items. Valuation of those inventories, by whatever method the company chooses, could be used to justify management decisions on consolidation of stock into one inventory. Inventory control would also be applied to stocks of both raw materials and finished products ready for shipment. While costing information on finished products would be slightly more difficult to gather, the standard inventory valuation methods would still be applicable.

THE SAMPLE RUN

This program performs two calculations, the cost per unit issued and the total cost of units issued, for any item issued from inventory, under the user's choice of three inventory costing methods: weighted average, LIFO, and FIFO. To do so, it conducts an input/output dialogue in the following sequence:

1. The user inputs the name and I.D. number (with check digit) of an inventory item, and the number of purchases made to supply that item in inventory.
2. The program prompts for the quantity purchased and the unit cost for each of the purchases.
3. The user then inputs the number of units of the item that have been issued from inventory.

4. By means of a recurring menu, the user may choose to examine the average and total costs of any of the three inventory costing methods. The menu also provides for input of a new inventory item or for termination of the program.

The sample run of the program appears in Figure 14.1. The first three screens show the input dialogue, and the subsequent screens show the menu and the individual costing method displays.

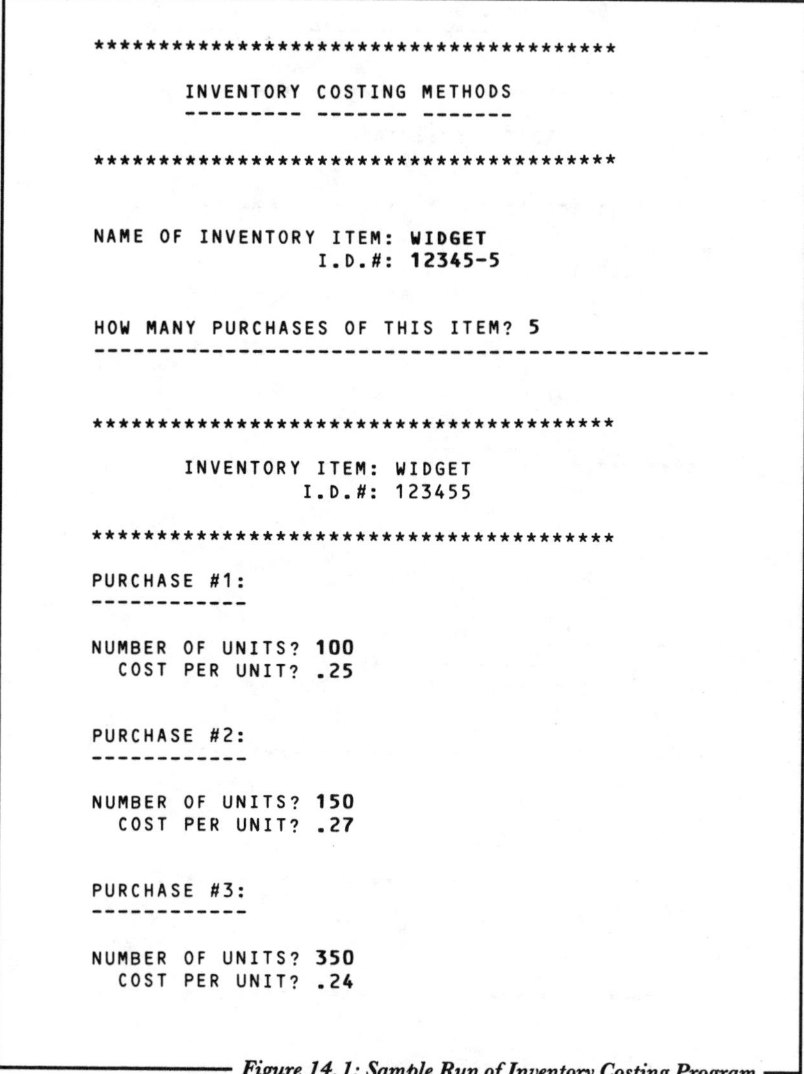

```
****************************************

       INVENTORY COSTING METHODS
       --------- ------- -------

****************************************


NAME OF INVENTORY ITEM: WIDGET
                I.D.#: 12345-5

HOW MANY PURCHASES OF THIS ITEM? 5
----------------------------------------------


****************************************

       INVENTORY ITEM: WIDGET
                I.D.#: 123455

****************************************

PURCHASE #1:
------------

NUMBER OF UNITS? 100
  COST PER UNIT? .25

PURCHASE #2:
------------

NUMBER OF UNITS? 150
  COST PER UNIT? .27

PURCHASE #3:
------------

NUMBER OF UNITS? 350
  COST PER UNIT? .24
```

Figure 14.1: Sample Run of Inventory Costing Program

```
PURCHASE #4:
------------

NUMBER OF UNITS? 125
  COST PER UNIT? .28


PURCHASE #5:
------------

NUMBER OF UNITS? 100
  COST PER UNIT? .29
-----------------------------------------------


****************************************

       INVENTORY ITEM: WIDGET
                I.D.#: 123455

****************************************

HOW MANY UNITS ISSUED
     FROM INVENTORY? 625
-----------------------------------------------


****************************************

       INVENTORY ITEM: WIDGET
                I.D.#: 123455

****************************************


WHICH COSTING METHOD?

         W(EIGHTED AVERAGE

         L(IFO
         F(IFO
         -----------------------
         A(NOTHER INVENTORY ITEM
         Q(UIT

****************************************

                    ? W
-----------------------------------------------


****************************************

       INVENTORY ITEM: WIDGET
                I.D.#: 123455

****************************************
```

Figure 14.1: Sample Run of Inventory Costing Program (cont.)

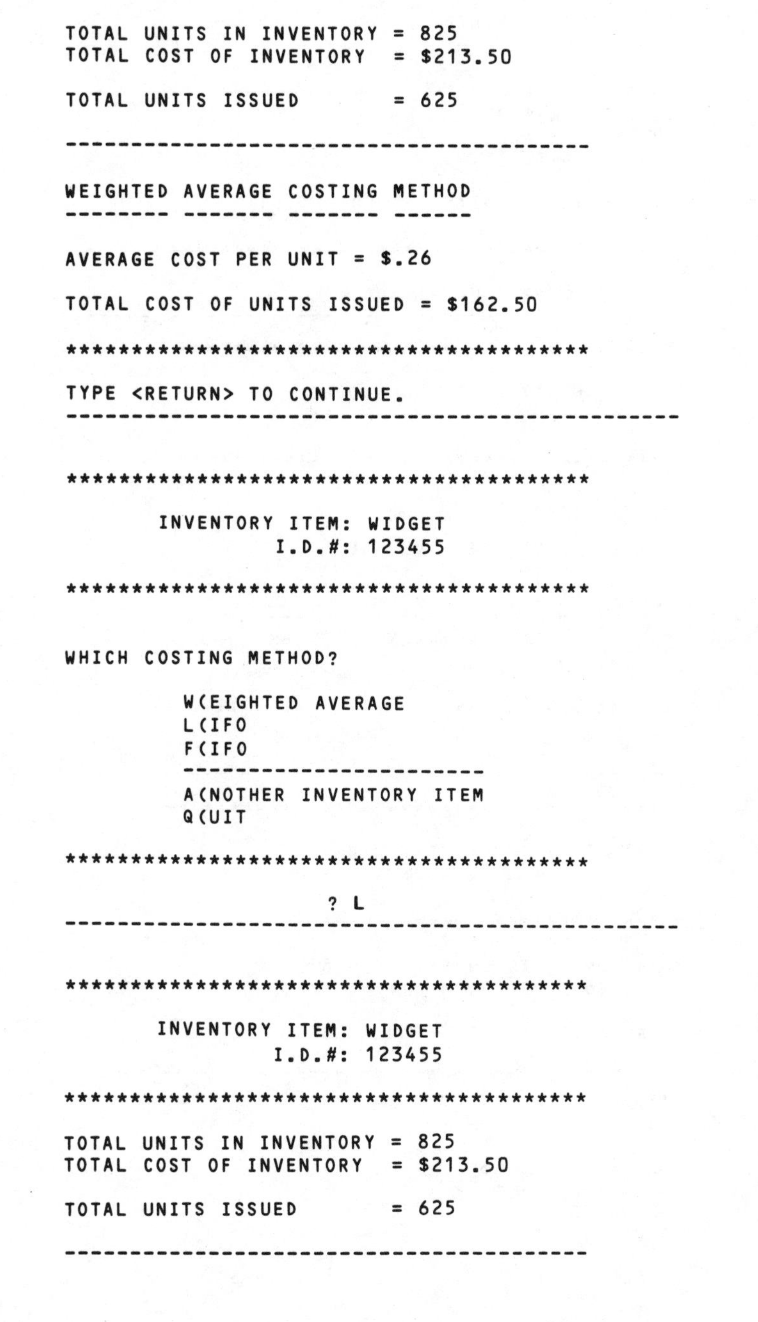

```
TOTAL UNITS IN INVENTORY = 825
TOTAL COST OF INVENTORY  = $213.50

TOTAL UNITS ISSUED       = 625

-----------------------------------------

WEIGHTED AVERAGE COSTING METHOD
-------- ------- ------- ------

AVERAGE COST PER UNIT = $.26

TOTAL COST OF UNITS ISSUED = $162.50

****************************************

TYPE <RETURN> TO CONTINUE.
------------------------------------------------


****************************************

       INVENTORY ITEM: WIDGET
               I.D.#: 123455

****************************************


WHICH COSTING METHOD?

         W(EIGHTED AVERAGE
         L(IFO
         F(IFO
         ----------------------
         A(NOTHER INVENTORY ITEM
         Q(UIT

****************************************

                   ? L
------------------------------------------------


****************************************

       INVENTORY ITEM: WIDGET
               I.D.#: 123455

****************************************

TOTAL UNITS IN INVENTORY = 825
TOTAL COST OF INVENTORY  = $213.50

TOTAL UNITS ISSUED       = 625

-----------------------------------------
```

Figure 14.1: Sample Run of Inventory Costing Program (cont.)

```
LIFO COSTING METHOD
---- ------- ------

100 UNITS @ $.29
125 UNITS @ $.28
350 UNITS @ $.24
50 UNITS @ $.27

TOTAL COST OF UNITS ISSUED = $161.50

****************************************

TYPE <RETURN> TO CONTINUE.
----------------------------------------------
****************************************

       INVENTORY ITEM: WIDGET
                I.D.#: 123455

****************************************

WHICH COSTING METHOD?

         W(EIGHTED AVERAGE
         L(IFO
         F(IFO
         -----------------------
         A(NOTHER INVENTORY ITEM
         Q(UIT

****************************************

                    ? F
----------------------------------------------
****************************************

       INVENTORY ITEM: WIDGET
                I.D.#: 123455

****************************************

TOTAL UNITS IN INVENTORY = 825
TOTAL COST OF INVENTORY  = $213.50

TOTAL UNITS ISSUED       = 625

----------------------------------------
FIFO COSTING METHOD
---- ------- ------

100 UNITS @ $.25
150 UNITS @ $.27
350 UNITS @ $.24
25 UNITS @ $.28

TOTAL COST OF UNITS ISSUED = $156.50
```

Figure 14.1: Sample Run of Inventory Costing Program (cont.)

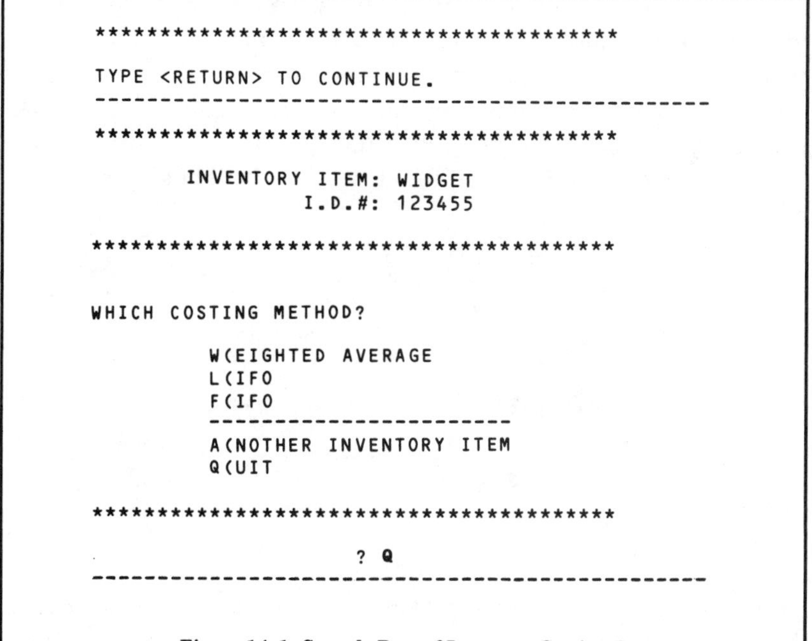

```
****************************************

TYPE <RETURN> TO CONTINUE.
-----------------------------------------------

****************************************

       INVENTORY ITEM: WIDGET
                I.D.#: 123455

****************************************


WHICH COSTING METHOD?

         W(EIGHTED AVERAGE
         L(IFO
         F(IFO
         ----------------------
         A(NOTHER INVENTORY ITEM
         Q(UIT

****************************************

                    ? Q
-----------------------------------------------
```

Figure 14.1: Sample Run of Inventory Costing Program (cont.)

THE PROGRAM

The central data structure of program INVENTORY, shown in Figure 14.2, is PURCHARY, an array of records. The record type PURCHASES has two fields, QUANTITY and COST:

```
PURCHASES = RECORD
   QUANTITY : INTEGER;
   COST     : LONG2
END;
```

PURCHARY is thus designed to store the information about the series of purchases for a given inventory item. As we will see, this structure simplifies the LIFO and FIFO costing calculations.

INVENTORY contains an assortment of short output procedures for producing legible and attractive output screens. LINEOFCHARS prints a line of characters across the screen. CONTINUE stops the action so the user can examine a screenful of information. REPORT-TOTALS and ECHOITEM both echo information about the current inventory item; these procedures are called from several points in the program.

The program also has two input routines. Procedure INITEM reads the name and number of the inventory item. Procedure INPURCH conducts the input dialogue for the purchases. It contains a small local procedure, ININT, designed to validate integer input. The purchase records are read within a FOR loop that increments I from 1 to the number of purchases, NUMPURCH. Using a WITH statement simplifies the code:

```
FOR I := 1 TO NUMPURCH DO
   WITH PURCHARY[I] DO
      BEGIN
         ...
         ININT(QUANTITY);
         ...
         INDOLLAR(COST);
         ...
      END;
```

This loop also accumulates the total number of units and the total cost of the inventory for the item:

```
TOTUNITS := TOTUNITS + QUANTITY;
TOTCOST := TOTCOST + COST * QUANTITY;
```

Finally, INPURCH reads the number of units that have been issued from inventory. This number cannot, of course, be greater than the total number of units purchased; a REPEAT loop verifies the input:

```
REPEAT
   ININT(ISSUES);
   IF ISSUES > TOTUNITS THEN
      BEGIN
         WRITELN('ONLY ', TOTUNITS, ' UNITS AVAILABLE.');
         WRITE('                    ? ');
      END
UNTIL ISSUES <= TOTUNITS;
```

Procedures WEIGHTED and IFO compute the cost of the issued units under the three costing methods. They are both called from procedure MENU. WEIGHTED is very short, but illustrates an algorithm for an important problem that we have not dealt with up to now: dividing a long integer by a regular integer. The average cost of the inventory is found by dividing the total cost (TOTCOST) by the total number of units (TOTUNITS). To perform this operation we first find the inverse of TOTUNITS:

```
INVERSE := 1.0 / TOTUNITS;
```

Notice that this statement also performs an *implicit type conversion*; INVERSE is of type REAL. We can now use procedure LONGMULT to multiply TOTCOST by INVERSE:

```
LONGMULT(TOTCOST, INVERSE, AVECOST);
```

The result, AVECOST, is returned to MENU.

As its ambiguous name implies, IFO calculates either the LIFO or the FIFO cost each time it is called. For this reason, a call to IFO has two arguments: the first, a VAR parameter, is a long integer of type LONG2, which receives the calculated total cost of the units issued from inventory; the second is a Boolean value sent to IFO from the calling program. A value of TRUE instructs IFO to return the FIFO cost; a FALSE returns the LIFO cost:

```
IFO(ISSUECOST,TRUE); (* FIFO *)
IFO(ISSUECOST,FALSE); (* LIFO *)
```

Procedure IFO receives this Boolean value in the variable FIFO and uses it to decide on the starting point and direction for working through the array of purchases. For FIFO, we start at the beginning of the array (i.e., the first purchase) and move forward:

```
IF FIFO THEN
  BEGIN
    INDEX := 1;
    DIRECTION := 1
  END
```

For LIFO, we start at the last purchase and move backward:

```
ELSE (* IF LIFO *)
  BEGIN
    INDEX := NUMPURCH;
    DIRECTION := -1
  END;
```

A WHILE loop is used to move through the array PURCHARY until all the issued units have been accounted for. First the temporary variable

TEMPQUANT is assigned the value of ISSUES:

```
TEMPQUANT := ISSUES;
```

Then the WHILE loop deducts units from TEMPQUANT, and accumulates the total cost, until TEMPQUANT equals zero:

```
WHILE TEMPQUANT > 0 DO
  WITH PURCHARY[INDEX] DO
    BEGIN
      ...
      TOTAL := TOTAL + QUANTITY * COST;
      TEMPQUANT := TEMPQUANT - QUANTITY;
      INDEX := INDEX + DIRECTION
      ...
    END;
```

If the last remaining portion of TEMPQUANT is less than the amount of the last relevant purchase, then only TEMPQUANT units are added to the total:

```
TOTAL := TOTAL + TEMPQUANT * COST;
```

In addition to calling the procedures for inventory costing, procedure MENU allows for input of a new inventory item when the user chooses the 'A' option from the menu. Since the variables that store the item and purchases information are global, MENU simply calls procedures INITEM and INPURCH to change this information:

```
'A' : BEGIN
        CLEARSCREEN;
        INITEM;
        INPURCH
      END;
```

```
(*$S+*)
PROGRAM INVENTORY;

USES
                    (*$U MONEYUNIT.CODE*)
MONEYUNIT,
                    (*$U CHECKUNIT.CODE*)
CHECKUNIT;
```

Figure 14.2: Listing of Program INVENTORY

```
CONST
  MAXPURCH = 30;

TYPE
  PURCHASES = RECORD
    QUANTITY : INTEGER;
    COST     : LONG2;
  END;

VAR
  PURCHARY : ARRAY[1..MAXPURCH] OF PURCHASES;
  ISSUES,
  NUMPURCH,
  TOTUNITS  : INTEGER;
  TOTCOST   : LONG2;
  DONE      : BOOLEAN;
  ITEMNUM   : LONG1;
  ITEMNAME  : STRING;


PROCEDURE INITEM;

  VAR
    DIGIT : BOOLEAN;

BEGIN
  WRITELN;
  WRITE('NAME OF INVENTORY ITEM: ');
  READLN(ITEMNAME);
  REPEAT
    WRITE('                    I.D.#: ');
    INVALUE(ITEMNUM, 6, DIGIT)
  UNTIL (DIGIT AND VERIFYCHECK(ITEMNUM))
END;   (* INITEM *)


PROCEDURE LINEOFCHARS(C : CHAR);

  CONST
    SCREENWIDTH = 40;

  VAR
    I : INTEGER;

BEGIN
  FOR I := 1 TO SCREENWIDTH DO
    WRITE(C);
  WRITELN
END;        (* LINEOFCHARS *)


PROCEDURE CONTINUE;

  VAR
    ANS : STRING;
```

Figure 14.2: Listing of Program INVENTORY (cont.)

```
BEGIN
  WRITELN;
  WRITE('TYPE <RETURN> TO CONTINUE.');
  READLN(ANS)
END;          (* CONTINUE *)



PROCEDURE REPORTTOTALS;

  VAR
    STTOTCOST : STRING;

BEGIN
  WRITELN;
  WRITELN('TOTAL UNITS IN INVENTORY = ', TOTUNITS);
  DOLLARFORM(TOTCOST,STTOTCOST);
  WRITELN('TOTAL COST OF INVENTORY  = ', STTOTCOST);
  WRITELN;
  WRITELN('TOTAL UNITS ISSUED       = ', ISSUES);
  WRITELN;
  LINEOFCHARS('-');
  WRITELN
END;         (* REPORTTOTALS *)


PROCEDURE ECHOITEM;

BEGIN
  WRITELN;
  LINEOFCHARS('*');
  WRITELN;
  WRITELN('        INVENTORY ITEM: ',ITEMNAME);
  WRITELN('                 I.D.#: ',ITEMNUM);
  WRITELN;
  LINEOFCHARS('*');
END;          (* ECHOITEM *)



PROCEDURE WEIGHTED (VAR AVECOST : LONG2);

  VAR
    INVERSE : REAL;


BEGIN   (* WEIGHTED *)
  INVERSE := 1.0 / TOTUNITS;
  LONGMULT(TOTCOST, INVERSE, AVECOST)
END;   (* WEIGHTED *)



PROCEDURE IFO (VAR TOTAL : LONG2;
                   FIFO  : BOOLEAN);
```

Figure 14.2: Listing of Program INVENTORY (cont.)

```
    VAR
      INDEX,
      TEMPQUANT,
      DIRECTION : INTEGER;
      STCOST : STRING;


  BEGIN
    IF FIFO THEN
      BEGIN
        INDEX := 1;       (* START AT FIRST PURCHASE *)
        DIRECTION := 1    (* AND GO FORWARD *)
      END
    ELSE  (* IF LIFO *)
      BEGIN
        INDEX := NUMPURCH;  (* START AT LAST PURCHASE *)
        DIRECTION := -1     (* AND GO BACKWARD *)
      END;


   TOTAL := 0;
   TEMPQUANT := ISSUES;


   WHILE TEMPQUANT > 0 DO
     WITH PURCHARY[INDEX] DO
       BEGIN
         DOLLARFORM(COST,STCOST);
         IF QUANTITY < TEMPQUANT THEN
           BEGIN
             WRITELN(QUANTITY, ' UNITS @ ', STCOST);
             TOTAL := TOTAL + QUANTITY * COST;
             TEMPQUANT := TEMPQUANT - QUANTITY;
             INDEX := INDEX + DIRECTION
           END
         ELSE
           BEGIN
             WRITELN(TEMPQUANT, ' UNITS @ ',STCOST);
             TOTAL := TOTAL + TEMPQUANT * COST;
             TEMPQUANT := 0
           END
       END (* WITH *)
END;  (* IFO *)



PROCEDURE INPURCH;

  VAR
    I : INTEGER;

  PROCEDURE ININT(VAR VAL : INTEGER);

    VAR
      GARBAGE : STRING;
```

Figure 14.2: Listing of Program INVENTORY (cont.)

```
    BEGIN
      GET(INPUT);
      IF INPUT^ IN ['0'..'9'] THEN
        READLN(VAL)
      ELSE
        BEGIN
          READLN(GARBAGE);
          ININT(VAL)
        END
    END;      (* ININT *)




    PROCEDURE ZEROPURCH;

      VAR
        I : INTEGER;

    BEGIN
      FOR I := 1 TO MAXPURCH DO
        WITH PURCHARY[I] DO
          BEGIN
            COST := 0;
            QUANTITY := 0
          END
    END;         (* ZEROPURCH *)




  BEGIN (* INPURCH *)
    REPEAT
      WRITELN;
      WRITELN;
      WRITE('HOW MANY PURCHASES OF THIS ITEM? ');
      ININT(NUMPURCH);
      IF (NUMPURCH > MAXPURCH) THEN
        BEGIN
          WRITELN(MAXPURCH, ' MAXIMUM');
          WRITELN
        END
    UNTIL (NUMPURCH <= MAXPURCH);

    CLEARSCREEN;
    ECHOITEM;
    WRITELN;

    TOTUNITS := 0;
    TOTCOST := 0;
    ZEROPURCH;
```

Figure 14.2: Listing of Program INVENTORY (cont.)

```
  FOR I := 1 TO NUMPURCH DO
    WITH PURCHARY[I] DO
      BEGIN
        WRITELN('PURCHASE #', I, ':');
        WRITELN('------------');
        WRITELN;
        WRITE('NUMBER OF UNITS? ');
        ININT(QUANTITY);
        TOTUNITS := TOTUNITS + QUANTITY;
        WRITE('  COST PER UNIT? ');
        INDOLLAR(COST);
        TOTCOST := TOTCOST + COST * QUANTITY;
        WRITELN;
        WRITELN
      END;

  CLEARSCREEN;
  ECHOITEM;




  WRITELN;
  WRITELN('HOW MANY UNITS ISSUED');
  WRITE('     FROM INVENTORY? ');

  REPEAT
    ININT(ISSUES);
    IF ISSUES > TOTUNITS THEN
      BEGIN
        WRITELN('ONLY ',TOTUNITS,' UNITS AVAILABLE');
        WRITELN('IN INVENTORY.');
        WRITE('                         ? ')
      END
  UNTIL (ISSUES <= TOTUNITS);

  CLEARSCREEN
END;   (* INPURCH *)





PROCEDURE MENU;

  VAR
    CHOICE : CHAR;
    AVERAGE,
    ISSUECOST : LONG2;
    STAVERAGE,
    STISSUECOST : STRING;

BEGIN
```

Figure 14.2: Listing of Program INVENTORY (cont.)

```
WRITELN;
ECHOITEM;
WRITELN;
WRITELN;
WRITELN('WHICH COSTING METHOD?');
WRITELN;
WRITELN('          W(EIGHTED AVERAGE');
WRITELN('          L(IFO');
WRITELN('          F(IFO');
WRITELN('          ----------------------');
WRITELN('          A(NOTHER INVENTORY ITEM');
WRITELN('          Q(UIT');
WRITELN;
LINEOFCHARS('*');
WRITELN;
REPEAT
  WRITE('                          ? ');
  READLN(CHOICE)
UNTIL CHOICE IN ['W','L','F','A','Q'];

IF (CHOICE IN ['W','L','F']) THEN
  BEGIN
    CLEARSCREEN;
    ECHOITEM;
    REPORTTOTALS
  END;

CASE CHOICE OF

  'W' : BEGIN
          WRITELN('WEIGHTED AVERAGE COSTING METHOD');
          WRITELN('-------- ------- ------- ------');
          WRITELN;
          WEIGHTED(AVERAGE);
          DOLLARFORM(AVERAGE,STAVERAGE);
          WRITELN('AVERAGE COST PER UNIT = ', STAVERAGE);
          ISSUECOST := ISSUES * AVERAGE
        END;

  'L' : BEGIN
          WRITELN('LIFO COSTING METHOD');
          WRITELN('---- ------- ------');
          WRITELN;
          IFO(ISSUECOST,FALSE)
        END;

  'F' : BEGIN
          WRITELN('FIFO COSTING METHOD');
          WRITELN('---- ------- ------');
          WRITELN;
          IFO(ISSUECOST,TRUE)
        END;

  'A' : BEGIN
          CLEARSCREEN;
```

Figure 14.2: Listing of Program INVENTORY (cont.)

```
            INITEM;
            INPURCH
          END;

    'Q' : DONE := TRUE

  END;  (* CASE *)

  IF (CHOICE IN ['W','F','L']) THEN
    BEGIN
      DOLLARFORM(ISSUECOST,STISSUECOST);
      WRITELN;
      WRITELN('TOTAL COST OF UNITS ISSUED = ', STISSUECOST);
      WRITELN;
      LINEOFCHARS('*');
      CONTINUE;
      CLEARSCREEN
    END

END;  (* MENU *)


BEGIN (* MAIN PROGRAM *)

  CLEARSCREEN;
  LINEOFCHARS('*');
  WRITELN;
  WRITELN('        INVENTORY COSTING METHODS');
  WRITELN('        --------- ------- -------');
  WRITELN;
  LINEOFCHARS('*');

  INITEM;
  INPURCH;
  DONE := FALSE;

  WHILE NOT DONE DO
    MENU

END.  (* MAIN PROGRAM *)
```

Figure 14.2: Listing of Program INVENTORY (cont.)

Chapter 15

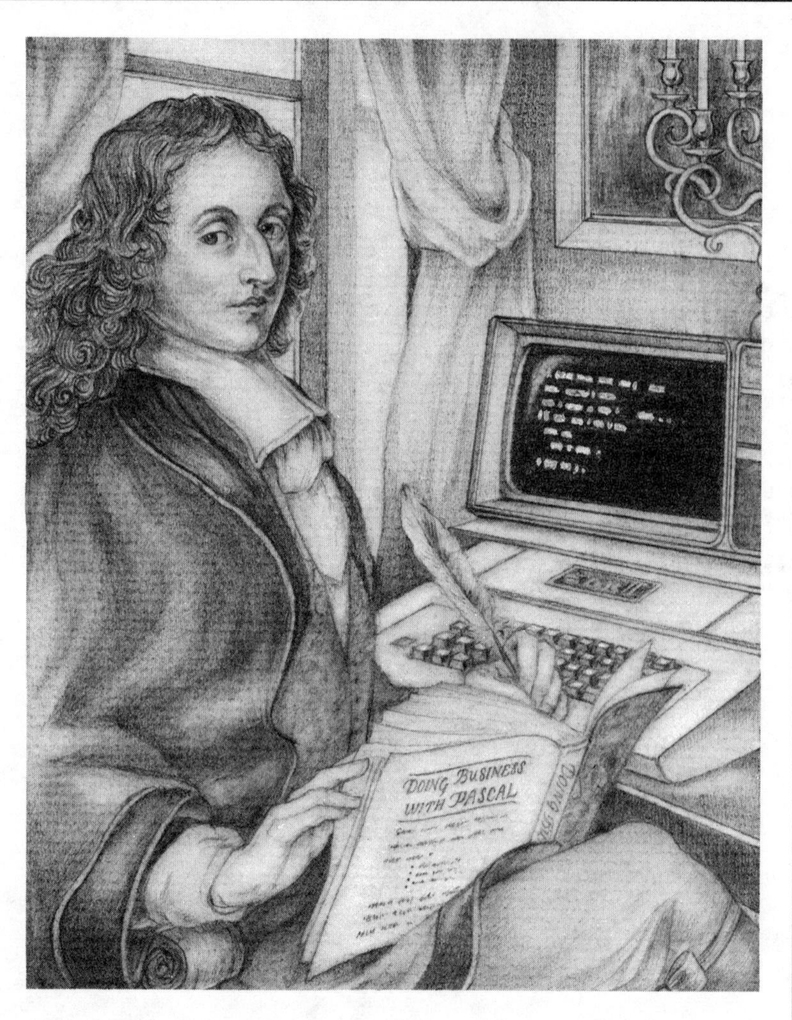

Economic Order Quantity

THE APPLICATION

The determination of the economic order quantity is a tool that nearly every management accounting textbook discusses. Several different formulas can be used in the calculation of the EOQ; a fairly simple one is implemented here. One problem with EOQ is that some of the most important data for input cannot be calculated exactly; they can only be estimated. How does one calculate the stockout cost per unit per year? The cost of placing one order? The storage cost per unit per year? Data gathered from a well-constructed business system can help provide more concrete information, but cannot provide the entire answer. Data processors frequently blame inaccurate results on the GIGO theory: garbage in—garbage out. Economic order quantity is probably more affected by this problem than any other application illustrated in this book.

Nevertheless, there are ways that a business system could help to make EOQ calculation more accurate. Certainly the annual demand, in units, could come directly from master file information for a particular inventory item. That in turn would have come from transaction files produced by the stock issues application. The cost of placing one order could be calculated as well, particularly if the purchasing department's costs were clearly identified. The costs of payroll, stock inventory items used by purchasing, and purchased services, and portions of depreciation expense for capital equipment all could be combined for the calculation of the cost of placing one order. The number of orders processed would also be a statistic kept by the stock issues/purchase order application.

Using the same methods, the storage costs per unit per year could be calculated based on the annual depreciation costs for the storage room and the number of square feet actually associated with the storage of a particular inventory item. This, plus the costs associated with stockroom personnel and equipment, could give a fairly accurate estimate of the storage costs.

A different approach would be to *estimate* each of these values and assume consistency for every inventory item the company has. Thus the values could be stored in the system profile and accessed by the EOQ application.

If management chooses to use the EOQ as a method for determining the quantity of orders, then specific reports could be generated that would report on exceptions to the EOQ standard. For instance, one report might show a month's worth of orders, comparing the actual quantities ordered with the EOQ calculations. The EOQ would thus serve as a *standard* (to measure actual data against) rather than an operational tool. The performance of the purchasing department could thus be measured; comparisons over time would allow for the modification of the standard itself.

THE SAMPLE RUN

This program presents the EOQ formula in one of its simplest forms. As we can see from the sample run, shown in Figure 15.1, the formula is computed with four items of input data: the annual demand (in units) of the inventory item, the cost of placing the order, the annual storage cost per unit, and the stockout cost per unit. From this information, the program calculates the optimal order quantity and the number of orders per year.

Missing from this version of the EOQ formula are two considerations that might be significant to some companies in some situations: the maximum inventory capacity, and the possibility of price discounts for large orders of the item. A more complete (and more complicated) program would include these two factors.

```
#######################################

        ECONOMIC ORDER QUANTITY

#######################################

NAME OF INVENTORY ITEM?          WIDGET
                 I.D.#?          12345-5

ANNUAL DEMAND IN UNITS?          4500
COST OF PLACING AN ORDER?        12.33
ANNUAL STORAGE COST PER UNIT?    .68
STOCKOUT COST PER UNIT PER YEAR? 2.40

#######################################

OPTIMAL ORDER QUANTITY = 458 UNITS

( 9.8 ORDERS PER YEAR)

#######################################

ANOTHER ITEM? N
-------------------------------------------
```

Figure 15.1: Sample Run of EOQ Program

THE PROGRAM

The listing of program EOQ is shown in Figure 15.2. Procedure INITEM reads the data for the inventory item, and procedure EOQCOMPUTE contains the EOQ formula.

The version of the formula used in this program is:

$$EOQ = \frac{2 \cdot C_o \cdot D_s}{C_h} \cdot \frac{C_h + C_s}{C_s}$$

where:

D = the annual demand, in units
C_o = the cost of placing one order
C_h = storage per unit per year
C_s = stockout cost per unit per year

Both terms of this equation contain fractions that have monetary values in the numerator and the denominator. Therefore, in our program we need a way of dividing one long integer by another and producing a quotient of type REAL. Function LDIVL performs this task by converting the most significant digits of both the numerator and the denominator to regular integers, and then finding their quotient. Both LDIVL and the built-in Pascal function SQRT appear in the implementation of the EOQ formula:

```
EOQUANT := SQRT(LDIVL((2*ORDER*DEMAND),(STORAGE))) *
           SQRT(LDIVL((STORAGE+STOCKOUT),STOCKOUT));
```

The number of orders per year is then computed as the demand divided by the economic order quantity:

```
NUMORDS := DEMAND / EOQUANT;
```

```
(*$S+*)
PROGRAM EOQ;

USES

TRANSCEND,
           (*$U MONEYUNIT.CODE*)
MONEYUNIT,
           (*$U CHECKUNIT.CODE*)
CHECKUNIT;

VAR
  ANSWER : STRING;
  DEMAND : INTEGER;
  ORDER,
  STORAGE,
  STOCKOUT : LONG2;

PROCEDURE LINEOFCHARS(C : CHAR);

CONST
  WIDTH = 40;

VAR
  I : INTEGER;

BEGIN
  FOR I := 1 TO WIDTH DO
    WRITE(C);
  WRITELN
END;         (* LINEOFCHARS *)

PROCEDURE INITEM;

  VAR
    NAME  : STRING;
    NUM   : LONG1;
    CHECK : BOOLEAN;
```

Figure 15.2: Listing of Program EOQ

```
    PROCEDURE ININT(VAR VAL : INTEGER);


      VAR
        GARBAGE : STRING;


      BEGIN
        GET(INPUT);
        IF (INPUT^ IN ['0'..'9']) THEN
          READLN(VAL)
        ELSE
          BEGIN
             READLN(GARBAGE);
             WRITELN('*** REDO');
             WRITE  ('        ? ');
             ININT(VAL)
           END
       END;       (* ININT *)


  BEGIN
    WRITELN;
    WRITE('NAME OF INVENTORY ITEM?            ');
    READLN(NAME);
    WRITE('                       I.D.#?      ');
    REPEAT
      INVALUE(NUM,6,CHECK)
    UNTIL (CHECK AND (VERIFYCHECK(NUM)));
    WRITELN;
    WRITE('ANNUAL DEMAND IN UNITS?            ');
    ININT(DEMAND);
    WRITE('COST OF PLACING AN ORDER?          ');
    INDOLLAR(ORDER);
    WRITE('ANNUAL STORAGE COST PER UNIT?      ');
    INDOLLAR(STORAGE);
    WRITE('STOCKOUT COST PER UNIT PER YEAR? ');
    INDOLLAR(STOCKOUT);
    WRITELN;
    LINEOFCHARS('#')
  END;       (* INITEM *)



  PROCEDURE EOQCOMPUTE;

    VAR
      EOQUANT,
      NUMORDS   : REAL;

    FUNCTION LDIVL(L1,L2 : LONG2): REAL;

      VAR
        HOLD1,
        HOLD2   : LONG2;
        R       : REAL;
```

Figure 15.2: Listing of Program EOQ (cont.)

```
      BEGIN
        HOLD1 := 1;
        WHILE L1 > MAXINT DO
          BEGIN
            L1 := L1 DIV 10;
            HOLD1 := HOLD1 * 10
          END;
        HOLD2 := 1;
        WHILE L2 > MAXINT DO
          BEGIN
            L2 := L2 DIV 10;
            HOLD2 := HOLD2 * 10

          END;
        R := TRUNC(L1) / TRUNC(L2);
        IF HOLD2 >= HOLD1 THEN
          BEGIN
            HOLD2 := HOLD2 DIV HOLD1;
            WHILE HOLD2 > 1 DO
              BEGIN
                R := R / 10.0;
                HOLD2 := HOLD2 DIV 10
              END
          END
        ELSE
          BEGIN
            HOLD1 := HOLD1 DIV HOLD2;
            WHILE HOLD1 > 1 DO
              BEGIN
                R := R * 10.0;
                HOLD1 := HOLD1 DIV 10
              END
          END;

        LDIVL := R
      END;            (* LDIVL *)

  BEGIN  (* EOQCOMPUTE *)
    WRITELN;
    EOQUANT := SQRT(LDIVL((2*ORDER*DEMAND),(STORAGE))) *
               SQRT(LDIVL((STORAGE + STOCKOUT),STOCKOUT));
    NUMORDS := DEMAND / EOQUANT;

    WRITELN('OPTIMAL ORDER QUANTITY = ',ROUND(EOQUANT),' UNITS');
    WRITELN;
    WRITELN('(',NUMORDS:4:1,' ORDERS PER YEAR)')
  END;   (* EOQCOMPUTE *)

  BEGIN       (* MAIN PROGRAM *)
    CLEARSCREEN;
    WRITELN;
    LINEOFCHARS('#');
    WRITELN;
    WRITELN('           ECONOMIC ORDER QUANTITY');
    WRITELN;
    LINEOFCHARS('#');
    WRITELN;
```

Figure 15.2: Listing of Program EOQ (cont.)

```
  REPEAT
    INITEM;
    EOQCOMPUTE;
    WRITELN;
    LINEOFCHARS('#');

    WRITELN;
    WRITE('ANOTHER ITEM? ');
    READLN(ANSWER);
    CLEARSCREEN
  UNTIL (ANSWER = 'N')
END.     (* MAIN PROGRAM *)
```

Figure 15.2: Listing of Program EOQ (cont.)

Chapter 16

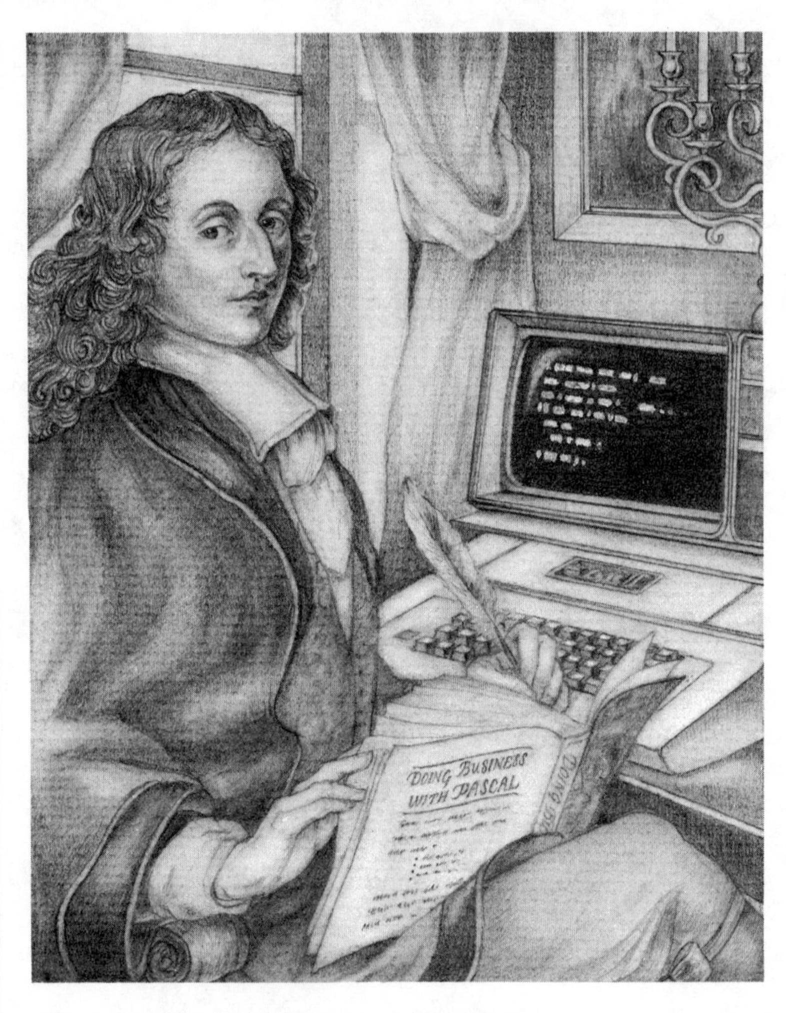

Cash Requirements

THE APPLICATION

The cash requirements application program predicts the cash needs of a business. It calculates the requirements by week for the first four weeks of the period and by month for the next two months, and displays a total for amounts due more than three months away. The application as given in this example allows for manual input through the keyboard and then verification on the screen. In a complete business system environment, the input would be quite different.

All input in the category of trade payables would come from the current invoices outstanding file of the accounts payable subsystem. Within that file would be an indication of the due date of each invoice. Due dates could be assigned so as to take advantage of trade discounts. Alternatively, two dates could be provided, one for the due date if all discounts are taken, another for a due date after which the company's credit rating might be in jeopardy. The cash requirements application could check for either date and report cash requirements accordingly.

Input would also be made from the payroll application. The system profile would be accessed to determine the frequency of the pay cycle, and then average payroll-related cash flows per cycle would be calculated and entered. Alternatively, the average payroll cash flow could be entered manually, carefully accounting for any annual cost-of-living pay raises. A detailed look at the evaluation date for each employee and the expected salary increase could also be made. Such accuracy, however, would normally not be required, as the cash requirements report would be used to predict general trends.

Information on leases and loans might well come from another file that shows repeating and constant cash outflows. Equipment obsolescence information, as reported by the capital assets subsystem, could also be factored in. Large outflows of cash for the purchase of fixed assets could then become part of the cash requirements report.

Any other items—one-time cash outflows, items paid out of a general funds account rather than from the accounts payable account, periodic stock dividends paid out, and so on—would all be entered into a file used solely by the cash requirements report; or these miscellaneous payables could be entered interactively.

The cash requirements report is only half of a complete cash-flow analysis. The other half is a prediction of cash receipts. The goal of the complete analysis is to measure the ability of the company to take advantage of investments, or the need to negotiate short-term loans. Cash receipts information could conceivably be generated from the accounts receivable file, from an estimate of gross sales (if the majority of the company's sales are on a cash basis), or from a combination of these two sources of information. Interest income and other kinds of non-operating income could also be included, either entered interactively or taken directly from other subsystem applications.

THE SAMPLE RUN

This program produces a table detailing cash requirements for the weeks and months forward from the current date. It reads input for payables under four categories—trade payables, payroll, leases and loans, and "other." For each payable the program reads the amount and the date due.

In the sample run shown in Figure 16.1, a total of 21 payables were entered. Notice that the program does not require that they be entered in chronological order. Following the input dialogue, the program presents the cash requirement table. The table shows totals for each of the four weeks following the current date, then for the second and third months, and finally for payables due beyond the third month. Subtotals for each of the categories are also shown for each period.

```
            CASH REQUIREMENTS
            ==== ============

TODAY'S DATE? 5-31-82

TRADE PAYABLES
--------------

HOW MANY ENTRIES? 8

1. AMOUNT?   2715.29
   DATE DUE?   6-10-82

2. AMOUNT?   850.50
   DATE DUE?   7-9-82

3. AMOUNT?   298.25
   DATE DUE?   7-23-82

4. AMOUNT?   640.00
   DATE DUE?   8-6-82

5. AMOUNT?   1852.18
   DATE DUE?   8-31-82

6. AMOUNT?   1650.10
   DATE DUE?   6-21-82

7. AMOUNT?   1829.50
   DATE DUE?   8-16-82

8. AMOUNT?   380.69
   DATE DUE?   7-5-82

PAYROLL
--------

HOW MANY ENTRIES? 6

1. AMOUNT?   45650
   DATE DUE?   6-2-82

2. AMOUNT?   45650
   DATE DUE?   6-16-82

3. AMOUNT?   45650
   DATE DUE?   6-30-82

4. AMOUNT?   45650
   DATE DUE?   7-14-82


5. AMOUNT?   49780
   DATE DUE?   7-28-82

6. AMOUNT?   49780
   DATE DUE?   8-11-82
```

Figure 16.1: Output of Cash Requirements Program

```
LEASES/LOANS
------------

HOW MANY ENTRIES? 5

1. AMOUNT?   4500
   DATE DUE?   6-1-82

2. AMOUNT?   1860
   DATE DUE?   7-15-82

3. AMOUNT?   4500
   DATE DUE?   7-1-82

4. AMOUNT?   1860
   DATE DUE?   8-16-82

5. AMOUNT?   4500
   DATE DUE?   8-2-82


OTHER
-----

HOW MANY ENTRIES? 2

1. AMOUNT?   1000
   DATE DUE?   6-2-82

2. AMOUNT?   1500
   DATE DUE?   8-26-82
-----------------------------------------------------

                          CASH REQUIREMENTS
                            MAY 31, 1982


        TRADE PAYABLES      PAYROLL LEASES/LOANS        OTHER         TOTAL

WEEKS:

  1                 --  $45,650.00   $4,500.00   $1,000.00  $51,150.00
  2          $2,715.29          --          --          --   $2,715.29
  3                 --  $45,650.00          --          --  $45,650.00
  4          $1,650.10          --          --          --   $1,650.10


MONTHS:

  2          $1,529.44  $91,300.00   $6,360.00          --  $99,189.44
  3          $2,469.50  $99,560.00   $6,360.00          -- $108,389.50


BEYOND THIRD MONTH:

             $1,852.18          --          --   $1,500.00   $3,352.18
```

Figure 16.1: Output of Cash Requirements Program (cont.)

THE PROGRAM

Program CASHREQ, shown in Figure 16.2, stores the input values in the two-dimensional array CASH:

```
TYPE
   ARY = ARRAY[1..MAXWEEK,1..MAXCATS] OF LONG2;

VAR
   CASH : ARY;
```

With the constant MAXWEEK set at 13, the CASH array can store cash requirements for twelve weeks into the future. The 13th element of the array is for any payables that fall due beyond the twelfth week. The constant MAXCATS is set at 4, for the four different categories of payables. In procedure INIT all the elements of the array CASH are initialized to zero. In addition, CATEGORY, an array of strings, receives the four string values that will be used in both the input dialogue and the cash requirements table.

Procedure INAMOUNTS conducts the input dialogue. A pair of nested loops control the action. The outer loop reads an input value for the number of entries for each payable category:

```
FOR I := 1 TO MAXCATS DO
   BEGIN
      WRITELN(CATEGORY[I]);
         ...
      WRITE('HOW MANY ENTRIES? ');
      ININT(ENTRIES);
```

Then the inner loop reads an amount and a date for each entry using input routines from MONEYUNIT and DATEUNIT:

```
FOR J := 1 TO ENTRIES DO
   BEGIN
      WRITE(J, '. AMOUNT? ');
      INDOLLAR(AMOUNT);
      WRITE('  DATE DUE? ');
      INDATE(DUE);
      DATECONVERT(DUE,SCDUE);
```

The week due is then calculated for each entry. SCTODAY, the scalar value of the current date, is a global value set in the main program section. The integer variable WEEK is the difference between SCTODAY and

SCDUE, divided by 7:

```
WEEK := TRUNC((SCDUE - SCTODAY) DIV 7 + 1);
```

All values due beyond the twelfth week are to be stored in the 13th element of CASH:

```
IF WEEK > MAXWEEK THEN
   WEEK := MAXWEEK;
```

Finally, we can use WEEK and I as indices into the CASH array to store each payable amount under its correct due date and its correct category:

```
CASH[WEEK,I] := CASH[WEEK,I] + AMOUNT;
```

By storing the input values in CASH, we avoid having to set up an additional array to keep track of the due date of each entry. In effect, we are organizing the output table itself in the input routine.

Procedure OUTTABLE contains three different sections that produce the three chronological parts of the cash requirements table. Each section uses procedure OUTCASH to print the cash entries of the table. OUTCASH, in turn, uses DOLLARFORM and RIGHTFIELD to prepare the long integer values for output:

```
IF AMT<>0 THEN
   BEGIN
      DOLLARFORM(AMT,STAMT);
      RIGHTFIELD(STAMT,12);
      WRITE(STAMT)
   END
```

To avoid entries of the form $.00, OUTCASH has an ELSE clause that prints a dash if the value of the entry is zero:

```
ELSE
   WRITE('      -')
```

```
(*$S+*)
PROGRAM CASHREQ;

USES
            (*$U MONEYUNIT.CODE*)
MONEYUNIT,
            (*$U DATEUNIT.CODE*)
DATEUNIT;
```

Figure 16.2: Listing of Program CASHREQ

```
CONST
  MAXWEEK = 13;       (* NUMBER OF WEEKS *)
  MAXCATS = 4;        (* NUMBER OF CASH CATEGORIES *)

TYPE
  ARY = ARRAY[1..MAXWEEK,1..MAXCATS] OF LONG2;

VAR
  CASH : ARY;
  CATEGORY : ARRAY[1..MAXCATS] OF STRING;
  TODAY   : DATEREC;
  SCTODAY : DATELONG;


PROCEDURE ININT(VAR VAL: INTEGER);

VAR
  GARBAGE : STRING;

BEGIN
  GET(INPUT);
  IF INPUT^ IN ['0'..'9'] THEN
    READLN(VAL)
  ELSE
    BEGIN
      READLN(GARBAGE);
      WRITELN('*** REDO');
      WRITE('         ? ');
      ININT(VAL)
    END
END;      (* ININT *)



PROCEDURE INIT;

VAR
  I,
  J : INTEGER;

BEGIN
  CATEGORY[1] := 'TRADE PAYABLES';
  CATEGORY[2] := 'PAYROLL ';
  CATEGORY[3] := 'LEASES/LOANS';
  CATEGORY[4] := 'OTHER';

  (*
   * INITIALIZE CASH ARRAY TO ZERO
   *)

  FOR I := 1 TO MAXWEEK DO
    FOR J := 1 TO MAXCATS DO
      CASH[I,J] := 0
END;


PROCEDURE INAMOUNTS;
```

Figure 16.2: Listing of Program CASHREQ (cont.)

```
VAR
  I,
  J,
  ENTRIES,
  WEEK   : INTEGER;
  AMOUNT : LONG2;
  DUE    : DATEREC;
  SCDUE  : DATELONG;

BEGIN  (* INAMOUNTS *)
  FOR I := 1 TO MAXCATS DO
    BEGIN
      WRITELN(CATEGORY[I]);
      FOR J := 1 TO LENGTH(CATEGORY[I]) DO
        WRITE('-');
      WRITELN;
      WRITELN;
      WRITE('HOW MANY ENTRIES? ');
      ININT(ENTRIES);
      WRITELN;
      FOR J := 1 TO ENTRIES DO
        BEGIN
          WRITE(J, '. AMOUNT?    ');
          INDOLLAR(AMOUNT);
          WRITE('    DATE DUE?    ');
          INDATE(DUE);
          DATECONVERT(DUE,SCDUE);
          WEEK := TRUNC((SCDUE - SCTODAY) DIV 7 + 1);

          (*
           *  THE LAST ELEMENT OF CASH
           *  IS FOR WEEKS BEYOND MAXWEEK.
           *)

          IF WEEK > MAXWEEK THEN
            WEEK := MAXWEEK;

          CASH[WEEK,I] := CASH[WEEK,I] + AMOUNT;
          WRITELN
        END;
        WRITELN
    END
END;    (* INAMOUNTS *)



PROCEDURE OUTTABLE;

  VAR
    I,
    J,
    K      : INTEGER;
    TOTAL,
    TEMPTOT : LONG2;


  PROCEDURE HEADING;
```

Figure 16.2: Listing of Program CASHREQ (cont.)

```
  VAR
    I : INTEGER;



  BEGIN
    WRITE('          ',CATEGORY[1]);
    FOR I := 2 TO 4 DO
      BEGIN
        RIGHTFIELD(CATEGORY[I],12);
        WRITE(CATEGORY[I])
      END;
    WRITELN('           TOTAL');
    WRITELN
  END;          (* HEADING *)



PROCEDURE OUTCASH(AMT : LONG2);

  VAR
    STAMT : STRING;



BEGIN
  IF AMT <> 0 THEN
    BEGIN
      DOLLARFORM(AMT,STAMT);
      RIGHTFIELD(STAMT,12);
      WRITE(STAMT)
    END
  ELSE
    WRITE('           --')
END;                    (* OUTCASH *)



BEGIN     (* OUTTABLE *)
  WRITELN;
  WRITELN('                         CASH REQUIREMENTS');
  WRITE('                           ');
  OUTDATE(TODAY);
  WRITELN;
  WRITELN;
  WRITELN;
  HEADING;

  WRITELN;
  WRITELN;

  (*
   * FIRST FOUR WEEKS
   *)
```

Figure 16.2: Listing of Program CASHREQ (cont.)

```
WRITELN('WEEKS:');
WRITELN;
FOR I := 1 TO 4 DO
  BEGIN
    TOTAL := 0;
    WRITE('  ',I,'        ');
    FOR J := 1 TO MAXCATS DO
      BEGIN
        TOTAL := TOTAL + CASH[I,J];
        OUTCASH(CASH[I,J])
      END;
    OUTCASH(TOTAL);
    WRITELN
  END;

(*
 *  SECOND AND THIRD MONTHS
 *)

WRITELN;
WRITELN;
WRITELN('MONTHS:');
WRITELN;

FOR I := 1 TO 2 DO
  BEGIN
    WRITE('  ',I+1,'        ');
    TOTAL := 0;
    FOR J := 1 TO MAXCATS DO
      BEGIN
        TEMPTOT := 0;
        FOR K := 1 TO 4 DO
          TEMPTOT := TEMPTOT + CASH[I*4+K,J];
        OUTCASH(TEMPTOT);
        TOTAL := TOTAL + TEMPTOT
      END;
    OUTCASH(TOTAL);
    WRITELN
  END;

(*
 *  .. AND BEYOND
 *)

WRITELN;
WRITELN;
WRITELN('BEYOND THIRD MONTH:');
WRITELN;

TOTAL := 0;
WRITE('           ');
FOR I := 1 TO MAXCATS DO
  BEGIN
    OUTCASH(CASH[MAXWEEK,I]);
    TOTAL := TOTAL + CASH[MAXWEEK,I]
  END;
OUTCASH(TOTAL);
```

Figure 16.2: Listing of Program CASHREQ (cont.)

```
    WRITELN

  END;     (* OUTTABLE *)

  BEGIN (* MAIN PROGRAM *)

    CLEARSCREEN;
    WRITELN;
    WRITELN('          CASH REQUIREMENTS');
    WRITELN('          ==== ============');
    WRITELN;
    WRITELN;
    WRITE('TODAY''S DATE? ');
    INDATE(TODAY);
    DATECONVERT(TODAY,SCTODAY);
    WRITELN;
    WRITELN;

    INIT;
    INAMOUNTS;

    CLEARSCREEN;
    OUTTABLE
  END.        (* MAIN PROGRAM *)
```

Figure 16.2: Listing of Program CASHREQ (cont.)

Chapter 17

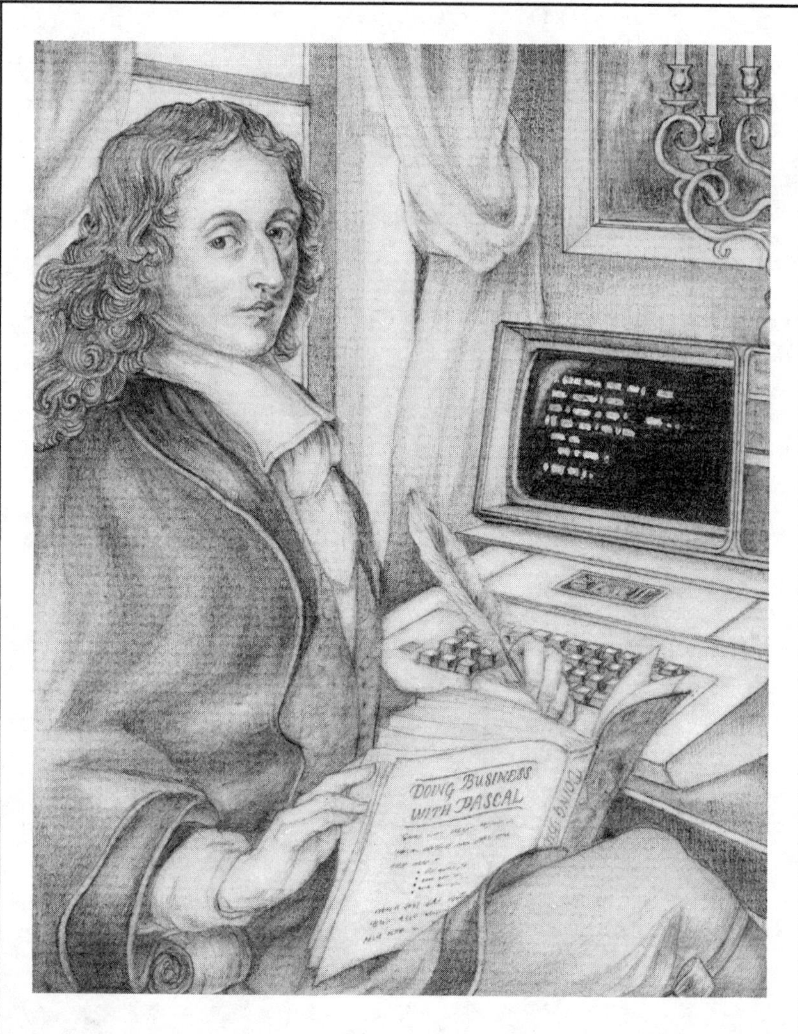

Fixed Asset Depreciation Methods

THE APPLICATION

In a complete business system, the information for depreciation reports like those produced by this application would be input completely from the capital assets master file. Little interactive input would be required, except to request the report. Even the choice of method used for depreciation of fixed assets would come from another file. The system profile would indicate the *standard* depreciation method. Then the fixed asset master file would indicate any exceptions to that standard method. The fixed asset master file would indicate the category of asset (building, type of equipment, and so on). The system profile might perhaps be expanded to allow for different depreciation methods for different kinds of assets, again with exceptions allowed for individual items.

The same application program could also be used to produce a report showing the effects of changing the depreciation methods for the entire fixed-asset base or perhaps for individual categories of assets. A slightly different program selection menu could be constructed, allowing as one option a search through the entire fixed asset master file to calculate depreciation by a new method. Following the recalculation of depreciation totals, financial statements might be printed to show the effect on the financial standing of the company. Accelerated depreciation methods are typically most valuable in times of rapidly changing rates of inflation, but the information from the various depreciation models could prove interesting to business management at any time.

The calculation of asset depreciation as discussed above is only one function of the capital assets subsystem. The ability to add and delete items from the fixed asset master file must also be provided for. The fixed asset file can then be used to monitor those assets that are approaching fully depreciated status. The decrease in depreciation as an expense can have considerable effect on the profitability of a business. Thus, one important report might list assets that will become fully depreciated over the next year, and show the impact of the resulting decrease in depreciation expense.

Also associated with the capital assets subsystem are management reports on the maintenance requirements of major items of equipment. Maintenance costs should be compared to the remaining undepreciated value of the asset. Also, maintenance schedules could be produced for management, to facilitate down-time scheduling or even employee vacation scheduling.

Finally, the analysis of capital purchasing decisions might also be automated and become part of the business system. Although some of the input items commonly used in capital purchase decision models are estimates (for example, the estimate of the cost of capital or of future inflation rates), the application that would do the calculations is fairly easy to automate, making reference to standard present value tables unnecessary.

In the design of the computer system, the application programmer should be careful to include all of the possible depreciation methods that the system user might require. In comparing depreciation methods, as in comparing inventory costing methods, nothing is more frustrating than attempting to use an application that does not provide for the full range of decisions.

THE SAMPLE RUN

The program presented in this chapter computes the annual depreciation of a fixed asset over its useful life by any of the four standard depreciation methods: straight-line, sum-of-the-year's-digits, double-declining-balance, and fixed-percentage-on-a-declining-base. It thus enables a user to compare the relative advantages of the four methods. Three items of input information are required for the calculation: its original cost, its residual value when fully depreciated, and its useful life in years.

The first screen of the dialogue produced by this program prompts the user for the asset information. In the sample run shown in Figure 17.1, the asset named MACHINE #1 has an original cost of $5,100, a residual value of $100, and a five-year useful life. The program echoes this information at the top of each screen.

The second screen shows the menu. Typing an integer from 1 to 4 produces the yearly depreciation figures for one of the four depreciation methods. Straight-line depreciation produces one amount, which is the same for each year of the useful life; the other methods display different amounts for each year. The user can call up the menu and select each method in turn. The program also allows the user to input a new asset in order to view another set of depreciation figures, by typing an 'A' as the menu choice.

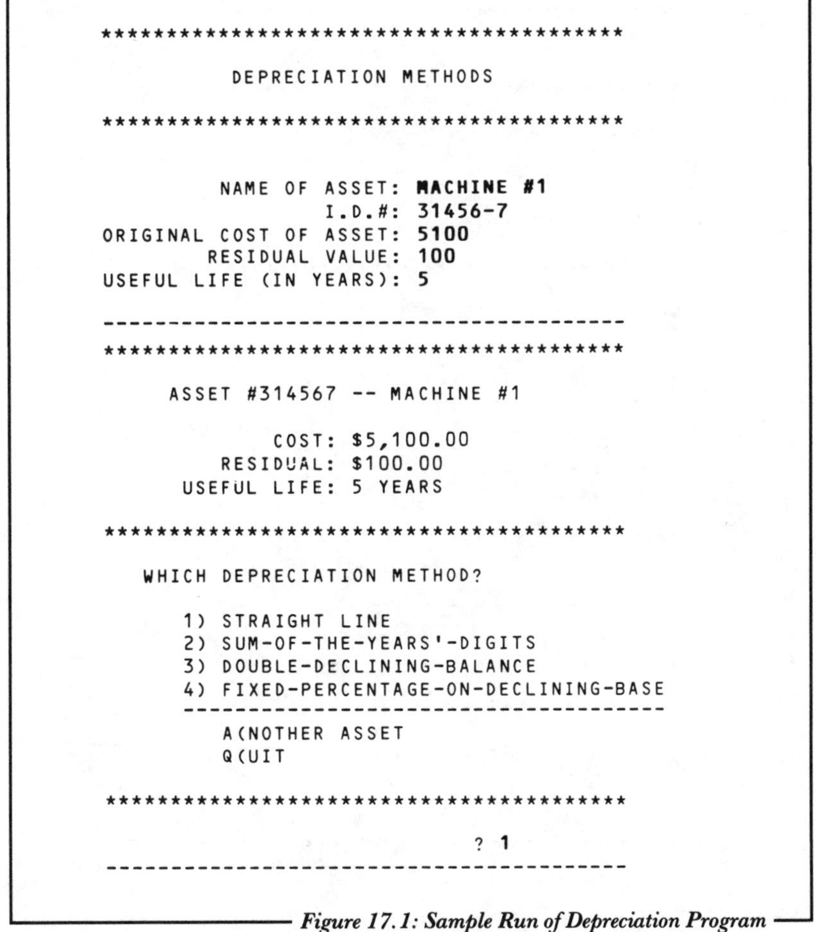

```
****************************************

          DEPRECIATION METHODS

****************************************


          NAME OF ASSET: MACHINE #1
                 I.D.#: 31456-7
ORIGINAL COST OF ASSET: 5100
        RESIDUAL VALUE: 100
USEFUL LIFE (IN YEARS): 5

----------------------------------------
****************************************

      ASSET #314567 -- MACHINE #1

             COST: $5,100.00
         RESIDUAL: $100.00
      USEFUL LIFE: 5 YEARS

****************************************

    WHICH DEPRECIATION METHOD?

      1) STRAIGHT LINE
      2) SUM-OF-THE-YEARS'-DIGITS
      3) DOUBLE-DECLINING-BALANCE
      4) FIXED-PERCENTAGE-ON-DECLINING-BASE
      ------------------------------------
         A(NOTHER ASSET
         Q(UIT

****************************************

                            ? 1
----------------------------------------
```

Figure 17.1: Sample Run of Depreciation Program

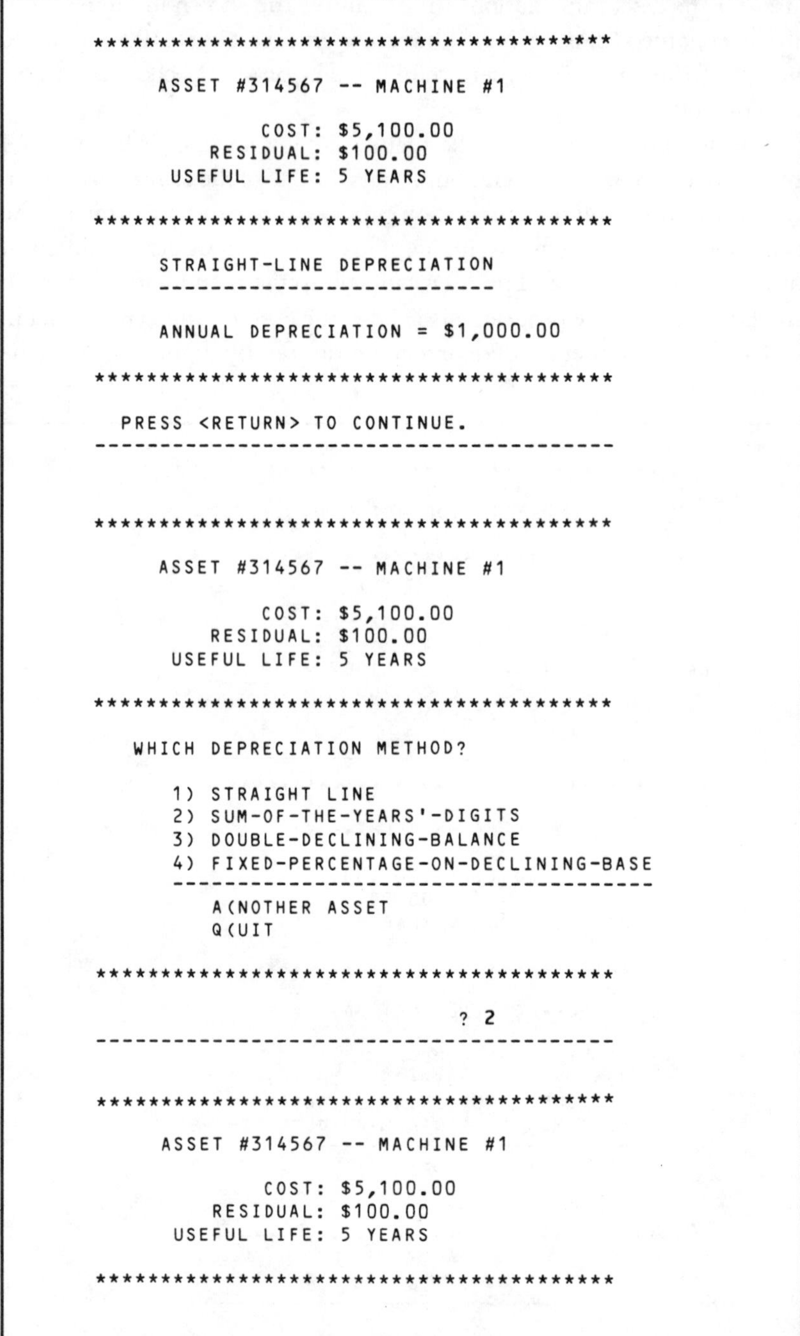

```
*****************************************

     ASSET #314567 -- MACHINE #1

             COST: $5,100.00
         RESIDUAL: $100.00
      USEFUL LIFE: 5 YEARS

*****************************************

     STRAIGHT-LINE DEPRECIATION
     --------------------------

     ANNUAL DEPRECIATION = $1,000.00

*****************************************

  PRESS <RETURN> TO CONTINUE.
-----------------------------------------


*****************************************

     ASSET #314567 -- MACHINE #1

             COST: $5,100.00
         RESIDUAL: $100.00
      USEFUL LIFE: 5 YEARS

*****************************************

   WHICH DEPRECIATION METHOD?

      1) STRAIGHT LINE
      2) SUM-OF-THE-YEARS'-DIGITS
      3) DOUBLE-DECLINING-BALANCE
      4) FIXED-PERCENTAGE-ON-DECLINING-BASE
      ------------------------------------
         A(NOTHER ASSET
         Q(UIT

*****************************************

                               ? 2
-----------------------------------------


*****************************************

     ASSET #314567 -- MACHINE #1

             COST: $5,100.00
         RESIDUAL: $100.00
      USEFUL LIFE: 5 YEARS

*****************************************
```

Figure 17.1: Sample Run of Depreciation Program (cont.)

```
SUM-OF-THE-YEARS'-DIGITS DEPRECIATION
-------------------------------------

     YEAR          DEPRECIATION

       1             $1,666.66
       2             $1,333.33
       3             $1,000.00
       4               $666.66
       5               $333.33

****************************************

  PRESS <RETURN> TO CONTINUE.

----------------------------------------


****************************************

     ASSET #314567 -- MACHINE #1

             COST: $5,100.00
         RESIDUAL: $100.00
      USEFUL LIFE: 5 YEARS

****************************************


   WHICH DEPRECIATION METHOD?

      1) STRAIGHT LINE
      2) SUM-OF-THE-YEARS'-DIGITS
      3) DOUBLE-DECLINING-BALANCE
      4) FIXED-PERCENTAGE-ON-DECLINING-BASE
      -------------------------------------
         A(NOTHER ASSET
         Q(UIT


****************************************
                              ? 3
----------------------------------------


****************************************

     ASSET #314567 -- MACHINE #1

             COST: $5,100.00
         RESIDUAL: $100.00
      USEFUL LIFE: 5 YEARS

****************************************
```

Figure 17.1: Sample Run of Depreciation Program (cont.)

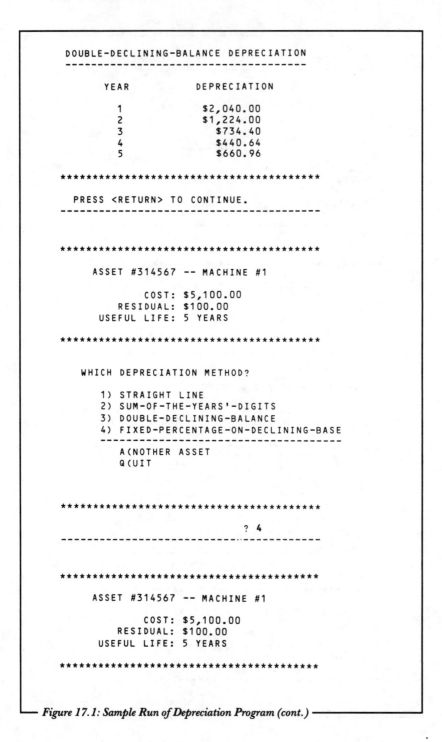

```
DOUBLE-DECLINING-BALANCE DEPRECIATION
-------------------------------------

     YEAR             DEPRECIATION

       1               $2,040.00
       2               $1,224.00
       3                 $734.40
       4                 $440.64
       5                 $660.96

***************************************

  PRESS <RETURN> TO CONTINUE.
---------------------------------------


***************************************

    ASSET #314567 -- MACHINE #1

            COST: $5,100.00
        RESIDUAL: $100.00
     USEFUL LIFE: 5 YEARS

***************************************


   WHICH DEPRECIATION METHOD?

      1) STRAIGHT LINE
      2) SUM-OF-THE-YEARS'-DIGITS
      3) DOUBLE-DECLINING-BALANCE
      4) FIXED-PERCENTAGE-ON-DECLINING-BASE
      ------------------------------------
         A(NOTHER ASSET
         Q(UIT


***************************************
                             ? 4
---------------------------------------


***************************************

    ASSET #314567 -- MACHINE #1

            COST: $5,100.00
        RESIDUAL: $100.00
     USEFUL LIFE: 5 YEARS

***************************************
```

Figure 17.1: Sample Run of Depreciation Program (cont.)

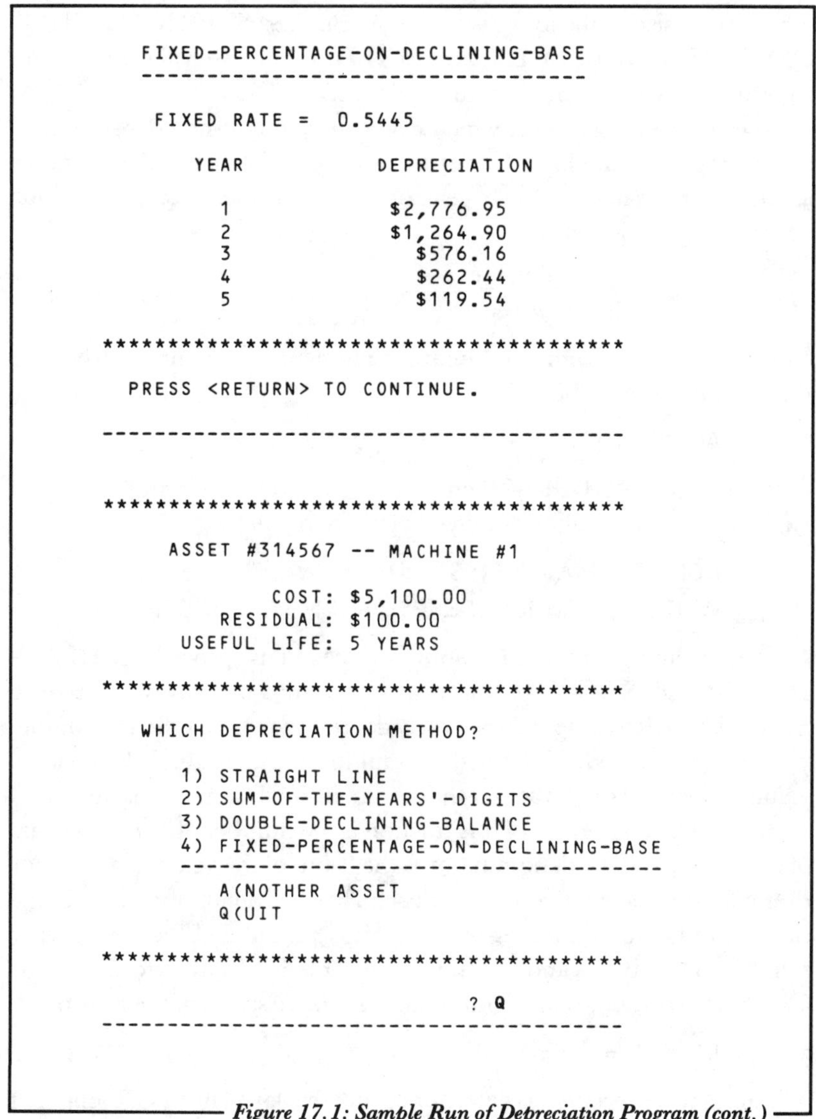

```
FIXED-PERCENTAGE-ON-DECLINING-BASE
----------------------------------

 FIXED RATE =  0.5445

    YEAR             DEPRECIATION

      1               $2,776.95
      2               $1,264.90
      3                 $576.16
      4                 $262.44
      5                 $119.54

****************************************

  PRESS <RETURN> TO CONTINUE.

----------------------------------------


****************************************

     ASSET #314567 -- MACHINE #1

              COST: $5,100.00
          RESIDUAL: $100.00
       USEFUL LIFE: 5 YEARS

****************************************

   WHICH DEPRECIATION METHOD?

      1) STRAIGHT LINE
      2) SUM-OF-THE-YEARS'-DIGITS
      3) DOUBLE-DECLINING-BALANCE
      4) FIXED-PERCENTAGE-ON-DECLINING-BASE
      ------------------------------------
         A(NOTHER ASSET
         Q(UIT

****************************************

                          ? Q
----------------------------------------
```

Figure 17.1: Sample Run of Depreciation Program (cont.)

THE PROGRAM

The listing of program DEPRECIATION is shown in Figure 17.2. The bulk of the program simply conducts the input/output dialogue. Procedure INASSET reads the asset information; procedures LINEOFCHARS, CONTINUE, ECHOASSET, HEADING, and MENU produce the various details of the output screens. The real heart of the program consists of the four depreciation routines: STRAIGHT, SUMOFYEARS, DOUBLEDEC, and FIXEDPERC. We will examine the algorithms of each of these routines in turn.

Procedure STRAIGHT, which calculates straight-line depreciation, is the simplest of the four. Under this method, the yearly depreciation amount is the same for each year of the useful life. The formula for determining this amount is:

$$\frac{\text{cost} - \text{residual value}}{\text{useful life (in years)}}$$

This formula is implemented in an assignment statement for ANDEP, the annual depreciation value:

```
ANDEP := (COST - RESIDUAL) DIV LIFE;
```

A call to DOLLARFORM then creates STANDEP, a string version of ANDEP, and the result is displayed on the screen:

```
DOLLARFORM(ANDEP, STANDEP);
WRITELN('   ANNUAL DEPRECIATION = ', STANDEP)
```

The remaining three depreciation routines all use procedures HEADING and FOURCOLUMN to display columns of figures. Procedure SUMOFYEARS computes the yearly depreciation under the sum-of-the-years'-digits method. This method multiplies the original depreciable value of the asset by a fraction that is determined from the useful life of the asset. The numerator of this fraction is the number of *remaining* years of useful life, and the denominator is the "sum of the years' digits." For example, if an asset has a five-year useful life, the denominator is 15 (the product of the total number of years of useful life and the next higher number, DIV two), and the numerator ranges from 1 to 5. SUMOFYEARS computes the denominator in the first line of the routine:

```
DENOM := (LIFE * (LIFE + 1)) DIV 2;
```

The annual depreciation is determined and displayed in a FOR loop that increments I from 1 to LIFE:

```
ANDEP := ((COST - RESIDUAL) * (LIFE - I + 1) DIV DENOM;
```

The double-declining-balance method is implemented in procedure DOUBLEDEC. This method ignores the residual value of the asset (a fact the user must keep in mind when examining the output for this method). An amount equal to twice the remaining value divided by the total number of years of useful life can be depreciated each year.

This formula appears in a FOR loop that increments the value of I from 1 to LIFE – 1:

```
ANDEP := (2 * (COST - TOTDEP)) DIV LIFE;
TOTDEP := TOTDEP + ANDEP;
```

The last year's depreciation is simply the total remaining value of the asset:

```
DOLLARFORM(COST - TOTDEP, STANDEP);
```

This value often exceeds the previous year's depreciation.

The fixed-percentage-on-a-declining-base method is the most accelerated of all the depreciation schedules, and is also the most difficult to compute. In this method, the *remaining* value of the asset is multiplied each year by a fixed percentage. This percentage is calculated in such a way that the residual value remains as the value of the asset at the end of the period of useful life. The formula for the fixed percentage is:

$$\text{rate} = 1.0 - \sqrt[y]{\frac{\text{residual value}}{\text{original cost}}}$$

where y is the number of years of useful life. Since the residual value is a factor in this equation, it must not be zero. If necessary, a nominal value of one dollar must be assigned to it. We use logarithms to implement this equation. Normally the following statement, using the LN and EXP functions, would do the job:

```
RATE := 1.0 - EXP(LN(RESIDUAL/COST)/LIFE);
```

Unfortunately, this statement cannot be used in program DEPRECIATION, because both RESIDUAL and COST are long integers, for which division is not defined. For this reason, procedure FIXEDPERC includes a long-integer division function, LDIVL. A call to this function takes two long integer parameters, L1 and L2, where L1 <= L2:

```
LDIVL(L1,L2)
```

The function thus returns a real number that is less than or equal to 1. LDIVL works as follows:

1. All but the four or five most significant digits of L1 and L2 are eliminated.
2. Both values are then converted to regular integers (using the TRUNC function).

3. The division is then performed, producing a result of type REAL.
4. The decimal point of the result is shifted left, according to the number of digits that were eliminated from L1 and L2.

The statement that calculates the fixed rate thus contains a call to function LDIVL to divide the residual value by the cost:

```
RATE := 1.0 - EXP((LN(LDIVL(RESIDUAL,COST)))/LIFE);
```

Once this rate is determined, the yearly depreciation calculation is simple, and is performed in a FOR loop. Procedure LONGMULT is used to multiply the remaining depreciable value (BASE) by the fixed rate, to produce the annual depreciation value:

```
LONGMULT(BASE,RATE,ANDEP);
BASE := BASE - ANDEP;
```

Notice that BASE is initially set to the value of COST.

```
(*$S+*)
PROGRAM DEPRECIATION;

USES
TRANSCEND,
                    (*$U MONEYUNIT.CODE*)
MONEYUNIT,
                    (*$U CHECKUNIT.CODE*)
CHECKUNIT;


VAR
  DONE : BOOLEAN;
  NAME : STRING;
  NUM  : LONG1;
  COST,
  RESIDUAL : LONG2;
  LIFE  : INTEGER;


PROCEDURE LINEOFCHARS(C : CHAR);

  CONST
    SCREENWIDTH = 40;

  VAR
    I : INTEGER;
```

Figure 17.2: Listing of Depreciation Program

```
BEGIN
  FOR I := 1 TO SCREENWIDTH DO
    WRITE(C);
  WRITELN
END;              (* LINEOFCHARS *)

PROCEDURE CONTINUE;

  VAR
    ANS : STRING;

BEGIN
  WRITE('  PRESS <RETURN> TO CONTINUE. ');
  READLN(ANS);
  CLEARSCREEN
END;            (* CONTINUE *)



PROCEDURE INASSET;

  VAR
    DIGIT : BOOLEAN;

  PROCEDURE ININT(VAR VAL : INTEGER);

    VAR
      GARBAGE : STRING;

  BEGIN
    GET(INPUT);
    IF INPUT^ IN ['0'..'9'] THEN
      READLN(VAL)
    ELSE
      BEGIN
        READLN(GARBAGE);
        ININT(VAL)
      END
  END;      (* ININT *)

BEGIN
  WRITE('          NAME OF ASSET: ');
  READLN(NAME);
  REPEAT
    WRITE('                  I.D.#: ');
    INVALUE(NUM,6,DIGIT)
  UNTIL (DIGIT AND (VERIFYCHECK(NUM)));
  WRITE('ORIGINAL COST OF ASSET: ');
  INDOLLAR(COST);
  WRITE('        RESIDUAL VALUE: ');
  INDOLLAR(RESIDUAL);
  WRITE('USEFUL LIFE (IN YEARS): ');
  ININT(LIFE);
  CLEARSCREEN
END;
```

Figure 17.2: Listing of Depreciation Program (cont.)

```
PROCEDURE ECHOASSET;

  VAR
    STCOST,
    STRESIDUAL : STRING;


BEGIN
  WRITELN;
  LINEOFCHARS('*');
  WRITELN;
  WRITELN('     ASSET #',NUM, ' -- ', NAME);
  WRITELN;
  DOLLARFORM(COST,STCOST);
  DOLLARFORM(RESIDUAL,STRESIDUAL);
  WRITELN('              COST: ',STCOST);
  WRITELN('          RESIDUAL: ',STRESIDUAL);
  WRITELN('       USEFUL LIFE: ',LIFE, ' YEARS');
  WRITELN;
  LINEOFCHARS('*');
  WRITELN
END;        (* ECHOASSET *)



PROCEDURE STRAIGHT;
  VAR
    ANDEP : LONG2;
    STANDEP : STRING;

  BEGIN
    ANDEP := (COST - RESIDUAL) DIV LIFE;
    DOLLARFORM(ANDEP,STANDEP);
    WRITELN('     ANNUAL DEPRECIATION = ', STANDEP)
  END;     (* STRAIGHT *)



PROCEDURE HEADING;

BEGIN
  FOURCOLUMN('YEAR','DEPRECIATION','','',11,21,0,0)
END;    (* HEADING *)

PROCEDURE SUMOFYEARS;

  VAR
    DENOM   : INTEGER;
    ANDEP   : LONG2;
    STANDEP,
    ST      : STRING;
    I       : INTEGER;

  BEGIN
    DENOM := (LIFE * (LIFE + 1)) DIV 2;
```

Figure 17.2: Listing of Depreciation Program (cont.)

```
      HEADING;
      WRITELN;
      FOR I := 1 TO LIFE DO
        BEGIN
          ANDEP := ((COST - RESIDUAL) * (LIFE - I + 1)) DIV DENOM;
          DOLLARFORM(ANDEP,STANDEP);
          STR(I,ST);
          FOURCOLUMN(ST,STANDEP,'','',10,20,0,0);
        END
    END;      (* SUMOFYEARS *)


  PROCEDURE DOUBLEDEC;
    VAR
      TOTDEP,
      ANDEP   : LONG2;
      ST,
      STANDEP : STRING;
      I       : INTEGER;

    BEGIN
      TOTDEP := 0;

      HEADING;
      WRITELN;
      FOR I := 1 TO LIFE - 1 DO
        BEGIN
          ANDEP := (2 * (COST - TOTDEP)) DIV LIFE;
          TOTDEP := TOTDEP + ANDEP;
          DOLLARFORM(ANDEP,STANDEP);
          STR(I,ST);
          FOURCOLUMN(ST,STANDEP,'','',10,20,0,0);
        END;

      (*
       * LAST YEAR
       *)

      DOLLARFORM(COST-TOTDEP,STANDEP);
      STR(LIFE,ST);
      FOURCOLUMN(ST,STANDEP,'','',10,20,0,0)
    END;      (* DOUBLEDEC *)


  PROCEDURE FIXEDPERC;

    VAR
      RATE : REAL:
      BASE,
      ANDEP : LONG2;
      STANDEP,
      ST      : STRING;
      I      : INTEGER;
```

Figure 17.2: Listing of Depreciation Program (cont.)

```
      FUNCTION LDIVL(L1,L2 : LONG2): REAL;

        (*
         * LDIVL EXPECTS THAT
         * L1 WILL BE SMALLER
         * THAN L2; THUS THE
         * RESULT WILL LESS THAN 1.
         *)

        VAR
          HOLD1,
          HOLD2   : LONG2;
          R       : REAL;

        BEGIN
          HOLD1 := 1;
          WHILE L1 > MAXINT DO
            BEGIN
              L1 := L1 DIV 10;
              HOLD1 := HOLD1 * 10
            END;
          HOLD2 := 1;
          WHILE L2 > MAXINT DO
            BEGIN
              L2 := L2 DIV 10;
              HOLD2 := HOLD2 * 10
            END;
          R := TRUNC(L1) / TRUNC(L2);
          HOLD2 := HOLD2 DIV HOLD1;
          WHILE HOLD2 > 1 DO
            BEGIN
              R := R / 10.0;
              HOLD2 := HOLD2 DIV 10
            END;
          LDIVL := R
        END;            (* LDIVL *)


    BEGIN  (* FIXEDPERC *)

      (*
       * IF THE RESIDUAL VALUE IS ZERO, THEN
       * WE MUST SET IT TO A NOMINAL SCRAP
       * VALUE OF $1 (OR 100, SINCE LONG2
       * IS IN CENTS).
       *)

      IF RESIDUAL = 0 THEN
        RESIDUAL := 100;

      RATE := 1.0 - EXP((LN(LDIVL(RESIDUAL,COST)))/LIFE);
      WRITELN('    FIXED RATE = ',RATE:4:4);
      WRITELN;
      HEADING;
      WRITELN;
```

Figure 17.2: Listing of Depreciation Program (cont.)

```
    BASE := COST;

    FOR I := 1 TO LIFE DO
      BEGIN
        LONGMULT(BASE,RATE,ANDEP);
        BASE := BASE - ANDEP;
        DOLLARFORM(ANDEP,STANDEP);
        STR(I,ST);
        FOURCOLUMN(ST,STANDEP,'','',10,20,0,0);
      END
  END;      (* FIXEDPERC *)


  PROCEDURE MENU;

    VAR
      CHOICE : CHAR;


  BEGIN
    ECHOASSET;
    WRITELN('    WHICH DEPRECIATION METHOD?');
    WRITELN;
    WRITELN('        1) STRAIGHT LINE');
    WRITELN('        2) SUM-OF-THE-YEARS''-DIGITS');
    WRITELN('        3) DOUBLE-DECLINING-BALANCE');
    WRITELN('        4) FIXED-PERCENTAGE-ON-DECLINING-BASE');
    WRITELN('        -------------------------------------');
    WRITELN('           A(NOTHER ASSET');
    WRITELN('           Q(UIT');
    WRITELN;

    LINEOFCHARS('*');
    WRITELN;
    REPEAT
      WRITE('                              ? ');
      READLN(CHOICE)
    UNTIL CHOICE IN ['1'..'4','A','Q'];

    IF CHOICE IN ['1'..'4'] THEN
      BEGIN
        CLEARSCREEN;
        ECHOASSET
      END;

    CASE CHOICE OF

      '1' : BEGIN
              WRITELN('      STRAIGHT-LINE DEPRECIATION');
              WRITELN('      --------------------------');
              WRITELN;
              STRAIGHT
            END;
```

Figure 17.2: Listing of Depreciation Program (cont.)

```
    '2' : BEGIN
            WRITELN(' SUM-OF-THE-YEARS''-DIGITS DEPRECIATION');
            WRITELN(' ---------------------------------------');
            WRITELN;
            SUMOFYEARS
          END;

    '3' : BEGIN
            WRITELN(' DOUBLE-DECLINING-BALANCE DEPRECIATION');
            WRITELN(' -------------------------------------');
            WRITELN;
            DOUBLEDEC
          END;

    '4' : BEGIN
            WRITELN('   FIXED-PERCENTAGE-ON-DECLINING-BASE');
            WRITELN('   ----------------------------------');
            WRITELN;
            FIXEDPERC
          END;

    'A' : BEGIN
            CLEARSCREEN;
            INASSET
          END;

    'Q' : DONE := TRUE

  END;  (* CASE *)

  IF CHOICE IN ['1'..'4'] THEN
    BEGIN
      WRITELN;
      LINEOFCHARS('*');
      WRITELN;
      CONTINUE
    END

END;  (* MENU *)

BEGIN (* MAIN PROGRAM *)
  CLEARSCREEN;
  WRITELN;
  LINEOFCHARS('*');
  WRITELN;
  WRITELN('          DEPRECIATION METHODS');
  WRITELN;
  LINEOFCHARS('*');
  WRITELN;
  WRITELN;
```

Figure 17.2: Listing of Depreciation Program (cont.)

```
    INASSET;
    DONE := FALSE;

    WHILE NOT DONE DO
      MENU

  END.  (* MAIN PROGRAM *)
```

Figure 17.2: Listing of Depreciation Program (cont.)

Chapter 18

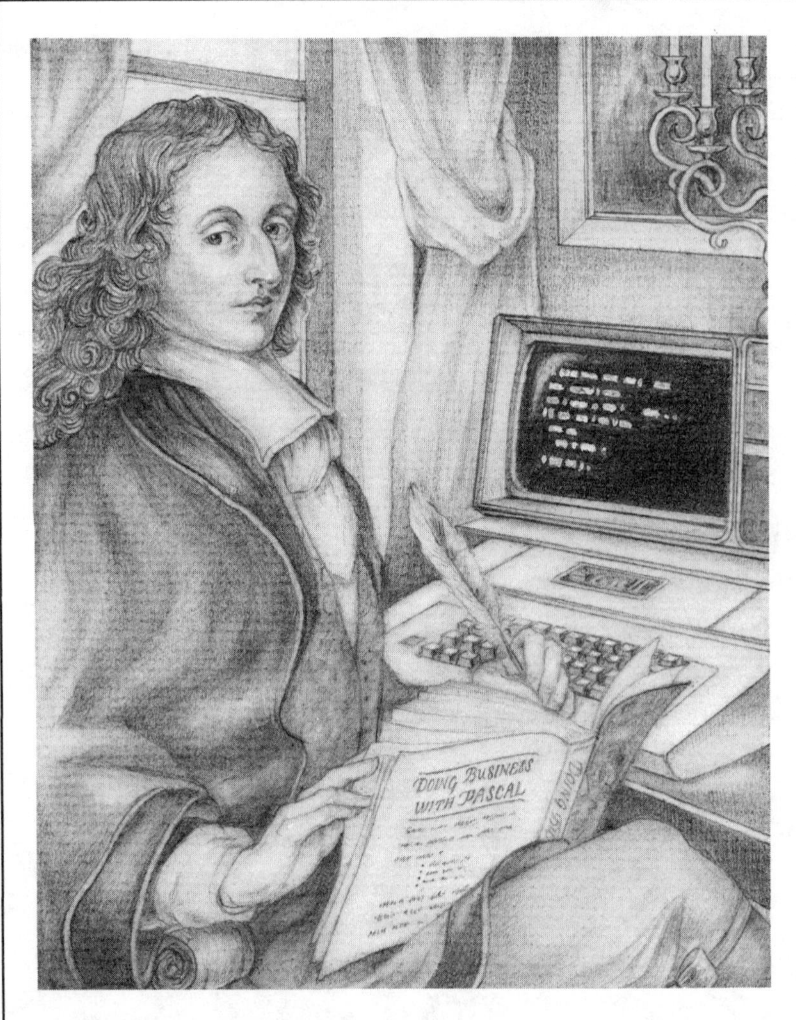

Accounts Receivable Aging Analysis

THE APPLICATION

One of the more significant assets of many companies—and often the asset which presents the most difficult management challenges—is the accounts receivable. The business system, in addition to producing the traditional accounts receivable reports, like detailed balance listings, statements at specified intervals, and the like, must produce summary reports that management can use to control the accounts receivable. Such management reports might include the analysis of bad-debt information by product type, by salesperson, and by region; and the sources of revenue and receivable by product line and by region. The report discussed in this chapter is an aging analysis of accounts receivable by account name, and within account name, by age of individual invoice. While this report categorizes accounts in standard aging divisions (up to 30 days, 31 to 60 days, and over 60 days), these actual divisions could be varied within the system by including them in the system profile (see Chapter 10), so as to provide information on accounts receivable at the point when it is critical to the management.

The movement of accounts receivable through the aging divisions, and the ultimate conversion of accounts receivable assets to cash, are tracked by this kind of report. The report is important not only at specific weekly intervals (for the on-going management of receivables), but also in the preparation of quarterly and yearly financial statements. Both internal and external auditors could use this kind of report in the determination of reserves for bad debt.

A number of possible enhancements might be included in a fully developed aging of accounts receivable. One such enhancement might include the percentage of total by aging categories for each account—thus indicating the relative value of accounts outstanding. Similarly, the report could indicate the percent of total for each aging category for the total report. This would require that the columns for each age grouping be totaled—a total that in itself would be an interesting statistic in the analysis of overall receivable collection efforts.

A complete business system might also include comparisons on a monthly, quarterly, or even yearly basis, with the ability to show significant changes in the status of the accounts receivable.

In addition, listings of accounts receivable (selected on the basis of invoice age or dollar amount due) might prove helpful in the management of the receivables asset. For instance, a report listing all accounts which show aging of over 61 days for any individual invoice might be used as a working document for the credit department, and perhaps even for the order/shipping department (to hold and delay orders until past-due accounts are resolved).

Finally, there are different ways of sorting the data presented in the report. We might sort by name of company or age of account (as we do in this example), but we could also sort on the basis of dollar amounts, with the account with the largest amount of dollars outstanding appearing at the top of the report. The selection of the aging type might then be a menu-driven input item at the beginning of the process.

THE SAMPLE RUN

The input dialogue from the accounts receivable aging program reads invoice information for a specified number of accounts. In the sample run, shown in Figure 18.1, we see input data for 10 different accounts receivable, and a total of 28 outstanding invoices. Each invoice input requires a date and a dollar amount.

From all this input data, the program produces a table entitled "Age of Accounts Receivable." The table contains five columns: the name of the account, the total amount due, and then the amounts due under three age categories. The table may be sorted either by the account names or by the age of the invoices, the oldest accounts first. The sample run shows examples of tables produced by both sorting methods.

```
        ACCOUNTS RECEIVABLE AGING
        ======== ========== =====


TODAY'S DATE? 6-7-82
HOW MANY ACCOUNTS? 10



NAME OF ACCOUNT? STANLEY CO
HOW MANY OUTSTANDING INVOICES FOR STANLEY CO? 3

DATE OF INVOICE #1? 4-5-82
AMOUNT OF INVOICE?  132.09

DATE OF INVOICE #2? 5-15-82
AMOUNT OF INVOICE?  371.93

DATE OF INVOICE #3? 5-21-82
AMOUNT OF INVOICE?  265.54


NAME OF ACCOUNT? VIM CO
HOW MANY OUTSTANDING INVOICES FOR VIM CO? 2

DATE OF INVOICE #1? 3-1-82
AMOUNT OF INVOICE?  468.88

DATE OF INVOICE #2? 3-15-82
AMOUNT OF INVOICE?  531.92


NAME OF ACCOUNT? JONES, INC
HOW MANY OUTSTANDING INVOICES FOR JONES, INC? 4

DATE OF INVOICE #1? 4-15-82
AMOUNT OF INVOICE?  879.44

DATE OF INVOICE #2? 5-1-82
AMOUNT OF INVOICE?  879.44

DATE OF INVOICE #3? 5-15-82
AMOUNT OF INVOICE?  956.32

DATE OF INVOICE #4? 6-1-82
AMOUNT OF INVOICE?  956.32


NAME OF ACCOUNT? COLLINS CO
HOW MANY OUTSTANDING INVOICES FOR COLLINS CO? 1

DATE OF INVOICE #1? 2-27-82
AMOUNT OF INVOICE?  650.00
```

Figure 18.1: Sample Run of Accounts Receivable Aging Program

```
NAME OF ACCOUNT? SMITH INC
HOW MANY OUTSTANDING INVOICES FOR SMITH INC? 5

DATE OF INVOICE #1? 4-3-82
AMOUNT OF INVOICE?  245.09

DATE OF INVOICE #2? 4-23-82
AMOUNT OF INVOICE?  245.09

DATE OF INVOICE #3? 5-3-82
AMOUNT OF INVOICE?  490.18

DATE OF INVOICE #4? 5-23-82
AMOUNT OF INVOICE?  490.18

DATE OF INVOICE #5? 6-3-82
AMOUNT OF INVOICE?  735.27


NAME OF ACCOUNT? ACME CO
HOW MANY OUTSTANDING INVOICES FOR ACME CO? 2

DATE OF INVOICE #1? 5-15-82
AMOUNT OF INVOICE?  478.95

DATE OF INVOICE #2? 5-30-82
AMOUNT OF INVOICE?  1089.73


NAME OF ACCOUNT? DAWSON,INC
HOW MANY OUTSTANDING INVOICES FOR DAWSON,INC? 3

DATE OF INVOICE #1? 4-1-82
AMOUNT OF INVOICE?  200.00

DATE OF INVOICE #2? 4-8-82
AMOUNT OF INVOICE?  245.87

DATE OF INVOICE #3? 4-15-82
AMOUNT OF INVOICE?  365.12


NAME OF ACCOUNT? ADAMS
HOW MANY OUTSTANDING INVOICES FOR ADAMS? 1

DATE OF INVOICE #1? 5-28-82
AMOUNT OF INVOICE?  57.45


NAME OF ACCOUNT? MELROSE CO
HOW MANY OUTSTANDING INVOICES FOR MELROSE CO? 2

DATE OF INVOICE #1? 5-13-82
AMOUNT OF INVOICE?  258.53
```

Figure 18.1: Sample Run of Accounts Receivable Aging Program (cont.)

```
DATE OF INVOICE #2? 5-27-82
AMOUNT OF INVOICE?  591.04


NAME OF ACCOUNT? PRINCE,INC
HOW MANY OUTSTANDING INVOICES FOR PRINCE,INC? 5

DATE OF INVOICE #1? 4-1-82
AMOUNT OF INVOICE?  235.86

DATE OF INVOICE #2? 4-15-82
AMOUNT OF INVOICE?  235.86

DATE OF INVOICE #3? 4-29-82
AMOUNT OF INVOICE?  235.86

DATE OF INVOICE #4? 5-14-82
AMOUNT OF INVOICE?  235.86

DATE OF INVOICE #5? 5-28-82
AMOUNT OF INVOICE?  235.86

---------------------------------------------

SORT BY N(AME OR BY A(GE? N


                  AGE OF ACCOUNTS RECEIVABLE
                  === == ======== ==========

                         JUNE 7, 1982

ACCOUNT        TOTAL DUE   TO 30 DAYS  31-60 DAYS    61+ DAYS
-------        ---------   ----------  ----------    --------

ACME CO        $1,568.68    $1,568.68          --          --
ADAMS             $57.45       $57.45          --          --
COLLINS CO       $650.00          --           --     $650.00
DAWSON,INC       $810.99          --      $610.99     $200.00
JONES, INC     $3,671.52    $1,912.64   $1,758.88          --
MELROSE CO       $849.57      $849.57          --          --
PRINCE,INC     $1,179.30      $471.72     $471.72     $235.86
SMITH INC      $2,205.81    $1,225.45     $735.27     $245.09
STANLEY CO       $769.56      $637.47          --     $132.09
VIM CO         $1,000.80          --           --   $1,000.80

ANOTHER REPORT FROM SAME DATA? Y

---------------------------------------------


     SORT BY N(AME OR BY A(GE? A
```

Figure 18.1: Sample Run of Accounts Receivable Aging Program (cont.)

```
                AGE OF ACCOUNTS RECEIVABLE
                === == ======== ==========

                      JUNE 7, 1982

ACCOUNT         TOTAL DUE   TO 30 DAYS  31-60 DAYS    61+ DAYS
-------         ---------   ----------  ----------    --------

VIM CO          $1,000.80           --          --   $1,000.80
COLLINS CO        $650.00           --          --     $650.00
SMITH INC       $2,205.81    $1,225.45     $735.27     $245.09
PRINCE,INC      $1,179.30      $471.72     $471.72     $235.86
DAWSON,INC        $810.99           --     $610.99     $200.00
STANLEY CO        $769.56      $637.47          --     $132.09
JONES, INC      $3,671.52    $1,912.64   $1,758.88          --
ACME CO         $1,568.68    $1,568.68          --          --
MELROSE CO        $849.57      $849.57          --          --
ADAMS              $57.45       $57.45          --          --


ANOTHER REPORT FROM SAME DATA? N
ANOTHER LIST OF ACCOUNTS? N
```

Figure 18.1: Sample Run of Accounts Receivable Aging Program (cont.)

THE PROGRAM

Figure 18.2 shows the listing of program ACCAGE. The data structure that holds the account information is ACCARY, an array of ACCOUNT records:

```
TYPE
   ACCOUNT = RECORD
      NAME : STRING[10];
      AMOUNT : NAME[1..3] OF LONG2

   END;

   ARY = ARRAY[1..MAXACCS] OF ACCOUNT;

VAR
   ACCARY : ARY;
```

The AMOUNT field of each ACCOUNT record is designed to store the account totals according to age. AMOUNT[1] is for receivables up to 30 days old; AMOUNT[2], 31 to 60 days old; and AMOUNT[3], 61 days or older.

Procedure INACCOUNTS reads the date of an invoice and calculates the age of the receivable:

```
WRITE('DATE OF INVOICE #',J,'? ');
INDATE(INVDATE);
DATECONVERT(INVDATE,SCINVDATE);
AGE := TRUNC(SCTODAY - SCINVDATE);
```

It then reads the amount of the invoice and stores it in the appropriate element of the array AMOUNT:

```
IF AGE > 60 THEN
   AMOUNT[3] := AMOUNT[3] + INVAMT
ELSE
   IF AGE > 30 THEN
      AMOUNT[2] := AMOUNT[2] + INVAMT
   ELSE
      AMOUNT[1] := AMOUNT[1] + INVAMT
```

With the input data already organized in a table-like data structure, the task of procedure OUTTABLE is simple. For each account, OUTTABLE calculates and outputs the total amount due:

```
FOR J := 1 TO 3 DO
   TOTAL := TOTAL + AMOUNT[J];
OUTCASH(TOTAL);
```

and then outputs the amounts due under each age category:

```
FOR J := 1 TO 3 DO
   OUTCASH(AMOUNT[J]);
```

The most difficult routine in this program is procedure SORTACCOUNTS. It can sort the array of account records, ACCARY, either by name or by age. The age sort is further complicated by the fact that there are three age categories, each of which may require a sort of its own. To simplify the coding we have used the bubble sort algorithm in this program rather than the Shell sort.

A call to BUBSORT, then, takes three parameters: the name of the array to be sorted, an integer representing the sort category, and an integer indicating where in the array the sort should begin. To sort by name, the category is 0 and the starting point is 1:

```
BUBSORT(ACCARY,0,1)
```

For the sort by age, I represents the age category, and FIRST is the top of the unsorted portion of the array:

```
BUBSORT(ACCARY,I,FIRST);
```

For the first age sort, FIRST equals 1; in subsequent sorts, FIRST is determined from a call to procedure NEXTSORT:

```
NEXTSORT(I,FIRST);
```

NEXTSORT simply searches age category I for the first zero value in the "column" of receivable amounts.

Procedure BUBSORT receives the sorting category and the starting point in the variables CATEGORY and POSN, respectively. It begins the sort at POSN and sorts to the end of the array:

```
N := NUMACCS;
FOR I := POSN TO N - 1 DO
  FOR J := I + 1 TO N DO
```

A CASE statement determines the sort key, and, in the case of the age sort, the age category:

```
CASE CATEGORY OF
  0 : IF A[I].NAME > A[J].NAME THEN
      SWAP(A[I],A[J]);
1,2,3 : IF A[I].AMOUNT[CATEGORY] <
      A[J].AMOUNT[CATEGORY] THEN
      SWAP(A[I],A[J])
END (* CASE *)
```

```
(*$S+*)
PROGRAM ACCAGE;

USES
                (*$U MONEYUNIT.CODE*)
MONEYUNIT,
                (*$U DATEUNIT.CODE*)
DATEUNIT;


CONST
  MAXACCS = 20;     (* MAXIMUM NUMBER OF ACCOUNTS PER REPORT *)
```

Figure 18.2: Listing of Program ACCAGE

```
TYPE
  ACCOUNT = RECORD
    NAME : STRING[10];
    AMOUNT : ARRAY[1..3] OF LONG2    (* AMOUNTS DUE *)
  END;

  ARY = ARRAY[1..MAXACCS] OF ACCOUNT;

VAR
  ACCARY : ARY;       (* ARRAY OF ACCOUNTS :)
  TODAY  : DATEREC;   (* CURRENT DATE *)
  SCTODAY: DATELONG;
  NUMACCS: INTEGER;   (* NUMBER OF ACCOUNTS IN A GIVEN REPORT *)
  ANS    : CHAR;


PROCEDURE ININT(VAR VAL : INTEGER);

(*
 * INTEGER INPUT VALIDATION.
 *)

  VAR
    GARBAGE : STRING;

  BEGIN
    GET(INPUT);
    IF INPUT^ IN ['0'..'9'] THEN
      READLN(VAL)
    ELSE
      BEGIN
        READLN(GARBAGE);
        WRITELN('*** REDO');
        WRITE('    ? ');
        ININT(VAL)
      END
  END;     (* ININT *)


PROCEDURE INACCOUNTS;

(*
 * READS ALL THE ACCOUNT INFORMATION,
 * AND ORGANIZES AMOUNTS DUE BY AGE.
 *)

  VAR
    I,
    J,
    AGE,
    INVOICES : INTEGER;
    INVDATE  : DATEREC;
    SCINVDATE: DATELONG;
    INVAMT   : LONG2;
```

Figure 18.2: Listing of Program ACCAGE (cont.)

```
BEGIN

  (* INITIALIZE AMOUNTS TO ZERO *)


  FOR I := 1 TO NUMACCS DO
    WITH ACCARY[I] DO
      FOR J := 1 TO 3 DO
        AMOUNT[J] := 0;


  FOR I := 1 TO NUMACCS DO
    WITH ACCARY[I] DO
      BEGIN
        WRITE('NAME OF ACCOUNT? ');
        READLN(NAME);
        WRITE('HOW MANY OUTSTANDING INVOICES FOR ',NAME,'? ');
        ININT(INVOICES);
        WRITELN;
        FOR J := 1 TO INVOICES DO
          BEGIN
            WRITE('DATE OF INVOICE #',J,'? ');
            INDATE(INVDATE);
            DATECONVERT(INVDATE,SCINVDATE);
            AGE := TRUNC(SCTODAY - SCINVDATE);

            WRITE('AMOUNT OF INVOICE?  ');
            INDOLLAR(INVAMT);
            WRITELN;

            (*
             * STORE AMOUNTS ACCORDING TO
             * AGE OF INVOICE.
             *)

            IF AGE > 60 THEN
              AMOUNT[3] := AMOUNT[3] + INVAMT
            ELSE
              IF AGE > 30 THEN
                AMOUNT[2] := AMOUNT[2] + INVAMT
              ELSE
                AMOUNT[1] := AMOUNT[1] + INVAMT
          END; (* FOR J *)
          WRITELN
      END (* WITH *)
END;  (* INACCOUNTS *)


PROCEDURE SORTACCOUNTS;

(*
 * SORTS ACCOUNTS BY NAME OR BY AGE.
 *)
```

Figure 18.2: Listing of Program ACCAGE (cont.)

```
VAR
  SORTTYPE : CHAR;
  I,
  FIRST    : INTEGER;
  DONE     : BOOLEAN;



  PROCEDURE NEXTSORT(COL : INTEGER;
                 VAR ROW : INTEGER);

   (*
    * DETERMINES WHERE TO START NEXT SORT.
    * USED FOR SORTING BY AGE CATEGORIES.
    *)

    VAR
      FOUND : BOOLEAN;

    BEGIN
      FOUND := FALSE;
      WHILE (ROW <= NUMACCS) AND (NOT FOUND) DO
        IF ACCARY[ROW].AMOUNT[COL] = 0 THEN
          FOUND := TRUE
        ELSE
          ROW := ROW + 1
    END;      (* NEXTSORT *)

PROCEDURE BUBSORT(VAR A : ARY;
                      CATEGORY,
                      POSN      : INTEGER);
  (*
   * BUBBLE SORT.
   * IF CATEGORY = 0 THEN SORT BY NAME;
   * OTHERWISE BY AGE.  SORT ARRAY
   * FROM POSN TO NUMACCS.
   *)

  VAR
    N,
    I,
    J : INTEGER;



  PROCEDURE SWAP(VAR P,Q : ACCOUNT);

    VAR
      HOLD : ACCOUNT;

    BEGIN
      HOLD := P;
      P := Q;
      Q := HOLD
    END;         (* SWAP *)
```

Figure 18.2: Listing of Program ACCAGE (cont.)

```
    BEGIN
      N := NUMACCS;

      FOR I := POSN TO N - 1 DO
        FOR J := I + 1 TO N DO
          CASE CATEGORY OF
            0 : IF A[I].NAME > A[J].NAME THEN
                  SWAP(A[I],A[J]);
        1,2,3 : IF A[I].AMOUNT[CATEGORY] <
                   A[J].AMOUNT[CATEGORY] THEN
                  SWAP(A[I],A[J])
          END (* CASE *)
    END;  (* BUBSORT *)


  BEGIN (* SORTACCOUNTS *)
    REPEAT
      WRITE('SORT BY N(AME OR BY A(GE? ');
      READLN(SORTTYPE)
    UNTIL SORTTYPE IN ['N','A'];
    WRITELN; WRITELN;

    IF SORTTYPE = 'N' THEN
      BUBSORT(ACCARY,0,1)    (* SORT BY NAME *)
    ELSE
      BEGIN   (* SORT BY AGE *)
        I := 3;   (* START WITH OLDEST ACCOUNTS *)
        FIRST := 1;
        DONE := FALSE;

        (*
         * UP TO 3 SORTS MAY BE REQUIRED, ONE FOR
         * EACH AGE CATEGORY.
         *)

        WHILE (NOT DONE) AND (I >= 1) DO
          BEGIN
            BUBSORT(ACCARY,I,FIRST);
            NEXTSORT(I,FIRST);
            IF FIRST >= NUMACCS THEN
              DONE := TRUE
            ELSE
              I := I - 1
          END  (* WHILE *)
      END  (* ELSE *)

  END;  (* SORTACCOUNTS *)


  PROCEDURE OUTTABLE;

    VAR
      I,
      J   : INTEGER;
      TOTAL : LONG2;
```

Figure 18.2: Listing of Program ACCAGE (cont.)

```
PROCEDURE HEADING;
  BEGIN
    WRITELN('AGE OF ACCOUNTS RECEIVABLE':42);
    WRITELN('=== == ======== ==========':42);
    WRITELN;
    WRITE(' ':22);
    OUTDATE(TODAY);
    WRITELN;
    WRITELN;
    WRITE('ACCOUNT     ');
    WRITELN('   TOTAL DUE  TO 30 DAYS  31-60 DAYS    61+ DAYS');
    WRITE('-------     ');
    WRITELN('   ---------  ----------  ----------    --------');
    WRITELN
  END;       (* HEADING *)

PROCEDURE OUTCASH (AMT : LONG2);

(*
 *  OUTPUTS ONE DOLLAR AND CENT AMOUNT.
 *)

  VAR
    STAMT : STRING;

  BEGIN
    IF AMT <> 0 THEN
      BEGIN
        DOLLARFORM(AMT,STAMT);
        RIGHTFIELD(STAMT,12);
        WRITE(STAMT)
      END
    ELSE
      WRITE('         --   ')
  END;      (* OUTCASH *)



BEGIN (* OUTTABLE *)
  HEADING;
  FOR I := 1 TO NUMACCS DO
    WITH ACCARY[I] DO
      BEGIN
        WRITE(NAME);
        FOR J := 1 TO (11 - LENGTH(NAME)) DO
          WRITE(' ');
        TOTAL := 0;

        (* TOTAL DUE COLUMN *)

        FOR J := 1 TO 3 DO
          TOTAL := TOTAL + AMOUNT[J];
        OUTCASH(TOTAL);

        (* AGE CATEGORIES *)
```

Figure 18.2: Listing of Program ACCAGE (cont.)

```
          FOR J := 1 TO 3 DO
            OUTCASH(AMOUNT[J]);

          WRITELN
        END;  (* WITH *)
    WRITELN;
    WRITELN
  END;        (* OUTTABLE *)

BEGIN (* MAIN PROGRAM *)

  CLEARSCREEN;
  WRITELN;
  WRITELN('ACCOUNTS RECEIVABLE AGING':32);
  WRITELN('======== ========== =====':32);
  WRITELN;
  WRITE('TODAY''S DATE? ');
  INDATE(TODAY);
  DATECONVERT(TODAY,SCTODAY);

  REPEAT
    WRITE('HOW MANY ACCOUNTS? ');
    ININT(NUMACCS);
    WRITELN;
    WRITELN;
    INACCOUNTS;
    REPEAT
      CLEARSCREEN;
      SORTACCOUNTS;
      OUTTABLE;
      WRITE('ANOTHER REPORT FROM SAME DATA? ');
      READLN(ANS)
    UNTIL (ANS = 'N');
    WRITE('ANOTHER LIST OF ACCOUNTS? ');
    READLN(ANS);
    CLEARSCREEN
  UNTIL (ANS = 'N')

END.  (* MAIN PROGRAM *)
```

Figure 18.2: Listing of Program ACCAGE (cont.)

Chapter 19

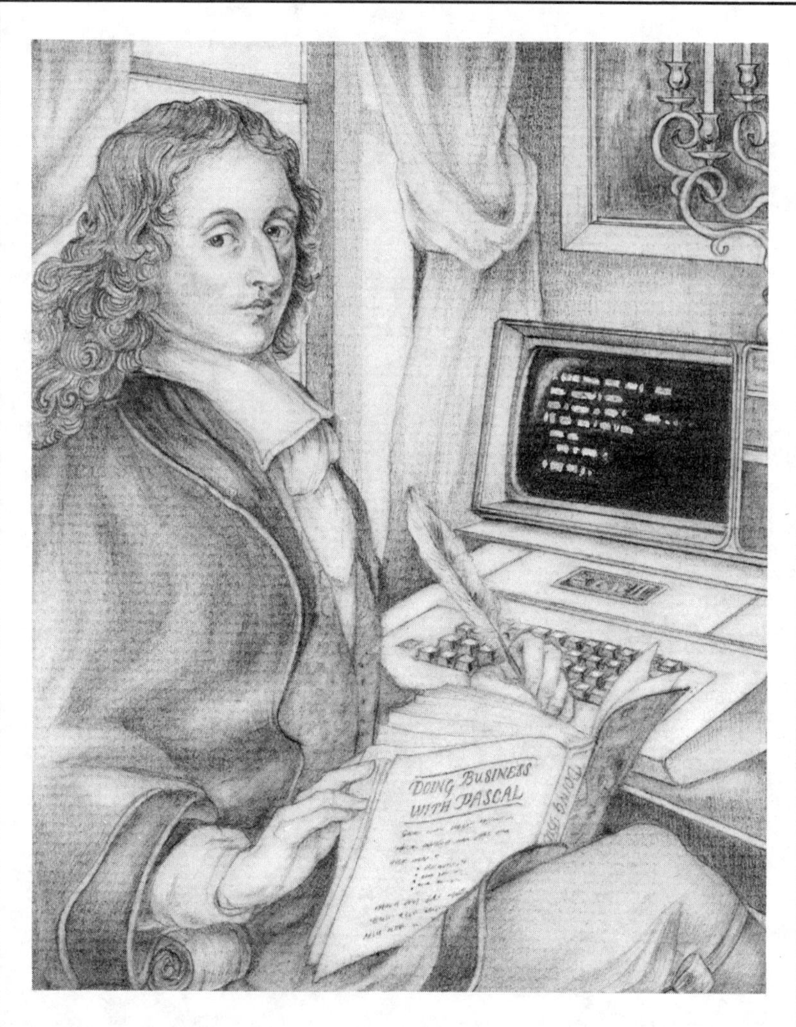

Sales Analysis

THE APPLICATION

The sales analysis program presented in this chapter would, in the business system we have described, receive its input from the revenue master file of the accounts receivable subsystem. As each sale is recorded, notation would be made of both the salesperson responsible for it and the specific product involved in the sale. This kind of information is easy to collect from sales invoices. The revenue master file must be designed to collect the data. The data collection cycle would run like this: Sales records, organized by both product and salesperson, would be entered interactively. This information, along with data on cash receipts at the time of sale, would be fed into the accounts receivable system. Accounts with balances outstanding would be flagged for production of invoices and for collection efforts. The transaction files produced in the recording of sales would then be summarized by product line, and within product line, by salesperson. This data would then be kept in the revenue master file. The sales analysis program would access that information and produce the report.

Once again, this is a management-level report. Just enough information is presented to help the manager make decisions. Quarterly statistics on products would be extremely significant in predicting sales trends or changes in the marketplace. Statistics on individual salespeople could indicate not only the relative skills of the members of the sales force, but also changes in the territory. In fact, a third use of the sales analysis application could focus on territory, especially if there is more than one salesperson covering a particular area.

This report, unlike the standard accounting reports that managers frequently have to wade through, presents its essential information in summary form. Furthermore, it requires very little in the way of special information gathering.

THE SAMPLE RUN

The sales analysis program presented in this chapter produces a table of quarterly gross sales revenues, detailed by salesperson. It provides a quick way of comparing the sales records of individual salespeople, in relation to total sales. The program could just as easily be used to compare sales figures for a series of products; as we will see, the program's essential algorithms would remain unchanged under this alternative use.

In the sample run, shown in Figure 19.1, quarterly sales figures for ten salespeople were entered in the input dialogue. Examining the resulting table, we see that the salespeople are sorted in order of annual performance, from best to worst. Also, three pieces of information are presented for each quarterly entry: the dollar amount of the individual's gross sales, the percentage of total sales represented by that amount and the individual's sales ranking. For example, for salesperson Macleish in the third quarter, we see the table entry:

```
$19,950.20
19%, #2
```

This shows that Macleish's third-quarter sales represented 19% of the total quarterly sales, ranking second for the quarter.

```
SALES ANALYSIS BY SALESPERSON
===== ======== == ===========

HOW MANY SALESPEOPLE? 10

NAME OF SALESPERSON? BARNES

GROSS SALES FOR QUARTER 1? 15371.15
GROSS SALES FOR QUARTER 2?  8115.20
GROSS SALES FOR QUARTER 3? 10200.00
GROSS SALES FOR QUARTER 4?   500.00
```

Figure 19.1: Output from the Sales Analysis Program

```
NAME OF SALESPERSON? CAEN

GROSS SALES FOR QUARTER 1? 22750
GROSS SALES FOR QUARTER 2? 8510.25
GROSS SALES FOR QUARTER 3? 17250
GROSS SALES FOR QUARTER 4? 5500


NAME OF SALESPERSON? GASSET

GROSS SALES FOR QUARTER 1? 0
GROSS SALES FOR QUARTER 2? 1500
GROSS SALES FOR QUARTER 3? 2750
GROSS SALES FOR QUARTER 4? 552.18


NAME OF SALESPERSON? HELLER

GROSS SALES FOR QUARTER 1? 6250
GROSS SALES FOR QUARTER 2? 7435.10
GROSS SALES FOR QUARTER 3? 1890.15
GROSS SALES FOR QUARTER 4? 985


NAME OF SALESPERSON? JAREIL

GROSS SALES FOR QUARTER 1? 25750
GROSS SALES FOR QUARTER 2? 27800
GROSS SALES FOR QUARTER 3? 6340
GROSS SALES FOR QUARTER 4? 1573


NAME OF SALESPERSON? MACLEISH

GROSS SALES FOR QUARTER 1? 18932.25
GROSS SALES FOR QUARTER 2? 14531
GROSS SALES FOR QUARTER 3? 19950.20
GROSS SALES FOR QUARTER 4? 3175.19


NAME OF SALESPERSON? SOUTHERN

GROSS SALES FOR QUARTER 1? 1459.33
GROSS SALES FOR QUARTER 2? 2087.14
GROSS SALES FOR QUARTER 3? 345.15
GROSS SALES FOR QUARTER 4? 940


NAME OF SALESPERSON? STEFFENS

GROSS SALES FOR QUARTER 1? 11950
GROSS SALES FOR QUARTER 2? 13500
GROSS SALES FOR QUARTER 3? 12000
GROSS SALES FOR QUARTER 4?  9510
```

Figure 19.1: Output from the Sales Analysis Program (cont.)

```
NAME OF SALESPERSON? WEBSTER

GROSS SALES FOR QUARTER 1? 18780
GROSS SALES FOR QUARTER 2? 25830.51
GROSS SALES FOR QUARTER 3? 31850.98
GROSS SALES FOR QUARTER 4?  9621.18

NAME OF SALESPERSON? WILSON

GROSS SALES FOR QUARTER 1? 872.15
GROSS SALES FOR QUARTER 2? 1310.29
GROSS SALES FOR QUARTER 3? 4468
GROSS SALES FOR QUARTER 4? 5782.25

-----------------------------------------

                         FOUR-QUARTER GROSS SALES
                              BY SALESPERSON

   NAME       QUARTER 1   QUARTER 2   QUARTER 3   QUARTER 4       TOTALS
   ----       ---------   ---------   ---------   ---------       ------

WEBSTER      $18,780.00  $25,830.51  $31,850.98   $9,621.18   $86,082.67
               15%, #4     23%, #2     30%, #1    25%, #1            23%

JAREIL       $25,750.00  $27,800.00   $6,340.00   $1,573.00   $61,463.00
               21%, #1     25%, #1      6%, #6     4%, #6            16%

MACLEISH     $18,932.25  $14,531.00  $19,950.20   $3,175.19   $56,588.64
               16%, #3     13%, #3     19%, #2     8%, #5            15%

CAEN         $22,750.00   $8,510.25  $17,250.00   $5,500.00   $54,010.25
               19%, #2      8%, #5     16%, #3    14%, #4            14%

STEFFENS     $11,950.00  $13,500.00  $12,000.00   $9,510.00   $46,960.00
               10%, #6     12%, #4     11%, #4    25%, #2            12%

BARNES       $15,371.15   $8,115.20  $10,200.00     $500.00   $34,186.35
               13%, #5      7%, #6     10%, #5    1%, #10             9%

HELLER        $6,250.00   $7,435.10   $1,890.15     $985.00   $16,560.25
                5%, #7      7%, #7      2%, #9     3%, #7             4%

WILSON          $872.15   $1,310.29   $4,468.00   $5,782.25   $12,432.69
                1%, #9     1%, #10      4%, #7    15%, #3             3%

SOUTHERN      $1,459.33   $2,087.14     $345.15     $940.00    $4,831.62
                1%, #8      2%, #8     0%, #10     2%, #8             1%

GASSET             $.00   $1,500.00   $2,750.00     $552.18    $4,802.18
               0%, #10      1%, #9      3%, #8     1%, #9             1%

**TOTALS**  $122,114.88 $110,619.49 $107,044.48  $38,138.80  $377,917.65

PRESS <RETURN> TO CONTINUE
```

Figure 19.1: Output from the Sales Analysis Program (cont.)

THE PROGRAM

Figure 19.2 shows the listing of program SALES. The TYPE declaration section defines the structures designed to hold the sales data:

```
TYPE
   RANKRANGE = 1..MAXSALES;
   ARY1 = ARRAY[1..5] OF LONG2;
   SALESPERSON = RECORD
      NAME : STRING[10];
      GROSS : ARY1;
      RANK : ARRAY[1..4] OF RANKRANGE
   END;
   ARY2 = ARRAY[1..MAXSALES] OF SALESPERSON;
```

Notice that two of the fields of the SALESPERSON record are arrays. GROSS holds the quarterly and total sales figures for a given salesperson, and RANK holds the integer values representing the performance rank for each quarter. The variables SALESARY and TOTAL are defined globally:

```
VAR
   SALESARY : ARY2;
   TOTAL : ARY1;
```

SALESARY is the array of salesperson records, and TOTAL is an array of total quarterly and annual sales.

Procedure INSALES simply reads the sales figures and calculates all the totals required for the table.

Procedure FINDRANKS, which contains a version of SHELLSORT as a local procedure, sorts SALESARY five times, to find the quarterly and then the annual ranks. After each of the first four sorts, the quarterly ranks are assigned to the RANK field:

```
FOR I := 1 TO 4 DO
   BEGIN
      SHELLSORT(SALESARY,I);
      FOR J := 1 TO NUMPEOPLE DO
         SALESARY[J].RANK[I] := J
   END;
```

Finally, the array is sorted by annual totals, in the order that is embodied in the table itself:

```
SHELLSORT(SALESARY,5);
```

Notice that the second parameter of the calls to this version of SHELLSORT is an index into an array, rather than the length of the array. (SHELLSORT gets the length of the salesperson array from the global variable NUMPEOPLE in this program.) This second parameter tells SHELLSORT which quarter's sales figures to use as the sort key; the "fifth quarter" represents the annual sales. SHELLSORT receives the value in the variable QUARTER, and compares the sales figures in the following IF statement:

```
IF A[J].GROSS[QUARTER] < A[I].GROSS[QUARTER] THEN
  ...
```

Procedure OUTTABLE contains three local procedures that aid in producing the table. OUTCASH writes the dollar-and-cent figures, and OUTSTATS outputs the ranks and percentages. The percentages are calculated using function LDIVL. Notice that the call to OUTSTATS contains three parameters: the percentage, the rank, and the width of the column in which these statistics are to be printed:

```
OUTCASH(ROUND(LDIVL(GROSS[5],TOTAL[5]) * 100.0),
         RANK[J],12);
```

```
(*$S+*)
PROGRAM SALES;

USES
          (*$U MONEYUNIT.CODE*)
MONEYUNIT;


CONST
  MAXSALES = 20;

TYPE
  RANKRANGE = 1..MAXSALES;
  ARY1 = ARRAY[1..5] OF LONG2;
  SALESPERSON = RECORD
    NAME : STRING[10];
    GROSS : ARY1;
    RANK : ARRAY[1..4] OF RANKRANGE
  END;
  ARY2 = ARRAY[1..MAXSALES] OF SALESPERSON;
```

Figure 19.2: Listing of Program SALES

```
VAR
  SALESARY : ARY2;
  TOTAL    : ARY1;
  NUMPEOPLE : INTEGER;


PROCEDURE CONTINUE;

  VAR
    ANS : STRING;

  BEGIN
    WRITE('PRESS <RETURN> TO CONTINUE ');
    READLN(ANS)
  END;       (* CONTINUE *)


PROCEDURE INSALES;

  VAR
    I,
    J   : INTEGER;

BEGIN
  (* INITIALIZE TOTALS ARRAY *)

  FOR I := 1 TO 5 DO
    TOTAL[I] := 0;



   (*
    * READ QUARTERLY GROSS SALES
    * FOR EACH SALESPERSON.
    *)


   FOR I := 1 TO NUMPEOPLE DO
     WITH SALESARY[I] DO
       BEGIN
         WRITE('NAME OF SALESPERSON? ');
         READLN(NAME);
         WRITELN;
         GROSS[5] := 0;
         FOR J := 1 TO 4 DO
           BEGIN
             WRITE('GROSS SALES FOR QUARTER ',J,'? ');
             INDOLLAR(GROSS[J]);



              (*
               * CALCULATE ANNUAL TOTALS AND
               * QUARTERLY TOTALS.
               *)
```

Figure 19.2: Listing of Program SALES (cont.)

```
                GROSS[5] := GROSS[5] + GROSS[J];
                TOTAL[J] := TOTAL[J] + GROSS[J]
              END;



            (*
             * TOTAL REVENUES FOR THE YEAR,
             * FOR ALL SALESPEOPLE.
             *)



            TOTAL[5] := TOTAL[5] + GROSS[5];
            WRITELN;
            WRITELN
          END  (* WITH *)
    END;  (* INSALES *)


    PROCEDURE FINDRANKS;

      VAR
        I,
        J   : INTEGER;



    PROCEDURE SHELLSORT(VAR A: ARY2;
                            QUARTER: INTEGER);



     (*
      * SORTS BY QUARTER, TO FIND THE RANKS.
      *)



     VAR
       DONE : BOOLEAN;
       JUMP,
       I,
       J,
       N    : INTEGER;


     PROCEDURE SWAP (VAR P, Q : SALESPERSON);
       VAR
         HOLD : SALESPERSON;
       BEGIN
         HOLD := P;
         P := Q;
         Q := HOLD
       END; (* SWAP *)
```

Figure 19.2: Listing of Program SALES (cont.)

```
BEGIN (* SHELLSORT *)
  N := NUMPEOPLE;   (* NUMPEOPLE IS GLOBAL *)
  JUMP := N;
  WHILE JUMP > 1 DO
  BEGIN
    JUMP := JUMP DIV 2;
      REPEAT
        DONE := TRUE;
          FOR J := 1 TO N - JUMP DO
            BEGIN
              I:= J + JUMP;
              IF A[J].GROSS[QUARTER] < A[I].GROSS[QUARTER] THEN
                BEGIN
                  SWAP(A[J],A[I]);
                  DONE := FALSE
                END (* IF *)
            END (* FOR *)
      UNTIL DONE
  END (* WHILE *)
END (* SHELLSORT *);



BEGIN (* FINDRANKS *)

  (*
   * QUARTERLY SORTS, TO FIND RANKS.
   *)

  FOR I := 1 TO 4 DO
    BEGIN
      SHELLSORT(SALESARY,I);
      FOR J := 1 TO NUMPEOPLE DO
        SALESARY[J].RANK[I] := J
    END;

    SHELLSORT(SALESARY,5);   (* FINAL SORT, BY TOTALS *)

END;  (* FINDRANKS *)



PROCEDURE OUTTABLE;



VAR
  I,
  J   : INTEGER;

PROCEDURE HEADING;

  VAR
    I : INTEGER;
```

Figure 19.2: Listing of Program SALES (cont.)

```
   BEGIN
     WRITELN('FOUR-QUARTER GROSS SALES':49);
     WRITELN('BY SALESPERSON':44);
     WRITELN; WRITELN;
     WRITE('NAME      ':11);
     FOR I := 1 TO 4 DO
       WRITE('  QUARTER ',I,' ');
     WRITELN('     TOTALS');
     WRITE('----      ':11);
     FOR I := 1 TO 4 DO
       WRITE('  --------- ');
     WRITELN('     ------');
     WRITELN
   END;       (* HEADING *)

 PROCEDURE OUTCASH (AMT: LONG2;
                  FIELD: INTEGER);

   VAR
     STAMT : STRING;

   BEGIN
     DOLLARFORM(AMT,STAMT);
     RIGHTFIELD(STAMT,FIELD);
     WRITE(STAMT)
   END;       (* OUTCASH *)

 PROCEDURE OUTSTATS (PERC,RNK,FIELD : INTEGER);

   (*
    *  OUTPUTS THE RANKS AND PERCENTAGES.
    *  IF RNK = 0 THEN ONLY THE PERCENTAGE IS
    *  WRITTEN.
    *)

   VAR
     STATS,
     STRANK : STRING;

   BEGIN
     STR(PERC,STATS);
     STATS := CONCAT(STATS,'%');
     IF RNK <> 0 THEN
       BEGIN
         STR(RNK,STRANK);
         STATS := CONCAT(STATS,', #',STRANK)
       END;
     STATS := CONCAT(STATS,'  ');
     RIGHTFIELD(STATS,FIELD);
     WRITE(STATS)
   END;    (* OUTSTATS *)

 FUNCTION LDIVL(L1,L2 : LONG2):REAL;

   (*
    * ASSUMES L1 < L2.
    *)
```

Figure 19.2: Listing of Program SALES (cont.)

```
    VAR
      HOLD1,
      HOLD2  : LONG2;
      R      : REAL;

    BEGIN
      HOLD1 := 1;
      WHILE L1 > MAXINT DO
        BEGIN
          L1 := L1 DIV 10;
          HOLD1 := HOLD1 * 10
        END;

      HOLD2 := 1;
      WHILE L2 > MAXINT DO
        BEGIN
          L2 := L2 DIV 10;
          HOLD2 := HOLD2 * 10
        END;

      R := TRUNC(L1) / TRUNC(L2);

      HOLD2 := HOLD2 DIV HOLD1;
      WHILE HOLD2 > 1 DO
        BEGIN
          R := R / 10.
          HOLD2 := HOLD2 DIV 10
        END;
      LDIVL := R
    END;      (* LDIVL *)


BEGIN (* OUTTABLE *)

  HEADING;

  FOR I := 1 TO NUMPEOPLE DO
    WITH SALESARY[I] DO
      BEGIN
        WRITE(NAME);
        FOR J := 1 TO (11 - LENGTH(NAME)) DO
          WRITE(' ');
        FOR J := 1 TO 4 DO
          OUTCASH(GROSS[J],12);
        OUTCASH(GROSS[5],14);    (* TOTAL *)
        WRITELN;
        WRITE('            ');
        FOR J := 1 TO 4 DO

          (* PRINT QUARTERLY PERCENTAGES AND RANKS *)

          OUTSTATS(ROUND(LDIVL(GROSS[J],TOTAL[J])*100.0),
                   RANK[J], 12);

        (* PRINT TOTAL PERCENTAGES *)
```

Figure 19.2: Listing of Program SALES (cont.)

```
            OUTSTATS(ROUND(LDIVL(GROSS[5],TOTAL[5])*100.0),0,14);
            WRITELN;
            WRITELN
          END;  (* WITH *)

    WRITE('**TOTALS** ');
    FOR I := 1 TO 4 DO
      OUTCASH(TOTAL[I],12);
    OUTCASH(TOTAL[5],14);
    WRITELN;WRITELN;WRITELN
  END;    (* OUTTABLE *)


  PROCEDURE ININT(VAR VAL:INTEGER);

    VAR
      GARBAGE : STRING;

    BEGIN
      GET(INPUT);
      IF INPUT^ IN ['0'..'9'] THEN
        READLN(VAL)
      ELSE
        BEGIN
          READLN(GARBAGE);
          WRITELN('*** REDO');
          WRITE('    ? ');
          ININT(VAL)
        END
    END;   (* ININT *)



  BEGIN   (* MAIN PROGRAM *)
    CLEARSCREEN;
    WRITELN;
    WRITELN('SALES ANALYSIS BY SALESPERSON');
    WRITELN('===== ======== == ===========');
    WRITELN;
    REPEAT
      WRITE('HOW MANY SALESPEOPLE? ');
      ININT(NUMPEOPLE)
    UNTIL NUMPEOPLE <= MAXSALES;
    WRITELN;
    WRITELN;

    INSALES;
    CLEARSCREEN;
    FINDRANKS;
    OUTTABLE;
    CONTINUE
  END.     (* MAIN PROGRAM *)
```

Figure 19.2: Listing of Program SALES (cont.)

Chapter 20

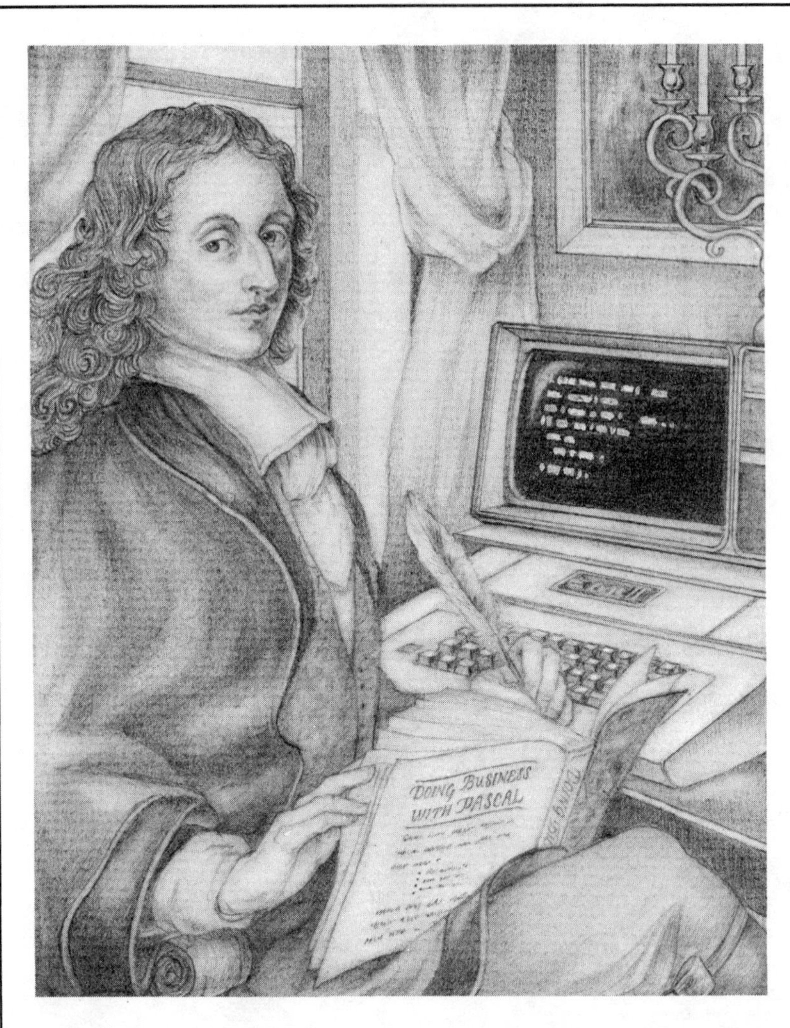

Financial Ratios

THE APPLICATION

Financial ratios are designed to aid in the prediction and control of a company's growth, by allowing comparison with other companies or previous periods. The specific ratios used—and even the methods of calculating them—vary from company to company, and from industry to industry. Among the categories of financial ratios are liquidity ratios, profitability ratios, and turnover ratios. In any given year, the ratios for a company might be compared with:

- average ratios for its industry during the same year;
- its own ratios from the previous several years.

Ratios are calculated from financial statement information. A given ratio may require two or more values from these statements. The financial statements, in turn, summarize the activity of the company for a specified period, or the net worth of the company at a given point in time. They are generated from the general ledger module of the system.

For the purposes of illustration, the program in this chapter reads eight values from the keyboard during the run of the program. These values are used to formulate financial statement summaries, and then the ratios themselves are computed from these summaries: the current ratio, the ratio of debts to assets, the profit margin, and the return on investment.

Although only those four ratios are given as examples, the program is designed so that additional ratios can easily be added. Some ratios might require more detailed financial statement information than is currently available to this program. For example, *inventory turnover* and *average collection period for receivables* are two ratios that might be calculated by submodules that feed into the general ledger module.

Finally, for the purpose of historical comparison, the financial ratios from the previous several years of company activity could conveniently be stored in the system profile.

THE SAMPLE RUN

A sample run of the program is shown in Figure 20.1. In the first two screens of the program dialogue, the information derived from the financial statements is input. Three values are required from the income statement:

- sales
- cost of goods sold
- operating expenses

and four values from the balance sheet:

- current assets
- fixed assets
- current liabilities
- long-term liabilities

The average tax rate for the company is also required.

From this information, the program calculates additional financial statement values and displays the statement summaries in the third screen of the dialogue. For the income statement summary, the following formulas are used:

gross margin = sales − cost of goods sold

pretax income = gross margin − operating expenses

net income = pretax income − income tax

The balance sheet summary shows the total assets and the total liabilities. A value for owners' equity is computed as follows:

owners' equity = total assets − total liabilities

Finally, the four ratios are calculated and displayed, one ratio to a screen. The specific financial statement categories used for the calculation of each ratio are also shown.

```
ENTER VALUES FROM INCOME STATEMENT
----- ------ ---- ------ ---------

SALES?                        3620000
COST OF GOODS SOLD?           2416000
OPERATING EXPENSES?            856000
---------------------------------------------



ENTER VALUES FROM BALANCE SHEET
----- ------ ---- ------- -----

CURRENT ASSETS?               2135000
FIXED ASSETS?                  390000
CURRENT LIABILITIES?           350000
LONG-TERM LIABILITIES?         600000

TAX RATE (%)? 46

---------------------------------------------



SUMMARY OF INCOME STATEMENT
------- -- ------ ---------

SALES                        $3,620,000.00
COST OF GOODS SOLD           $2,416,000.00
GROSS MARGIN                 $1,204,000.00
OPERATING EXPENSES             $856,000.00
PRETAX INCOME                  $348,000.00
INCOME TAX                     $160,080.00
NET INCOME                     $187,920.00



SUMMARY OF BALANCE SHEET
------- -- ------- -----

CURRENT ASSETS               $2,135,000.00
FIXED ASSETS                   $390,000.00
TOTAL ASSETS                 $2,525,000.00
CURRENT LIABILITIES            $350,000.00
LONG-TERM LIABILITIES          $600,000.00
TOTAL LIABILITIES              $950,000.00
OWNERS' EQUITY               $1,575,000.00

PRESS <RETURN> TO CONTINUE.
---------------------------------------------
```

Figure 20.1: Sample Run of the Financial Ratio Program

```
CURRENT RATIO
======= =====

             CURRENT ASSETS
            -------------------
            CURRENT LIABILITIES

            =====>   6.10 TIMES

PRESS <RETURN> TO CONTINUE.
------------------------------------------------


DEBTS TO ASSETS
===== == ======

                TOTAL LIABILITIES
                -----------------
                  TOTAL ASSETS

                =====>   37.62%

PRESS <RETURN> TO CONTINUE.
------------------------------------------------


PROFIT MARGIN
====== ======

          AFTER-TAX INCOME
          ----------------
               SALES

          =====>   5.19%

PRESS <RETURN> TO CONTINUE.
------------------------------------------------


RETURN ON INVESTMENT
====== == ==========

                 AFTER-TAX INCOME
                 ----------------
                  OWNERS' EQUITY

                 =====>   11.93%

PRESS <RETURN> TO CONTINUE.
------------------------------------------------
```

Figure 20.1: Sample Run of the Financial Ratio Program (cont.)

THE PROGRAM

The listing of program FINRATIO is shown in Figure 20.2. The main program section shows clearly that the activity of the program is performed by four major procedures: INITSTRINGS, INVALUES, OUTSTATE, and RATIOS.

The essential data type of this program is STATEMENT, which is an array of records. The record type, LINE, consists of two fields—a string and a long integer:

```
TYPE
   LINE = RECORD
      ITEM : STRING;
      AMOUNT : LONG2
   END;

   STATEMENT = ARRAY[1..CATEGORIES] OF LINE;
```

The array variables INCOME and BALANCE, which are designed to hold the financial statement summaries, are both of type STATEMENT:

```
VAR
   INCOME : STATEMENT;
   BALANCE : STATEMENT;
```

Procedure INITSTRINGS initializes the string ITEM fields of these two arrays. The items are used first as prompts for the input routine, and then again in the routine that displays the financial statements.

Procedure INVALUES has two FOR loops that read the required input values—first the income statement values, then the balance sheet values. Procedure CALCTOTS, which is local to procedure INVALUES, calculates seven additional values for the two statements.

Procedure OUTSTATE displays the financial statements. Since the strings and the long integer values needed for the statements are all stored in the two arrays INCOME and BALANCE, the output procedure is very simple. The display of each financial statement is controlled by a FOR loop. Procedures DOLLARFORM and RIGHTFIELD, from MONEYUNIT, convert the long integer values into right-justified dollar-and-cent strings:

```
DOLLARFORM(INCOME[I].AMOUNT,TEMPSTR);
RIGHTFIELD(TEMPSTR,15);
```

Procedure RATIOS has a series of local procedures that calculate and display the financial ratios: CURRENT (for the current ratio); DTOA (for the debts to assets ratio); PM (for the profit margin); and ROI (for the return on investment). Thus, to include additional ratios in the program we can simply write more routines in the same format as the procedures that already exist. Notice that function LDIVL is also included in procedure RATIOS. LDIVL, which we have seen in previous application programs, divides one long integer by another and returns a value of type REAL. Each of the local procedures uses this function in calculating a ratio.

```
PROGRAM FINRATIO;

(*
 * ADAPTED FROM THE PROGRAM "FINANCIAL ANALYSIS BY RATIOS" IN
 * EXECUTIVE PLANNING WITH BASIC BY X.T. BUI, BY PERMISSION OF
 * THE AUTHOR
 *)

USES
            (*$U MONEYUNIT.CODE*)
MONEYUNIT;


CONST
  CATEGORIES = 7;

TYPE
  LINE = RECORD
    ITEM : STRING;
    AMOUNT : LONG2
  END;

  STATEMENT = ARRAY[1..CATEGORIES] OF LINE;


VAR
  INCOME : STATEMENT;
  BALANCE : STATEMENT;


PROCEDURE CONTINUE;

  VAR
    ANSWER : STRING;

BEGIN
  WRITELN;
  WRITE('PRESS <RETURN> TO CONTINUE. ');
  READLN(ANSWER);
  CLEARSCREEN;
  WRITELN
END;         (* CONTINUE *)
```

Figure 20.2: Listing of the Financial Ratio Program

```
PROCEDURE INITSTRINGS;

BEGIN
  INCOME[1].ITEM := 'SALES';
  INCOME[2].ITEM := 'COST OF GOODS SOLD';
  INCOME[3].ITEM := 'GROSS MARGIN';
  INCOME[4].ITEM := 'OPERATING EXPENSES';
  INCOME[5].ITEM := 'PRETAX INCOME';
  INCOME[6].ITEM := 'INCOME TAX';
  INCOME[7].ITEM := 'NET INCOME';

  BALANCE[1].ITEM := 'CURRENT ASSETS';
  BALANCE[2].ITEM := 'FIXED ASSETS';
  BALANCE[3].ITEM := 'TOTAL ASSETS';
  BALANCE[4].ITEM := 'CURRENT LIABILITIES';
  BALANCE[5].ITEM := 'LONG-TERM LIABILITIES';
  BALANCE[6].ITEM := 'TOTAL LIABILITIES';
  BALANCE[7].ITEM := 'OWNERS'' EQUITY';
END;


PROCEDURE INVALUES;

(*
 * READS FINANCIAL STATEMENT VALUES,
 * AND COMPUTES STATEMENT TOTALS.
 *)

  VAR
    I : INTEGER;
    TEMP : LONG2;
    TXRATE : REAL;


PROCEDURE CALCTOTS;

(*
 * COMPUTES INCOME STATEMENT AND
 * BALANCE SHEET TOTALS.
 *)

BEGIN
  INCOME[3].AMOUNT := INCOME[1].AMOUNT
                    - INCOME[2].AMOUNT; (* GROSS MARGIN *)

  INCOME[5].AMOUNT := INCOME[3].AMOUNT
                    - INCOME[4].AMOUNT; (* PRETAX INCOME *)

  LONGMULT(INCOME[5].AMOUNT,TXRATE,INCOME[6].AMOUNT); (* TAX *)

  INCOME[7].AMOUNT := INCOME[5].AMOUNT
                    - INCOME[6].AMOUNT; (* NET INCOME *)


  BALANCE[3].AMOUNT := BALANCE[1].AMOUNT
                     + BALANCE[2].AMOUNT;    (* TOTAL ASSETS *)
```

Figure 20.2: Listing of the Financial Ratio Program (cont.)

```
    BALANCE[6].AMOUNT := BALANCE[4].AMOUNT
                       + BALANCE[5].AMOUNT;   (* TOTAL LIABILITIES *)

    BALANCE[7].AMOUNT := BALANCE[3].AMOUNT
                       - BALANCE[6].AMOUNT;   (* OWNER'S EQUITY *)

  END;     (* CALCTOTS *)

  BEGIN
    CLEARSCREEN;
    WRITELN;
    WRITELN('ENTER VALUES FROM INCOME STATEMENT');
    WRITELN('----- ------ ---- ------ ---------');
    WRITELN;

    FOR I := 1 TO 4 DO
      IF I <> 3 THEN
        BEGIN
          WRITE(INCOME[I].ITEM,'?  ');
          INDOLLAR(INCOME[I].AMOUNT)
        END;

    CLEARSCREEN;

    WRITELN;
    WRITELN('ENTER VALUES FROM BALANCE SHEET');
    WRITELN('----- ------ ---- ------- -----');
    WRITELN;

    FOR I := 1 TO 5 DO
      IF I <> 3 THEN
        BEGIN
          WRITE(BALANCE[I].ITEM,'?  ');
          INDOLLAR(BALANCE[I].AMOUNT)
        END;

    WRITELN;
    WRITE('TAX RATE (%)?  ');
    INDOLLAR(TEMP);
    TXRATE := TRUNC(TEMP)/10000;

    CALCTOTS   (* COMPUTE TOTALS *)
  END;         (* INVALUES *)



  PROCEDURE OUTSTATE;

  (*
   * DISPLAYS FINANCIAL STATEMENT SUMMARIES.
   *)

    VAR
      I,
      J : INTEGER;
      TEMPSTR : STRING;
```

Figure 20.2: Listing of the Financial Ratio Program (cont.)

```
BEGIN
  CLEARSCREEN;
  WRITELN;
  WRITELN('SUMMARY OF INCOME STATEMENT');
  WRITELN('------- -- ------ ---------');
  WRITELN;
  FOR I := 1 TO CATEGORIES DO
    BEGIN
      DOLLARFORM(INCOME[I].AMOUNT,TEMPSTR);
      RIGHTFIELD(TEMPSTR,15);
      WRITE(INCOME[I].ITEM);
      FOR J := 1 TO (25 - LENGTH(INCOME[I].ITEM)) DO
        WRITE(' ');
      WRITELN(TEMPSTR)
    END;



  WRITELN;
  WRITELN;
  WRITELN('SUMMARY OF BALANCE SHEET');
  WRITELN('------- -- ------- -----');
  WRITELN;
  FOR I := 1 TO CATEGORIES DO
    BEGIN
      DOLLARFORM(BALANCE[I].AMOUNT,TEMPSTR);
      RIGHTFIELD(TEMPSTR,15);
      WRITE(BALANCE[I].ITEM);
      FOR J := 1 TO (25 - LENGTH(BALANCE[I].ITEM)) DO
        WRITE(' ');
      WRITELN(TEMPSTR)
    END;
  CONTINUE

END;      (* OUTSTATE *)



PROCEDURE RATIOS;

(*
 * COMPUTES AND DISPLAYS FINANCIAL RATIOS.
 *)

FUNCTION LDIVL(L1,L2 : LONG2): REAL;

 (*
  * DIVIDES L1 BY L2;
  * RESULT IS OF TYPE REAL.
  *)

  VAR
    HOLD1,
    HOLD2  : LONG2;
    R      : REAL;
```

Figure 20.2: Listing of the Financial Ratio Program (cont.)

```
    BEGIN
      HOLD1 := 1;
      WHILE L1 > MAXINT DO
        BEGIN
          L1 := L1 DIV 10;
          HOLD1 := HOLD1 * 10
        END;
      HOLD2 := 1;
      WHILE L2 > MAXINT DO
        BEGIN
          L2 := L2 DIV 10;
          HOLD2 := HOLD2 * 10
        END;
      R := TRUNC(L1) / TRUNC(L2);

      IF HOLD2 >= HOLD1 THEN
        BEGIN
          HOLD2 := HOLD2 DIV HOLD1;
          WHILE HOLD2 > 1 DO
            BEGIN
              R := R / 10.0;
              HOLD2 := HOLD2 DIV 10
            END
        END
      ELSE
        BEGIN
          HOLD1 := HOLD1 DIV HOLD2;
          WHILE HOLD1 > 1 DO
            BEGIN
              R := R * 10.0;
              HOLD1 := HOLD1 DIV 10
            END
        END;

      LDIVL := R
  END;                  (* LDIVL *)


  PROCEDURE CURRENT;



  BEGIN
    WRITELN('CURRENT RATIO');
    WRITELN('======= =====');
    WRITELN;
    WRITELN('              CURRENT ASSETS');
    WRITELN('            -------------------');
    WRITELN('            CURRENT LIABILITIES');
    WRITELN;
    WRITELN;
    WRITE('          =====>   ');
    WRITELN(LDIVL(BALANCE[1].AMOUNT,BALANCE[4].AMOUNT):5:2, ' TIMES');
    CONTINUE
  END;          (* CURRENT *)
```

Figure 20.2: Listing of the Financial Ratio Program (cont.)

```
PROCEDURE DTOA;

  VAR
    R : REAL;

BEGIN

  WRITELN('DEBTS TO ASSETS');
  WRITELN('===== == ======');
  WRITELN;
  WRITELN('                  TOTAL LIABILITIES');
  WRITELN('                  -----------------');
  WRITELN('                    TOTAL ASSETS');
  WRITELN;
  WRITELN;
  WRITE('                  =====>   ');
  R := LDIVL(BALANCE[6].AMOUNT,BALANCE[3].AMOUNT) * 100;
  WRITELN(R:5:2,'%');
  CONTINUE
END;          (* DTOA *)


PROCEDURE PM;

  VAR
    R : REAL;


BEGIN
  WRITELN('PROFIT MARGIN');
  WRITELN('====== ======');
  WRITELN;
  WRITELN('                AFTER-TAX INCOME');
  WRITELN('                ----------------');
  WRITELN('                     SALES');
  WRITELN;
  WRITELN;
  WRITE('                =====>   ');
  R := LDIVL(INCOME[7].AMOUNT,INCOME[1].AMOUNT) * 100;
  WRITELN(R:5:2,'%');
  CONTINUE
END;          (* PM *)


PROCEDURE ROI;

  VAR
    R : REAL;
```

Figure 20.2: Listing of the Financial Ratio Program (cont.)

```
BEGIN
  WRITELN('RETURN ON INVESTMENT');
  WRITELN('====== == ==========');
  WRITELN;
  WRITELN('                       AFTER-TAX INCOME');
  WRITELN('                       ----------------');
  WRITELN('                        OWNERS'' EQUITY');
  WRITELN;
  WRITELN;
  WRITE('                     =====>  ');
  R := LDIVL(INCOME[7].AMOUNT,BALANCE[7].AMOUNT) * 100;
  WRITELN(R:5:2,'%');
  CONTINUE
END;          (* ROI *)


BEGIN  (* RATIOS *)
  CURRENT;
  DTOA;
  PM;
  ROI
END;   (* RATIOS *)


BEGIN (* MAIN PROGRAM *)
  INITSTRINGS;
  INVALUES;
  OUTSTATE;
  RATIOS
END.  (* MAIN PROGRAM *)
```

Figure 20.2: Listing of the Financial Ratio Program (cont.)

Appendix: Pascal Extensions for Business Programming

In Part II of this book we discussed three extensions to standard Pascal that are especially important for business programming. In UCSD Pascal, these extensions are the long integer type, random-access files, and units. Features equivalent to these are available on many versions of Pascal; some are presented in the accompanying table. The terminology used is the manufacturers' own.

	Double-precision numerical data type	*Direct- (or random) access data files*	*Pre-compilable program modules*
UCSD	long integer	random-access files	units
Pascal-80,86 (Intel)	*	random-access files	components
Pascal-2 (OMSI)	15-digit double-precision reals	direct-access files	external modules
Pascal/Z (Ithaca Inter-sytems, Inc.)	Fixed-point decimal	direct-access files	separate compilation of modules
Pascal MT + (Digital Research)	BCD real: 18 digits, 4 fixed decimal places	random-access files	Module (modular (compilation)
HP 1000	15-digit double-precision reals	random-access files with OPEN statement	*
JRT Pascal	14-digit reals	random files up to 8K bytes	external procedures and modules

*Information not available at publication date. Sybex welcomes additional information concerning these or other versions of Pascal.

Bibliography

Anthony, Robert N. and James S. Reece. *Management Accounting: Text and Cases.* Homewood, Ill.: Richard D. Irwin, 1973.

Apple Computer, Inc. *Apple Pascal Reference Manual.* Cupertino, Calif.: Apple Computer, 1979.

Athey, Thomas H. *Systematic Systems Approach.* Englewood Cliffs, N.J.: Prentice-Hall, 1982.

Atwood, Jerry W. *The Systems Analyst.* Rochelle Park, N.J.: Hayden Book Company, 1977.

Bowles, Kenneth L. *Beginner's Guide for the UCSD Pascal System.* Peterborough, N.H.: Byte Books, 1980.

__________. "Pascal versus COBOL: Where Pascal Gets Down to Business". In *The Byte Book of Pascal,* edited by Blaise W. Liffick. Peterborough, N.H.: Byte Publications, 1979.

Dopuch, Nicholas and Jacob G. Birnberg. *Cost Accounting: Accounting Data for Management's Decisions.* New York: Harcourt, Brace & World, 1969.

Grant, Charles W. and Jon Butah. *Introduction to the UCSD p-System.* Berkeley: Sybex, 1982.

Grogono, Peter. *Programming in Pascal.* Reading, Mass.: Addison-Wesley Publishing Company, 1980.

Hennessy, Jr., J.H. *Financial Manager's Handbook.* Englewood Cliffs, N.J.: Prentice-Hall, 1977.

Hermanson, Roger H., Stephen E. Loeb, John M. Saada and Robert H. Strawser. *Auditing Theory and Practice.* Homewood, Ill.: Richard D. Irwin, 1976.

Hillier, Frederick S. and Gerald J. Lieberman. *Introduction to Operations Research.* San Francisco: Holden-Day, 1980.

Horngren, Charles T. *Introduction to Management Accounting.* Englewood Cliffs, N.J.: Prentice-Hall, 1978.

Jensen, Kathleen and Niklaus Wirth. *Pascal User Manual and Report.* New York: Springer-Verlag, 1978.

Katzan, Jr., Harry. *Computer Data Management and Data Base Technology.* New York: Van Nostrand Reinhold, 1975.

Kennedy, Ralph Dale, and Stewart Yarwood McMullen. *Financial Statements: Forms, Analysis, Interpretation.* Homewood, Ill.: Richard D. Irwin, 1976.

Kernighan, Brian W. and P. J. Plauger. *Software Tools in Pascal.* Reading, Mass.: Addison-Wesley Publishing Company, 1981.

Knuth, Donald E. *The Art of Computer Programming. Vol. 3: Sorting and Searching.* Reading, Mass.: Addison-Wesley Publishing Company, 1973.

Kohler, Eric L. *A Dictionary for Accountants.* Englewood Cliffs, N.J.: Prentice-Hall, 1977.

Kuck, David J. *The Structure of Computers and Computation,* Vol. 1. New York: John Wiley and Sons, 1978.

Lewis, T. G. *Pascal Programming for the Apple.* Reston, Va.: Reston Publishing Company, 1981.

McGowan, Roger A. and Ried Henderson. *CDP Review Manual: A Data Processing Handbook.* New York: Petrocelli/Charter, 1975.

Miller, Alan R. *Pascal Programs for Scientists and Engineers.* Berkeley: Sybex, 1981.

Muller, Martin A. *Muller's Comprehensive GAAP Guide.* New York: Harcourt, Brace and Jovanovich, 1979.

Neuner, John J.W. *Cost Accounting: Principles and Practice.* Homewood, Ill.: Richard D. Irwin, 1973.

Niswonger, C. Rollin and Philip E. Fess. *Accounting Principles.* 11th Ed. Cincinnati: South-Western Publishing Company, 1973.

Pescow, Jerome K., Jack Horn, and Marvin Bachman. *Handbook of Successful Data Processing Applications.* Englewood Cliffs, N.J.: Prentice-Hall, 1973.

Tiberghien, Jacques. *The Pascal Handbook.* Berkeley: Sybex, 1981.

Welsch, Glenn A., and Robert N. Anthony. *Fundamentals of Financial Accounting.* Homewood, Ill.: Richard D. Irwin, 1977.

Wixon, Rufus. *Accountants' Handbook.* New York: Ronald Press Company, 1965.

Zaks, Rodnay. *Introduction to Pascal, Including UCSD Pascal.* Berkeley: Sybex, 1981.

General Index

Procedures Index

Note: the following is a list of the major procedures presented in the book. References are to both the explanation of a procedure and the source code listing for that procedure. Procedures are also listed in the general index.

SYBEX